The History of Herodotus - Volume 1

By Herodotus

Translated by G. C. Macaulay

Published by Pantianos Classics

ISBN-13: 978-1536824001

First published in 1890

Contents

Preface 4

The History of Herodotus.......................... 5

Book I 5
BookII... 48
Book III 83
Book IV..115

Preface

If a new translation of Herodotus does not justify itself, it will hardly be justified in a preface; therefore the question whether it was needed may be left here without discussion. The aim of the translator has been above all things faithfulness—faithfulness to the manner of expression and to the structure of sentences, as well as to the meaning of the Author. At the same time it is conceived that the freedom and variety of Herodotus is not always best reproduced by such severe consistency of rendering as is perhaps desirable in the case of the Epic writers before and the philosophical writers after his time: nor again must his simplicity of thought and occasional quaintness be reproduced in the form of archaisms of language; and that not only because the affectation of an archaic style would necessarily be offensive to the reader, but also because in language Herodotus is not archaic. His style is the "best canon of the Ionic speech," marked, however, not so much by primitive purity as by eclectic variety. At the same time it is characterised largely by the poetic diction of the Epic and Tragic writers; and while the translator is free to employ all the resources of modern English, so far as he has them at his command, he must carefully retain this poetical colouring and by all means avoid the courtier phrase by which the style of Herodotus has too often been made "more noble."

As regards the text from which this translation has been made, it is based upon that of Stein's critical edition (Berlin, -), that is to say the estimate there made of the comparative value of the authorities has been on the whole accepted as a just one, rather than that which depreciates the value of the Medicean MS. and of the class to which it belongs. On the other hand the conjectural emendations proposed by Stein have very seldom been adopted, and his text has been departed from in a large number of other instances also, which will for the most part be found recorded in the notes.

As it seemed that even after Stein's re-collation of the Medicean MS. there were doubts felt by some scholars as to the true reading in some places of this MS., which is very generally acknowledged to be the most important, I thought it right to examine it myself in all those passages where questions about text arise which concern a translator, that is in nearly five hundred places altogether; and the results, when they are worth observing, are recorded in the notes. At the same time, by the suggestion of Dr. Stein, I re-collated a large part of the third book in the MS. which is commonly referred to as F (i.e. Florentinus), called by Stein C, and I examined this MS. also in a certain number of other places. It should be understood that wherever in the notes I mention the reading of any particular MS. by name, I do so on my own authority.

The notes have been confined to a tolerably small compass. Their purpose is, first, in cases where the text is doubtful, to indicate the reading adopted by the translator and any other which may seem to have reasonable probability, but without discussion of the authorities; secondly, where the rendering is not quite literal (and in other cases where it seemed desirable), to quote the words of the original or to give a more literal version; thirdly, to add an alternative version in cases where there seems to be a doubt as to the true meaning; and lastly, to give occasionally a short explanation, or a reference from one passage of the author to another.

For the orthography of proper names reference may be made to the note prefixed to the index. No consistent system has been adopted, and the result will therefore be open to criticism in many details; but the aim has been to avoid on the one hand the pedantry of seriously altering the form of those names which are fairly established in the English language of literature, as distinguished from that of scholarship, and on the other hand the absurdity of looking to Latin rather than to Greek for the orthography of the names which are not so established. There is no intention to put forward any theory about pronunciation.

The index of proper names will, it is hoped, be found more complete and accurate than those hitherto published. The best with which I was acquainted I found to have so many errors and omissions that I was compelled to do the work again from the beginning. In a collection of more than ten thousand references there must in all probability be mistakes, but I trust they will be found to be few.

My acknowledgments of obligation are due first to Dr. Stein, both for his critical work and also for his most excellent commentary, which I have had always by me. After this I have made most use of the editions of Krüger, Bähr, Abicht, and (in the first two books) Mr. Woods. As to translations, I have had Rawlinson's before me while revising my own work, and I have referred also occasionally to the translations of Littlebury (perhaps the best English version as regards style, but full of gross errors), Taylor, and Larcher. In the second book I have also used the version of B. R. reprinted by Mr. Lang: of the first book of this translation I have access only to a fragment written out some years ago, when the British Museum was within my reach. Other particular obligations are acknowledged in the notes.

The History of Herodotus

Book I

The First Book of the Histories, Called Clio

This is the Showing forth of the Inquiry of Herodotus of Halicarnassos, to the end that neither the deeds of men may be forgotten by lapse of time, nor the works great and marvellous, which have been produced some by Hellenes and some by Barbarians, may lose their renown; and especially that the causes may be remembered for which these waged war with one another.

Those of the Persians who have knowledge of history declare that the Phenicians first began the quarrel. These, they say, came from that which is called the Erythraian Sea to this of ours; and having settled in the land where they continue even now to dwell, set themselves forthwith to make long voyages by sea. And conveying merchandise of Egypt and of Assyria they arrived at other places and also at Argos; now Argos was at that time in all points the first of the States within that land which is now called Hellas;—the Phenicians arrived then at this land of Argos, and began to dispose of their ship's cargo: and on the fifth or sixth day after they had arrived, when their goods had been almost all sold, there came down to the sea a great company of women, and among them the daughter of the king; and her name, as the Hellenes also agree, was Io the daughter of Inachos. These standing near to the stern of the ship were buying of the wares such as pleased them most, when of a sudden the Phenicians, passing the word from one to another, made a rush upon them; and the greater part of the women escaped by flight, but Io and certain others were carried off. So they put them on board their ship, and forthwith departed, sailing away to Egypt.

In this manner the Persians report that Io came to Egypt, not agreeing therein with the Hellenes, and this they say was the first beginning of wrongs. Then after this, they say, certain Hellenes (but the name of the people they are not able to report) put in to the city of Tyre in Phenicia and carried off the king's daughter Europa;—these would doubtless be Cretans;—and so they were quits for the former injury. After this however the Hellenes, they say, were the authors of the second wrong; for they sailed in to Aia of Colchis and to the river Phasis with a ship of war, and from thence, after they had done the other business for which they came, they carried off the king's daughter Medea: and the king of Colchis sent a herald to the land of Hellas and demanded satisfaction for the rape and to have his daughter back; but they answered that, as the Barbarians had given them no satisfaction for the rape of Io the Argive, so neither would they give satisfaction to the Barbarians for this.

In the next generation after this, they say, Alexander the son of Priam, having heard of these things, desired to get a wife for himself by violence from Hellas, being fully assured that he would not be compelled to give any satisfaction for this wrong, inasmuch as the Hellenes gave none for theirs. So he carried off Helen, and the Hellenes resolved to send messengers first and to demand her back with satisfaction for the rape; and when they put forth this demand, the others alleged to them the rape of Medea, saying that the Hellenes were now desiring satisfaction to be given to them by others, though they had given none themselves nor had surrendered the person when demand was made.

Up to this point, they say, nothing more happened than the carrying away of women on both sides; but after this the Hellenes were very greatly to blame; for they set the first example of war, making an expedition into Asia before the Barbarians made any into Europe. Now they say that in their judgment, though it is an act of wrong to carry away women by force, it is a folly to set one's heart on taking vengeance for their rape, and the wise course is to pay no regard when they have been carried away; for it is evident that they would never be carried away if they were not themselves willing to go. And the Persians say that they, namely the people of Asia, when their women were carried away by force, had made it a matter of no account, but the Hellenes on account of a woman of Lacedemon gathered together a great armament, and then came to Asia and destroyed the dominion of Priam; and that from this time forward they had always considered the Hellenic race to be their enemy: for Asia and the Barbarian races which dwell there the Persians claim as belonging to them; but Europe and the Hellenic race they consider to be parted off from them.

The Persians for their part say that things happened thus; and they conclude that the beginning of their quarrel with the Hellenes was on account of the taking of Ilion: but as regards Io the Phenicians do not agree with the Persians in telling the tale thus; for they deny that they carried her off to Egypt by violent means, and they say on the other hand that when they were in Argos she was intimate with the master of their ship, and perceiving that she was with child, she was ashamed to confess it to her parents, and therefore sailed away with the Phenicians of her own will, for fear of being found out. These are the tales told by the Persians and the Phenicians severally: and concerning these things I am not going to say that they happened thus or thus, but when I have pointed to the man who first within my own knowledge began to commit wrong against the Hellenes, I shall go forward further with the story, giving an account of the cities of men, small as well as great: for those which in old times were great have for the most part become small, while those that were in my own time great used in former times to be small: so then, since I know that human prosperity never continues steadfast, I shall make mention of both indifferently.

Croesus was Lydian by race, the son of Alyattes and ruler of the nations which dwell on this side of the river Halys; which river, flowing from the South between the Syrians and the Paphlagonians, runs out towards the North Wind into that Sea which is called the Euxine. This Croesus, first of all the Barbarians of whom we have knowledge, subdued certain of the Hellenes and forced them to pay tribute, while others he gained over and made them his friends. Those whom he subdued were the Ionians, the Aiolians, and the Dorians who dwell in Asia; and those whom he made his friends were the Lacedemonians. But before the reign of Croesus all the Hellenes were free; for the expedition of the Kimmerians, which came upon Ionia before the time of Croesus, was not a conquest of the cities but a plundering incursion only.

Now the supremacy which had belonged to the Heracleidai came to the family of Croesus, called Mermnadai, in the following manner:—Candaules, whom the Hellenes call Myrsilos, was ruler of Sardis and a descendant of Alcaios, son of Heracles: for Agron, the son of Ninos, the son of Belos, the son of Alcaios, was the first of the Heracleidai who became king of Sardis, and Candaules the son of Myrsos was the last; but those who were kings over this land before Agrond, were descendants of Lydos the son of Atys, whence this whole nation was called Lydian, having been before called Meonian. From these the Heracleidai, descended from Heracles and the slave-girl of Iardanos, obtained the government, being charged with it by reason of an oracle; and they reigned for two-and-twenty generations of men, five hundred and five years, handing on the power from father to son, till the time of Clandaules the son of Myrsos.

This Candaules then of whom I speak had become passionately in love with his own wife; and having become so, he deemed that his wife was fairer by far than all other women; and thus deeming, to Gyges the son of Daskylos (for he of all his spearmen was the most pleasing to him), to this Gyges, I say, he used to impart as well the more weighty of his affairs as also the beauty of his wife, praising it above measure: and after no long time, since it was destined that evil should happen to Candaules, he said to Gyges as follows: "Gyges, I think that thou dost not believe me when I tell thee of the beauty of my wife, for it happens that men's ears are less apt of belief than their eyes: contrive therefore means by which thou mayest look upon her naked." But he cried aloud and said: "Master, what word of unwisdom is this which thou dost utter, bidding me look upon my mistress naked? When a woman puts off her tunic she puts off her modesty also. Moreover of old time those fair sayings have been found out by men, from which we ought to learn wisdom; and of these one is this,—that each man should look on his own: but I believe indeed that she is of all women the fairest and I entreat thee not to ask of me that which it is not lawful for me to do."

With such words as these he resisted, fearing lest some evil might come to him from this; but the king answered him thus: "Be of good courage, Gyges, and have no fear, either of me, that I am saying these words to try thee, or of my wife, lest any harm may happen to thee from her. For I will contrive it so from the first that she shall not even perceive that she has been seen by thee. I will place thee in the room where we sleep, behind the open door; and after I have gone in, my wife also will come to lie down. Now there is a seat near the entrance of the room, and upon this she will lay her garments as she takes them off one by one; and so thou wilt be able to gaze upon her at full leisure. And when she goes from the chair to the bed and thou shalt be behind her back, then let it be thy part to take care that she sees thee not as thou goest through the door."

He then, since he might not avoid it, gave consent: and Candaules, when he considered that it was time to rest, led Gyges to the chamber; and straightway after this the woman also appeared: and Gyges looked upon her after she came in and as she laid down her garments; and when she had her back turned towards him, as she went to the bed, then he slipped away from his hiding-place and was going forth. And as he went out, the woman caught sight of him, and perceiving that which had been done by her husband she did not cry out, though struck with shame, but she made as though she had not perceived the matter, meaning to avenge herself upon Candaules: for among the Lydians as also among most other Barbarians it is a shame even for a man to be seen naked.

At the time then she kept silence, as I say, and made no outward sign; but as soon as day had dawned, and she made ready those of the servants whom she perceived to be the most attached to herself, and after that she sent to summon Gyges. He then, not supposing that anything of that which had been done was known to her, came upon her summons; for he had been accustomed before to go whenever the queen summoned him. And when Gyges was come, the woman said to him these words: "There are now two ways open to thee, Gyges, and I give thee the choice which of the two thou wilt prefer to take. Either thou must slay Candaules and possess both me and the kingdom of Lydia, or thou must thyself here on the spot be slain, so that thou mayest not in future, by obeying Candaules in all things, see that which thou shouldest not. Either he must die who formed this design, or thou who hast looked upon me naked and done that which is not accounted lawful." For a time then Gyges was amazed at these words, and afterwards he began to entreat her that she would not bind him by necessity to make such a choice: then however, as he could not prevail with her, but saw that necessity was in truth set before him either to slay his master or to be himself slain by others, he made the choice to live himself; and he inquired further as follows: "Since thou dost compel me to take my master's life against my own will, let me hear from thee also what is the manner in which we shall lay hands upon him." And she answering said: "From that same place shall the attempt be, where he displayed me naked; and we will lay hands upon him as he sleeps."

So after they had prepared the plot, when night came on, (for Gyges was not let go nor was there any way of escape for him, but he must either be slain himself or slay Candaules), he followed the woman to the bedchamber; and she gave him a dagger and concealed him behind that very same door. Then afterwards, while Candaules was sleeping, Gyges came privily up to him and slew him, and he obtained both his wife and his kingdom: of him moreover Archilochos the Parian, who lived about that time, made mention in a trimeter iambic verse.

He obtained the kingdom however and was strengthened in it by means of the Oracle at Delphi; for when the Lydians were angry because of the fate of Candaules, and had risen in arms, a treaty was made between the followers of Gyges and the other Lydians to this effect, that if the Oracle should give answer that he was to be king of the Lydians, he should be king, and if not, he should give back the power to the sons of Heracles. So the Oracle gave answer, and Gyges accordingly became king: yet the Pythian prophetess said this also, that vengeance for the Heracleidai should come upon the descendants of Gyges in the fifth generation. Of this oracle the Lydians and their kings made no account until it was in fact fulfilled.

Thus the Mermnadai obtained the government having driven out from it the Heracleidai: and Gyges when he became ruler sent votive offerings to Delphi not a few, for of all the silver offerings at Delphi his are more in number than those of any other man; and besides the silver he offered a vast quantity of gold, and especially one offering which is more worthy of mention than the rest, namely six golden mixing-bowls, which are dedicated there as his gift: of these the weight is thirty talents, and they stand in the treasury of the Corinthians, (though in truth this treasury does not belong to the State of the Corinthians, but is that of Kypselos the son of Aëtion). This Gyges was the first of the Barbarians within our knowledge who dedicated votive offerings at Delphi, except only Midas the son of Gordias king of Phrygia, who dedicated for an offering the royal throne on which he sat before all to decide causes; and this throne, a sight worth seeing, stands in the same place with the bowls of Gyges. This gold and silver which Gyges dedicated is called Gygian by the people of Delphi, after the name of him who offered it.

Now Gyges also, as soon as he became king, led an army against Miletos and Smyrna, and he took the lower town of Colophon: but no other great deed did he do in his reign, which lasted eight-and-thirty years, therefore we will pass him by with no more mention than has already been made, and I will speak now of Ardys the son of Gyges, who became king after Gyges. He took Priene and made an invasion against Miletos; and while he was ruling over Sardis, the Kimmerians driven from their abodes by the nomad Scythians came to Asia and took Sardis except the citadel.

Now when Ardys had been king for nine-and-forty years, Sadyattes his son succeeded to his kingdom, and reigned twelve years; and after him Alyattes. This last made war against Kyaxares the descendant of Deïokes and against the Medes, and he drove the Kimmerians forth out of Asia, and he took Smyrna which had been founded from Colophon, and made an invasion against Clazomenai. From this he returned not as he desired, but with great loss: during his reign however he performed other deeds very worthy of mention as follows:—

He made war with those of Miletos, having received this war as an inheritance from his father: for he used to invade their land and besiege Miletos in the following manner:—whenever there were ripe crops upon the land, then he led an army into their confines, making his march to the sound of pipes and harps and flutes both of male and female tone: and when he came to the Milesian land, he neither pulled down the houses that were in the fields, nor set fire to them nor tore off their doors, but let them stand as they were; the trees however and the crops that were upon the land he destroyed, and then departed by the way he came: for the men of Miletos had command of the sea, so that it was of no use for his army to blockade them: and he abstained from pulling down the houses to the end that the Milesians might have places to dwell in while they sowed and tilled the land, and by the means of their labour he might have somewhat to destroy when he made his invasion.

Thus he continued to war with them for eleven years; and in the course of these years the Milesians suffered two great defeats, once when they fought a battle in the district of Limenion in their own land, and again in the plain of Maiander. Now for six of the eleven years Sadyattes the son of Ardys was still ruler of the Lydians, the same who was wont to invade the land of Miletos at the times mentioned; for this Sadyattes was he who first began the war: but for the five years which followed these first six the war was carried on by Alyattes the son of Sadyattes, who received it as an inheritance from his father (as I have already said) and applied himself to it earnestly. And none of the Ionians helped those of Miletos bear the burden of this war except only the men of Chios. These came to their aid to pay back like with like, for the Milesians had formerly assisted the Chians throughout their war with the people of Erythrai.

. Then in the twelfth year of the war, when standing corn was being burnt by the army of the Lydians, it happened as follows:—as soon as the corn was kindled, it was driven by a violent wind and set fire to the temple of Athene surnamed of Assessos; and the temple being set on fire was burnt down to the ground. Of this no account was made then; but afterwards when the army had returned to Sardis, Alyattes fell sick, and as his sickness lasted long, he sent messengers to inquire of the Oracle at Delphi, either being advised to do so by some one, or because he himself thought it best to send and inquire of the god concerning his sickness. But when these arrived at Delphi, the Pythian prophetess said that she would give them no answer, until they should have built up again the temple of Athene which they had burnt at Assessos in the land of Miletos.

Thus much I know by the report of the people of Delphi; but the Milesians add to this that Periander the son of Kypselos, being a special guest-friend of Thrasybulos the then despot of Miletos, heard of the oracle which had been given to Alyattes, and sending a messenger told Thrasybulos, in order that he might have knowledge of it beforehand and take such counsel as the case required. This is the story told by the Milesians.

And Alyattes, when this answer was reported to him, sent a herald forthwith to Miletos, desiring to make a truce with Thrasybulos and the Milesians for so long a time as he should be building the temple. He then was being sent as envoy to Miletos; and Thrasybulos in the meantime being informed beforehand of the whole matter and knowing what Alyattes was meaning to do, contrived this device:—he gathered together in the market-place all the store of provisions which was found in the city, both his own and that which belonged to private persons; and he proclaimed to the Milesians that on a signal given by him they should all begin to drink and make merry with one another.

This Thrasybulos did and thus proclaimed to the end that the herald from Sardis, seeing a vast quantity of provisions carelessly piled up, and the people feasting, might report this to Alyattes: and so on fact it happened; for when the herald returned to Sardis after seeing this and delivering to Thrasybulos the charge which was given to him by the king of Lydia, the peace which was made, came about, as I am informed, merely because of this. For Alyattes, who thought that there was a great famine in Miletos and that the people had been worn down to the extreme of misery, heard from the herald, when he returned from Miletos, the opposite to that which he himself supposed. And after this the peace was made between them on condition of being guest-friends and allies to one another, and Alyattes built two temples to Athene at Assessos in place of one, and himself recovered from his sickness. With regard then to the war waged by Alyattes with the Milesians and Thrasybulos things went thus.

As for Periander, the man who gave information about the oracle to Thrasybulos, he was the son of Kypselos, and despot of Corinth. In his life, say the Corinthians, (and with them agree the Lesbians), there happened to him a very great marvel, namely that Arion of Methymna was carried ashore at Tainaron upon a dolphin's back. This man was a harper second to none of those who then lived, and the first, so far as we know, who composed a dithyramb, naming it so and teaching it to a chorus at Corinth.

This Arion, they say, who for the most part of his time stayed with Periander, conceived a desire to sail to Italy and Sicily; and after he had there acquired large sums of money, he wished to return again to Corinth. He set forth therefore from Taras, and as he had faith in Corinthians more than in other men, he hired a ship with a crew of Corinthians. These, the story says, when out in open sea, formed a plot to cast Arion overboard and so possess his wealth; and he having obtained knowledge of this made entreaties to them, offering them his wealth and asking them to grant him his life. With this however he did not prevail upon them, but the men who were conveying him bade him either slay himself there, that he might receive burial on the land, or leap straightway into the sea. So Arion being driven to a strait entreated them that, since they were so minded, they would allow him to take his stand in full minstrel's garb upon the deck of the ship and sing; and he promised to put himself to death after he had sung. They then, well pleased to think that they should hear the best of all minstrels upon earth, drew back from the stern towards the middle of the ship; and he put on the full minstrel's garb and took his lyre, and standing on the deck performed the Orthian measure. Then as the measure ended, he threw himself into the sea just as he was, in his full minstrel's garb; and they went on sailing away to Corinth, but him, they say, a dolphin supported on its back and brought him to shore at Tainaron: and when he had come to land he proceeded to Corinth with his minstrel's garb. Thither having arrived he related all that had been done; and Periander doubting of his story kept Arion in guard and would let him go nowhere, while he kept careful watch for those who had conveyed him. When these came, he called them and inquired of them if they had any report to make of Arion; and when they said that he was safe in Italy and that they had left him at Taras faring well, Arion suddenly appeared before them in the same guise as when he made his leap from the ship; and they being struck with amazement were no longer able to deny when they were questioned. This is the tale told by the Corinthians and Lesbians alike, and there is at Tainaron a votive offering of Arion of no great size, namely a bronze figure of a man upon a dolphin's back.

Alyattes the Lydian, when he had thus waged war against the Milesians, afterwards died, having reigned seven-and-fifty years. This king, when he recovered from his sickness, dedicated a votive offering at Delphi (being the second of his house who had so done), namely a great mixing-bowl of silver with a stand for it of iron welded together, which last is a sight worth seeing above all the offerings at Delphi and the work of Glaucos the Chian, who of all men first found out the art of welding iron.

After Alyattes was dead Croesus the son of Alyattes received the kingdom in succession, being five-and-thirty years of age. He (as I said) fought against the Hellenes and of them he attacked the Ephesians first. The Ephesians then, being besieged by him, dedicated their city to Artemis and tied a rope from the temple to the wall of the city: now the distance between the ancient city, which was then being besieged, and the temple is seven furlongs. These, I say, where the first upon whom Croesus laid hands, but afterwards he did the same to the other Ionian and Aiolian cities one by one, alleging against them various causes of complaint, and making serious charges against those in whose cases he could find serious grounds, while against others of them he charged merely trifling offences.

Then when the Hellenes in Asia had been conquered and forced to pay tribute, he designed next to build for himself ships and to lay hands upon those who dwelt in the islands; and when all was prepared for his building of ships, they say that Bias of Priene (or, according to another account, Pittacos of Mytilene) came to Sardis, and being asked by Croesus whether there was any new thing doing in Hellas, brought to an end his building of ships by this saying: "O king," said he, "the men of the islands are hiring a troop of ten thousand horse, and with this they mean to march to Sardis and fight against thee." And Croesus, supposing that what he reported was true, said: "May the gods put it into the minds of the dwellers of the islands to come with horses against the sons of the Lydians!" And he answered and said: "O king, I perceive that thou dost earnestly desire to catch the men of the islands on the mainland riding upon horses; and it is not unreasonable that thou shouldest wish for this: what else however thinkest thou the men of the islands desire and have been praying for ever since the time they heard that thou wert about to build ships against them, than that they might catch the Lydians upon the sea, so as to take vengeance upon thee for the Hellenes who dwell upon the mainland, whom thou dost hold enslaved?" Croesus, they say, was greatly pleased with this conclusion, and obeying his suggestion, for he judged him to speak suitably, he stopped his building of ships; and upon that he formed a friendship with the Ionians dwelling in the islands.As time went on, when nearly all those dwelling on this side the river Halys had been subdued, (for except the Kilikians and Lykians Croesus subdued and kept under his rule all the nations, that is to say Lydians, Phrygians, Mysians, Mariandynoi, Chalybians, Paphlagonians, Thracians both Thynian and Bithynian, Carians, Ionians, Dorians, Aiolians, and Pamphylians), when these, I say, had been subdued, and while he was still adding to his Lydian dominions, there came to Sardis, then at the height of its wealth, all the wise men of the Hellas who chanced to be alive at that time, brought thither severally by various occasions; and of them one was Solon the Athenian, who after he had made laws for the Athenians at their bidding, left his native country for ten years and sailed away saying that he desired to visit various lands, in order that he might not be compelled to repeal any of the laws which he had proposed. For of themselves the Athenians were not competent to do this, having bound themselves by solemn oaths to submit for ten years to the laws which Solon should propose for them.

. So Solon, having left his native country for this reason and for the sake of seeing various lands, came to Amasis in Egypt, and also to Croesus at Sardis. Having there arrived he was entertained as a guest by Croesus in the king's palace; and afterwards, on the third or fourth day, at the bidding of Croesus his servants led Solon round to see his treasuries; and they showed him all things, how great and magnificent they were: and after he had looked upon them all and examined them as he had occasion, Croesus asked him as follows: "Athenian guest, much report of thee has come to us, both in regard to thy wisdom and thy wanderings, how that in thy search for wisdom thou hast traversed many lands to see them; now therefore a desire has come upon me to ask thee whether thou hast seen any whom thou deemest to be of all men the most happy." This he asked supposing that he himself was the happiest of men; but Solon, using no flattery but the truth only, said: "Yes, O king, Tellos the Athenian." And Croesus, marvelling at that which he said, asked him earnestly: "In what respect dost thou judge Tellos to be the most happy?" And he said: "Tellos, in the first place, living while his native State was prosperous, had sons fair and good and saw from all of them children begotten and living to grow up; and secondly he had what with us is accounted wealth, and after his life a most glorious end: for when a battle was fought by the Athenians at Eleusis against the neighbouring people, he brought up supports and routed the foe and there died by a most fair death; and the Athenians buried him publicly where he fell, and honoured him greatly."

So when Solon had moved Croesus to inquire further by the story of Tellos, recounting how many points of happiness he had, the king asked again whom he had seen proper to be placed next after this man, supposing that he himself would certainly obtain at least the second place; but he replied: "Cleobis and Biton: for these, who were of Argos by race, possessed a sufficiency of wealth and, in addition to this, strength of body such as I shall tell. Both equally had won prizes in the games, and moreover the following tale is told of them:—There was a feast of Hera among the Argives and it was by all means necessary that their mother should be borne in a car to the temple. But since their oxen were not brought up in time from the field, the young men, barred from all else by lack of time, submitted themselves to the yoke and drew the wain, their mother being borne by them upon it; and so they brought it on for five-and-forty furlongs, and came to the temple. Then after they had done this and had been seen by the assembled crowd, there came to their life a most excellent ending; and in this the deity declared that it was better for man to die than to continue to live. For the Argive men were standing round and extolling the strength of the young men, while the Argive women were extolling the mother to whose lot it had fallen to have such sons; and the mother being exceedingly rejoiced both by the deed itself and by the report made of it, took her stand in front of the image of the goddess and prayed that she would give to Cleobis and Biton her sons, who had honoured her greatly, that gift which is best for man to receive: and after this prayer, when they had sacrificed and feasted, the young men lay down to sleep within the temple itself, and never rose again, but were held bound in this last end. And the Argives made statues in the likeness of them and dedicated them as offerings at Delphi, thinking that they had proved themselves most excellent."

Thus Solon assigned the second place in respect of happiness to these: and Croesus was moved to anger and said: "Athenian guest, hast thou then so cast aside our prosperous state as worth nothing, that thou dost prefer to us even men of private station?" And he said: "Croesus, thou art inquiring about human fortunes of one who well knows that the Deity is altogether envious and apt to disturb our lot. For in the course of long time a man may see many things which he would not desire to see, and suffer also many things which he would not desire to suffer. The limit of life for a man I lay down at seventy years: and these seventy years give twenty-five thousand and two hundred days, not reckoning for any intercalated month. Then if every other one of these years shall be made longer by one month, that the seasons may be caused to come round at the due time of the year, the intercalated months will be in number five-and-thirty besides the seventy years; and of these months the days will be one thousand and fifty. Of all these days, being in number twenty-six thousand two hundred and fifty, which go to the seventy years, one day produces nothing at all which resembles what another brings with it. Thus then, O Croesus, man is altogether a creature of accident. As for thee, I perceive that thou art both great in wealth and king of many men, but that of which thou didst ask me I cannot call thee yet, until I learn that thou hast brought thy life to a fair ending: for the very rich man is not at all to be accounted more happy than he who has but his subsistence from day to day, unless also the fortune go with him of ending his life well in possession of all things fair. For many very wealthy men are not happy, while many who have but a moderate living are fortunate; and in truth the very rich man who is not happy has two advantages only as compared with the poor man who is fortunate, whereas this latter has many as compared with the rich man who is not happy. The rich man is able better to fulfil his desire, and also to endure a great calamity if it fall upon him; whereas the other has advantage over him in these things which follow:—he is not indeed able equally with the rich man to endure a calamity or to fulfil his desire, but these his good fortune keeps away from him, while he is sound of limb, free from disease, untouched by suffering, the father of fair children and himself of comely form; and if in addition to this he shall end his life well, he is worthy to be called that which thou seekest, namely a happy man; but before he comes to his end it is well to hold back and not to call him yet happy but only fortunate. Now to possess all these things together is impossible for one who is mere man, just as no single land suffices to supply all things for itself, but one thing it has and another it lacks, and the land that has the greatest number of things is the best: so also in the case of a man, no single person is complete in himself, for one thing he has and another he lacks; but whosoever of men continues to the end in possession of the greatest number of these things and then has a gracious ending of his life, he is by me accounted worthy, O king, to receive this name. But we must of every thing examine the end and how it will turn out at the last, for to many God shows but a glimpse of happiness and then plucks them up by the roots and overturns them."

Thus saying he refused to gratify Croesus, who sent him away from his presence holding him in no esteem, and thinking him utterly senseless in that he passed over present good things and bade men look to the end of every matter.

After Solon had departed, a great retribution from God came upon Croesus, probably because he judged himself to be the happiest of all men. First there came and stood by him a dream, which showed to him the truth of the evils that were about to come to pass in respect of his son. Now Croesus had two sons, of whom one was deficient, seeing that he was deaf and dumb, while the other far surpassed his companions of the same age in all things: and the name of this last was Atys. As regards this Atys then, the dream signified to Croesus that he should lose him by the blow of an iron spear-point: and when he rose up from sleep and considered the matter with himself, he was struck with fear on account of the dream; and first he took for his son a wife; and whereas his son had been wont to lead the armies of the Lydians, he now no longer sent him forth anywhere on any such business; and the javelins and lances and all such things which men use for fighting he conveyed out of the men's apartments and piled them up in the inner bed-chambers, for fear lest something hanging up might fall down upon his son.

Then while he was engaged about the marriage of his son, there came to Sardis a man under a misfortune and with hands not clean, a Phrygian by birth and of the royal house. This man came to the house of Croesus, and according to the customs which prevail in that land made request that he might have cleansing; and Croesus gave him cleansing: now the manner of cleansing among the Lydians is the same almost as that which the Hellenes use. So when Croesus had done that which was customary, he asked of him whence he came and who he was, saying as follows: "Man, who art thou, and from what region of Phrygia didst thou come to sit upon my hearth? And whom of men or women didst thou slay?" And he replied: "O king, I am the son of Gordias, the son of Midas, and I am called Adrastos; and I slew my own brother against my will, and therefore am I here, having been driven forth by my father and deprived of all that I had." And Croesus answered thus: "Thou art, as it chances, the offshoot of men who are our friends and thou hast come to friends, among whom thou shalt want of nothing so long as thou shalt remain in our land: and thou wilt find it most for thy profit to bear this misfortune as lightly as may be." So he had his abode with Croesus.

. During this time there was produced in the Mysian Olympos a boar of monstrous size. This, coming down from the mountain aforesaid, ravaged the fields of the Mysians, and although the Mysians went out against it often, yet they could do it no hurt, but rather received hurt themselves from it; so at length messengers came from the Mysians to Croesus and said: "O king, there has appeared in our land a boar of monstrous size, which lays waste our fields; and we, desiring eagerly to take it, are not able: now therefore we ask of thee to send with us thy son and also a chosen band of young men with dogs, that we may destroy it out of our land." Thus they made request, and Croesus calling to mind the words of the dream spoke to them as follows: "As touching my son, make no further mention of him in this matter; for I will not send him with you, seeing that he is newly married and is concerned now with the affairs of his marriage: but I will send with you chosen men of the Lydians and the whole number of my hunting dogs, and I will give command to those who go, to be as zealous as may be in helping you to destroy the wild beast out of your land."

Thus he made reply, and while the Mysians were being contented with this answer, there came in also the son of Croesus, having heard of the request made by the Mysians: and when Croesus said that he would not send his son with them, the young man spoke as follows: "My father, in times past the fairest and most noble part was allotted to us, to go out continually to wars and to the chase and so have good repute; but now thou hast debarred me from both of these, although thou hast not observed in me any cowardly or faint-hearted spirit. And now with what face must I appear when I go to and from the market-place of the city? What kind of a man shall I be esteemed by the citizens, and what kind of a man shall I be esteemed by my newly-married wife? With what kind of a husband will she think that she is mated? Therefore either let me go to the hunt, or persuade me by reason that these things are better for me done as now they are."

And Croesus made answer thus: "My son, not because I have observed in thee any spirit of cowardice or any other ungracious thing, do I act thus; but a vision of a dream came and stood by me in my sleep and told me that thou shouldest be short-lived, and that thou shouldest perish by a spear-point of iron. With thought of this vision therefore I both urged on this marriage for thee, and I refuse now to send thee upon the matter which is being taken in hand, having a care of thee that I may steal thee from thy fate at least for the period of my own life, if by any means possible for me to do so. For thou art, as it chances, my only son: the other I do not reckon as one, seeing that he is deficient in hearing."

The young man made answer thus: "It may well be forgiven in thee, O my father, that thou shouldest have a care of me after having seen such a vision; but that which thou dost not understand, and in which the meaning of the dream has escaped thee, it is right that I should expound to thee. Thou sayest the dream declared that I should end my life by means of a spear-point of iron: but what hands has a boar, or what spear-point of iron, of which thou art afraid? If the dream had told thee that I should end my life by a tusk, or any other thing which resembles that, it would be right for thee doubtless to do as thou art doing; but it said 'by a spear-point.' Since therefore our fight will not be with men, let me now go."

Croesus made answer: "My son, thou dost partly prevail with me by declaring thy judgment about the dream; therefore, having been prevailed upon by thee, I change my resolution and allow thee to go to the chase."

Having thus said Croesus went to summon Adrastos the Phrygian; and when he came, he addressed him thus: "Adrastos, when thou wast struck with a grievous misfortune (with which I reproach thee not), I cleansed thee, and I have received thee into my house supplying all thy costs. Now therefore, since having first received kindness from me thou art bound to requite me with kindness, I ask of thee to be the protector of my son who goes forth to the chase, lest any evil robbers come upon you by the way to do you harm; and besides this thou too oughtest to go where thou mayest become famous by thy deeds, for it belongs to thee as an inheritance from thy fathers so to do, and moreover thou hast strength for it."

Adrastos made answer: "O king, but for this I should not have been going to any such contest of valour; for first it is not fitting that one who is suffering such a great misfortune as mine should seek the company of his fellows who are in prosperity, and secondly I have no desire for it; and for many reasons I should have kept myself away. But now, since thou art urgent with me, and I ought to gratify thee (for I am bound to requite thee with kindness), I am ready to do this: expect therefore that thy son, whom thou commandest me to protect, will return home to thee unhurt, so far as his protector may avail to keep him safe."

When he had made answer to Croesus in words like these, they afterwards set forth provided with chosen young men and with dogs. And when they were come to Mount Olympos, they tracked the animal; and having found it and taken their stand round in a circle, they were hurling against it their spears. Then the guest, he who had been cleansed of manslaughter, whose name was Adrastos, hurling a spear at it missed the boar and struck the son of Croesus. So he being struck by the spear-point fulfilled the saying of the dream. And one ran to report to Croesus that which had come to pass, and having come to Sardis he signified to him of the combat and of the fate of his son. And Croesus was very greatly disturbed by the death of his son, and was much the more moved to complaining by this, namely that his son was slain by the man whom he had himself cleansed of manslaughter. And being grievously troubled by the misfortune he called upon Zeus the Cleanser, protesting to him that which he had suffered from his guest, and he called moreover upon the Protector of Suppliants and the Guardian of Friendship, naming still the same god, and calling upon him as the Protector of Suppliants because when he received the guest into his house he had been fostering ignorantly the slayer of his son, and as the Guardian of Friendship because having sent him as a protector he had found him the worst of foes.

After this the Lydians came bearing the corpse, and behind it followed the slayer: and he taking his stand before the corpse delivered himself up to Croesus, holding forth his hands and bidding the king slay him over the corpse, speaking of his former misfortune and saying that in addition to this he had now been the destroyer of the man who had cleansed him of it; and that life for him was no more worth living. But Croesus hearing this pitied Adrastos, although he was himself suffering so great an evil of his own, and said to him: "Guest, I have already received from thee all the satisfaction that is due, seeing that thou dost condemn thyself to suffer death; and not thou alone art the cause of this evil, except in so far as thou wert the instrument of it against thine own will, but some one, as I suppose, of the gods, who also long ago signified to me that which was about to be." So Croesus buried his son as was fitting: but Adrastos the son of Gordias, the son of Midas, he who had been the slayer of his own brother and the slayer also of the man who had cleansed him, when silence came of all men round about the tomb, recognising that he was more grievously burdened by misfortune than all men of whom he knew, slew himself upon the grave.

For two years then Croesus remained quiet in his mourning, because he was deprived of his son: but after this period of time the overthrowing of the rule of Astyages the son of Kyaxares by Cyrus the son of Cambyses, and the growing greatness of the Persians caused Croesus to cease from his mourning, and led him to a care of cutting short the power of the Persians, if by any means he might, while yet it was in growth and before they should have become great.

So having formed this design he began forthwith to make trial of the Oracles, both those of the Hellenes and that in Libya, sending messengers some to one place and some to another, some to go to Delphi, others to Abai of the Phokians, and others to Dodona; and some were sent to the shrine of Amphiaraos and to that of Trophonios, others to Branchidai in the land of Miletos: these are the Oracles of the Hellenes to which Croesus sent messengers to seek divination; and others he sent to the shrine of Ammon in Libya to inquire there. Now he was sending the messengers abroad to the end that he might try the Oracles and find out what knowledge they had, so that if they should be found to have knowledge of the truth, he might send and ask them secondly whether he should attempt to march against the Persians.

And to the Lydians whom he sent to make trial of the Oracles he gave charge as follows,—that from the day on which they set out from Sardis they should reckon up the number of the days following and on the hundredth day they should consult the Oracles, asking what Croesus the son of Alyattes king of the Lydians chanced then to be doing: and whatever the Oracles severally should prophesy, this they should cause to be written down and bear it back to him. Now what the other Oracles prophesied is not by any reported, but at Delphi, so soon as the Lydians entered the sanctuary of the temple to consult the god and asked that which they were commanded to ask, the Pythian prophetess spoke thus in hexameter measure:

"But the number of sand I know, and the measure of drops in the ocean;

The dumb man I understand, and I hear the speech of the speechless:

And there hath come to my soul the smell of a strong-shelled tortoise

Boiling in caldron of bronze, and the flesh of a lamb mingled with it;

Under it bronze is laid, it hath bronze as a clothing upon it."

When the Pythian prophetess had uttered this oracle, the Lydians caused the prophecy to be written down, and went away at once to Sardis. And when the rest also who had been sent round were there arrived with the answers of the Oracles, then Croesus unfolded the writings one by one and looked upon them: and at first none of them pleased him, but when he heard that from Delphi, forthwith he did worship to the god and accepted the answer, judging that the Oracle at Delphi was the only true one, because it had found out what he himself had done. For when he had sent to the several Oracles his messengers to consult the gods, keeping well in mind the appointed day he contrived the following device,—he thought of something which it would be impossible to discover or to conceive of, and cutting up a tortoise and a lamb he boiled them together himself in a caldron of bronze, laying a cover of bronze over them.

This then was the answer given to Croesus from Delphi; and as regards the answer of Amphiaraos, I cannot tell what he replied to the Lydians after they had done the things customary in his temple, for there is no record of this any more than of the others, except only that Croesus thought that he also possessed a true Oracle.

After this with great sacrifices he endeavoured to win the favour of the god at Delphi: for of all the animals that are fit for sacrifice he offered three thousand of each kind, and he heaped up couches overlaid with gold and overlaid with silver, and cups of gold, and robes of purple, and tunics, making of them a great pyre, and this he burnt up, hoping by these means the more to win over the god to the side of the Lydians: and he proclaimed to all the Lydians that every one of them should make sacrifice with that which each man had. And when he had finished the sacrifice, he melted down a vast quantity of gold, and of it he wrought half-plinths making them six palms in length and three in breadth, and in height one palm; and their number was one hundred and seventeen. Of these four were of pure gold weighing two talents and a half each, and others of gold alloyed with silver weighing two talents. And he caused to be made also an image of a lion of pure gold weighing ten talents; which lion, when the temple of Delphi was being burnt down, fell from off the half-plinths, for upon these it was set, and is placed now in the treasury of the Corinthians, weighing six talents and a half, for three talents and a half were melted away from it.

So Croesus having finished all these things sent them to Delphi, and with them these besides:—two mixing bowls of great size, one of gold and the other of silver, of which the golden bowl was placed on the right hand as one enters the temple, and the silver on the left, but the places of these also were changed after the temple was burnt down, and the golden bowl is now placed in the treasury of the people of Clazomenai, weighing eight and a half talents and twelve pounds over, while the silver one is placed in the corner of the vestibule and holds six hundred amphors (being filled with wine by the Delphians on the feast of the Theophania): this the people of Delphi say is the work of Theodoros the Samian, and, as I think, rightly, for it is evident to me that the workmanship is of no common kind: moreover Croesus sent four silver wine-jars, which stand in the treasury of the Corinthians, and two vessels for lustral water, one of gold and the other of silver, of which the gold one is inscribed "from the Lacedemonians," who say that it is their offering: therein however they do not speak rightly; for this also is from Croesus, but one of the Delphians wrote the inscription upon it, desiring to gratify the Lacedemonians; and his name I know but will not make mention of it. The boy through whose hand the water flows is from the Lacedemonians, but neither of the vessels for lustral water. And many other votive offerings Croesus sent with these, not specially distinguished, among which are certain castings of silver of a round shape, and also a golden figure of a woman three cubits high, which the Delphians say is a statue of the baker of Croesus. Moreover Croesus dedicated the ornaments from his wife's neck and her girdles.

These are the things which he sent to Delphi; and to Amphiaraos, having heard of his valour and of his evil fate, he dedicated a shield made altogether of gold throughout, and a spear all of solid gold, the shaft being of gold also as well as the two points, which offerings were both remaining even to my time at Thebes in the temple of Ismenian Apollo.

To the Lydians who were to carry these gifts to the temples Croesus gave charge that they should ask the Oracles this question also,—whether Croesus should march against the Persians, and if so, whether he should join with himself any army of men as his friends. And when the Lydians had arrived at the places to which they had been sent and had dedicated the votive offerings, they inquired of the Oracles and said: "Croesus, king of the Lydians and of other nations, considering that these are the only true Oracles among men, presents to you gifts such as your revelations deserve, and asks you again now whether he shall march against the Persians, and if so, whether he shall join with himself any army of men as allies." They inquired thus, and the answers of both the Oracles agreed in one, declaring to Croesus that if he should march against the Persians he should destroy a great empire: and they counselled him to find out the most powerful of the Hellenes and join these with himself as friends.

So when the answers were brought back and Croesus heard them, he was delighted with the oracles, and expecting that he would certainly destroy the kingdom of Cyrus, he sent again to Pytho, and presented to the men of Delphi, having ascertained the number of them, two staters of gold for each man: and in return for this the Delphians gave to Croesus and to the Lydians precedence in consulting the Oracle and freedom from all payments, and the right to front seats at the games, with this privilege also for all time, that any one of them who wished should be allowed to become a citizen of Delphi.

And having made presents to the men of Delphi, Croesus consulted the Oracle the third time; for from the time when he learnt the truth of the Oracle, he made abundant use of it. And consulting the Oracle he inquired whether his monarchy would endure for a long time. And the Pythian prophetess answered him thus:

"But when it cometh to pass that a mule of the Medes shall be monarch

Then by the pebbly Hermos, O Lydian delicate-footed,

Flee and stay not, and be not ashamed to be callèd a coward."

By these lines when they came to him Croesus was pleased more than by all the rest, for he supposed that a mule would never be ruler of the Medes instead of a man, and accordingly that he himself and his heirs would never cease from their rule. Then after this he gave thought to inquire which people of the Hellenes he should esteem the most powerful and gain over to himself as friends. And inquiring he found that the Lacedemonians and the Athenians had the pre-eminence, the first of the Dorian and the others of the Ionian race. For these were the most eminent races in ancient time, the second being a Pelasgian and the first a Hellenic race: and the one never migrated from its place in any direction, while the other was very exceedingly given to wanderings; for in the reign of Deucalion this race dwelt in Pthiotis, and in the time of Doros the son of Hellen in the land lying below Ossa and Olympos, which is called Histiaiotis; and when it was driven from Histiaiotis by the sons of Cadmos, it dwelt in Pindos and was called Makednian; and thence it moved afterwards to Dryopis, and from Dryopis it came finally to Peloponnesus, and began to be called Dorian.

What language however the Pelasgians used to speak I am not able with certainty to say. But if one must pronounce judging by those that still remain of the Pelasgians who dwelt in the city of Creston above the Tyrsenians, and who were once neighbours of the race now called Dorian, dwelling then in the land which is now called Thessaliotis, and also by those that remain of the Pelasgians who settled at Plakia and Skylake in the region of the Hellespont, who before that had been settlers with the Athenians, and of the natives of the various other towns which are really Pelasgian, though they have lost the name,—if one must pronounce judging by these, the Pelasgians used to speak a Barbarian language. If therefore all the Pelasgian race was such as these, then the Attic race, being Pelasgian, at the same time when it changed and became Hellenic, unlearnt also its language. For the people of Creston do not speak the same language with any of those who dwell about them, nor yet do the people of Phakia, but they speak the same language one as the other: and by this it is proved that they still keep unchanged the form of language which they brought with them when they migrated to these places.

As for the Hellenic race, it has used ever the same language, as I clearly perceive, since it first took its rise; but since the time when it parted off feeble at first from the Pelasgian race, setting forth from a small beginning it has increased to that great number of races which we see, and chiefly because many Barbarian races have been added to it besides. Moreover it is true, as I think, of the Pelasgian race also, that so far as it remained Barbarian it never made any great increase.

Of these races then Croesus was informed that the Athenian was held subject and torn with faction by Peisistratos the son of Hippocrates, who then was despot of the Athenians. For to Hippocrates, when as a private citizen he went to view the Olympic games, a great marvel had occurred. After he had offered the sacrifice, the caldrons which were standing upon the hearth, full of pieces of flesh and of water, boiled without fire under them and ran over. And Chilon the Lacedemonian, who chanced to have been present and to have seen the marvel, advised Hippocrates first not to bring into his house a wife to bear him children, and secondly, if he happened to have one already, to dismiss her, and if he chanced to have a son, to disown him. When Chilon had thus recommended, Hippocrates, they say, was not willing to be persuaded, and so there was born to him afterwards this Peisistratos; who, when the Athenians of the shore were at feud with those of the plain, Megacles the son of Alcmaion being leader of the first faction, and Lycurgos the son of Aristolaïdes of that of the plain, aimed at the despotism for himself and gathered a third party. So then, after having collected supporters and called himself leader of the men of the mountain-lands, he contrived a device as follows:—he inflicted wounds upon himself and upon his mules, and then drove his car into the market-place, as if he had just escaped from his opponents, who, as he alleged, had desired to kill him when he was driving into the country: and he asked the commons that he might obtain some protection from them, for before this he had gained reputation in his command against the Megarians, during which he took Nisaia and performed other signal service. And the commons of the Athenians being deceived gave him those men chosen from the dwellers in the city who became not indeed the spear-men of Peisistratos but his club-men; for they followed behind him bearing wooden clubs. And these made insurrection with Peisistratos and obtained possession of the Acropolis. Then Peisistratos was ruler of the Athenians, not having disturbed the existing magistrates nor changed the ancient laws; but he administered the State under that constitution of things which was already established, ordering it fairly and well.

However, no long time after this the followers of Megacles and those of Lycurgos joined together and drove him forth. Thus Peisistratos had obtained possession of Athens for the first time, and thus he lost the power before he had it firmly rooted. But those who had driven out Peisistratos became afterwards at feud with one another again. And Megacles, harassed by the party strife, sent a message to Peisistratos asking whether he was willing to have his daughter to wife on condition of becoming despot. And Peisistratos having accepted the proposal and made an agreement on these terms, they contrived with a view to his return a device the most simple by far, as I think, that ever was practised, considering at least that it was devised at a time when the Hellenic race had been long marked off from the Barbarian as more skilful and further removed from foolish simplicity, and among the Athenians who are accounted the first of the Hellenes in ability. In the deme of Paiania there was a woman whose name was Phya, in height four cubits all but three fingers, and also fair of form. This woman they dressed in full armour and caused her to ascend a chariot and showed her the bearing in which she might best beseem her part, and so they drove to the city, having sent on heralds to run before them, who, when they arrived at the city, spoke that which had been commanded them, saying as follows: "O Athenians, receive with favour Peisistratos, whom Athene herself, honouring him most of all men, brings back to her Acropolis." So the heralds went about hither and thither saying this, and straightway there came to the demes in the country round a report that Athene was bringing Peisistratos back, while at the same time the men of the city, persuaded that the woman was the very goddess herself, were paying worship to the human creature and receiving Peisistratos.

So having received back the despotism in the manner which has been said, Peisistratos according to the agreement made with Megacles married the daughter of Megacles; but as he had already sons who were young men, and as the descendants of Alcmaion were said to be under a curse, therefore not desiring that children should be born to him from his newly-married wife, he had commerce with her not in the accustomed manner. And at first the woman kept this secret, but afterwards she told her mother, whether in answer to her inquiry or not I cannot tell; and the mother told her husband Megacles. He then was very indignant that he should be dishonoured by Peisistratos; and in his anger straightway he proceeded to compose his quarrel with the men of his faction. And when Peisistratos heard of that which was being done against himself, he departed wholly from the land and came to Eretria, where he took counsel together with his sons: and the advice of Hippias having prevailed, that they should endeavour to win back the despotism, they began to gather gifts of money from those States which owed them obligations for favours received: and many contributed great sums, but the Thebans surpassed the rest in the giving of money. Then, not to make the story long, time elapsed and at last everything was prepared for their return. For certain Argives came as mercenaries from the Peloponnesus, and a man of Naxos had come to them of his own motion, whose name was Lygdamis, and showed very great zeal in providing both money and men.

So starting from Eretria after the lapse of ten years they returned back; and in Attica the first place of which they took possession was Marathon. While they were encamping here, their partisans from the city came to them, and also others flowed in from the various demes, to whom despotic rule was more welcome than freedom. So these were gathering themselves together; but the Athenians in the city, so long as Peisistratos was collecting the money, and afterwards when he took possession of Marathon, made no account of it; but when they heard that he was marching from Marathon towards the city, then they went to the rescue against him. These then were going in full force to fight against the returning exiles, and the forces of Peisistratos, as they went towards the city starting from Marathon, met them just when they came to the temple of Athene Pallenis, and there encamped opposite to them. Then moved by divine guidance there came into the presence of Peisistratos Amphilytos the Arcarnanian, a soothsayer, who approaching him uttered an oracle in hexameter verse, saying thus:

"But now the cast hath been made and the net hath been widely extended,

And in the night the tunnies will dart through the moon-lighted waters."

This oracle he uttered to him being divinely inspired, and Peisistratos, having understood the oracle and having said that he accepted the prophecy which was uttered, led his army against the enemy. Now the Athenians from the city were just at that time occupied with the morning meal, and some of them after their meal with games of dice or with sleep; and the forces of Peisistratos fell upon the Athenians and put them to flight. Then as they fled, Peisistratos devised a very skilful counsel, to the end that the Athenians might not gather again into one body but might remain scattered abroad. He mounted his sons on horseback and sent them before him; and overtaking the fugitives they said that which was commanded them by Peisistratos, bidding them be of good cheer and that each man should depart to his own home.

Thus then the Athenians did, and so Peisistratos for the third time obtained possession of Athens, and he firmly rooted his despotism by many foreign mercenaries and by much revenue of money, coming partly from the land itself and partly from about the river Strymon, and also by taking as hostages the sons of those Athenians who had remained in the land and had not at once fled, and placing them in the hands of Naxos; for this also Peisistratos conquered by war and delivered into the charge of Lygdamis. Moreover besides this he cleansed the island of Delos in obedience to the oracles; and his cleansing was of the following kind:—so far as the view from the temple extended he dug up all the dead bodies which were buried in this part and removed them to another part of Delos. So Peisistratos was despot of the Athenians; but of the Athenians some had fallen in the battle, and others of them with the sons of Alcmaion were exiles from their native land.

Such was the condition of things which Croesus heard was prevailing among the Athenians during this time; but as to the Lacedemonians he heard that they had escaped from great evils and had now got the better of the Tegeans in the war. For when Leon and Hegesicles were kings of Sparta, the Lacedemonians, who had good success in all their other wars, suffered disaster in that alone which they waged against the men of Tegea. Moreover in the times before this they had the worst laws of almost all the Hellenes, both in matters which concerned themselves alone and also in that they had no dealings with strangers. And they made their change to a good constitution of laws thus:—Lycurgos, a man of the Spartans who was held in high repute, came to the Oracle at Delphi, and as he entered the sanctuary of the temple, straightway the Pythian prophetess said as follows:

"Lo, thou art come, O Lycurgos, to this rich shrine of my temple,

Loved thou by Zeus and by all who possess the abodes of Olympos.

Whether to call thee a god, I doubt, in my voices prophetic,

God or a man, but rather a god I think, O Lycurgos."

Some say in addition to this that the Pythian prophetess also set forth to him the order of things which is now established for the Spartans; but the Lacedemonians themselves say that Lycurgos having become guardian of Leobotes his brother's son, who was king of the Spartans, brought in these things from Crete. For as soon as he became guardian, he changed all the prevailing laws, and took measures that they should not transgress his institutions: and after this Lycurgos established that which appertained to war, namely Enomoties and Triecads and Common Meals, and in addition to this the Ephors and the Senate. Having changed thus, the Spartans had good laws; and to Lycurgos after he was dead they erected a temple, and they pay him great worship. So then, as might be supposed, with a fertile land and with no small number of men dwelling in it, they straightway shot up and became prosperous: and it was no longer sufficient for them to keep still; but presuming that they were superior in strength to the Arcadians, they consulted the Oracle at Delphi respecting conquest of the whole of Arcadia; and the Pythian prophetess gave answer thus:

"The land of Arcadia thou askest; thou askest me much; I refuse it;

Many there are in Arcadian land, stout men, eating acorns;

These will prevent thee from this: but I am not grudging towards thee;

Tegea beaten with sounding feet I will give thee to dance in,

And a fair plain I will give thee to measure with line and divide it."

When the Lacedemonians heard report of this, they held off from the other Arcadians, and marched against the Tegeans with fetters in their hands, trusting to a deceitful oracle and expecting that they would make slaves of the men of Tegea. But having been worsted in the encounter, those of them who were taken alive worked wearing the fetters which they themselves brought with them and having "measured with line and divided" the plain of the Tegeans. And these fetters with which they had been bound were preserved even to my own time at Tegea, hanging about the temple of Athene Alea.

In the former war then I say they struggled against the Tegeans continually with ill success; but in the time of Croesus and in the reign of Anaxandrides and Ariston at Lacedemon the Spartans had at length become victors in the war; and they became so in the following manner:—As they continued to be always worsted in the war by the men of Tegea, they sent messengers to consult the Oracle at Delphi and inquired what god they should propitiate in order to get the better of the men of Tegea in the war: and the Pythian prophetess made answer to them that they should bring into their land the bones of Orestes the son of Agamemnon. Then as they were not able to find the grave of Orestes, they sent men again to go to the god and to inquire about the spot where Orestes was laid: and when the messengers who were sent asked this, the prophetess said as follows:

"Tegea there is, in Arcadian land, in a smooth place founded;

Where there do blow two blasts by strong compulsion together;

Stroke too there is and stroke in return, and trouble on trouble.

There Agamemnon's son in the life-giving earth is reposing;

Him if thou bring with thee home, of Tegea thou shalt be master."

When the Lacedemonians had heard this they were none the less far from finding it out, though they searched all places; until the time that Lichas, one of those Spartans who are called "Well-doers," discovered it. Now the "Well-doers" are of the citizens the eldest who are passing from the ranks of the "Horsemen," in each year five; and these are bound during that year in which they pass out from the "Horsemen," to allow themselves to be sent without ceasing to various places by the Spartan State.

Lichas then, being one of these, discovered it in Tegea by means both of fortune and ability. For as there were at that time dealings under truce with the men of Tegea, he had come to a forge there and was looking at iron being wrought;

and he was in wonder as he saw that which was being done. The smith therefore, perceiving that he marvelled at it, ceased from his work and said: "Surely, thou stranger of Lacedemon, if thou hadst seen that which I once saw, thou wouldst have marvelled much, since now it falls out that thou dost marvel so greatly at the working of this iron; for I, desiring in this enclosure to make a well, lighted in my digging upon a coffin of seven cubits in length; and not believing that ever there had been men larger than those of the present day, I opened it, and I saw that the dead body was equal in length to the coffin: then after I had measured it, I filled in the earth over it again." He then thus told him of that which he had seen; and the other, having thought upon that which was told, conjectured that this was Orestes according to the saying of the Oracle, forming his conjecture in the following manner:—whereas he saw that the smith had two pairs of bellows, he concluded that these were the winds spoken of, and that the anvil and the hammer were the stroke and the stroke in return, and that the iron which was being wrought was the trouble laid upon trouble, making comparison by the thought that iron has been discovered for the evil of mankind. Having thus conjectured he came back to Sparta and declared the whole matter to the Lacedemonians; and they brought a charge against him on a fictitious pretext and drove him out into exile. So having come to Tegea, he told the smith of his evil fortune and endeavoured to hire from him the enclosure, but at first he would not allow him to have it: at length however Lichas persuaded him and he took up his abode there; and he dug up the grave and gathered together the bones and went with them away to Sparta. From that time, whenever they made trial of one another, the Lacedemonians had much the advantage in the war; and by now they had subdued to themselves the greater part of Peloponnesus besides.

Croesus accordingly being informed of all these things was sending messengers to Sparta with gifts in their hands to ask for an alliance, having commanded them what they ought to say: and they when they came said: "Croesus king of the Lydians and also of other nations sent us hither and saith as follows: O Lacedemonians, whereas the god by an oracle bade me join with myself the Hellene as a friend, therefore, since I am informed that ye are the chiefs of Hellas, I invite you according to the oracle, desiring to be your friend and your ally apart from all guile and deceit." Thus did Croesus announce to the Lacedemonians through his messengers; and the Lacedemonians, who themselves also had heard of the oracle given to Croesus, were pleased at the coming of the Lydians and exchanged oaths of friendship and alliance: for they were bound to Croesus also by some services rendered to them even before this time; since the Lacedemonians had sent to Sardis and were buying gold there with purpose of using it for the image of Apollo which is now set up on Mount Thornax in the Lacedemonian land; and Croesus, when they desired to buy it, gave it them as a gift.

For this reason therefore the Lacedemonians accepted the alliance, and also because he chose them as his friends, preferring them to all the other Hellenes. And not only were they ready themselves when he made his offer, but they caused a mixing-bowl to be made of bronze, covered outside with figures round the rim and of such a size as to hold three hundred amphors, and this they conveyed, desiring to give it as a gift in return to Croesus. This bowl never came to Sardis for reasons of which two accounts are given as follows:—The Lacedemonians say that when the bowl was on its way to Sardis and came opposite the land of Samos, the men of Samos having heard of it sailed out with ships of war and took it away; but the Samians themselves say that the Lacedemonians who were conveying the bowl, finding that they were too late and hearing that Sardis had been taken and Croesus was a prisoner, sold the bowl in Samos, and certain private persons bought it and dedicated it as a votive offering in the temple of Hera; and probably those who had sold it would say when they returned to Sparta that it had been taken from them by the Samians.

Thus then it happened about the mixing-bowl: but meanwhile Croesus, mistaking the meaning of the oracle, was making a march into Cappadokia, expecting to overthrow Cyrus and the power of the Persians: and while Croesus was preparing to march against the Persians, one of the Lydians, who even before this time was thought to be a wise man but in consequence of this opinion got a very great name for wisdom among the Lydians, had advised Croesus as follows (the name of the man was Sandanis):—"O king, thou art preparing to march against men who wear breeches of leather, and the rest of their clothing is of leather also; and they eat food not such as they desire but such as they can obtain, dwelling in a land which is rugged; and moreover they make no use of wine but drink water; and no figs have they for dessert, nor any other good thing. On the one hand, if thou shalt overcome them, what wilt thou take away from them, seeing they have nothing? and on the other hand, if thou shalt be overcome, consider how many good things thou wilt lose; for once having tasted our good things, they will cling to them fast and it will not be possible to drive them away. I for my own part feel gratitude to the gods that they do not put it into the minds of the Persians to march against the Lydians." Thus he spoke not persuading Croesus: for it is true indeed that the Persians before they subdued the Lydians had no luxury nor any good thing.

Now the Cappadokians are called by the Hellenes Syrians; and these Syrians, before the Persians had rule, were subjects of the Medes, but at this time they were subjects of Cyrus. For the boundary between the Median empire and the Lydian was the river Halys; and this flows from the mountain-land of Armenia through the Kilikians, and afterwards, as it flows, it has the Matienians on the right hand and the Phrygians on the other side; then passing by these and flowing up towards the North Wind, it bounds on the one side the Cappadokian Syrians and on the left hand the Paphlagonians. Thus the river Halys cuts off from the rest almost all the lower parts of Asia by a line extending from the sea that is opposite Cyprus to the Euxine. And this tract is the neck of the whole peninsula, the distance of the journey being such that five days are spent on the way by a man without encumbrance.

Now for the following reasons Croesus was marching into Cappadokia:—first because he desired to acquire the land in addition to his own possessions, and then especially because he had confidence in the oracle and wished to take vengeance on Cyrus for Astyages. For Cyrus the son of Cambyses had conquered Astyages and was keeping him in captivity, who was brother by marriage to Croesus and king of the Medes: and he had become the brother by marriage of Croesus in this manner:—A horde of the nomad Scythians at feud with the rest withdrew and sought refuge in the land of the Medes: and at this time the ruler of the Medes was Kyaxares the son of Phraortes, the son of Deïokes, who at first dealt well with these Scythians, being suppliants for his protection; and esteeming them very highly he delivered boys to them to learn their speech and the art of shooting with the bow. Then time went by, and the Scythians used to go out continually to the chase and always brought back something; till once it happened that they took nothing, and when they returned with empty hands Kyaxares (being, as he showed on this occasion, not of an eminently good disposition) dealt with them very harshly and used insult towards them. And they, when they had received this treatment from Kyaxares, considering that they had suffered indignity, planned to kill and to cut up one of the boys who were being instructed among them, and having dressed his flesh as they had been wont to dress the wild animals, to bear it to Kyaxares and give it to him, pretending that it was game taken in hunting; and when they had given it, their design was to make their way as quickly as possible to Alyattes the son of Sadyattes at Sardis. This then was done; and Kyaxares with the guests who ate at his table tasted of that meat, and the Scythians having so done became suppliants for the protection of Alyattes.

After this, seeing that Alyattes would not give up the Scythians when Kyaxares demanded them, there had arisen war between the Lydians and the Medes lasting five years; in which years the Medes often discomfited the Lydians and the Lydians often discomfited the Medes (and among others they fought also a battle by night): and as they still carried on the war with equally balanced fortune, in the sixth year a battle took place in which it happened, when the fight had begun, that suddenly the day became night. And this change of the day Thales the Milesian had foretold to the Ionians laying down as a limit this very year in which the change took place. The Lydians however and the Medes, when they saw that it had become night instead of day, ceased from their fighting and were much more eager both of them that peace should be made between them. And they who brought about the peace between them were Syennesis the Kilikian and Labynetos the Babylonian: these were they who urged also the taking of the oath by them, and they brought about an interchange of marriages; for they decided that Alyattes should give his daughter Aryenis to Astyages the son of Kyaxares, seeing that without the compulsion of a strong tie agreements are apt not to hold strongly together. Now these nations observe the same ceremonies in taking oaths as the Hellenes, and in addition to them they make incision into the skin of their arms, and then lick up the blood each of the other.

This Astyages then, being his mother's father, Cyrus had conquered and made prisoner for a reason which I shall declare in the history which comes after. This then was the complaint which Croesus had against Cyrus when he sent to the Oracles to ask if he should march against the Persians; and when a deceitful answer had come back to him, he marched into the dominion of the Persians, supposing that the answer was favourable to himself. And when Croesus came to the river Halys, then, according to my account, he passed his army across by the bridges which there were; but, according to the account which prevails among the Hellenes, Thales the Milesian enabled him to pass his army across. For, say they, when Croesus was at a loss how his army should pass over the river (since, they add, there were not yet at that time the bridges which now there are), Thales being present in the army caused the river, which flowed then on the left hand of the army, to flow partly also on the right; and he did it thus:—beginning above the camp he proceeded to dig a deep channel, directing it in the form of a crescent moon, so that the river might take the camp there pitched in the rear, being turned aside from its ancient course by this way along the channel, and afterwards passing by the camp might fall again into its ancient course; so that as soon as the river was thus parted in two it became fordable by both branches: and some say even that the ancient course of the river was altogether dried up. But this tale I do not admit as true, for how then did they pass over the river as they went back?

And Croesus, when he had passed over with his army, came to that place in Cappadokia which is called Pteria (now Pteria is the strongest place in this country, and is situated somewhere about in a line with the city of Sinope on the Euxine). Here he encamped and ravaged the fields of the Syrians. Moreover he took the city of the Pterians, and sold the people into slavery, and he took also all the towns that lay about it; and the Syrians, who were not guilty of any wrong, he forced to remove from their homes. Meanwhile Cyrus, having gathered his own forces and having taken up in addition to them all who dwelt in the region between, was coming to meet Croesus. Before he began however to lead forth his army, he had sent heralds to the Ionians and tried to induce them to revolt from Croesus; but the Ionians would not do as he said. Then when Cyrus was come and had encamped over against Croesus, they made trial of one another by force of arms in the land of Pteria: and after hard fighting, when many had fallen on both sides, at length, night having come on, they parted from one the other with no victory on either side.

Thus the two armies contended with one another: and Croesus being ill satisfied with his own army in respect of number (for the army which he had when he fought was far smaller than that of Cyrus), being dissatisfied with it I say on this account, as Cyrus did not attempt to advance against him on the following day, marched back to Sardis, having it in his mind to call the Egyptians to his help according to the oath which they had taken (for he had made an alliance with Amasis king of Egypt before he made the alliance with the Lacedemonians), and to summon the Babylonians as well (for with these also an alliance had been concluded by him, Labynetos being at that time ruler of the Babylonians), and moreover to send a message to the Lacedemonians bidding them appear at a fixed time: and then after he had got all these together and had gathered his own army, his design was to let the winter go by and at the coming of spring to march against the Persians. So with these thoughts in his mind, as soon as he came to Sardis he proceeded to send heralds to his several allies to give them notice that by the fifth month from that time they should assemble at Sardis: but the army which he had with him and which had fought with the Persians, an army which consisted of mercenary troops, he let go and disbanded altogether, never expecting that Cyrus, after having contended against him with such even fortune, would after all march upon Sardis.

When Croesus had these plans in his mind, the suburb of the city became of a sudden all full of serpents; and when these had appeared, the horses leaving off to feed in their pastures came constantly thither and devoured them. When Croesus saw this he deemed it to be a portent, as indeed it was: and forthwith he despatched messengers to the dwelling of the Telmessians, who interpret omens: and the messengers who were sent to consult arrived there and learnt from the Telmessians what the portent meant to signify, but they did not succeed in reporting the answer to Croesus, for before they sailed back to Sardis Croesus had been taken prisoner. The Telmessians however gave decision thus: that an army speaking a foreign tongue was to be looked for by Croesus to invade his land, and that this when it came would subdue the native inhabitants; for they said that the serpent was born of the soil, while the horse was an enemy and a stranger. The men of Telmessos thus made answer to Croesus after he was already taken prisoner, not knowing as yet anything of the things which had happened to Sardis and to Croesus himself.

Cyrus, however, so soon as Croesus marched away after the battle which had been fought in Pteria, having learnt that Croesus meant after he had marched away to disband his army, took counsel with himself and concluded that it was good for him to march as quickly as possible to Sardis, before the power of the Lydians should be again gathered together. So when he had resolved upon this, he did it without delay: for he marched his army into Lydia with such speed that he was himself the first to announce his coming to Croesus. Then Croesus, although he had come to a great strait, since his affairs had fallen out altogether contrary to his own expectation, yet proceeded to lead forth the Lydians into battle. Now there was at this time no nation in Asia more courageous or more stout in battle than the Lydian; and they fought on horseback carrying long spears, the men being excellent in horsemanship.

So when the armies had met in that plain which is in front of the city of Sardis,—a plain wide and open, through which flow rivers (and especially the river Hyllos) all rushing down to join the largest called Hermos, which flows from the mountain sacred to the Mother surnamed "of Dindymos" and runs out into the sea by the city of Phocaia,—then Cyrus, when he saw the Lydians being arrayed for battle, fearing their horsemen, did on the suggestion of Harpagos a Mede as follows:—all the camels which were in the train of his army carrying provisions and baggage he gathered together, and he took off their burdens and set men upon them provided with the equipment of cavalry: and having thus furnished them forth he appointed them to go in front of the rest of the army towards the horsemen of Croesus; and after the camel-troop he ordered the infantry to follow; and behind the infantry he placed his whole force of cavalry. Then when all his men had been placed in their several positions, he charged them to spare none of the other Lydians, slaying all who might come in their way, but Croesus himself they were not to slay, not even if he should make resistance when he was captured. Such was his charge: and he set the camels opposite the horsemen for this reason,—because the horse has a fear of the camel and cannot endure either to see his form or to scent his smell: for this reason then the trick had been devised, in order that the cavalry of Croesus might be useless, that very force wherewith the Lydian king was expecting most to shine. And as they were coming together to the battle, so soon as the horses scented the camels and saw them they turned away back, and the hopes of Croesus were at once brought to nought. The Lydians however for their part did not upon that act as cowards, but when they perceived what was coming to pass they leapt from their horses and fought with the Persians on foot. At length, however, when many had fallen on either side, the Lydians turned to flight; and having been driven within the wall of their fortress they were besieged by the Persians.

By these then a siege had been established: but Croesus, supposing that the siege would last a long time, proceeded to send from the fortress other messengers to his allies. For the former messengers were sent round to give notice that they should assemble at Sardis by the fifth month, but these he was sending out to ask them to come to his assistance as quickly as possible, because Croesus was being besieged.

So then in sending to his other allies he sent also to Lacedemon. But these too, the Spartans I mean, had themselves at this very time (for so it had fallen out) a quarrel in hand with the Argives about the district called Thyrea. For this Thyrea, being part of the Argive possessions, the Lacedemonians had cut off and taken for themselves. Now the whole region towards the west extending as far down as Malea was then possessed by the Argives, both the parts situated on the mainland and also the island of Kythera with the other islands. And when the Argives had come to the rescue to save their territory from being cut off from them, then the two sides came to a parley together and agreed that three hundred should fight of each side, and whichever side had the better in the fight that nation should possess the disputed land: they agreed moreover that the main body of each army should withdraw to their own country, and not stand by while the contest was fought, for fear lest, if the armies were present, one side seeing their countrymen suffering defeat should come up to their support. Having made this agreement they withdrew; and chosen men of both sides were left behind and engaged in fight with one another. So they fought and proved themselves to be equally matched; and there were left at last of six hundred men three, on the side of the Argives Alkenor and Chromios, and on the side of the Lacedemonians Othryades: these were left alive when night came on. So then the two men of the Argives, supposing that they were the victors, set off to run to Argos, but the Lacedemonian Othryades, after having stripped the corpses of the Argives and carried their arms to his own camp, remained in his place. On the next day both the two sides came thither to inquire about the result; and for some time both claimed the victory for themselves, the one side saying that of them more had remained alive, and the others declaring that these had fled away, whereas their own man had stood his ground and had stripped the corpses of the other party: and at length by reason of this dispute they fell upon one another and began to fight; and after many had fallen on both sides, the Lacedemonians were the victors. The Argives then cut their hair short, whereas formerly they were compelled by law to wear it long, and they made a law with a curse attached to it, that from that time forth no man of the Argives should grow the hair long nor their women wear ornaments of gold, until they should have won back Thyrea. The Lacedemonians however laid down for themselves the opposite law to this, namely that they should wear long hair from that time forward, whereas before that time they had not their hair long. And they say that the one man who was left alive of the three hundred, namely Othryades, being ashamed to return to Sparta when all his comrades had been slain, slew himself there in Thyrea.

Such was the condition of things at Sparta when the herald from Sardis arrived asking them to come to the assistance of Croesus, who was being besieged. And they notwithstanding their own difficulties, as soon as they heard the news from the herald, were eager to go to his assistance; but when they had completed their preparations and their ships were ready, there came another message reporting that the fortress of the Lydians had been taken and that Croesus had been made prisoner. Then (and not before) they ceased from their efforts, being grieved at the event as at a great calamity.

. Now the taking of Sardis came about as follows:—When the fourteenth day came after Croesus began to be besieged, Cyrus made proclamation to his army, sending horsemen round to the several parts of it, that he would give gifts to the man who should first scale the wall. After this the army made an attempt; and when it failed, then after all the rest had ceased from the attack, a certain Mardian whose name was Hyroiades made an attempt to approach on that side of the citadel where no guard had been set; for they had no fear that it would ever be taken from that side, seeing that here the citadel is precipitous and unassailable. To this part of the wall alone Meles also, who formerly was king of Sardis, did not carry round the lion which his concubine bore to him, the Telmessians having given decision that if the lion should be carried round the wall, Sardis should be safe from capture: and Meles having carried it round the rest of the wall, that is to say those parts of the citadel where the fortress was open to attack, passed over this part as being unassailable and precipitous: now this is a part of the city which is turned towards Tmolos. So then this Mardian

Hyroiades, having seen on the day before how one of the Lydians had descended on that side of the citadel to recover his helmet which had rolled down from above, and had picked it up, took thought and cast the matter about in his own mind. Then he himself ascended first, and after him came up others of the Persians, and many having thus made approach, Sardis was finally taken and the whole city was given up to plunder.

Meanwhile to Croesus himself it happened thus:—He had a son, of whom I made mention before, who was of good disposition enough but deprived of speech. Now in his former time of prosperity Croesus had done everything that was possible for him, and besides other things which he devised he had also sent messengers to Delphi to inquire concerning him. And the Pythian prophetess spoke to him thus:

"Lydian, master of many, much blind to destiny, Croesus,

Do not desire to hear in thy halls that voice which is prayed for,

Voice of thy son; much better if this from thee were removèd,

Since he shall first utter speech in an evil day of misfortune."

Now when the fortress was being taken, one of the Persians was about to slay Croesus taking him for another; and Croesus for his part, seeing him coming on, cared nothing for it because of the misfortune which was upon him, and to him it was indifferent that he should be slain by the stroke; but this voiceless son, when he saw the Persian coming on, by reason of terror and affliction burst the bonds of his utterance and said: "Man, slay not Croesus." This son, I say, uttered voice then first of all, but after this he continued to use speech for the whole time of his life.

The Persians then had obtained possession of Sardis and had taken Croesus himself prisoner, after he had reigned fourteen years and had been besieged fourteen days, having fulfilled the oracle in that he had brought to an end his own great empire. So the Persians having taken him brought him into the presence of Cyrus: and he piled up a great pyre and caused Croesus to go up upon it bound in fetters, and along with him twice seven sons of Lydians, whether it was that he meant to dedicate this offering as first-fruits of his victory to some god, or whether he desired to fulfil a vow, or else had heard that Croesus was a god-fearing man and so caused him to go up on the pyre because he wished to know if any one of the divine powers would save him, so that he should not be burnt alive. He, they say, did this; but to Croesus as he stood upon the pyre there came, although he was in such evil case, a memory of the saying of Solon, how he had said with divine inspiration that no one of the living might be called happy. And when this thought came into his mind, they say that he sighed deeply and groaned aloud, having been for long silent, and three times he uttered the name of Solon. Hearing this, Cyrus bade the interpreters ask Croesus who was this person on whom he called; and they came near and asked. And Croesus for a time, it is said, kept silence when he was asked this, but afterwards being pressed he said: "One whom more than much wealth I should have desired to have speech with all monarchs." Then, since his words were of doubtful import, they asked again of that which he said; and as they were urgent with him and gave him no peace, he told how once Solon an Athenian had come, and having inspected all his wealth had made light of it, with such and such words; and how all had turned out for him according as Solon had said, not speaking at all especially with a view to Croesus himself, but with a view to the whole human race and especially those who seem to themselves to be happy men. And while Croesus related these things, already the pyre was lighted and the edges of it round about were burning. Then they say that Cyrus, hearing from the interpreters what Croesus had said, changed his purpose and considered that he himself also was but a man, and that he was delivering another man, who had been not inferior to himself in felicity, alive to the fire; and moreover he feared the requital, and reflected that there was nothing of that which men possessed which was secure; therefore, they say, he ordered them to extinguish as quickly as possible the fire that was burning, and to bring down Croesus and those who were with him from the pyre; and they using endeavours were not able now to get the mastery of the flames.

Then it is related by the Lydians that Croesus, having learned how Cyrus had changed his mind, and seeing that every one was trying to put out the fire but that they were no longer able to check it, cried aloud entreating Apollo that if any gift had ever been given by him which had been acceptable to the god, he would come to his aid and rescue him from the evil which was now upon him. So he with tears entreated the god, and suddenly, they say, after clear sky and calm weather clouds gathered and a storm burst, and it rained with a very violent shower, and the pyre was extinguished. Then Cyrus, having perceived that Croesus was a lover of the gods and a good man, caused him to be brought down from the pyre and asked him as follows: "Croesus, tell me who of all men was it who persuaded thee to march upon my land and so to become an enemy to me instead of a friend?" and he said: "O king, I did this to thy felicity and to my own misfortune, and the causer of this was the god of the Hellenes, who incited me to march with my army. For no one is so senseless as to choose of his own will war rather peace, since in peace the sons bury their fathers, but in war the fathers bury their sons. But it was pleasing, I suppose, to the divine powers that these things should come to pass thus."

So he spoke, and Cyrus loosed his bonds and caused him to sit near himself and paid to him much regard, and he marvelled both himself and all who were about him at the sight of Croesus. And Croesus wrapt in thought was silent; but after a time, turning round and seeing the Persians plundering the city of the Lydians, he said: "O king, must I say to thee that which I chance to have in my thought, or must I keep silent in this my present fortune?" Then Cyrus bade him say boldly whatsoever he desired; and he asked him saying: "What is the business that this great multitude of men is doing with so much eagerness?" and he said: "They are plundering thy city and carrying away thy wealth." And Croesus answered: "Neither is it my city that they are plundering nor my wealth which they are carrying away; for I have no longer any property in these things: but it is thy wealth that they are carrying and driving away."

And Cyrus was concerned by that which Croesus had said, and he caused all the rest to withdraw and asked Croesus what he discerned for his advantage as regards that which was being done; and he said: "Since the gods gave me to thee as a slave, I think it right if I discern anything more than others to signify it to thee. The Persians, who are by nature unruly, are without wealth: if therefore thou shalt suffer them to carry off in plunder great wealth and to take possession of it, then it is to be looked for that thou wilt experience this result, thou must expect namely that whosoever gets possession of the largest share will make insurrection against thee. Now therefore, if that which I say is pleasing to thee, do this:—set spearmen of thy guard to watch at all the gates, and let these take away the things, and say to the men who were bearing them out of the city that they must first be tithed for Zeus: and thus thou on the one hand wilt not be hated by them for taking away the things by force, and they on the other will willingly let the things go, acknowledging within themselves that thou art doing that which is just."

Hearing this, Cyrus was above measure pleased, because he thought that Croesus advised well; and he commended him much and enjoined the spearmen of his guard to perform that which Croesus had advised: and after that he spoke to Croesus thus: "Croesus, since thou art prepared, like a king as thou art, to do good deeds and speak good words, therefore ask me for a gift, whatsoever thou desirest to be given thee forthwith." And he said: "Master, thou wilt most do me a pleasure if thou wilt permit me to send to the god of the Hellenes, whom I honoured most of all gods, these fetters, and to ask him whether it is accounted by him right to deceive those who do well to him." Then Cyrus asked him what accusation he made against the god, that he thus requested; and Croesus repeated to him all that had been in his mind, and the answers of the Oracles, and especially the votive offerings, and how he had been incited by the prophecy to march upon the Persians: and thus speaking he came back again to the request that it might be permitted to him to make this reproach against the god. And Cyrus laughed and said: "Not this only shalt thou obtain from me, Croesus, but also whatsoever thou mayst desire of me at any time." Hearing this Croesus sent certain of the Lydians to Delphi, enjoining them to lay the fetters upon the threshold of the temple and to ask the god whether he felt no shame that he had incited Croesus by his prophecies to march upon the Persians, persuading him that he should bring to an end the empire of Cyrus, seeing that these were the first-fruits of spoil which he had won from it,—at the same time displaying the fetters. This they were to ask, and moreover also whether it was thought right by the gods of the Hellenes to practice ingratitude.

When the Lydians came and repeated that which they were enjoined to say, it is related that the Pythian prophetess spoke as follows: "The fated destiny it is impossible even for a god to escape. And Croesus paid the debt due for the sin of his fifth ancestor, who being one of the spearmen of the Heracleidai followed the treacherous device of a woman, and having slain his master took possession of his royal dignity, which belonged not to him of right. And although Loxias eagerly desired that the calamity of Sardis might come upon the sons of Croesus and not upon Croesus himself, it was not possible for him to draw the Destinies aside from their course; but so much as these granted he brought to pass, and gave it as a gift to Croesus: for he put off the taking of Sardis by three years; and let Croesus be assured that he was taken prisoner later by these years than the fated time: moreover secondly, he assisted him when he was about to be burnt. And as to the oracle which was given, Croesus finds fault with good ground: for Loxias told him beforehand that if he should march upon the Persians he should destroy a great empire: and he upon hearing this, if he wished to take counsel well, ought to have sent and asked further whether the god meant his own empire or that of Cyrus: but as he did not comprehend that which was uttered and did not ask again, let him pronounce himself to be the cause of that which followed. To him also when he consulted the Oracle for the last time Loxias said that which he said concerning a mule; but this also he failed to comprehend: for Cyrus was in fact this mule, seeing that he was born of parents who were of two different races, his mother being of nobler descent and his father of less noble: for she was a Median woman, daughter of Astyages and king of the Medes, but he was a Persian, one of a race subject to the Medes, and being inferior in all respects he was the husband of one who was his royal mistress." Thus the Pythian prophetess replied to the Lydians, and they brought the answer back to Sardis and repeated it to Croesus; and he, when he heard it, acknowledged that the fault was his own and not that of the god. With regard then to the empire of Croesus and the first conquest of Ionia, it happened thus.

Now there are in Hellas many other votive offerings made by Croesus and not only those which have been mentioned: for first at Thebes of the Boeotians there is a tripod of gold, which he dedicated to the Ismenian Apollo; then at Ephesos there are the golden cows and the greater number of the pillars of the temple; and in the temple of Athene Pronaia at Delphi a large golden shield. These were still remaining down to my own time, but others of his votive offerings have perished: and the votive offerings of Croesus at Branchidai of the Milesians were, as I am told, equal in weight and similar to those at Delphi. Now those which he sent to Delphi and to the temple of Amphiaraos he dedicated of his own goods and as first-fruits of the wealth inherited from his father; but the other offerings were made of the substance of a man who was his foe, who before Croesus became king had been factious against him and had joined in endeavouring to make Pantaleon ruler of the Lydians. Now Pantaleon was a son of Alyattes and a brother of Croesus, but not by the same mother, for Croesus was born to Alyattes of a Carian woman, but Pantaleon of an Ionian. And when Croesus had gained possession of the kingdom by the gift of his father, he put to death the man who opposed him, drawing him upon the carding-comb; and his property, which even before that time he had vowed to dedicate, he then offered in the manner mentioned to those shrines which have been named. About his votive offerings let it suffice to have said so much.

Of marvels to be recorded the land of Lydia has no great store as compared with other lands, excepting the gold-dust which is carried down from Tmolos; but one work it has to show which is larger far than any other except only those in Egypt and Babylon: for there is there the sepulchral monument of Alyattes the father of Croesus, of which the base is made of larger stones and the rest of the monument is of earth piled up. And this was built by contributions of those who practised trade and of the artisans and the girls who plied their traffic there; and still there existed to my own time boundary-stones five in number erected upon the monument above, on which were carved inscriptions telling how much of the work was done by each class; and upon measurement it was found that the work of the girls was the greatest in amount. For the daughters of the common people in Lydia practice prostitution one and all, to gather for themselves dowries, continuing this until the time when they marry; and the girls give themselves away in marriage. Now the circuit of the monument is six furlongs and two hundred feet, and the breadth is thirteen hundred feet. And adjoining the monument is a great lake, which the Lydians say has a never-failing supply of water, and it is called the lake of Gyges. Such is the nature of this monument.

Now the Lydians have very nearly the same customs as the Hellenes, with the exception that they prostitute their female children; and they were the first of men, so far as we know, who struck and used coin of gold or silver; and also they were the first retail-traders. And the Lydians themselves say that the games which are now in use among them and among the Hellenes were also their invention. These they say were invented among them at the same time as they colonised Tyrsenia, and this is the account they give of them:—In the reign of Atys the son of Manes their king there came to be a grievous dearth over the whole of Lydia; and the Lydians for a time continued to endure it, but afterwards, as it did not cease, they sought for remedies; and one devised one thing and another of them devised another thing. And then were discovered, they say, the ways of playing with the dice and the knucklebones and the ball, and all the other games excepting draughts (for the discovery of this last is not claimed by the Lydians). These games they invented as a resource against the famine, and thus they used to do:—on one of the days they would play games all the time in order that they might not feel the want of food, and on the next they ceased from their games and had food: and thus they went on for eighteen years. As however the evil did not slacken but pressed upon them ever more and more, therefore their king divided the whole Lydian people into two parts, and he appointed by lot one part to remain and the other to go forth from the land; and the king appointed himself to be over that one of the parts which had the lot to stay in the land, and his son to be over that which was departing; and the name of his son was Tyrsenos. So the one party of them, having obtained the lot to go forth from the land, went down to the sea at Smyrna and built ships for themselves, wherein they placed all the movable goods which they had and sailed away to seek for means of living and a land to dwell in; until after passing by many nations they came at last to the land of the Ombricans, and there they founded cities and dwell up to the present time: and changing their name they were called after the king's son who led them out from home, not Lydians but Tyrsenians, taking the name from him.

The Lydians then had been made subject to the Persians as I say: and after this our history proceeds to inquire about Cyrus, who he was that destroyed the empire of Croesus, and about the Persians, in what manner they obtained the lead of Asia. Following then the report of some of the Persians,—those I mean who do not desire to glorify the history of Cyrus but to speak that which is in fact true,—according to their report, I say, I shall write; but I could set forth also the other forms of the story in three several ways.

The Assyrians ruled Upper Asia for five hundred and twenty years, and from them the Medes were the first who made revolt. These having fought for their freedom with the Assyrians proved themselves good men, and thus they pushed off the yoke of slavery from themselves and were set free; and after them the other nations also did the same as the Medes: and when all on the continent were thus independent, they returned again to despotic rule as follows:—

There appeared among the Medes a man of great ability whose name was Deïokes, and this man was the son of Phraortes. This Deïokes, having formed a desire for despotic power, did thus:—whereas the Medes dwelt in separate villages, he, being even before that time of great repute in his own village, set himself to practise just dealing much more and with greater zeal than before; and this he did although there was much lawlessness throughout the whole of Media, and although he knew that injustice is ever at feud with justice. And the Medes of the same village, seeing his manners, chose him for their judge. So he, since he was aiming at power, was upright and just, and doing thus he had no little praise from his fellow-citizens, insomuch that those of the other villages learning that Deïokes was a man who more than all others gave decision rightly, whereas before this they had been wont to suffer from unjust judgments, themselves also when they heard it came gladly to Deïokes to have their causes determined, and at last they trusted the business to no one else.

Then, as more and more continually kept coming to him, because men learnt that his decisions proved to be according to the truth, Deïokes perceiving that everything was referred to himself would no longer sit in the place where he used formerly to sit in public to determine causes, and said that he would determine causes no more, for it was not profitable for him to neglect his own affairs and to determine causes for his neighbours all through the day. So then, since robbery and lawlessness prevailed even much more in the villages than they did before, the Medes having assembled together in one place considered with one another and spoke about the state in which they were: and I suppose the friends of Deïokes spoke much to this effect: "Seeing that we are not able to dwell in the land under the present order of things, let us set up a king from among ourselves, and thus the land will be well governed and we ourselves shall turn to labour, and shall not be ruined by lawlessness." By some such words as these they persuaded themselves to have a king.

And when they straightway proposed the question whom they should set up to be king, Deïokes was much put forward and commended by every one, until at last they agreed that he should be their king. And he bade them build for him a palace worthy of the royal dignity and strengthen him with a guard of spearmen. And the Medes did so: for they built him a large and strong palace in that part of the land which he told them, and they allowed him to select spearmen from all the Medes. And when he had obtained the rule over them, he compelled the Medes to make one fortified city and pay chief attention to this, having less regard to the other cities. And as the Medes obeyed him in this also, he built large and strong walls, those which are now called Agbatana, standing in circles one within the other. And this wall is so contrived that one circle is higher than the next by the height of the battlements alone. And to some extent, I suppose, the nature of the ground, seeing that it is on a hill, assists towards this end; but much more was it produced by art, since the circles are in all seven in number. And within the last circle are the royal palace and the treasure-houses. The largest of these walls is in size about equal to the circuit of the wall round Athens; and of the first circle the battlements are white, of the second black, of the third crimson, of the fourth blue, of the fifth red; thus are the battlements of all the circles coloured with various tints, and the two last have their battlements one of them overlaid with silver and the other with gold.

These walls then Deïokes built for himself and round his own palace, and the people he commanded to dwell round about the wall. And after all was built, Deïokes established the rule, which he was the first to establish, ordaining that none should enter into the presence of the king, but that they deal with him always through messengers; and that the king should be seen by no one; and moreover that to laugh or to spit in presence is unseemly, and this last for every one without exception. Now he surrounded himself with this state to the end that his fellows, who had been brought up with him and were of no meaner family nor behind him in manly virtue, might not be grieved by seeing him and make plots against him, but that being unseen by them he might be thought to be of different mould.

Having set these things in order and strengthened himself in his despotism, he was severe in preserving justice; and the people used to write down their causes and send them in to his presence, and he determined the questions which were brought in to him and sent them out again. Thus he used to do about the judgment of causes; and he also took order for this, that is to say, if he heard that any one was behaving in an unruly manner, he sent for him and punished him according as each act of wrong deserved, and he had watchers and listeners about all the land over which he ruled.

Deïokes then united the Median race alone, and was ruler of this: and of the Medes there are the tribes which here follow, namely, Busai, Paretakenians, Struchates, Arizantians, Budians, Magians: the tribes of the Medes are so many in number.

Now the son of Deïokes was Phraortes, who when Deïokes was dead, having been king for three-and-fifty years, received the power in succession; and having received it he was not satisfied to be ruler of the Medes alone, but marched upon the Persians; and attacking them first before others, he made these first subject to the Medes. After this, being ruler of these two nations and both of them strong, he proceeded to subdue Asia going from one nation to another, until at last he marched against the Assyrians, those Assyrians I mean who dwelt at Nineveh, and who formerly had been rulers of the whole, but at that time they were left without support their allies having revolted from them, though at home they were prosperous enough. Phraortes marched, I say, against these, and was both himself slain, after he had reigned two-and-twenty years, and the greater part of his army was destroyed.

When Phraortes had brought his life to an end, Kyaxares the son of Phraortes, the son of Deïokes, received the power. This king is said to have been yet much more warlike than his forefathers; and he first banded the men of Asia into separate divisions, that is to say, he first arrayed apart from one another the spearmen and the archers and the horsemen, for before that time they were all mingled together without distinction. This was he who fought with the Lydians when the day became night as they fought, and who also united under his rule the whole of Asia above the river Halys. And having gathered together all his subjects he marched upon Nineveh to avenge his father, and also because he desired to conquer that city. And when he had fought a battle with the Assyrians and had defeated them, while he was sitting down before Nineveh there came upon him a great army of Scythians, and the leader of them was Madyas the son of Protohyas, king of the Scythians. These had invaded Asia after driving the Kimmerians out of Europe, and in pursuit of them as they fled they had come to the land of Media.

Now from the Maiotian lake to the river Phasis and to the land of the Colchians is a journey of thirty days for one without encumbrance; and from Colchis it is not far to pass over to Media, for there is only one nation between them, the Saspeirians, and passing by this nation you are in Media. However the Scythians did not make their invasion by this way, but turned aside from it to go by the upper road which is much longer, keeping Mount Caucasus on their right hand. Then the Medes fought with the Scythians, and having been worsted in the battle they lost their power, and the Scythians obtained rule over all Asia.

Thence they went on to invade Egypt; and when they were in Syria which is called Palestine, Psammetichos king of Egypt met them; and by gifts and entreaties he turned them from their purpose, so that they should not advance any further: and as they retreated, when they came to the city of Ascalon in Syria, most of the Scythians passed through without doing any damage, but a few of them who had stayed behind plundered the temple of Aphrodite Urania. Now this temple, as I find by inquiry, is the most ancient of all the temples which belong to this goddess; for the temple in Cyprus was founded from this, as the people of Cyprus themselves report, and it was the Phenicians who founded the temple in Kythera, coming from this land of Syria. So these Scythians who had plundered the temple at Ascalon, and their descendants for ever, were smitten by the divinity with a disease which made them women instead of men: and the Scythians say that it was for this reason that they were diseased, and that for this reason travellers who visit Scythia now, see among them the affection of those who by the Scythians are called Enareës.

For eight-and-twenty years then the Scythians were rulers of Asia, and by their unruliness and reckless behaviour everything was ruined; for on the one hand they exacted that in tribute from each people which they laid upon them, and apart from the tribute they rode about and carried off by force the possessions of each tribe. Then Kyaxares with the Medes, having invited the greater number of them to a banquet, made them drunk and slew them; and thus the Medes recovered their power, and had rule over the same nations as before; and they also took Nineveh,—the manner how it was taken I shall set forth in another history,—and made the Assyrians subject to them excepting only the land of Babylon.

After this Kyaxares died, having reigned forty years including those years during which the Scythians had rule, and Astyages son of Kyaxares received from him the kingdom. To him was born a daughter whom he named Mandane; and in his sleep it seemed to him that there passed from her so much water as to fill his city and also to flood the whole of Asia. This dream he delivered over to the Magian interpreters of dreams, and when he heard from them the truth at each point he became afraid. And afterwards when this Mandane was of an age to have a husband, he did not give her in marriage to any one of the Medes who were his peers, because he feared the vision; but he gave her to a Persian named Cambyses, whom he found to be of a good descent and of a quiet disposition, counting him to be in station much below a Mede of middle rank.

And when Mandane was married to Cambyses, in the first year Astyages saw another vision. It seemed to him that from the womb of this daughter a vine grew, and this vine overspread the whole of Asia. Having seen this vision and delivered it to the interpreters of dreams, he sent for his daughter, being then with child, to come from the land of the Persians. And when she had come he kept watch over her, desiring to destroy that which should be born of her; for the Magian interpreters of dreams signified to him that the offspring of his daughter should be king in his room. Astyages then desiring to guard against this, when Cyrus was born, called Harpagos, a man who was of kin near him and whom he trusted above all the other Medes, and had made him manager of all his affairs; and to him he said as follows: "Neglect not by any means, Harpagos, the matter which I shall lay upon thee to do, and beware lest thou set me aside, and choosing the advantage of others instead, bring thyself afterwards to destruction. Take the child which Mandane bore, and carry it to thy house and slay it; and afterwards bury it in whatsoever manner thou thyself desirest." To this he made answer: "O king, never yet in any past time didst thou discern in me an offence against thee, and I keep watch over myself also with a view to the time that comes after, that I may not commit any error towards thee. If it is indeed thy pleasure that this should so be done, my service at least must be fitly rendered."

Thus he made answer, and when the child had been delivered to him adorned as for death, Harpagos went weeping to his wife all the words which had been spoken by Astyages. And she said to him: "Now, therefore, what is it in thy mind to do?" and he made answer: "Not according as Astyages enjoined: for not even if he shall come to be yet more out of his senses and more mad than he now is, will I agree to his will or serve him in such a murder as this. And for many reasons I will not slay the child; first because he is a kin to me, and then because Astyages is old and without male issue, and if after he is dead the power shall come through me, does not the greatest of dangers then await me? To secure me, this child must die; but one of the servants of Astyages must be the slayer of it, and not one of mine."

Thus he spoke, and straightway sent a messenger to that one of the herdsmen of Astyages who he knew fed his herds on the pastures which were most suitable for his purpose, and on the mountains most haunted by wild beasts. The name of this man was Mitradates, and he was married to one who was his fellow-slave; and the name of the woman to whom he was married was Kyno in the tongue of the Hellenes and in the Median tongue Spaco, for what the Hellenes call kyna (bitch) the Medes call spaca. Now, it was on the skirts of the mountains that this herdsman had his cattle-pastures, from Agbatana towards the North Wind and towards the Euxine Sea. For here in the direction of the Saspeirians the Median land is very mountainous and lofty and thickly covered with forests; but the rest of the land of Media is all level plain. So when this herdsman came, being summoned with much urgency, Harpagos said these words: "Astyages bids thee take this child and place it on the most desolate part of the mountains, so that it may perish as quickly as possible. And he bade me to say that if thou do not kill it, but in any way shalt preserve it from death, he will slay thee by the most evil kind of destruction: and I have been appointed to see that the child is laid forth."

Having heard this and having taken up the child, the herdsman went back by the way he came, and arrived at his dwelling. And his wife also, as it seems, having been every day on the point of bearing a child, by a providential chance brought her child to birth just at that time, when the herdsman was gone to the city. And both were in anxiety, each for the other, the man having fear about the child-bearing of his wife, and the woman about the cause why Harpagos had sent to summon her husband, not having been wont to do so aforetime. So as soon as he returned and stood before her, the woman seeing him again beyond her hopes was the first to speak, and asked him for what purpose Harpagos had sent for him so urgently. And he said: "Wife, when I came to the city I saw and heard that which I would I had not seen, and which I should wish had never chanced to those whom we serve. For the house of Harpagos was all full of mourning, and I being astonished thereat went within: and as soon as I entered I saw laid out to view an infant child gasping for breath and screaming, which was adorned with gold ornaments and embroidered clothing: and when Harpagos saw me he bade me forthwith to take up the child and carry it away and lay it on that part of the mountains which is most haunted by wild beasts, saying that it was Astyages who laid this task upon me, and using to me many threats, if I should fail to do this. And I took it up and bore it away, supposing that it was the child of some one of the servants of the house, for never could I have supposed whence it really was; but I marvelled to see it adorned with gold and raiment, and I marvelled also because mourning was made for it openly in the house of Harpagos. And straightway as we went by the road, I learnt the whole of the matter from the servant who went with me out of the city and placed in my hands the babe, namely that it was in truth the son of Mandane the daughter of Astyages, and of Cambyses the son of Cyrus, and that Astyages bade slay it. And now here it is."

And as he said this the herdsman uncovered it and showed it to her. And she, seeing that the child was large and of fair form, wept and clung to the knees of her husband, beseeching him by no means to lay it forth. But he said that he could not do otherwise than so, for watchers would come backwards and forwards sent by Harpagos to see that this was done, and he would perish by a miserable death if he should fail to do this. And as she could not after all persuade her husband, the wife next said as follows: "Since then I am unable to persuade thee not to lay it forth, do thou this which I shall tell thee, if indeed it needs must be seen laid forth. I also have borne a child, but I have borne it dead. Take this and expose it, and let us rear the child of the daughter of Astyages as if it were our own. Thus thou wilt not be found out doing a wrong to those whom we serve, nor shall we have taken ill counsel for ourselves; for the dead child will obtain a royal burial and the surviving one will not lose his life."

To the herdsman it seemed that, the case standing thus, his wife spoke well, and forthwith he did so. The child which he was bearing to put to death, this he delivered to his wife, and his own, which was dead, he took and placed in the chest in which he had been bearing the other; and having adorned it with all the adornment of the other child, he bore it to the most desolate part of the mountains and placed it there. And when the third day came after the child had been laid forth, the herdsman went to the city, leaving one of his under-herdsmen to watch there, and when he came to the house of Harpagos he said that he was ready to display the dead body of the child; and Harpagos sent the most trusted of his spearmen, and through them he saw and buried the herdsman's child. This then had had burial, but him who was afterwards called Cyrus the wife of the herdsman had received, and was bringing him up, giving him no doubt some other name, not Cyrus.

And when the boy was ten years old, it happened with regard to him as follows, and this made him known. He was playing in the village in which were stalls for oxen, he was playing there, I say, with other boys of his age in the road. And the boys in their play chose as their king this one who was called the son of the herdsman: and he set some of them to build palaces and others to be spearmen of his guard, and one of them no doubt he appointed to be the eye of the king, and to one he gave the office of bearing the messages, appointing a work for each one severally. Now one of these boys who was playing with the rest, the son of Artembares a man of repute among the Medes, did not do that which Cyrus appointed him to do; therefore Cyrus bade the other boys seize him hand and foot, and when they obeyed his command he dealt with the boy very roughly, scourging him. But he, so soon as he was let go, being made much more angry because he considered that he had been treated with indignity, went down to the city and complained to his father of the treatment which he had met with from Cyrus, calling him not Cyrus, for this was not yet his name, but the son of the herdsman of Astyages. And Artembares in the anger of the moment went at once to Astyages, taking the boy with him, and he declared that he had suffered things that were unfitting and said: "O king, by thy slave, the son of a herdsman, we have been thus outraged," showing him the shoulders of his son.

And Astyages having heard and seen this, wishing to punish the boy to avenge the honour of Artembares, sent for both the herdsman and his son. And when both were present, Astyages looked at Cyrus and said: "Didst thou dare, being the son of so mean a father as this, to treat with such unseemly insult the son of this man who is first in my favour?" And he replied thus: "Master, I did so to him with right. For the boys of the village, of whom he also was one, in their play set me up as king over them, for I appeared to them most fitted for this place. Now the other boys did what I commanded them, but this one disobeyed and paid no regard, until at last he received the punishment due. If therefore for this I am worthy to suffer any evil, here I stand before thee."

While the boy thus spoke, there came upon Astyages a sense of recognition of him and the lineaments of his face seemed to him to resemble his own, and his answer appeared to be somewhat over free for his station, while the time of the laying forth seemed to agree with the age of the boy. Being struck with amazement by these things, for a time he was speechless; and having at length with difficulty recovered himself, he said, desiring to dismiss Artembares, in order that he might get the herdsman by himself alone and examine him: "Artembares, I will so order these things that thou and thy son shall have no cause to find fault"; and so he dismissed Artembares, and the servants upon the command of Astyages led Cyrus within. And when the herdsman was left alone with the king, Astyages being alone with him asked whence he had received the boy, and who it was who had delivered the boy to him. And the herdsman said that he was his own son, and that the mother was living with him still as his wife. But Astyages said that he was not well advised in desiring to be brought to extreme necessity, and as he said this he made a sign to the spearmen of his guard to seize him. So he, as he was being led away to the torture, then declared the story as it really was; and beginning from the beginning he went through the whole, telling the truth about it, and finally ended with entreaties, asking that he would grant him pardon.

So when the herdsman had made known the truth, Astyages now cared less about him, but with Harpagos he was very greatly displeased and bade his spearmen summon him. And when Harpagos came, Astyages asked him thus: "By what death, Harpagos, didst thou destroy the child whom I delivered to thee, born of my daughter?" and Harpagos, seeing that the herdsman was in the king's palace, turned not to any false way of speech, lest he should be convicted and found out, but said as follows: "O king, so soon as I received the child, I took counsel and considered how I should do according to thy mind, and how without offence to thy command I might not be guilty of murder against thy daughter and against thyself. I did therefore thus:—I called this herdsman and delivered the child to him, saying first that thou wert he who bade him slay it—and in this at least I did not lie, for thou didst so command. I delivered it, I say, to this man commanding him to place it upon a desolate mountain, and to stay by it and watch it until it should die, threatening him with all kinds of punishment if he should fail to accomplish this. And when he had done that which was ordered and the child was dead, I sent the most trusted of my eunuchs and through them I saw and buried the child. Thus, O king, it happened about this matter, and the child had this death which I say."

So Harpagos declared the truth, and Astyages concealed the anger which he kept against him for that which had come to pass, and first he related the matter over again to Harpagos according as he had been told it by the herdsman, and afterwards, when it had been thus repeated by him, he ended by saying that the child was alive and that that which had come to pass was well, "for," continued he, "I was greatly troubled by that which had been done to this child, and I thought it no light thing that I had been made at variance with my daughter. Therefore consider that this is a happy change of fortune, and first send thy son to be with the boy who is newly come, and then, seeing that I intend to make a sacrifice of thanksgiving for the preservation of the boy to those gods to whom that honour belongs, be here thyself to dine with me."

When Harpagos heard this, he did reverence and thought it a great matter that his offence had turned out for his profit and moreover that he had been invited to dinner with happy augury; and so he went to his house. And having entered it straightway, he sent forth his son, for he had one only son of about thirteen years old, bidding him go to the palace of Astyages and do whatsoever the king should command; and he himself being overjoyed told his wife that which had befallen him. But Astyages, when the son of Harpagos arrived, cut his throat and divided him limb from limb, and having roasted some pieces of the flesh and boiled others he caused them to be dressed for eating and kept them ready. And when the time arrived for dinner and the other guests were present and also Harpagos, then before the other guests and before Astyages himself were placed tables covered with flesh of sheep; but before Harpagos was placed the flesh of his own son, all but the head and the hands and the feet, and these were laid aside covered up in a basket. Then when it seemed that Harpagos was satisfied with food, Astyages asked him whether he had been pleased with the banquet; and when Harpagos said that he had been very greatly pleased, they who had been commanded to do this brought to him the head of his son covered up, together with the hands and the feet; and standing near they bade Harpagos uncover and take of them that which he desired. So when Harpagos obeyed and uncovered, he saw the remains of his son; and seeing them he was not overcome with amazement but contained himself: and Astyages asked him whether he perceived of what animal he had been eating the flesh: and he said that he perceived, and that whatsoever the king might do was well pleasing to him. Thus having made answer and taking up the parts of the flesh which still remained he went to his house; and after that, I suppose, he would gather all the parts together and bury them.

On Harpagos Astyages laid this penalty; and about Cyrus he took thought, and summoned the same men of the Magians who had given judgment about his dream in the manner which has been said: and when they came, Astyages asked how they had given judgment about his vision; and they spoke according to the same manner, saying that the child must have become king if he had lived on and had not died before. He made answer to them thus: "The child is alive and not dead: and while he was dwelling in the country, the boys of the village appointed him king; and he performed completely all those things which they do who are really kings; for he exercised rule, appointed to their places spearmen of the guard and doorkeepers and bearers of messages and all else. Now therefore, to what does it seem to you that these things tend?" The Magians said: "If the child is still alive and became king without any arrangement, be thou confident concerning him and have good courage, for he shall not be ruler again the second time; since some even of our oracles have had but small results, and that at least which has to do with dreams comes often in the end to a feeble accomplishment." Astyages made answer in these words: "I myself also, O Magians, am most disposed to believe that this is so, namely that since the boy was named king the dream has had its fulfilment and that this boy is no longer a source of danger to me. Nevertheless give counsel to me, having well considered what is likely to be most safe both for my house and for you." Replying to this the Magians said: "To us also, O king, it is of great consequence that thy rule should stand firm; for in the other case it is transferred to strangers, coming round to this boy who is a Persian, and we being Medes are made slaves and become of no account in the eyes of the Persians, seeing that we are of different race; but while thou art established as our king, who art one of our own nation, we both have our share of rule and receive great honours from thee. Thus then we must by all means have a care of thee and of thy rule. And now, if we saw in this anything to cause fear, we would declare all to thee beforehand: but as the dream has had its issue in a trifling manner, both we ourselves are of good cheer and we exhort thee to be so likewise: and as for this boy, send him away from before thine eyes to the Persians and to his parents."

When he heard this Astyages rejoiced, and calling Cyrus spoke to him thus: "My son, I did thee wrong by reason of a vision of a dream which has not come to pass, but thou art yet alive by thine own destiny; now therefore go in peace to the land of the Persians, and I will send with thee men to conduct thee: and when thou art come thither, thou shalt find a father and a mother not after the fashion of Mitradates the herdsman and his wife."

Thus having spoken Astyages sent Cyrus away; and when he had returned and come to the house of Cambyses, his parents received him; and after that, when they learnt who he was, they welcomed him not a little, for they had supposed without doubt that their son had perished straightway after his birth; and they inquired in what manner he had survived. And he told them, saying that before this he had not known but had been utterly in error; on the way, however, he had learnt all his own fortunes: for he had supposed without doubt that he was the son of the herdsman of Astyages, but since his journey from the city began he had learnt the whole story from those who conducted him. And he said that he had been brought up by the wife of the herdsman, and continued to praise her throughout, so that Kyno was the chief person in his tale. And his parents took up this name from him, and in order that their son might be thought by the Persians to have been preserved in a more supernatural manner, they set on foot a report that Cyrus when he was exposed had been reared by a bitch: and from that source has come this report.

Then as Cyrus grew to be a man, being of all those of his age the most courageous and the best beloved, Harpagos sought to become his friend and sent him gifts, because he desired to take vengeance on Astyages. For he saw not how from himself, who was in a private station, punishment should come upon Astyages; but when he saw Cyrus growing up, he endeavoured to make him an ally, finding a likeness between the fortunes of Cyrus and his own. And even before that time he had effected something: for Astyages being harsh towards the Medes, Harpagos communicated severally with the chief men of the Medes, and persuaded them that they must make Cyrus their leader and cause Astyages to cease from being king. When he had effected this and when all was ready, then Harpagos wishing to make known his design to Cyrus, who lived among the Persians, could do it no other way, seeing that the roads were watched, but devised a scheme as follows:—he made ready a hare, and having cut open its belly but without pulling off any of the fur, he put into it, just as it was, a piece of paper, having written upon it that which he thought good; and then he sewed up again the belly of the hare, and giving nets as if he were a hunter to that one of his servants whom he trusted most, he sent him away to the land of the Persians, enjoining him by word of mouth to give the hare to Cyrus, and to tell him at the same time to open it with his own hands and let no one else be present when he did so.

This then was accomplished, and Cyrus having received from him the hare, cut it open; and having found within it the paper he took and read it over. And the writing said this: "Son of Cambyses, over thee the gods keep guard, for otherwise thou wouldst never have come to so much good fortune. Do thou therefore take vengeance on Astyages who is thy murderer, for so far as his will is concerned thou art dead, but by the care of the gods and of me thou art still alive; and this I think thou hast long ago learnt from first to last, both how it happened about thyself, and also what things I have suffered from Astyages, because I did not slay thee but gave thee to the herdsman. If therefore thou wilt be guided by me, thou shalt be ruler of all that land over which now Astyages is ruler. Persuade the Persians to revolt, and march any army against the Medes: and whether I shall be appointed leader of the army against thee, or any other of the Medes who are in repute, thou hast what thou desirest; for these will be the first to attempt to destroy Astyages, revolting from him and coming over to thy party. Consider then that here at least all is ready, and therefore do this and do it with speed."

Cyrus having heard this began to consider in what manner he might most skilfully persuade the Persians to revolt, and on consideration he found that this was the most convenient way, and so in fact he did:—He wrote first on a paper that which he desired to write, and he made an assembly of the Persians. Then he unfolded the paper and reading from it said that Astyages appointed him commander of the Persians; "and now, O Persians," he continued, "I give you command to come to me each one with a reaping-hook." Cyrus then proclaimed this command. (Now there are of the Persians many tribes, and some of them Cyrus gathered together and persuaded to revolt from the Medes, namely those, upon which all the other Persians depend, the Pasargadai, the Maraphians and the Maspians, and of these the Pasargadai are the most noble, of whom also the Achaimenidai are a clan, whence are sprung the Perseïd kings. But other Persian tribes there are, as follows:—the Panthaliaians, the Derusiaians and the Germanians, these are all tillers of the soil; and the rest are nomad tribes, namely the Daoi, Mardians, Dropicans and Sagartians.)

Now there was a certain region of the Persian land which was overgrown with thorns, extending some eighteen or twenty furlongs in each direction; and when all had come with that which they had been before commanded to bring, Cyrus bade them clear this region for cultivation within one day: and when the Persians had achieved the task proposed, then he bade them come to him on the next day bathed and clean. Meanwhile Cyrus, having gathered together in one place all the flocks of goats and sheep and the herds of cattle belonging to his father, slaughtered them and prepared with them to entertain the host of the Persians, and moreover with wine and other provisions of the most agreeable kind. So when the Persians came on the next day, he made them recline in a meadow and feasted them. And when they had finished dinner, Cyrus asked them whether that which they had on the former day or that which they had now seemed to them preferable. They said that the difference between them was great, for the former day had for them nothing but evil, and the present day nothing but good. Taking up this saying Cyrus proceeded to lay bare his whole design, saying: "Men of the Persians, thus it is with you. If ye will do as I say, ye have these and ten thousand other good things, with no servile labour; but if ye will not do as I say, ye have labours like that of yesterday innumerable. Now therefore do as I say and make yourselves free: for I seem to myself to have been born by providential fortune to take these matters in hand; and I think that ye are not worse men than the Medes, either in other matters or in those which have to do with war. Consider then that this is so, and make revolt from Astyages forthwith."

So the Persians having obtained a leader willingly attempted to set themselves free, since they had already for a long time been indignant to be ruled by the Medes: but when Astyages heard that Cyrus was acting thus, he sent a messenger and summoned him; and Cyrus bade the messenger report to Astyages that he would be with him sooner than he would himself desire. So Astyages hearing this armed all the Medes, and blinded by divine providence he appointed Harpagos to be the leader of the army, forgetting what he had done to him. Then when the Medes had marched out and began to fight with the Persians, some of them continued the battle, namely those who had not been made partakers in the design, while others went over to the Persians; but the greater number were wilfully slack and fled.

So when the Median army had been shamefully dispersed, so soon as Astyages heard of it he said, threatening Cyrus: "But not even so shall Cyrus at least escape punishment." Thus having spoken he first impaled the Magian interpreters of dreams who had persuaded him to let Cyrus go, and then he armed those of the Medes, youths and old men, who had been left behind in the city. These he led out and having engaged battle with the Persians he was worsted, and Astyages himself was taken alive, and he lost also those of the Medes whom he had led forth.

Then when Astyages was a prisoner, Harpagos came and stood near him and rejoiced over him and insulted him; and besides other things which he said to grieve him, he asked him especially how it pleased him to be a slave instead of a king, making reference to that dinner at which Astyages had feasted him with the flesh of his own son. He looking at him asked him in return whether he claimed the work of Cyrus as his own deed: and Harpagos said that since he had written the letter, the deed was justly his. Then Astyages declared him to be at the same time the most unskilful and the most unjust of men; the most unskilful because, when it was in his power to become king (as it was, if that which had now been done was really brought about by him), he had conferred the chief power on another, and the most unjust, because on account of that dinner he had reduced the Medes to slavery. For if he must needs confer the kingdom on some other and not keep it himself, it was more just to give this good thing to one of the Medes rather than to one of the Persians; whereas now the Medes, who were guiltless of this, had become slaves instead of masters, and the Persians who formerly were slaves of the Medes had now become their masters.

Astyages then, having been king for five-and-thirty years, was thus caused to cease from being king; and the Medes stooped under the yoke of the Persians because of his cruelty, after they had ruled Asia above the river Halys for one hundred and twenty-eight years, except during that period for which the Scythians had rule. Afterwards however it repented them that they had done this, and they revolted from Dareios, and having revolted they were subdued again, being conquered in a battle. At this time then, I say, in the reign of Astyages, the Persians with Cyrus rose up against the Medes and from that time forth were rulers of Asia: but as for Astyages, Cyrus did no harm to him besides, but kept him with himself until he died. Thus born and bred Cyrus became king; and after this he subdued Croesus, who was the first to begin the quarrel, as I have before said; and having subdued him he then became ruler of all Asia.

These are the customs, so far as I know, which the Persians practise:—Images and temples and altars they do not account it lawful to erect, nay they even charge with folly those who do these things; and this, as it seems to me, because they do not account the gods to be in the likeness of men, as do the Hellenes. But it is their wont to perform sacrifices to Zeus going up to the most lofty of the mountains, and the whole circle of the heavens they call Zeus: and they sacrifice to the Sun and the Moon and the Earth, to Fire and to Water and to the Winds: these are the only gods to whom they have sacrificed ever from the first; but they have learnt also to sacrifice to Aphrodite Urania, having learnt it both from the Assyrians and the Arabians; and the Assyrians call Aphrodite Mylitta, the Arabians Alitta, and the Persians Mitra.

Now this is the manner of sacrifice for the gods aforesaid which is established among the Persians:—they make no altars neither do they kindle fire; and when they mean to sacrifice they use no libation nor music of the pipe nor chaplets nor meal for sprinkling; but when a man wishes to sacrifice to any one of the gods, he leads the animal for sacrifice to an unpolluted place and calls upon the god, having his tiara wreathed round generally with a branch of myrtle. For himself alone separately the man who sacrifices may not request good things in his prayer, but he prays that it may be well with all the Persians and with the king; for he himself also is included of course in the whole body of Persians. And when he has cut up the victim into pieces and boiled the flesh, he spreads a layer of the freshest grass and especially clover, upon which he places forthwith all the pieces of flesh; and when he has placed them in order, a Magian man stands by them and chants over them a theogony (for of this nature they say that their incantation is), seeing that without a Magian it is not lawful for them to make sacrifices. Then after waiting a short time the sacrificer carries away the flesh and uses it for whatever purpose he pleases.

And of all days their wont is to honour most that on which they were born, each one: on this they think it right to set out a feast more liberal than on other days; and in this feast the wealthier of them set upon the table an ox or a horse or a camel or an ass, roasted whole in an oven, and the poor among them set out small animals in the same way. They have few solid dishes, but many served up after as dessert, and these not in a single course; and for this reason the Persians say that the Hellenes leave off dinner hungry, because after dinner they have nothing worth mentioning served up as dessert, whereas if any good dessert were served up they would not stop eating so soon. To wine-drinking they are very much given, and it is not permitted for a man to vomit or to make water in presence of another. Thus do they provide against these things; and they are wont to deliberate when drinking hard about the most important of their affairs, and whatsoever conclusion has pleased them in their deliberation, this on the next day, when they are sober, the master of the house in which they happen to be when they deliberate lays before them for discussion: and if it pleases them when they are sober also, they adopt it, but if it does not please them, they let it go: and that on which they have had the first deliberation when they are sober, they consider again when they are drinking.

When they meet one another in the roads, by this you may discern whether those who meet are of equal rank,—for instead of greeting by words they kiss one another on the mouth; but if one of them is a little inferior to the other, they kiss one another on the cheeks, and if one is of much less noble rank than the other, he falls down before him and does worship to him. And they honour of all most after themselves those nations which dwell nearest to them, and next those which dwell next nearest, and so they go on giving honour in proportion to distance; and they hold least in honour those who dwell furthest off from themselves, esteeming themselves to be by far the best of all the human race on every point, and thinking that others possess merit according to the proportion which is here stated, and that those who dwell furthest from themselves are the worst. And under the supremacy of the Medes the various nations used also to govern one another according to the same rule as the Persians observe in giving honour, the Medes governing the whole and in particular those who dwelt nearest to themselves, and these having rule over those who bordered upon them, and those again over the nations that were next to them: for the race went forward thus ever from government by themselves to government through others.

The Persians more than any other men admit foreign usages; for they both wear the Median dress judging it to be more comely than their own, and also for fighting the Egyptian corslet: moreover they adopt all kinds of luxuries when they hear of them, and in particular they have learnt from the Hellenes to have commerce with boys. They marry each one several lawful wives, and they get also a much larger number of concubines.

It is established as a sign of manly excellence next after excellence in fight, to be able to show many sons; and to those who have most the king sends gifts every year: for they consider number to be a source of strength. And they educate their children, beginning at five years old and going on till twenty, in three things only, in riding, in shooting, and in speaking the truth: but before the boy is five years old he does not come into the presence of his father, but lives with the women; and it is so done for this reason, that if the child should die while he is being bred up, he may not be the cause of any grief to his father.

I commend this custom of theirs, and also the one which is next to be mentioned, namely that neither the king himself shall put any to death for one cause alone, nor any of the other Persians for one cause alone shall do hurt that is irremediable to any of his own servants; but if after reckoning he finds that the wrongs done are more in number and greater than the services rendered, then only he gives vent to his anger. Moreover they say that no one ever killed his own father or mother, but whatever deeds have been done which seemed to be of this nature, if examined must necessarily, they say, be found to be due either to changelings or to children of adulterous birth; for, say they, it is not reasonable to suppose that the true parent would be killed by his own son.

Whatever things it is not lawful for them to do, these it is not lawful for them even to speak of: and the most disgraceful thing in their estimation is to tell an lie, and next to this to owe money, this last for many other reasons, but especially because it is necessary, they say, for him who owes money, also sometimes to tell lies: and whosoever of the men of the city has leprosy or whiteness of skin, he does not come into a city nor mingle with the other Persians; and they say that he has these diseases because he has offended in some way against the Sun: but a stranger who is taken by these diseases, in many regions they drive out of the country altogether, and also white doves, alleging against them the same cause. And into a river they neither make water nor spit, neither do they wash their hands in it, nor allow any other to do these things, but they reverence rivers very greatly.

This moreover also has chanced to them, which the Persians have themselves failed to notice but I have not failed to do so:—their names, which are formed to correspond with their bodily shapes or their magnificence of station, end all with the same letter, that letter which the Dorians call san and the Ionians sigma; with this you will find, if you examine the matter, that all the Persian names end, not some with this and others with other letters, but all alike.

So much I am able to say for certain from my own knowledge about them: but what follows is reported about their dead as a secret mystery and not with clearness, namely that the body of a Persian man is not buried until it has been torn by a bird or a dog. (The Magians I know for a certainty have this practice, for they do it openly.) However that may be, the Persians cover the body with wax and then bury it in the earth. Now the Magians are distinguished in many ways from other men, as also from the priests in Egypt: for these last esteem it a matter of purity to kill no living creature except the animals which they sacrifice; but the Magians kill with their own hands all creatures except dogs and men, and they even make this a great end to aim at, killing both ants and serpents and all other creeping and flying things. About this custom then be it as it was from the first established; and I return now to the former narrative.

The Ionians and Aiolians, as soon as the Lydians had been subdued by the Persians, sent messengers to Cyrus at Sardis, desiring to be his subjects on the same terms as they had been subjects of Croesus. And when he heard that which they proposed to him, he spoke to them a fable, saying that a certain player on the pipe saw fishes in the sea and played on his pipe, supposing that they would come out to land; but being deceived in his expectation, he took a casting-net and enclosed a great multitude of the fishes and drew them forth from the water: and when he saw them leaping about, he said to the fishes: "Stop dancing I pray you now, seeing that ye would not come out and dance before when I piped." Cyrus spoke this fable to the Ionians and Aiolians for this reason, because the Ionians had refused to comply before, when Cyrus himself by a messenger requested them to revolt from Croesus, while now when the conquest had been made they were ready to submit to Cyrus. Thus he said to them in anger, and the Ionians, when they heard this answer brought back to their cities, put walls round about them severally, and gathered together to the Panionion, all except the men of Miletos, for with these alone Cyrus had sworn an agreement on the same terms as the Lydians had granted. The rest of the Ionians resolved by common consent to send messengers to Sparta, to ask the Spartans to help the Ionians.

These Ionians to whom belongs the Panionion had the fortune to build their cities in the most favourable position for climate and seasons of any men whom we know: for neither the regions above Ionia nor those below, neither those towards the East nor those towards the West, produce the same results as Ionia itself, the regions in the one direction being oppressed by cold and moisture, and those in the other by heat and drought. And these do not use all the same speech, but have four different variations of language. First of their cities on the side of the South lies Miletos, and next to it Myus and Priene. These are settlements made in Caria, and speak the same language with one another; and the following are in Lydia,—Ephesos, Colophon, Lebedos, Teos, Clazomenai, Phocaia: these cities resemble not at all those mentioned before in the speech which they use, but they agree one with another. There remain besides three Ionian cities, of which two are established in the islands of Samos and Chios, and one is built upon the mainland, namely Erythrai: now the men of Chios and of Erythrai use the same form of language, but the Samians have one for themselves alone. Thus there result four separate forms of language.

Of these Ionians then those of Miletos were sheltered from danger, since they had sworn an agreement; and those of them who lived in islands had no cause for fear, for the Phenicians were not yet subjects of the Persians and the Persians themselves were not sea-men. Now these were parted off from the other Ionians for no other reason than this:—The whole Hellenic nation was at that time weak, but of all its races the Ionian was much the weakest and of least account: except Athens, indeed, it had no considerable city. Now the other Ionians, and among them the Athenians, avoided the name, not wishing to be called Ionians, nay even now I perceive that the greater number of them are ashamed of the name: but these twelve cities not only prided themselves on the name but established a temple of their own, to which they gave the name of Panionion, and they made resolution not to grant a share in it to any other Ionians (nor indeed did any ask to share it except those of Smyrna); just as the Dorians of that district which is now called the Five Cities but was formerly called the Six Cities, take care not to admit any of the neighbouring Dorians to the temple of Triopion, and even exclude from sharing in it those of their own body who commit any offence as regards the temple. For example, in the games of the Triopian Apollo they used formerly to set bronze tripods as prizes for the victors, and the rule was that those who received them should not carry them out of the temple but dedicate them then and there to the god. There was a man then of Halicarnassos, whose name was Agasicles, who being a victor paid no regard to this rule, but carried away the tripod to his own house and hung it up there upon a nail. On this ground the other five cities, Lindos, Ialysos and Cameiros, Cos and Cnidos, excluded the sixth city Halicarnassos from sharing in the temple.

Upon these they laid this penalty: but as for the Ionians, I think that the reason why they made of themselves twelve cities and would not receive any more into their body, was because when they dwelt in Peloponnesus there were of them twelve divisions, just as now there are twelve divisions of the Achaians who drove the Ionians out: for first, (beginning from the side of Sikyon) comes Pellene, then Aigeira and Aigai, in which last is the river Crathis with a perpetual flow (whence the river of the same name in Italy received its name), and Bura and Helike, to which the Ionians fled for refuge when they were worsted by the Achaians in fight, and Aigion and Rhypes and Patreis and Phareis and Olenos, where is the great river Peiros, and Dyme and Tritaieis, of which the last alone has an inland position. These form now twelve divisions of the Achaians, and in former times they were divisions of the Ionians.

. For this reason then the Ionians also made for themselves twelve cities; for at any rate to say that these are any more Ionians than the other Ionians, or have at all a nobler descent, is mere folly, considering that a large part of them are Abantians from Euboea, who have no share even in the name of Ionia, and Minyai of Orchomenos have been mingled with them, and Cadmeians and Dryopians and Phokians who seceded from their native State and Molossians and Pelasgians of Arcadia and Dorians of Epidauros and many other races have been mingled with them; and those of them who set forth to their settlements from the City Hall of Athens and who esteem themselves the most noble by descent of the Ionians, these, I say, brought no women with them to their settlement, but took Carian women, whose parents they slew: and on account of this slaughter these women laid down for themselves a rule, imposing oaths on one another, and handed it on to their daughters, that they should never eat with their husbands, nor should a wife call her own husband by name, for this reason, because the Ionians had slain their fathers and husbands and children and then having done this had them to wife. This happened at Miletos.

Moreover some of them set Lykian kings over them, descendants of Glaucos and Hippolochos, while others were ruled by Cauconians of Pylos, descendants of Codros the son of Melanthos, and others again by princes of the two races combined. Since however these hold on to the name more than the other Ionians, let them be called, if they will, the Ionians of truly pure descent; but in fact all are Ionians who have their descent from Athens and who keep the feast of Apaturia; and this all keep except the men of Ephesos and Colophon: for these alone of all the Ionians do not keep the Apaturia, and that on the ground of some murder committed.

Now the Panionion is a sacred place on the north side of Mycale, set apart by common agreement of the Ionians for Poseidon of Helike ; and this Mycale is a promontory of the mainland running out Westwards towards Samos, where the Ionians gathering together from their cities used to hold a festival which they called the Panionia. (And not only the feasts of the Ionians but also those of all the Hellenes equally are subject to this rule, that their names all end in the same letter, just like the names of the Persians.)

These then are the Ionian cities: and those of Aiolia are as follows:—Kyme, which is called Phriconis, Larisai, Neonteichos, Temnos, Killa, Notion, Aigiroëssa, Pitane, Aigaiai, Myrina, Gryneia; these are the ancient cities of the Aiolians, eleven in number, since one, Smyrna, was severed from them by the Ionians; for these cities, that is those on the mainland, used also formerly to be twelve in number. And these Aiolians had the fortune to settle in a land which is more fertile than that of the Ionians but in respect of climate less favoured.

. Now the Aiolians lost Smyrna in the following manner:—certain men of Colophon, who had been worsted in party strife and had been driven from their native city, were received there for refuge: and after this the Colophonian exiles watched for a time when the men of Smyrna were celebrating a festival to Dionysos outside the walls, and then they closed the gates against them and got possession of the city. After this, when the whole body of Aiolians came to the rescue, they made an agreement that the Ionians should give up the movable goods, and that on this condition the Aiolians should abandon Smyrna. When the men of Smyrna had done this, the remaining eleven cities divided them amongst themselves and made them their own citizens.

These then are the Aiolian cities upon the mainland, with the exception of those situated on Mount Ida, for these are separate from the rest. And of those which are in the islands, there are five in Lesbos, for the sixth which was situated in Lesbos, namely Arisba, was enslaved by the men of Methymna, though its citizens were of the same race as they; and in Tenedos there is one city, and another in what are called the "Hundred Isles." Now the Lesbians and the men of Tenedos, like those Ionians who dwelt in the islands, had no cause for fear; but the remaining cities came to a common agreement to follow the Ionians whithersoever they should lead.

Now when the messengers from the Ionians and Aiolians came to Sparta (for this business was carried out with speed), they chose before all others to speak for them the Phocaian, whose name was Pythermos. He then put upon him a purple cloak, in order that as many as possible of the Spartans might hear of it and come together, and having been introduced before the assembly he spoke at length, asking the Spartans to help them. The Lacedemonians however would not listen to him, but resolved on the contrary not to help the Ionians. So they departed, and the Lacedemonians, having dismissed the messengers of the Ionians, sent men notwithstanding in a ship of fifty oars, to find out, as I imagine, about the affairs of Cyrus and about Ionia. These when they came to Phocaia sent to Sardis the man of most repute among them, whose name was Lacrines, to report to Cyrus the saying of the Lacedemonians, bidding him do hurt to no city of the Hellas, since they would not permit it.

When the herald had spoken thus, Cyrus is said to have asked those of the Hellenes whom he had with him, what men the Lacedemonians were and how many in number, that they made this proclamation to him; and hearing their answer he said to the Spartan herald: "Never yet did I fear men such as these, who have a place appointed in the midst of their city where they gather together and deceive one another by false oaths: and if I continue in good health, not the misfortunes of the Ionians will be for them a subject of talk, but rather their own." These words Cyrus threw out scornfully with reference to the Hellenes in general, because they have got for themselves markets and practise buying and selling there; for the Persians themselves are not wont to use markets nor have they any market-place at all. After this he entrusted Sardis to Tabalos a Persian, and the gold both of Croesus and of the other Lydians he gave to Pactyas a Lydian to take charge of, and himself marched away to Agbatana, taking with him Croesus and making for the present no account of the Ionians. For Babylon stood in his way still, as also the Bactrian nation and the Sacans and the Egyptians; and against these he meant to make expeditions himself, while sending some other commander about the Ionians.

But when Cyrus had marched away from Sardis, Pactyas caused the Lydians to revolt from Tabalos and from Cyrus. This man went down to the sea, and having in his possession all the gold that there had been in Sardis, he hired for himself mercenaries and persuaded the men of the sea-coast to join his expedition. So he marched on Sardis and besieged Tabalos, having shut himself up in the citadel.

Hearing this on his way, Cyrus said to Croesus as follows: "Croesus, what end shall I find of these things which are coming to pass? The Lydians will not cease as it seems, from giving trouble to me and from having it themselves. I doubt me if it were not best to sell them all as slaves; for as it is, I see that I have done in like manner as if one should slay the father and then spare his sons: just so I took prisoner and am carrying away thee, who wert much more than the father of the Lydians, while to the Lydians themselves I delivered up their city; and can I feel surprise after this that they have revolted from me?" Thus he said what was in his mind, but Croesus answered him as follows, fearing lest he should destroy Sardis: "O king, that which thou hast said is not without reason; but do not thou altogether give vent to thy wrath, nor destroy an ancient city which is guiltless both of the former things and also of those which have come to pass now: for as to the former things it was I who did them and I bear the consequences heaped upon my head; and as for what is now being done, since the wrongdoer is Pactyas to whom thou didst entrust the charge of Sardis, let him pay the penalty. But the Lydians I pray thee pardon, and lay upon them commands as follows, in order that they may not revolt nor be a cause of danger to thee:—send to them and forbid them to possess weapons of war, but bid them on the other hand put on tunics under their outer garments and be shod with buskins, and proclaim to them that they train their sons to play the lyre and the harp and to be retail-dealers; and soon thou shalt see, O king, that they have become women instead of men, so that there will be no fear that they will revolt from thee."

Croesus, I say, suggested to him this, perceiving that this was better for the Lydians than to be reduced to slavery and sold; for he knew that if he did not offer a sufficient reason, he would not persuade Cyrus to change his mind, and he feared lest at some future time, if they should escape the present danger, the Lydians might revolt from the Persians and be destroyed. And Cyrus was greatly pleased with the suggestion made and slackened from his wrath, saying that he agreed with his advice. Then he called Mazares a Mede, and laid charge upon him to proclaim to the Lydians that which Croesus suggested, and moreover to sell into slavery all the rest who had joined with the Lydians in the expedition to Sardis, and finally by all means to bring Pactyas himself alive to Cyrus.

Having given this charge upon the road, he continued his march to the native land of the Persians; but Pactyas hearing that an army was approaching to fight against him was struck with fear and fled away forthwith to Kyme. Then Mazares the Mede marched upon Sardis with a certain portion of the army of Cyrus, and as he did not find Pactyas or his followers any longer at Sardis, he first compelled the Lydians to perform the commands of Cyrus, and by his commands the Lydians changed the whole manner of their life. After this Mazares proceeded to send messengers to Kyme bidding them give up Pactyas: and the men of Kyme resolved to refer to the god at Branchidai the question what counsel they should follow. For there was there an Oracle established of old time, which all the Ionians and Aiolians were wont to consult; and this place is in the territory of Miletos above the port of Panormos.

So the men of Kyme sent messengers to the Branchidai to inquire of the god, and they asked what course they should take about Pactyas so as to do that which was pleasing to the gods. When they thus inquired, the answer was given them that they should deliver up Pactyas to the Persians: and the men of Kyme, having heard this answer reported, were disposed to give him up. Then when the mass of the people were thus disposed, Aristodicos the son of Heracleides, a man of repute among the citizens, stopped the men of Kyme from doing so, having distrust of the answer and thinking that those sent to inquire were not speaking the truth; until at last other messengers were sent to the Oracle to ask a second time about Pactyas, and of them Aristodicos was one.

When these came to Branchidai, Aristodicos stood forth from the rest and consulted the Oracle, asking as follows: Lord, there came to us a suppliant for protection Pactyas the Lydian, flying from a violent death at the hands of the Persians, and they demand him from us, bidding the men of Kyme give him up. But we, though we fear the power of the Persians, yet have not ventured up to this time to deliver to them the suppliant, until thy counsel shall be clearly manifested to us, saying which of the two things we ought to do." He thus inquired, but the god again declared to them the same answer, bidding them deliver up Pactyas to the Persians. Upon this Aristodicos with deliberate purpose did as follows:—he went all round the temple destroying the nests of the sparrows and of all the other kinds of birds which had been hatched on the temple: and while he was doing this, it is said that a voice came from the inner shrine directed to Aristodicos and speaking thus: "Thou most impious of men, why dost thou dare to do this? Dost thou carry away by force from my temple the suppliants for my protection?" And Aristodicos, it is said, not being at all at a loss replied to this: "Lord, dost thou thus come to the assistance of thy suppliants, and yet biddest the men of Kyme deliver up theirs?" and the god answered him again thus: "Yea, I bid you do so, that ye may perish the more quickly for your impiety; so that ye may not at any future time come to the Oracle to ask about delivering up of suppliants."

When the men of Kyme heard this saying reported, not wishing either to be destroyed by giving him up or to be besieged by keeping him with them, they sent him away to Mytilene. Those of Mytilene however, when Mazares sent messages to them, were preparing to deliver up Pactyas for a price, but what the price was I cannot say for certain, since the bargain was never completed; for the men of Kyme, when they learnt that this was being done by the Mytilenians, sent a vessel to Lesbos and conveyed away Pactyas to Chios. After this he was dragged forcibly from the temple of Athene Poliuchos by the Chians and delivered up: and the Chians delivered him up receiving Atarneus in return, (now this Atarneus is a region of Mysia opposition Lesbos). So the Persians having received Pactyas kept him under guard, meaning to produce him before Cyrus. And a long time elapsed during which none of the Chians either used barley-meal grown in this region of Atarneus, for pouring out in sacrifice to any god, or baked cakes for offering of the corn which grew there, but all the produce of this land was excluded from every kind of sacred service.

The men of Chios had then delivered up Pactyas; and after this Mazares made expedition against those who had joined in besieging Tabalos: and first he reduced to slavery those of Priene, then he overran the whole plain of the Maiander making spoil of it for his army, and Magnesia in the same manner: and straightway after this he fell sick and died.

After he was dead, Harpagos came down to take his place in command, being also a Mede by race (this was the man whom the king of the Medes Astyages feasted with the unlawful banquet, and who helped to give the kingdom to Cyrus). This man, being appointed commander then by Cyrus, came to Ionia and proceeded to take the cities by throwing up mounds against them: for when he had enclosed any people within their walls, then he threw up mounds against the walls and took their city by storm; and the first city of Ionia upon which he made an attempt was Phocaia.

Now these Phocaians were the first of the Hellenes who made long voyages, and these are they who discovered the Adriatic and Tyrsenia and Iberia and Tartessos: and they made voyages not in round ships, but in vessels of fifty oars. These came to Tartessos and became friends with the king of the Tartessians whose name was Arganthonios: he was ruler of the Tartessians for eighty years and lived in all one hundred and twenty. With this man, I say, the Phocaians became so exceedingly friendly, that first he bade them leave Ionia and dwell wherever they desired in his own land; and as he did not prevail upon the Phocaians to do this, afterwards, hearing from them of the Mede how his power was increasing, he gave them money to build a wall about their city: and he did this without sparing, for the circuit of the wall is many furlongs in extent, and it is built all of large stones closely fitted together.

The wall of the Phocaians was made in this manner: and Harpagos having marched his army against them began to besiege them, at the same time holding forth to them proposals and saying that it was enough to satisfy him if the Phocaians were willing to throw down one battlement of their wall and dedicate one single house. But the Phocaians, being very greatly grieved at the thought of subjection, said that they wished to deliberate about the matter for one day and after that they would give their answer; and they asked him to withdraw his army from the wall while they were deliberating. Harpagos said that he knew very well what they were meaning to do, nevertheless he was willing to allow them to deliberate. So in the time that followed, when Harpagos had withdrawn his army from the wall, the Phocaians drew down their fifty-oared galleys to the sea, put into them their children and women and all their movable goods, and besides them the images out of the temples and the other votive offerings except such as were made of bronze or stone or consisted of paintings, all the rest, I say, they put into the ships, and having embarked themselves they sailed towards Chios; and the Persians obtained possession of Phocaia, the city being deserted of the inhabitants.

But as for the Phocaians, since the men of Chios would not sell them at their request the islands called Oinussai, from the fear lest these islands might be made a seat of trade and their island might be shut out, therefore they set out for Kyrnos: for in Kyrnos twenty years before this they had established a city named Alalia, in accordance with an oracle, (now Arganthonios by that time was dead). And when they were setting out for Kyrnos they first sailed to Phocaia and slaughtered the Persian garrison, to whose charge Harpagos had delivered the city; then after they had achieved this they made solemn imprecations on any one of them who should be left behind from their voyage, and moreover they sank a mass of iron in the sea and swore that not until that mass should appear again on the surface would they return to Phocaia. However as they were setting forth to Kyrnos, more than half of the citizens were seized with yearning and regret for their city and for their native land, and they proved false to their oath and sailed back to Phocaia. But those of them who kept the oath still, weighed anchor from the islands of Oinussai and sailed.

When these came to Kyrnos, for five years they dwelt together with those who had come thither before, and they founded temples there. Then, since they plundered the property of all their neighbours, the Tyrsenians and Carthaginians made expedition against them by agreement with one another, each with sixty ships. And the Phocaians also manned their vessels, sixty in number, and came to meet the enemy in that which is called the Sardinian sea: and when they encountered one another in the sea-fight the Phocaians won a kind of Cadmean victory, for forty of their ships were destroyed and the remaining twenty were disabled, having had their prows bent aside. So they sailed in to Alalia and took up their children and their women and their other possessions as much as their ships proved capable of carrying, and then they left Kyrnos behind them and sailed to Rhegion.

But as for the crews of the ships that were destroyed, the Carthaginians and Tyrsenians obtained much the greater number of them, and these they brought to land and killed by stoning. After this the men of Agylla found that everything which passed by the spot where the Phocaians were laid after being stoned, became either distorted, or crippled, or paralysed, both small cattle and beasts of burden and human creatures: so the men of Agylla sent to Delphi desiring to purge themselves of the offence; and the Pythian prophetess bade them do that which the men of Agylla still continue to perform, that is to say, they make great sacrifices in honour of the dead, and hold at the place a contest of athletics and horse-racing. These then of the Phocaians had the fate which I have said; but those of them who took refuge at Rhegion started from thence and took possession of that city in the land of Oinotria which now is called Hyele. This they founded having learnt from a man of Poseidonia that the Pythian prophetess by her answer meant them to found a temple to Kyrnos, who was a hero, and not to found a settlement in the island of Kyrnos.

About Phocaia in Ionia it happened thus, and nearly the same thing also was done by the men of Teos: for as soon as Harpagos took their wall with a mound, they embarked in their ships and sailed straightway for Thrace; and there they founded the city of Abdera, which before them Timesios of Clazomenai founded and had no profit therefrom, but was driven out by the Thracians; and now he is honoured as a hero by the Teïans in Abdera.

. These alone of all the Ionians left their native cities because they would not endure subjection: but the other Ionians except the Milesians did indeed contend in arms with Harpagos like those who left their homes, and proved themselves brave men, fighting each for his own native city; but when they were defeated and captured they remained all in their own place and performed that which was laid upon them: but the Milesians, as I have also said before, had made a sworn agreement with Cyrus himself and kept still. Thus for the second time Ionia had been reduced to subjection. And when Harpagos had conquered the Ionians on the mainland, then the Ionians who dwelt in the islands, being struck with fear by these things, gave themselves over to Cyrus.

. When the Ionians had been thus evilly entreated but were continuing still to hold their gatherings as before at the Panionion, Bias a man of Priene set forth to the Ionians, as I am informed, a most profitable counsel, by following which they might have been the most prosperous of all the Hellenes. He urged that the Ionians should set forth in one common expedition and sail to Sardinia, and after that found a single city for all the Ionians: and thus they would escape subjection and would be prosperous, inhabiting the largest of all islands and being rulers over others; whereas, if they remained in Ionia, he did not perceive, he said, that freedom would any longer exist for them. This was the counsel given by Bias of Priene after the Ionians had been ruined; but a good counsel too was given before the ruin of Ionia by Thales a man of Miletos, who was by descent of Phenician race. He advised the Ionians to have one single seat of government, and that this should be at Teos (for Teos, he said, was in the centre of Ionia), and that the other cities should be inhabited as before, but accounted just as if they were demes.

These men set forth to them counsels of the kind which I have said: but Harpagos, after subduing Ionia, proceeded to march against the Carians and Caunians and Lykians, taking also Ionians and Aiolians to help him. Of these the Carians came to the mainland from the islands; for being of old time subjects of Minos and being called Leleges, they used to dwell in the islands, paying no tribute, so far back as I am able to arrive by hearsay, but whenever Minos required it, they used to supply his ships with seamen: and as Minos subdued much land and was fortunate in his fighting, the Carian nation was of all nations by much the most famous at that time together with him. And they produced three inventions of which the Hellenes adopted the use; that is to say, the Carians were those who first set the fashion of fastening crests on helmets, and of making the devices which are put onto shields, and these also were the first who made handles for their shields, whereas up to that time all who were wont to use shields carried them without handles and with leathern straps to guide them, having them hung about their necks and their left shoulders. Then after the lapse of a long time the Dorians and Ionians drove the Carians out of the islands, and so they came to the mainland. With respect to the Carians the Cretans relate that it happened thus; the Carians themselves however do not agree with this account, but suppose that they are dwellers on the mainland from the beginning, and that they went always by the same name which they have now: and they point as evidence of this to an ancient temple of Carian Zeus at Mylasa, in which the Mysians and Lydians share as being brother races of the Carians, for they say that Lydos and Mysos were brothers of Car; these share in it, but those who being of another race have come to speak the same language as the Carians, these have no share in it.

It seems to me however that the Caunians are dwellers there from the beginning, though they say themselves that they came from Crete: but they have been assimilated to the Carian race in language, or else the Carians to the Caunian race, I cannot with certainty determine which. They have customs however in which they differ very much from all other men as well as from the Carians; for example the fairest thing in their estimation is to meet together in numbers for drinking, according to equality of age or friendship, both men, women, and children; and again when they had founded temples for foreign deities, afterwards they changed their purpose and resolved to worship only their own native gods, and the whole body of Caunian young men put on their armour and made pursuit as far as the borders of the Calyndians, beating the air with their spears; and they said that they were casting the foreign gods out of the land. Such are the customs which these have.

The Lykians however have sprung originally from Crete (for in old time the whole of Crete was possessed by Barbarians): and when the sons of Europa, Sarpedon and Minos, came to be at variance in Crete about the kingdom, Minos having got the better in the strife of parties drove out both Sarpedon himself and those of his party: and they having been expelled came to the land of Milyas in Asia, for the land which now the Lykians inhabit was anciently called Milyas, and the Milyans were then called Solymoi. Now while Sarpedon reigned over them, they were called by the name which they had when they came thither, and by which the Lykians are even now called by the neighbouring tribes, namely Termilai; but when from Athens Lycos the son of Pandion came to the land of the Termilai and to Sarpedon, he too having been driven out by his brother namely Aigeus, then by the name taken from Lycos they were called after a time Lykians. The customs which these have are partly Cretan and partly Carian; but one custom they have which is peculiar to them, and in which they agree with no other people, that is they call themselves by their mothers and not by their fathers; and if one asks his neighbour who he is, he will state his parentage on the mother's side and enumerate his mother's female ascendants: and if a woman who is a citizen marry a slave, the children are accounted to be of gentle birth; but if a man who is a citizen, though he were the first man among them, have a slave for wife or concubine, the children are without civil rights.

Now the Carians were reduced to subjection by Harpagos without any brilliant deed displayed either by the Carians themselves or by those of the Hellenes who dwell in this land. Of these last there are besides others the men of Cnidos, settlers from Lacedemon, whose land runs out into the sea, being in fact the region which is called Triopion, beginning from the peninsula of Bybassos: and since all the land of Cnidos except a small part is washed by the sea (for the part of it which looks towards the North is bounded by the Gulf of Keramos, and that which looks to the South by the sea off Syme and Rhodes), therefore the men of Cnidos began to dig through this small part, which is about five furlongs across, while Harpagos was subduing Ionia, desiring to make their land an island: and within the isthmus all was theirs, for where the territory of Cnidos ends in the direction of the mainland, here is the isthmus which they were digging across. And while the Cnidians were working at it with a great number of men, it was perceived that the men who worked suffered injury much more than might have been expected and in a more supernatural manner, both in other parts of their bodies and especially in their eyes, when the rock was being broken up; so they sent men to ask the Oracle at Delphi what the cause of the difficulty was. And the Pythian prophetess, as the men of Cnidos themselves report, gave them this reply in trimeter verse:—

"Fence not the place with towers, nor dig the isthmus through;

Zeus would have made your land an island, had he willed."

When the Pythian prophetess had given this oracle, the men of Cnidos not only ceased from their digging but delivered themselves to Harpagos without resistance, when he came against them with his army.

There were also the Pedasians, who dwelt in the inland country above Halicarnassos; and among these, whenever anything hurtful is about to happen either to themselves or to their neighbours, the priestess of Athene has a great beard: this befell them three times. These of all about Caria were the only men who held out for any time against Harpagos, and they gave him trouble more than any other people, having fortified a mountain called Lide.

After a time the Pedasians were conquered; and the Lykians, when Harpagos marched his army into the plain of Xanthos, came out against him and fought, few against many, and displayed proofs of valour; but being defeated and confined within their city, they gathered together into the citadel their wives and their children, their property and their servants, and after that they set fire to this citadel, so that it was all in flames, and having done so and sworn terrible oaths with one another, they went forth against the enemy and were slain in fight, that is to say all the men of Xanthos: and of the Xanthians who now claim to be Lykians the greater number have come in from abroad, except only eighty households; but these eighty households happened at that time to be away from their native place, and so they escaped destruction. Thus Harpagos obtained possession of Caunos, for the men of Caunos imitated in most respects the behaviour of the Lykians.

So Harpagos was conquering the coast regions of Asia; and Cyrus himself meanwhile was doing the same in the upper parts of it, subduing every nation and passing over none. Now most of these actions I shall pass over in silence, but the undertakings which gave him trouble more than the rest and which are the most worthy of note, of these I shall make mention.

Cyrus, so soon as he had made subject to himself all other parts of the mainland, proceeded to attack the Assyrians. Now Assyria has doubtless many other great cities, but the most famous and the strongest, and the place where the seat of their monarchy had been established after Nineveh was destroyed, was Babylon; which was a city such as I shall say.—It lies in a great plain, and in size it is such that each face measures one hundred and twenty furlongs, the shape of the whole being square; thus the furlongs of the circuit of the city amount in all to four hundred and eighty. Such is the size of the city of Babylon, and it had a magnificence greater than all other cities of which we have knowledge. First there runs round it a trench deep and broad and full of water; then a wall fifty royal cubits in thickness and two hundred cubits in height: now the royal cubit is larger by three fingers than the common cubit.

I must also tell in addition to this for what purpose the earth was used, which was taken out of the trench, and in what manner the wall was made. As they dug the trench they made the earth which was carried out of the excavation into bricks, and having moulded enough bricks they baked them in kilns; and then afterwards, using hot asphalt for mortar and inserting reed mats at every thirty courses of brickwork, they built up first the edges of the trench and then the wall itself in the same manner: and at the top of the wall along the edges they built chambers of one story facing one another; and between the rows of chambers they left space to drive a four-horse chariot. In the circuit of the wall there are set a hundred gates made of bronze throughout, and the gate-posts and lintels likewise. Now there is another city distant from Babylon a space of eight days' journey, of which the name is Is; and there is a river there of no great size, and the name of the river is also Is, and it sends its stream into the river Euphrates. This river Is throws up together with its water lumps of asphalt in great abundance, and thence was brought the asphalt for the wall of Babylon.

Babylon then was walled in this manner; and there are two divisions of the city; for a river whose name is Euphrates parts it in the middle. This flows from the land of the Armenians and is large and deep and swift, and it flows out into the Erythraian sea. The wall then on each side has its bends carried down to the river, and from this point the return walls stretch along each bank of the stream in the form of a rampart of baked bricks: and the city itself is full of houses of three and four stories, and the roads by which it is cut up run in straight lines, including the cross roads which lead to the river; and opposite to each road there were set gates in the rampart which ran along the river, in many in number as the ways, and these also were of bronze and led like the ways to the river itself.

This wall then which I have mentioned is as it were a cuirass for the town, and another wall runs round within it, not much weaker for defence than the first but enclosing a smaller space. And in each division of the city was a building in the midst, in the one the king's palace of great extent and strongly fortified round, and in the other the temple of Zeus Belos with bronze gates, and this exists still up to my time and measures two furlongs each way, being of a square shape: and in the midst of the temple is built a solid tower measuring a furlong both in length and in breadth, and on this tower another tower has been erected, and another again upon this, and so on up to the number of eight towers. An ascent to these has been built running outside round about all the towers; and when one reaches about the middle of the ascent one finds a stopping-place and seats to rest upon, on which those who ascend sit down and rest: and on the top of the last tower there is a large cell, and in the cell a large couch is laid, well covered, and by it is placed a golden table: and there is no image there set up nor does any human being spend the night there except only one woman of the natives of the place, whomsoever the god shall choose from all the woman, as say the Chaldeans who are the priests of this god.

These same men say also, but I do not believe them, that the god himself comes often to the cell and rests upon the couch, as happens likewise in the Egyptian Thebes according to the report of the Egyptians, for there also a woman sleeps in the temple of the Theban Zeus (and both these women are said to abstain from commerce with men), and as happens also with the prophetess of the god in Patara of Lykia, whenever there is one, for there is not always an Oracle there, but whenever there is one, then she is shut up during the nights in the temple within the cell.

There is moreover in the temple at Babylon another cell below, wherein is a great image of Zeus sitting, made of gold, and by it is placed a large table of gold, and his footstool and seat are of gold also; and, as the Chaldeans reported, the weight of the gold of which these things are made is eight hundred talents. Outside this cell is an altar of gold; and there is also another altar of great size, where full-grown animals are sacrificed, whereas on the golden altar it is not lawful to sacrifice any but young sucklings only: and also on the larger altar the Chaldeans offer one thousand talents of frankincense every year at the time when they celebrate the feast in honour of this god. There was moreover in these precincts still remaining at the time of Cyrus, a statue twelve cubits high, of gold and solid. This I did not myself see, but that which is related by the Chaldeans I relate. Against this statue Dareios the son of Hystaspes formed a design, but he did not venture to take it: it was taken however by Xerxes the son of Dareios, who also killed the priest when he forbade him to meddle with the statue. This temple, then, is thus adorned with magnificence, and there are also many private votive-offerings.

Of this Babylon, besides many other rulers, of whom I shall make mention in the Assyrian history, and who added improvement to the walls and temples, there were also two who were women. Of these, the one who ruled first, named Semiramis, who lived five generations before the other, produced banks of earth in the plain which are a sight worth seeing; and before this the river used to flood like a sea over the whole plain.

The queen who lived after her time, named Nitocris, was wiser than she who had reigned before; and in the first place she left behind her monuments which I shall tell of; then secondly, seeing that the monarchy of the Medes was great and not apt to remain still, but that besides other cities even Nineveh had been captured by it, she made provision against it in so far as she was able. First, as regards the river Euphrates which flows through the midst of their city, whereas before this it flowed straight, she by digging channels above made it so winding that it actually comes three times in its course to one of the villages in Assyria; and the name of the village to which the Euphrates comes is Ardericca; and at this day those who travel from this Sea of ours to Babylon, in their voyage down the river Euphrates arrive three times at this same village and on three separate days. This she did thus; and she also piled up a mound along each bank of the river, which is worthy to cause wonder for its size and height: and at a great distance above Babylon, she dug a basin for a lake, which she caused to extend along at a very small distance from the river, excavating it everywhere of such depth as to come to water, and making the extent such that the circuit of it measured four hundred and twenty furlongs: and the earth which was dug out of this excavation she used up by piling it in mounds along the banks of the river: and when this had been dug by her she brought stones and set them all round it as a facing wall. Both these two things she did, that is she made the river to have a winding course, and she made the place which was dug out all into a swamp, in order that the river might run more slowly, having its force broken by going round many bends, and that the voyages might be winding to Babylon, and after the voyages there might succeed a long circuit of the pool. These works she carried out in that part where the entrance to the country was, and the shortest way to it from Media, so that the Medes might not have dealings with her kingdom and learn of her affairs.

These defences she cast round her city from the depth; and she made the following addition which was dependent upon them:—The city was in two divisions, and the river occupied the space between; and in the time of the former rulers, when any one wished to pass over from the one division to the other, he had to pass over in a boat, and that, as I imagine, was troublesome: she however made provision also for this; for when she was digging the basin for the lake she left this other monument of herself derived from the same work, that is, she caused stones to be cut of very great length, and when the stones were prepared for her and the place had been dug out, she turned aside the whole stream of the river into the place which she had been digging; and while this was being filled with water, the ancient bed of the river being dried up in the meantime, she both built up with baked bricks after the same fashion as the wall the edges of the river, where it flows through the city, and the places of descent leading from the small gateways to the river; and also about the middle of the city, as I judge, with the stones which she had caused to be dug out she proceeded to build a bridge, binding together the stones with iron and lead: and upon the top she laid squared timbers across, to remain there while it was daytime, over which the people of Babylon made the passage across; but at night they used to take away these timbers for this reason, namely that they might not go backwards and forwards by night and steal from one another: and when the place dug out had been made into a lake full of water by the river, and at the same time the bridge had been completed, then she conducted the Euphrates back into its ancient channel from the lake, and so the place dug out being made into a swamp was thought to have served a good purpose, and there had been a bridge set up for the men of the city.

This same queen also contrived a snare of the following kind:—Over that gate of the city through which the greatest number of people passed she set up for herself a tomb above the very gate itself. And on the tomb she engraved writing which said thus: "If any of the kings of Babylon who come after me shall be in want of wealth, let him open my tomb and take as much as he desires; but let him not open it for any other cause, if he be not in want; for that will not be well." This tomb was undisturbed until the kingdom came to Dareios; but to Dareios it seemed that it was a monstrous thing not to make any use of this gate, and also, when there was money lying there, not to take it, considering that the money itself invited him to do so. Now the reason why he would not make any use of this gate was because the corpse would have been above his head as he drove through. He then, I say, opened the tomb and found not indeed money but the corpse, with writing which said thus: "If thou hadst not been insatiable of wealth and basely covetous, thou wouldest not have opened the resting-places of the dead."

This queen then is reported to have been such as I have described: and it was the son of this woman, bearing the same name as his father, Labynetos, and being ruler over the Assyrians, against whom Cyrus was marching. Now the great king makes his marches not only well furnished from home with provisions for his table and with cattle, but also taking with him water from the river Choaspes, which flows by Susa, of which alone and of no other river the king drinks: and of this water of the Choaspes boiled, a very great number of waggons, four-wheeled and drawn by mules, carry a supply in silver vessels, and go with him wherever he may march at any time.

Now when Cyrus on his way towards Babylon arrived at the river Gyndes,—of which river the springs are in the mountains of the Matienians, and it flows through the Dardanians and runs into another river, the Tigris, which flowing by the city of Opis runs out into the Erythraian Sea,—when Cyrus, I say, was endeavouring to cross this river Gyndes, which is a navigable stream, then one of his sacred white horses in high spirit and wantonness went into the river and endeavoured to cross, but the stream swept it under water and carried it off forthwith. And Cyrus was greatly moved with anger against the river for having done thus insolently, and he threatened to make it so feeble that for the future even women could cross it easily without wetting the knee. So after this threat he ceased from his march against Babylon and divided his army into two parts; and having divided it he stretched lines and marked out straight channels, one hundred and eighty on each bank of the Gyndes, directed every way, and having disposed his army along them he commanded them to dig: so, as a great multitude was working, the work was completed indeed, but they spent the whole summer season at this spot working.

. When Cyrus had taken vengeance on the river Gyndes by dividing it into three hundred and sixty channels, and when the next spring was just beginning, then at length he continued his advance upon Babylon: and the men of Babylon had marched forth out of their city and were awaiting him. So when in his advance he came near to the city, the Babylonians joined battle with him, and having been worsted in the fight they were shut up close within their city. But knowing well even before this that Cyrus was not apt to remain still, and seeing him lay hands on every nation equally, they had brought in provisions beforehand for very many years. So while these made no account of the siege, Cyrus was in straits what to do, for much time went by and his affairs made no progress onwards.

Therefore, whether it was some other man who suggested it to him when he was in a strait what to do, or whether he of himself perceived what he ought to do, he did as follows:—The main body of his army he posted at the place where the river runs into the city, and then again behind the city he set others, where the river issues forth from the city; and he proclaimed to his army that so soon as they should see that the stream had become passable, they should enter by this way into the city. Having thus set them in their places and in this manner exhorted them he marched away himself with that part of his army which was not fit for fighting: and when he came to the lake, Cyrus also did the same things which the queen of the Babylonians had done as regards the river and the lake; that is to say, he conducted the river by a channel into the lake, which was at that time a swamp, and so made the former course of the river passable by the sinking of the stream. When this had been done in such a manner, the Persians who had been posted for this very purpose entered by the bed of the river Euphrates into Babylon, the stream having sunk so far that it reached about to the middle of a man's thigh. Now if the Babylonians had had knowledge of it beforehand or had perceived that which was being done by Cyrus, they would have allowed the Persians to enter the city and then destroyed them miserably; for if they had closed all the gates that led to the river and mounted themselves upon the ramparts which were carried along the banks of the stream, they would have caught them as it were in a fish-wheal: but as it was, the Persians came upon them unexpectedly; and owing to the size of the city (so it is said by those who dwell there) after those about the extremities of the city had suffered capture, those Babylonians who dwelt in the middle did not know that they had been captured; but as they chanced to be holding a festival, they went on dancing and rejoicing during this time until they learnt the truth only too well.

Babylon then had thus been taken for the first time: and as to the resources of the Babylonians how great they are, I shall show by many other proofs and among them also by this:—For the support of the great king and his army, apart from the regular tribute the whole land of which he is ruler has been distributed into portions. Now whereas twelve months go to make up the year, for four of these he has his support from the territory of Babylon, and for the remaining eight months from the whole of the rest of Asia; thus the Assyrian land is in regard to resources the third part of all Asia: and the government, or satrapy as it is called by the Persians, of this territory is of all the governments by far the best; seeing that when Tritantaichmes son of Artabazos had this province from the king, there came in to him every day an artab full of silver coin (now the artab is a Persian measure and holds more than the medimnos of Attica by three Attic choinikes); and of horses he had in this province as his private property, apart from the horses for use in war, eight hundred stallions and sixteen thousand mares, for each of these stallions served twenty mares: of Indian hounds moreover such a vast number were kept that four large villages in the plain, being free from other contributions, had been appointed to provide food for the hounds.

Such was the wealth which belonged to the ruler of Babylon. Now the land of the Assyrians has but little rain; and this little gives nourishment to the root of the corn, but the crop is ripened and the ear comes on by the help of watering from the river, not as in Egypt by the coming up of the river itself over the fields, but the crop is watered by hand or with swing-buckets. For the whole Babylonian territory like the Egyptian is cut up into channels, and the largest of the channels is navigable for ships and runs in the direction of the sunrising in winter from the Euphrates to another river, namely the Tigris, along the bank of which lay the city of Nineveh. This territory is of all that we know the best by far for producing corn: as to trees, it does not even attempt to bear them, either fig or vine or olive, but for producing corn it is so good that it returns as much as two-hundred-fold for the average, and when it bears at its best it produces three-hundred-fold. The leaves of the wheat and barley there grow to be full four fingers broad; and from millet and sesame seed how large a tree grows, I know myself but shall not record, being well aware that even what has already been said relating to the crops produced has been enough to cause disbelief in those who have not visited the Babylonian land. They use no oil of olives, but only that which they make of sesame seed; and they have date-palms growing over all the plain, most of them fruit-bearing, of which they make both solid food and wine and honey; and to these they attend in the same manner as to fig-trees, and in particular they take the fruit of those palms which the Hellenes call male-palms, and tie them upon the date-bearing palms, so that their gall-fly may enter into the date and ripen it and that the fruit of the palm may not fall off: for the male-palm produces gall-flies in its fruit just as the wild-fig does.

. But the greatest marvel of all the things in the land after the city itself, to my mind is this which I am about to tell: Their boats, those I mean which go down the river to Babylon, are round and all of leather: for they make ribs for them of willow which they cut in the land of the Armenians who dwell above the Assyrians, and round these they stretch hides which serve as a covering outside by way of hull, not making broad the stern nor gathering in the prow to a point, but making the boats round like a shield: and after that they stow the whole boat with straw and suffer it to be carried down the stream full of cargo; and for the most part these boats bring down casks of palm-wood filled with wine. The boat is kept straight by two steering-oars and two men standing upright, and the man inside pulls his oar while the man outside pushes. These vessels are made both of very large size and also smaller, the largest of them having a burden of as much as five thousand talents' weight; and in each one there is a live ass, and in those of larger size several. So when they have arrived at Babylon in their voyage and have disposed of their cargo, they sell by auction the ribs of the boat and all the straw, but they pack the hides upon their asses and drive them off to Armenia: for up the stream of the river it is not possible by any means to sail, owing to the swiftness of the current; and for this reason they make their boats not of timber but of hides. Then when they have come back to the land of the Armenians, driving their asses with them, they make other boats in the same manner.

Such are their boats; and the following is the manner of dress which they use, namely a linen tunic reaching to the feet, and over this they put on another of wool, and then a white mantle thrown round, while they have shoes of a native fashion rather like the Boeotian slippers. They wear their hair long and bind their heads round with fillets, and they are anointed over the whole of their body with perfumes. Each man has a seal and a staff carved by hand, and on each staff is carved either an apple or a rose or a lily or an eagle or some other device, for it is not their custom to have a staff without a device upon it.

Such is the equipment of their bodies: and the customs which are established among them are as follows, the wisest in our opinion being this, which I am informed that the Enetoi in Illyria also have. In every village once in each year it was done as follows:—When the maidens grew to the age for marriage, they gathered these all together and brought them in a body to one place, and round them stood a company of men: and the crier caused each one severally to stand up, and proceeded to sell them, first the most comely of all, and afterwards, when she had been sold and had fetched a large sum of money, he would put up another who was the most comely after her: and they were sold for marriage. Now all the wealthy men of the Babylonians who were ready to marry vied with one another in bidding for the most beautiful maidens; those however of the common sort who were ready to marry did not require a fine form, but they would accept money together with less comely maidens. For when the crier had made an end of selling the most comely of the maidens, then he would cause to stand up that one who was least shapely, or any one of them who might be crippled in any way, and he would make proclamation of her, asking who was willing for least gold to have her in marriage, until she was assigned to him who was willing to accept least: and the gold would be got from the sale of the comely maidens, and so those of beautiful form provided dowries for those which were unshapely or crippled; but to give in marriage one's own daughter to whomsoever each man would, was not allowed, nor to carry off the maiden after buying her without a surety; for it was necessary for the man to provide sureties that he would marry her, before he took her away; and if they did not agree well together, the law was laid down that he should pay back the money. It was allowed also for any one who wished it to come from another village and buy. This then was their most honourable custom; it does not however still exist at the present time, but they have found out of late another way, in order that the men may not ill-treat them or take them to another city: for since the time when being conquered they were oppressed and ruined, each one of the common people when he is in want of livelihood prostitutes his female children.

Next in wisdom to that, is this other custom which was established among them:—they bear out the sick into the market-place; for of physicians they make no use. So people come up to the sick man and give advice about his disease, if any one himself has ever suffered anything like that which the sick man has, or saw any other who had suffered it; and coming near they advise and recommend those means by which they themselves got rid of a like disease or seen some other get rid of it: and to pass by the sick man in silence is not permitted to them, nor until one has asked what disease he has.

They bury their dead in honey, and their modes of lamentation are similar to those used in Egypt. And whenever a Babylonian man has intercourse with his wife, he sits by incense offered, and his wife does the same on the other side, and when it is morning they wash themselves, both of them, for they will touch no vessel until they have washed themselves: and the Arabians do likewise in this matter.

Now the most shameful of the customs of the Babylonians is as follows: every woman of the country must sit down in the precincts of Aphrodite once in her life and have commerce with a man who is a stranger: and many women who do not deign to mingle with the rest, because they are made arrogant by wealth, drive to the temple with pairs of horses in covered carriages, and so take their place, and a large number of attendants follow after them; but the greater number do thus,—in the sacred enclosure of Aphrodite sit great numbers of women with a wreath of cord about their heads; some come and others go; and there are passages in straight lines going between the women in every direction, through which the strangers pass by and make their choice. Here when a woman takes her seat she does not depart again to her house until one of the strangers has thrown a silver coin into her lap and has had commerce with her outside the temple, and after throwing it he must say these words only: "I demand thee in the name of the goddess Mylitta": now Mylitta is the name given by the Assyrians to Aphrodite: and the silver coin may be of any value; whatever it is she will not refuse it, for that is not lawful for her, seeing that this coin is made sacred by the act: and she follows the man who has first thrown and does not reject any: and after that she departs to her house, having acquitted herself of her duty to the goddess, nor will you be able thenceforth to give any gift so great as to win her. So then as many as have attained to beauty and stature are speedily released, but those of them who are unshapely remain there much time, not being able to fulfil the law; for some of them remain even as much as three or four years: and in some parts of Cyprus too there is a custom similar to this.

These customs then are established among the Babylonians: and there are of them three tribes which eat nothing but fish only: and when they have caught them and dried them in the sun they do thus,—they throw them into brine, and then pound them with pestles and strain them through muslin; and they have them for food either kneaded into a soft cake, or baked like bread, according to their liking.

When this nation also had been subdued by Cyrus, he had a desire to bring the Massagetai into subjection to himself. This nation is reputed to be both great and warlike, and to dwell towards the East and the sunrising, beyond the river Araxes and over against the Issedonians: and some also say that this nation is of Scythian race.

Now the Araxes is said by some to be larger and by others to be smaller than the Ister: and they say that there are many islands in it about equal in size to Lesbos, and in them people dwelling who feed in the summer upon roots of all kinds which they dig up and certain fruits from trees, which have been discovered by them for food, they store up, it is said, in the season when they are ripe and feed upon them in the winter. Moreover it is said that other trees have been discovered by them which yield fruit of such a kind that when they have assembled together in companies in the same place and lighted a fire, they sit round in a circle and throw some of it into the fire, and they smell the fruit which is thrown on, as it burns, and are intoxicated by the scent as the Hellenes are with wine, and when more of the fruit is thrown on they become more intoxicated, until at last they rise up to dance and begin to sing. This is said to be their manner of living: and as to the river Araxes, it flows from the land of the Matienians, whence flows the Gyndes which Cyrus divided into the three hundred and sixty channels, and it discharges itself by forty branches, of which all except one end in swamps and shallow pools; and among them they say that men dwell who feed on fish eaten raw, and who are wont to use as clothing the skins of seals: but the one remaining branch of the Araxes flows with unimpeded course into the Caspian Sea.

Now the Caspian Sea is apart by itself, not having connection with the other Sea: for all that Sea which the Hellenes navigate, and the Sea beyond the Pillars, which is called Atlantis, and the Erythraian Sea are in fact all one, but the Caspian is separate and lies apart by itself. In length it is a voyage of fifteen days if one uses oars, and in breadth, where it is broadest, a voyage of eight days. On the side towards the West of this Sea the Caucasus runs along by it, which is of all mountain-ranges both the greatest in extent and the loftiest: and the Caucasus has many various races of men dwelling in it, living for the most part on the wild produce of the forests; and among them there are said to be trees which produce leaves of such a kind that by pounding them and mixing water with them they paint figures upon their garments, and the figures do not wash out, but grow old with the woollen stuff as if they had been woven into it at the first: and men say that the sexual intercourse of these people is open like that of cattle.

On the West then of this Sea which is called Caspian the Caucasus is the boundary, while towards the East and the rising sun a plain succeeds which is of limitless extent to the view. Of this great plain then the Massagetai occupy a large part, against whom Cyrus had become eager to march; for there were many strong reasons which incited him to it and urged him onwards,—first the manner of his birth, that is to say the opinion held of him that he was more than a mere mortal man, and next the success which he had met with in his wars, for whithersoever Cyrus directed his march, it was impossible for that nation to escape.

Now the ruler of the Massagetai was a woman, who was queen after the death of her husband, and her name was Tomyris. To her Cyrus sent and wooed her, pretending that he desired to have her for his wife: but Tomyris understanding that he was wooing not herself but rather the kingdom of the Massagetai, rejected his approaches: and Cyrus after this, as he made no progress by craft, marched to the Araxes, and proceeded to make an expedition openly against the Massagetai, forming bridges of boats over the river for his army to cross, and building towers upon the vessels which gave them passage across the river.

While he was busied about this labour, Tomyris sent a herald and said thus: "O king of the Medes, cease to press forward the work which thou art now pressing forward; for thou canst not tell whether these things will be in the end for thy advantage or no; cease to do so, I say, and be king over thine own people, and endure to see us ruling those whom we rule. Since however I know that thou wilt not be willing to receive this counsel, but dost choose anything rather than to be at rest, therefore if thou art greatly anxious to make trial of the Massagetai in fight, come now, leave that labour which thou hast in yoking together the banks of the river, and cross over into our land, when we have first withdrawn three days' journey from the river: or if thou desirest rather to receive us into your land, do thou this same thing thyself." Having heard this Cyrus called together the first men among the Persians, and having gathered these together he laid the matter before them for discussion, asking their advice as to which of the two things he should do: and their opinions all agreed in one, bidding him receive Tomyris and her army into his country.

. But Croesus the Lydian, being present and finding fault with this opinion, declared an opinion opposite to that which had been set forth, saying as follows: "O king, I told thee in former time also, that since Zeus had given me over to thee, I would avert according to my power whatever occasion of falling I might see coming near thy house: and now my sufferings, which have been bitter, have proved to be lessons of wisdom to me. If thou dost suppose that thou art immortal and that thou dost command an army which is also immortal, it will be of no use for me to declare to thee my judgment; but if thou hast perceived that thou art a mortal man thyself and dost command others who are so likewise, then learn this first, that for the affairs of men there is a revolving wheel, and that this in its revolution suffers not the same persons always to have good fortune. I therefore now have an opinion about the matter laid before us, which is opposite to that of these men: for if we shall consent to receive the enemy into our land, there is for thee this danger in so doing:—if thou shalt be worsted thou wilt lose in addition all thy realm, for it is evident that if the Massagetai are victors they will not turn back and fly, but will march upon the provinces of thy realm; and on the other hand if thou shalt be the victor, thou wilt not be victor so fully as if thou shouldest overcome the Massagetai after crossing over into their land and shouldest pursue them when they fled. For against that which I said before I will set the same again here, and say that thou, when thou hast conquered, wilt march straight against the realm of Tomyris. Moreover besides that which has been said, it is a disgrace and not to be endured that Cyrus the son of Cambyses should yield to a woman and so withdraw from her land. Now therefore it seems good to me that we should cross over and go forward from the crossing as far as they go in their retreat, and endeavour to get the better of them by doing as follows:—The Massagetai, as I am informed, are without experience of Persian good things, and have never enjoyed any great luxuries. Cut up therefore cattle without stint and dress the meat and set out for these men a banquet in our camp: moreover also provide without stint bowls of unmixed wine and provisions of every kind; and having so done, leave behind the most worthless part of thy army and let the rest begin to retreat from the camp towards the river: for if I am not mistaken in my judgment, they when they see a quantity of good things will fall to the feast, and after that it remains for us to display great deeds."

These were the conflicting opinions; and Cyrus, letting go the former opinion and choosing that of Croesus, gave notice to Tomyris to retire, as he was intending to cross over to her. She then proceeded to retire, as she had at first engaged to do, but Cyrus delivered Croesus into the hands of his son Cambyses, to whom he meant to give the kingdom, and gave him charge earnestly to honour him and to treat him well, if the crossing over to go against the Massagetai should not be prosperous. Having thus charged him and sent these away to the land of the Persians, he crossed over the river both himself and his army.

. And when he had passed over the Araxes, night having come on he saw a vision in his sleep in the land of the Massagetai, as follows:—in his sleep it seemed to Cyrus that he saw the eldest of the sons of Hystaspes having upon his shoulders wings, and that with the one of these he overshadowed Asia and with the other Europe. Now of Hystaspes the son of Arsames, who was a man of the Achaimenid clan, the eldest son was Dareios, who was then, I suppose, a youth of about twenty years of age, and he had been left behind in the land of the Persians, for he was not yet of full age to go out to the wars. So then when Cyrus awoke he considered with himself concerning the vision: and as the vision seemed to him to be of great import, he called Hystaspes, and having taken him apart by himself he said: "Hystaspes, thy son has been found plotting against me and against my throne: and how I know this for certain I will declare to thee:—The gods have a care of me and show me beforehand all the evils that threaten me. So in the night that is past while sleeping I saw the eldest of thy sons having upon his shoulders wings, and with the one of these he overshadowed Asia and with the other Europe. To judge by this vision then, it cannot be but that he is plotting against me. Do thou therefore go by the quickest way back to Persia and take care that, when I return thither after having subdued these regions, thou set thy son before me to be examined."

Cyrus said thus supposing that Dareios was plotting against him; but in fact the divine powers were showing him beforehand that he was destined to find his end there and that his kingdom was coming about to Dareios. To this then Hystaspes replied as follows: "O king, heaven forbid that there should be any man of Persian race who would plot against thee, and if there be any, I pray that he perish as quickly as may be; seeing that thou didst make the Persians to be free instead of slaves, and to rule all nations instead of being ruled by others. And if any vision announces to thee that my son is planning rebellion against thee, I deliver him over to thee to do with him whatsoever thou wilt."

Hystaspes then, having made answer with these words and having crossed over the Araxes, was going his way to the Persian land to keep watch over his son Dareios for Cyrus; and Cyrus meanwhile went forward and made a march of one day from the Araxes according to the suggestion of Croesus. After this when Cyrus and the best part of the army of the Persians had marched back to the Araxes, and those who were unfit for fighting had been left behind, then a third part of the army of the Massagetai came to the attack and proceeded to slay, not without resistance, those who were left behind of the army of Cyrus; and seeing the feast that was set forth, when they had overcome their enemies they lay down and feasted, and being satiated with food and wine they went to sleep. Then the Persians came upon them and slew many of them, and took alive many more even than they slew, and among these the son of the queen Tomyris, who was leading the army of the Massagetai; and his name was Spargapises.

. She then, when she heard that which had come to pass concerning the army and also the things concerning her son, sent a herald to Cyrus and said as follows: "Cyrus, insatiable of blood, be not elated with pride by this which has come to pass, namely because with that fruit of the vine, with which ye fill yourselves and become so mad that as the wine descends into your bodies, evil words float up upon its stream,—because setting a snare, I say, with such a drug as this thou didst overcome my son, and not by valour in fight. Now therefore receive the word which I utter, giving thee good advice:—Restore to me my son and depart from this land without penalty, triumphant over a third part of the army of the Massagetai: but if thou shalt not do so, I swear to thee by the Sun, who is lord of the Massagetai, that surely I will give thee thy fill of blood, insatiable as thou art."

When these words were reported to him Cyrus made no account of them; and the son of the queen Tomyris, Spargapises, when the wine left him and he learnt in what evil case he was, entreated Cyrus that he might be loosed from his chains and gained his request, and then so soon as he was loosed and had got power over his hands he put himself to death.

He then ended his life in this manner; but Tomyris, as Cyrus did not listen to her, gathered together all her power and joined battle with Cyrus. This battle of all the battles fought by Barbarians I judge to have been the fiercest, and I am informed that it happened thus:—first, it is said, they stood apart and shot at one another, and afterwards when their arrows were all shot away, they fell upon one another and engaged in close combat with their spears and daggers; and so they continued to be in conflict with one another for a long time, and neither side would flee; but at last the Massagetai got the better in the fight: and the greater part of the Persian army was destroyed there on the spot, and Cyrus himself brought his life to an end there, after he had reigned in all thirty years wanting one. Then Tomyris filled a skin with human blood and had search made among the Persian dead for the corpse of Cyrus: and when she found it, she let his head down into the skin and doing outrage to the corpse she said at the same time this: "Though I yet live and have overcome thee in fight, nevertheless thou didst undo me by taking my son with craft: but I according to my threat will give thee thy fill of blood." Now as regards the end of the life of Cyrus there are many tales told, but this which I have related is to my mind the most worthy of belief.

As to the Massagetai, they wear a dress which is similar to that of the Scythians, and they have a manner of life which is also like theirs; and there are of them horsemen and also men who do not ride on horses (for they have both fashions), and moreover there are both archers and spearmen, and their custom it is to carry battle-axes; and for everything they use either gold or bronze, for in all that has to do with spear-points or arrow-heads or battle-axes they use bronze, but for head-dresses and girdles and belts round the arm-pits they employ gold as ornament: and in like manner as regards their horses, they put breast-plates of bronze about their chests, but on their bridles and bits and cheek-pieces they employ gold. Iron however and silver they use not at all, for they have them not in their land, but gold and bronze in abundance.

These are the customs which they have:—Each marries a wife, but they have their wives in common; for that which the Hellenes say that the Scythians do, is not in fact done by the Scythians but by the Massagetai, that is to say, whatever woman a man of the Massagetai may desire he hangs up his quiver in front of the waggon and has commerce with her freely. They have no precise limit of age laid down for their life, but when a man becomes very old, his nearest of kin come together and slaughter him solemnly and cattle also with him; and then after that they boil the flesh and banquet upon it. This is considered by them the happiest lot; but him who has ended his life by disease they do not eat, but cover him up in the earth, counting it a misfortune that he did not attain to being slaughtered. They sow no crops but live on cattle and on fish, which last they get in abundance from the river Araxes; moreover they are drinkers of milk. Of gods they reverence the Sun alone, and to him they sacrifice horses: and the rule of the sacrifice is this:—to the swiftest of the gods they assign the swiftest of all mortal things.

Book II

The Second Book of the Histories, Called Euterpe

When Cyrus had brought his life to an end, Cambyses received the royal power in succession, being the son of Cyrus and of Cassandane the daughter of Pharnaspes, for whose death, which came about before his own, Cyrus had made great mourning himself and also had proclaimed to all those over whom he bore rule that they should make mourning for her: Cambyses, I say, being the son of this woman and of Cyrus, regarded the Ionians and Aiolians as slaves inherited from his father; and he proceeded to march an army against Egypt, taking with him as helpers not only the other nations of which he was the ruler, but also those of the Hellenes over whom he had power besides.

Now the Egyptians, before the time when Psammetichos became king over them, were wont to suppose that they had come into being first of all men; but since the time when Psammetichos having become king desired to know what men had come into being first, they suppose that the Phrygians came into being before themselves, but they themselves before all other men. Now Psammetichos, when he was not able by inquiry to find out any means of knowing who had come into being first of all men, contrived a device of the following kind:—Taking two new-born children belonging to persons of the common sort he gave them to a shepherd to bring up at the place where his flocks were, with a manner of bringing up such as I shall say, charging him namely that no man should utter any word in their presence, and that they should be placed by themselves in a room where none might come, and at the proper time he should bring to them she-goats, and when he had satisfied them with milk he should do for them whatever else was needed. These things Psammetichos did and gave him this charge wishing to hear what word the children would let break forth first, after they had ceased from wailings without sense. And accordingly so it came to pass; for after a space of two years had gone by, during which the shepherd went on acting so, at length, when he opened the door and entered, both the children fell before him in entreaty and uttered the word bekos, stretching forth their hands. At first when he heard this the shepherd kept silence; but since this word was often repeated, as he visited them constantly and attended to them, at last he declared the matter to his master, and at his command he brought the children before his face. Then Psammetichos having himself also heard it, began to inquire about what nation of men named anything bekos, and inquiring he found that the Phrygians had this name for bread. In this manner and guided by an indication such as this, the Egyptians were brought to allow that the Phrygians were a more ancient people than themselves.

That so it came to pass I heard from the priests of that Hephaistos who dwells at Memphis; but the Hellenes relate, besides many other idle tales, that Psammetichos cut out the tongues of certain women, and then caused the children to live with these women.

With regard then to the rearing of the children they related so much as I have said: and I heard also other things at Memphis when I had speech with the priests of Hephaistos. Moreover I visited both Thebes and Heliopolis for this very cause, namely because I wished to know whether the priests at these places would agree in their accounts with those at Memphis; for the men of Heliopolis are said to be the most learned in records of the Egyptians. Those of their narrations which I heard with regard to the gods I am not earnest to relate in full, but I shall name them only, because I consider that all men are equally ignorant of these matters: and whatever things of them I may record, I shall record only because I am compelled by the course of the story.

But as to those matters which concern men, the priests agreed with one another in saying that the Egyptians were the first of all men on earth to find out the course of the year, having divided the seasons into twelve parts to make up the whole; and this they said they found out from the stars: and they reckon to this extent more wisely than the Hellenes, as it seems to me, inasmuch as the Hellenes throw in an intercalated month every other year, to make the seasons right, whereas the Egyptians, reckoning the twelve months at thirty days each, bring in also every year five days beyond the number, and thus the circle of their seasons is completed and comes round to the same point whence it set out. They said moreover that the Egyptians were the first who brought into use appellations for the twelve gods and the Hellenes took up the use from them; and that they were the first who assigned altars and images and temples to the gods, and who engraved figures on stones; and with regard to the greater number of these things they showed me by actual facts that they had happened so. They said also that the first man who became king of Egypt was Min; and that in his time all Egypt except the district of Thebes was a swamp, and none of the regions were then above water which now lie below the lake of Moiris, to which lake it is a voyage of seven days up the river from the sea: and I thought that they said well about the land; for it is manifest in truth even to a person who has not heard it beforehand but has only seen, at least if he have understanding, that the Egypt to which the Hellenes come in ships is a land which has been won by the Egyptians as an addition, and that it is a gift of the river: moreover the regions which lie above this lake also for a distance of three days' sail, about which they did not go on to say anything of this kind, are nevertheless another instance of the same thing: for the nature of the land of Egypt is as follows:—First when you are still approaching it in a ship and are distant a day's run from the land, if you let down a sounding-line you will bring up mud and will find yourself in eleven fathoms. This then so far shows that there is a silting forward of the land.

Then secondly, as to Egypt itself, the extent of it along the sea is sixty schoines, according to our definition of Egypt as extending from the Gulf of Plinthine to the Serbonian lake, along which stretches Mount Casion; from this lake then the sixty schoines are reckoned: for those of men who are poor in land have their country measured by fathoms, those who are less poor by furlongs, those who have much land by parasangs, and those who have land in very great abundance by schoines: now the parasang is equal to thirty furlongs, and each schoine, which is an Egyptian measure, is equal to sixty furlongs. So there would be an extent of three thousand six hundred furlongs for the coast-land of Egypt.

From thence and as far as Heliopolis inland Egypt is broad, and the land is all flat and without springs of water and formed of mud: and the road as one goes inland from the sea to Heliopolis is about the same in length as that which leads from the altar of the twelve gods at Athens to Pisa and the temple of Olympian Zeus: reckoning up you would find the difference very small by which these roads fail of being equal in length, not more indeed than fifteen furlongs; for the road from Athens to Pisa wants fifteen furlongs of being fifteen hundred, while the road to Heliopolis from the sea reaches that number completely.

From Heliopolis however, as you go up, Egypt is narrow; for on the one side a mountain-range belonging to Arabia stretches along by the side of it, going in a direction from North towards the midday and the South Wind, tending upwards without a break to that which is called the Erythraian Sea, in which range are the stone-quarries which were used in cutting stone for the pyramids at Memphis. On this side then the mountain ends where I have said, and then takes a turn back; and where it is widest, as I was informed, it is a journey of two months across from East to West; and the borders of it which turn towards the East are said to produce frankincense. Such then is the nature of this mountain-range; and on the side of Egypt towards Libya another range extends, rocky and enveloped in sand: in this are the pyramids, and it runs in the same direction as those parts of the Arabian mountains which go towards the midday. So then, I say, from Heliopolis the land has no longer a great extent so far as it belongs to Egypt, and for about four days' sail up the river Egypt properly so called is narrow: and the space between the mountain-ranges which have been mentioned is plain-land, but where it is narrowest it did not seem to me to exceed two hundred furlongs from the Arabian mountains to those which are called the Libyan. After this again Egypt is broad.

. Such is the nature of this land: and from Heliopolis to Thebes is a voyage up the river of nine days, and the distance of the journey in furlongs is four thousand eight hundred and sixty, the number of the schoines being eighty-one. If these measures of Egypt in furlongs be put together the result is as follows:—I have already before this shown that the distance along the sea amounts to three thousand six hundred furlongs, and I will now declare what the distance is inland from the sea to Thebes, namely six thousand one hundred and twenty furlongs: and again the distance from Thebes to the city called Elephantine is one thousand eight hundred furlongs.

Of this land then, concerning which I have spoken, it seemed to myself also, according as the priests said, that the greater part had been won as an addition by the Egyptians; for it was evident to me that the space between the aforesaid mountain-ranges, which lie above the city of Memphis, once was a gulf of the sea, like the regions about Ilion and Teuthrania and Ephesos and the plain of the Maiander, if it be permitted to compare small things with great; and small these are in comparison, for of the rivers which heaped up the soil in those regions none is worthy to be compared in volume with a single one of the mouths of the Nile, which has five mouths. Moreover there are other rivers also, not in size at all equal to the Nile, which have performed great feats; of which I can mention the names of several, and especially the Acheloös, which flowing through Acarnania and so issuing out into the sea has already made half of the Echinades from islands into mainland.

Now there is in the land of Arabia, not far from Egypt, a gulf of the sea running in from that which is called the Erythraian Sea, very long and narrow, as I am about to tell. With respect to the length of the voyage along it, one who set out from the innermost point to sail out through it into the open sea, would spend forty days upon the voyage, using oars; and with respect to breadth, where the gulf is broadest it is half a day's sail across: and there is in it an ebb and flow of tide every day. Just such another gulf I suppose that Egypt was, and that the one ran in towards Ethiopia from the Northern Sea, and the other, the Arabian, of which I am about to speak, tended from the South towards Syria, the gulfs boring in so as almost to meet at their extreme points, and passing by one another with but a small space left between. If then the stream of the Nile should turn aside into this Arabian gulf, what would hinder that gulf from being filled up with silt as the river continued to flow, at all events within a period of twenty thousand years? indeed for my part I am of opinion that it would be filled up even within ten thousand years. How, then, in all the time that has elapsed before I came into being should not a gulf be filled up even of much greater size than this by a river so great and so active?

As regards Egypt then, I both believe those who say that things are so, and for myself also I am strongly of opinion that they are so; because I have observed that Egypt runs out into the sea further than the adjoining land, and that shells are found upon the mountains of it, and an efflorescence of salt forms upon the surface, so that even the pyramids are being eaten away by it, and moreover that of all the mountains of Egypt, the range which lies above Memphis is the only one which has sand: besides which I notice that Egypt resembles neither the land of Arabia, which borders upon it, nor Libya, nor yet Syria (for they are Syrians who dwell in the parts of Arabia lying along the sea), but that it has soil which is black and easily breaks up, seeing that it is in truth mud and silt brought down from Ethiopia by the river: but the soil of Libya, we know, is reddish in colour and rather sandy, while that of Arabia and Syria is somewhat clayey and rocky.

The priests also gave me a strong proof concerning this land as follows, namely that in the reign of king Moiris, whenever the river reached a height of at least eight cubits it watered Egypt below Memphis; and not yet nine hundred years had gone by since the death of Moiris, when I heard these things from the priests: now however, unless the river rises to sixteen cubits, or fifteen at the least, it does not go over the land. I think too that those Egyptians who dwell below the lake of Moiris and especially in that region which is called the Delta, if that land continues to grow in height according to this proportion and to increase similarly in extent, will suffer for all remaining time, from the Nile not overflowing their land, that same thing which they themselves said that the Hellenes would at some time suffer: for hearing that the whole land of the Hellenes has rain and is not watered by rivers as theirs is, they said that the Hellenes would at some time be disappointed of a great hope and would suffer the ills of famine. This saying means that if the god shall not send them rain, but shall allow drought to prevail for a long time, the Hellenes will be destroyed by hunger; for they have in fact no other supply of water to save them except from Zeus alone.

This has been rightly said by the Egyptians with reference to the Hellenes: but now let me tell how matters are with the Egyptians themselves in their turn. If, in accordance with what I before said, their land below Memphis (for this is that which is increasing) shall continue to increase in height according to the same proportion as in past time, assuredly those Egyptians who dwell here will suffer famine, if their land shall not have rain nor the river be able to go over their fields. It is certain however that now they gather in fruit from the earth with less labour than any other men and also with less than the other Egyptians; for they have no labour in breaking up furrows with a plough nor in hoeing nor in any other of those labours which other men have about a crop; but when the river has come up of itself and watered their fields and after watering has left them again, then each man sows his own field and turns into it swine, and when he has trodden the seed into the ground by means of the swine, after that he waits for the harvest; and when he has threshed the corn by means of the swine, then he gathers it in.

If we desire to follow the opinions of the Ionians as regards Egypt, who say that the Delta alone is Egypt, reckoning its sea-coast to be from the watch-tower called of Perseus to the fish-curing houses of Pelusion, a distance of forty schoines, and counting it to extend inland as far as the city of Kercasoros, where the Nile divides and runs to Pelusion and Canobos, while as for the rest of Egypt, they assign it partly to Libya and partly to Arabia,—if, I say, we should follow this account, we should thereby declare that in former times the Egyptians had no land to live in; for, as we have seen, their Delta at any rate is alluvial, and has appeared (so to speak) lately, as the Egyptians themselves say and as my opinion is. If then at the first there was no land for them to live in, why did they waste their labour to prove that they had come into being before all other men? They needed not to have made trial of the children to see what language they would first utter. However I am not of opinion that the Egyptians came into being at the same time as that which is called by the Ionians the Delta, but that they existed always ever since the human race came into being, and that as their land advanced forwards, many of them were left in their first abodes and many came down gradually to the lower parts. At least it is certain that in old times Thebes had the name of Egypt, and of this the circumference measures six thousand one hundred and twenty furlongs.

If then we judge aright of these matters, the opinion of the Ionians about Egypt is not sound: but if the judgment of the Ionians is right, I declare that neither the Hellenes nor the Ionians themselves know how to reckon since they say that the whole earth is made up of three divisions, Europe, Asia, and Libya: for they ought to count in addition to these the

Delta of Egypt, since it belongs neither to Asia nor to Libya; for at least it cannot be the river Nile by this reckoning which divides Asia from Libya, but the Nile is cleft at the point of this Delta so as to flow round it, and the result is that this land would come between Asia and Libya.

We dismiss then the opinion of the Ionians, and express a judgment of our own in this matter also, that Egypt is all that land which is inhabited by Egyptians, just as Kilikia is that which is inhabited by Kilikians and Assyria that which is inhabited by Assyrians, and we know of no boundary properly speaking between Asia and Libya except the borders of Egypt. If however we shall adopt the opinion which is commonly held by the Hellenes, we shall suppose that the whole of Egypt, beginning from the Cataract and the city of Elephantine, is divided into two parts and that it thus partakes of both the names, since one side will thus belong to Libya and the other to Asia; for the Nile from the Cataract onwards flows to the sea cutting Egypt through the midst; and as far as the city of Kercasoros the Nile flows in one single stream, but from this city onwards it is parted into three ways; and one, which is called the Pelusian mouth, turns towards the East; the second of the ways goes towards the West, and this is called the Canobic mouth; but that one of the ways which is straight runs thus,—when the river in its course downwards comes to the point of the Delta, then it cuts the Delta through the midst and so issues out to the sea. In this we have a portion of the water of the river which is not the smallest nor the least famous, and it is called the Sebennytic mouth. There are also two other mouths which part off from the Sebennytic and go to the sea, and these are called, one the Saïtic, the other the Mendesian mouth. The Bolbitinitic and Bucolic mouths, on the other hand, are not natural but made by digging.

Moreover also the answer given by the Oracle of Ammon bears witness in support of my opinion that Egypt is of the extent which I declare it to be in my account; and of this answer I heard after I had formed my own opinion about Egypt. For those of the city of Marea and of Apis, dwelling in the parts of Egypt which border on Libya, being of opinion themselves that they were Libyans and not Egyptians, and also being burdened by the rules of religious service, because they desired not to be debarred from the use of cows' flesh, sent to Ammon saying that they had nought in common with the Egyptians, for they dwelt outside the Delta and agreed with them in nothing; and they said they desired that it might be lawful for them to eat everything without distinction. The god however did not permit them to do so, but said that that land which was Egypt which the Nile came over and watered, and that those were Egyptians who dwelling below the city of Elephantine drank of that river. Thus it was answered to them by the Oracle about this: and the Nile, when it is in flood, goes over not only the Delta but also of the land which is called Libyan and of that which is called Arabian sometimes as much as two days' journey on each side, and at times even more than this or at times less.

As regards the nature of the river, neither from the priests nor yet from any other man was I able to obtain any knowledge: and I was desirous especially to learn from them about these matters, namely why the Nile comes down increasing in volume from the summer solstice onwards for a hundred days, and then, when it has reached the number of these days, turns and goes back, failing in its stream, so that through the whole winter season it continues to be low, and until the summer solstice returns. Of none of these things was I able to receive any account from the Egyptians, when I inquired of them what power the Nile has whereby it is of a nature opposite to that of other rivers. And I made inquiry, desiring to know both this which I say and also why, unlike all other rivers, it does not give rise to any breezes blowing from it.

However some of the Hellenes who desired to gain distinction for cleverness have given an account of this water in three different ways: two of these I do not think it worth while even to speak of except only to indicate their nature; of which the one says that the Etesian Winds are the cause that makes the river rise, by preventing the Nile from flowing out into the sea. But often the Etesian Winds fail and yet the Nile does the same work as it is wont to do; and moreover, if these were the cause, all the other rivers also which flow in a direction opposed to the Etesian Winds ought to have been affected in the same way as the Nile, and even more, in as much as they are smaller and present to them a feebler flow of stream: but there are many of these rivers in Syria and many also in Libya, and they are affected in no such manner as the Nile.

The second way shows more ignorance than that which has been mentioned, and it is more marvellous to tell; for it says that the river produces these effects because it flows from the Ocean, and that the Ocean flows round the whole earth.

The third of the ways is much the most specious, but nevertheless it is the most mistaken of all: for indeed this way has no more truth in it than the rest, alleging as it does that the Nile flows from melting snow; whereas it flows out of Libya through the midst of the Ethiopians, and so comes out into Egypt. How then should it flow from snow, when it flows from the hottest parts to those which are cooler? And indeed most of the facts are such as to convince a man (one at least who is capable of reasoning about such matters), that it is not at all likely that it flows from snow. The first and greatest evidence is afforded by the winds, which blow hot from these regions; the second is that the land is rainless always and without frost, whereas after snow has fallen rain must necessarily come within five days, so that if it snowed in those parts rain would fall there; the third evidence is afforded by the people dwelling there, who are of a black colour by reason of the burning heat. Moreover kites and swallows remain there through the year and do not leave the land; and cranes flying from the cold weather which comes on in the region of Scythia come regularly to these parts for wintering: if then it snowed ever so little in that land through which the Nile flows and in which it has its rise, none of these things would take place, as necessity compels us to admit.

As for him who talked about the Ocean, he carried his tale into the region of the unknown, and so he need not be refuted; since I for my part know of no river Ocean existing, but I think that Homer or one of the poets who were before him invented the name and introduced it into his verse.

If however after I have found fault with the opinions proposed, I am bound to declare an opinion of my own about the matters which are in doubt, I will tell what to my mind is the reason why the Nile increases in the summer. In the winter season the Sun, being driven away from his former path through the heaven by the stormy winds, comes to the upper parts of Libya. If one would set forth the matter in the shortest way, all has now been said; for whatever region this god approaches most and stands directly above, this it may reasonably be supposed is most in want of water, and its native streams of rivers are dried up most.

However, to set it forth at greater length, thus it is:—the Sun passing in his course by the upper parts of Libya, does thus, that is to say, since at all times the air in those parts is clear and the country is warm, because there are no cold winds, in passing through it the Sun does just as he was wont to do in the summer, when going through the midst of the heaven, that is he draws to himself the water, and having drawn it he drives it away to the upper parts of the country, and the winds take it up and scattering it abroad melt it into rain; so it is natural that the winds which blow from this region, namely the South and South-west Winds, should be much the most rainy of all the winds. I think however that the Sun does not send away from himself all the water of the Nile of each year, but that he also lets some remain behind with himself. Then when the winter becomes milder, the Sun returns back again to the midst of the heaven, and from that time onwards he draws equally from all rivers; but in the meanwhile they flow in large volume, since water of rain mingles with them in great quantity, because their country receives rain then and is filled with torrent streams. In summer however they are weak, since not only the showers of rain fail then, but also they are drawn by the Sun. The Nile however, alone of all rivers, not having rain and being drawn by the Sun, naturally flows during this time of winter in much less than its proper volume, that is much less than in summer; for then it is drawn equally with all the other waters, but in winter it bears the burden alone. Thus I suppose the Sun to be the cause of these things.

He is also the cause in my opinion that the air in these parts is dry, since he makes it so by scorching up his path through the heaven: thus summer prevails always in the upper parts of Libya. If however the station of the seasons had been changed, and where now in the heaven are placed the North Wind and winter, there was the station of the South Wind and of the midday, and where now is placed the South Wind, there was the North, if this had been so, the Sun being driven from the midst of the heaven by the winter and the North Wind would go to the upper parts of Europe, just as now he comes to the upper parts of Libya, and passing in his course throughout the whole of Europe I suppose that he would do to the Ister that which he now works upon the Nile.

As to the breeze, why none blows from the river, my opinion is that from very hot places it is not natural that anything should blow, and that a breeze is wont to blow from something cold.

Let these matters then be as they are and as they were at the first: but as to the sources of the Nile, not one either of the Egyptians or of the Libyans or of the Hellenes, who came to speech with me, professed to know anything, except the scribe of the sacred treasury of Athene at the city of Saïs in Egypt. To me however this man seemed not to be speaking seriously when he said that he had certain knowledge of it; and he said as follows, namely that there were two mountains of which the tops ran up to a sharp point, situated between the city of Syene, which is in the district of Thebes, and Elephantine, and the names of the mountains were, of the one Crophi and of the other Mophi. From the middle between these two mountains flowed (he said) the sources of the Nile, which were fathomless in depth, and half of the water flowed to Egypt and towards the North Wind, the other half to Ethiopia and the South Wind. As for the fathomless depth of the source, he said that Psammetichos king of Egypt came to a trial of this matter; for he had a rope twisted of many thousands of fathoms and let it down in this place, and it found no bottom. By this the scribe (if this which he told me was really as he said) gave me to understand that there were certain strong eddies there and a backward flow, and that since the water dashed against the mountains, therefore the sounding-line could not come to any bottom when it was let down.

From no other person was I able to learn anything about this matter; but for the rest I learnt so much as here follows by the most diligent inquiry; for I went myself as an eye-witness as far as the city of Elephantine and from that point onwards I gathered knowledge by report. From the city of Elephantine as one goes up the river there is country which slopes steeply; so that here one must attach ropes to the vessel on both sides, as one fastens an ox, and so make one's way onward; and if the rope break, the vessel is gone at once, carried away by the violence of the stream. Through this country it is a voyage of about four days in length, and in this part the Nile is winding like the river Maiander, and the distance amounts to twelve schoines, which one must traverse in this manner. Then you will come to a level plain, in which the Nile flows round an island named Tachompso. (Now in the regions above Elephantine there dwell Ethiopians at once succeeding, who also occupy half of the island, and Egyptians the other half.) Adjoining this island there is a great lake, round which dwell Ethiopian nomad tribes; and when you have sailed through this you will come to the stream of the Nile again, which flows into this lake. After this you will disembark and make a journey by land of forty days; for in the Nile sharp rocks stand forth out of the water, and there are many reefs, by which it is not possible for a vessel to pass. Then after having passed through this country in the forty days which I have said, you will embark again in another vessel and sail for twelve days; and after this you will come to a great city called Meroe. This city is said to be the mother-city of all the other Ethiopians: and they who dwell in it reverence of the gods Zeus and Dionysos alone, and these they greatly honour; and they have an Oracle of Zeus established, and make warlike marches whensoever this god commands them by prophesyings and to whatsoever place he commands.

Sailing from this city you will come to the "Deserters" in another period of time equal to that in which you came from Elephantine to the mother-city of the Ethiopians. Now the name of these "Deserters" is Asmach, and this word signifies, when translated into the tongue of the Hellenes, "those who stand on the left hand of the king." These were two hundred and forty thousand Egyptians of the warrior class, who revolted and went over to the Ethiopians for the following cause:—In the reign of Psammetichos garrisons were set, one towards the Ethiopians at the city of Elephantine, another towards the Arabians and Assyrians at Daphnai of Pelusion, and another towards Libya at Marea: and even in my own time the garrisons of the Persians too are ordered in the same manner as these were in the reign of Psammetichos, for both at Elephantine and at Daphnai the Persians have outposts. The Egyptians then of whom I speak had served as outposts for three years and no one relieved them from their guard; accordingly they took counsel together, and adopting a common plan they all in a body revolted from Psammetichos and set out for Ethiopia. Hearing this Psammetichos set forth in pursuit, and when he came up with them he entreated them much and endeavoured to persuade them not to desert the gods of their country and their children and wives: upon which it is said that one of them pointed to his privy member and said that wherever this was, there would they have both children and wives. When these came to Ethiopia they gave themselves over to the king of the Ethiopians; and he rewarded them as follows:—there were certain of the Ethiopians who had come to be at variance with him; and he bade them drive these out and dwell in their land. So since these men settled in the land of the Ethiopians, the Ethiopians have come to be of milder manners, from having learnt the customs of the Egyptians.

The Nile then, besides that part of its course which is in Egypt, is known as far as a four months' journey by river and land: for that is the number of months which are found by reckoning to be spent in going from Elephantine to these "Deserters": and the river runs from the West and the setting of the sun. But what comes after that no one can clearly say; for this land is desert by reason of the burning heat.

Thus much however I heard from men of Kyrene, who told me that they had been to the Oracle of Ammon, and had come to speech with Etearchos king of the Ammonians: and it happened that after speaking of other matters they fell to discourse about the Nile and how no one knew the sources of it; and Etearchos said that once there had come to him men of the Nasamonians (this is a Libyan race which dwells in the Syrtis, and also in the land to the East of the Syrtis reaching to no great distance), and when the Nasamonians came and were asked by him whether they were able to tell him anything more than he knew about the desert parts of Libya, they said that there had been among them certain sons of chief men, who were of unruly disposition; and these when they grew up to be men had devised various other extravagant things and also they had told off by lot five of themselves to go to see the desert parts of Libya and to try whether they could discover more than those who had previously explored furthest: for in those parts of Libya which are by the Northern Sea, beginning from Egypt and going as far as the headland of Soloeis, which is the extreme point of Libya, Libyans (and of them many races) extend along the whole coast, except so much as the Hellenes and Phenicians hold; but in the upper parts, which lie above the sea-coast and above those people whose land comes down to the sea, Libya is full of wild beasts; and in the parts above the land of wild beasts it is full of sand, terribly waterless and utterly desert. These young men then (said they), being sent out by their companions well furnished with supplies of water and provisions, went first through the inhabited country, and after they had passed through this they came to the country of wild beasts, and after this they passed through the desert, making their journey towards the West Wind; and having passed through a great tract of sand in many days, they saw at last trees growing in a level place; and having come up to them, they were beginning to pluck the fruit which was upon the trees: but as they began to pluck it, there came upon them small men, of less stature than men of the common size, and these seized them and carried them away; and neither could the Nasamonians understand anything of their speech nor could those who were carrying them off understand anything of the speech of the Nasamonians: and they led them (so it was said) through very great swamps, and after passing through these they came to a city in which all the men were in size like those who carried them off and in colour of skin black; and by the city ran a great river, which ran from the West towards the sunrising, and in it were seen crocodiles.

Of the account given by Etearchos the Ammonian let so much suffice as is here said, except that, as the men of Kyrene told me, he alleged that the Nasamonians returned safe home, and that the people to whom they had come were all wizards. Now this river which ran by the city, Etearchos conjectured to be the Nile, and moreover reason compels us to think so; for the Nile flows from Libya and cuts Libya through in the midst, and as I conjecture, judging of what is not known by that which is evident to the view, it starts at a distance from its mouth equal to that of the Ister: for the river Ister begins from the Keltoi and the city of Pyrene and so runs that it divides Europe in the midst (now the Keltoi are outside the Pillars of Heracles and border upon the Kynesians, who dwell furthest towards the sunset of all those who have their dwelling in Europe); and the Ister ends, having its course through the whole of Europe, by flowing into the Euxine Sea at the place where the Milesians have their settlement of Istria.

Now the Ister, since it flows through land which is inhabited, is known by the reports of many; but of the sources of the Nile no one can give an account, for the part of Libya through which it flows is uninhabited and desert. About its course however so much as it was possible to learn by the most diligent inquiry has been told; and it runs out into Egypt. Now Egypt lies nearly opposite to the mountain districts of Kilikia; and from thence to Sinope, which lies upon the Euxine Sea, is a journey in the same straight line of five days for a man without encumbrance; and Sinope lies opposite to the place where the Ister runs out into the sea: thus I think that the Nile passes through the whole of Libya and is of equal measure with the Ister.

Of the Nile then let so much suffice as has been said.

. Of Egypt however I shall make my report at length, because it has wonders more in number than any other land, and works too it has to show as much as any land, which are beyond expression great: for this reason then more shall be said concerning it.

The Egyptians in agreement with their climate, which is unlike any other, and with the river, which shows a nature different from all other rivers, established for themselves manners and customs in a way opposite to other men in almost all matters: for among them the women frequent the market and carry on trade, while the men remain at home and weave; and whereas others weave pushing the woof upwards, the Egyptians push it downwards: the men carry their burdens upon their heads and the women upon their shoulders: the women make water standing up and the men crouching down: they ease themselves in their houses and they eat without in the streets, alleging as reason for this that it is right to do secretly the things that are unseemly though necessary, but those which are not unseemly, in public: no woman is a minister either of male or female divinity, but men of all, both male and female: to support their parents the sons are in no way compelled, if they do not desire to do so, but the daughters are forced to do so, be they never so unwilling.

The priests of the gods in other lands wear long hair, but in Egypt they shave their heads: among other men the custom is that in mourning those whom the matter concerns most nearly have their hair cut short, but the Egyptians, when deaths occur, let their hair grow long, both that on the head and that on the chin, having before been close shaven: other men have their daily living separated from beasts, but the Egyptians have theirs together with beasts: other men live on wheat and barley, but to any one of the Egyptians who makes his living on these it is a great reproach; they make their bread of maize, which some call spelt; they knead dough with their feet and clay with their hands, with which also they gather up dung: and whereas other men, except such as have learnt otherwise from the Egyptians, have their members as nature made them, the Egyptians practise circumcision: as to garments, the men wear two each and the women but one: and whereas others make fast the rings and ropes of the sails outside the ship, the Egyptians do this inside: finally in the writing of characters and reckoning with pebbles, while the Hellenes carry the hand from the left to the right, the Egyptians do this from the right to the left; and doing so they say that they do it themselves rightwise and the Hellenes leftwise: and they use two kinds of characters for writing, of which the one kind is called sacred and the other common.

They are religious excessively beyond all other men, and with regard to this they have customs as follows:—they drink from cups of bronze and rinse them out every day, and not some only do this but all: they wear garments of linen always newly washed, and this they make a special point of practice: they circumcise themselves for the sake of cleanliness, preferring to be clean rather than comely. The priests shave themselves all over their body every other day, so that no lice or any other foul thing may come to be upon them when they minister to the gods; and the priests wear garments of linen only and sandals of papyrus, and any other garment they may not take nor other sandals; these wash themselves in cold water twice in the day and twice again in the night; and other religious services they perform (one may almost say) of infinite number. They enjoy also good things not a few, for they do not consume or spend anything of their own substance, but there is sacred bread baked for them and they have each great quantity of flesh of oxen and geese coming in to them each day, and also wine of grapes is given to them; but it is not permitted to them to taste of fish: beans moreover the Egyptians do not at all sow in their land, and those which grow they neither eat raw nor boil for food; nay the priests do not endure even to look upon them, thinking this to be an unclean kind of pulse: and there is not one priest only for each of the gods but many, and of them one is chief-priest, and whenever a priest dies his son is appointed to his place.

The males of the ox kind they consider to belong to Epaphos, and on account of him they test them in the following manner:—If the priest sees one single black hair upon the beast he counts it not clean for sacrifice; and one of the priests who is appointed for the purpose makes investigation of these matters, both when the beast is standing upright and when it is lying on its back, drawing out its tongue moreover, to see if it is clean in respect of the appointed signs, which I shall tell of in another part of the history: he looks also at the hairs of the tail to see if it has them growing in the natural manner: and if it be clean in respect of all these things, he marks it with a piece of papyrus, rolling this round the horns, and then when he has plastered sealing-earth over it he sets upon it the seal of his signet-ring, and after that they take the animal away. But for one who sacrifices a beast not sealed the penalty appointed is death.

In this way then the beast is tested; and their appointed manner of sacrifice is as follows:—they lead the sealed beast to the altar where they happen to be sacrificing and then kindle a fire: after that, having poured libations of wine over the altar so that it runs down upon the victim and having called upon the god, they cut its throat, and having cut its throat they sever the head from the body. The body then of the beast they flay, but upon the head they make many imprecations first, and then they who have a market and Hellenes sojourning among them for trade, these carry it to the market-place and sell it, while they who have no Hellenes among them cast it away into the river: and this is the form of imprecation which they utter upon the heads, praying that if any evil be about to befall either themselves who are offering sacrifice or the land of Egypt in general, it may come rather upon this head. Now as regards the heads of the beasts which are sacrificed and the pouring over them of the wine, all the Egyptians have the same customs equally for all their sacrifices; and by reason of this custom none of the Egyptians eat of the head either of this or of any other kind of animal: but the manner of disembowelling the victims and of burning them is appointed among them differently for different sacrifices; I shall speak however of the sacrifices to that goddess whom they regard as the greatest of all, and to whom they celebrate the greatest feast.—When they have flayed the bullock and made imprecation, they take out the whole of its lower entrails but leave in the body the upper entrails and the fat; and they sever from it the legs and the end of the loin and the shoulders and the neck: and this done, they fill the rest of the body of the animal with consecrated loaves and honey and raisins and figs and frankincense and myrrh and every other kind of spices, and having filled it with these they offer it, pouring over it great abundance of oil. They make their sacrifice after fasting, and while the offerings are being burnt, they all beat themselves for mourning, and when they have finished beating themselves they set forth as a feast that which they left unburnt of the sacrifice.

The clean males then of the ox kind, both full-grown animals and calves, are sacrificed by all the Egyptians; the females however they may not sacrifice, but these are sacred to Isis; for the figure of Isis is in the form of a woman with cow's horns, just as the Hellenes present Io in pictures, and all the Egyptians without distinction reverence cows far more than any other kind of cattle; for which reason neither man nor woman of Egyptian race would kiss a man who is a Hellene on the mouth, nor will they use a knife or roasting-spits or a caldron belonging to a Hellene, nor taste of the flesh even of a clean animal if it has been cut with the knife of a Hellene. And the cattle of this kind which die they bury in the following manner:—the females they cast into the river, but the males they bury, each people in the suburb of their town, with one of the horns, or sometimes both, protruding to mark the place; and when the bodies have rotted away and the appointed time comes on, then to each city comes a boat from that which is called the island of Prosopitis (this is in the Delta, and the extent of its circuit is nine schoines). In this island of Prosopitis is situated, besides many other cities, that one from which the boats come to take up the bones of the oxen, and the name of the city is Atarbechis, and in it there is set up a holy temple of Aphrodite. From this city many go abroad in various directions, some to one city and others to another, and when they have dug up the bones of the oxen they carry them off, and coming together they bury them in one single place. In the same manner as they bury the oxen they bury also their other cattle when they die; for about them also they have the same law laid down, and these also they abstain from killing.

Now all who have a temple set up to the Theban Zeus or who are of the district of Thebes, these, I say, all sacrifice goats and abstain from sheep: for not all the Egyptians equally reverence the same gods, except only Isis and Osiris (who they say is Dionysos), these they all reverence alike: but they who have a temple of Mendes or belong to the Mendesian district, these abstain from goats and sacrifice sheep. Now the men of Thebes and those who after their example abstain from sheep, say that this custom was established among them for the cause which follows:—Heracles (they say) had an earnest desire to see Zeus, and Zeus did not desire to be seen of him; and at last when Heracles was urgent in entreaty Zeus contrived this device, that is to say, he flayed a ram and held in front of him the head of the ram which he had cut off, and he put on over him the fleece and then showed himself to him. Hence the Egyptians make the image of Zeus into the face of a ram; and the Ammonians do so also after their example, being settlers both from the Egyptians and from the Ethiopians, and using a language which is a medley of both tongues: and in my opinion it is from this god that the Ammonians took the name which they have, for the Egyptians call Zeus Amun. The Thebans then do not sacrifice rams but hold them sacred for this reason; on one day however in the year, on the feast of Zeus, they cut up in the same manner and flay one single ram and cover with its skin the image of Zeus, and then they bring up to it another image of Heracles. This done, all who are in the temple beat themselves in lamentation for the ram, and then they bury it in a sacred tomb.

About Heracles I heard the account given that he was of the number of the twelve gods; but of the other Heracles whom the Hellenes know I was not able to hear in any part of Egypt: and moreover to prove that the Egyptians did not take the name of Heracles from the Hellenes, but rather the Hellenes from the Egyptians,—that is to say those of the Hellenes who gave the name Heracles to the son of Amphitryon,—of that, I say, besides many other evidences there is chiefly this, namely that the parents of this Heracles, Amphitryon and Alcmene, were both of Egypt by descent, and also that the Egyptians say that they do not know the names either of Poseidon or of the Dioscuroi, nor have these been accepted by them as gods among the other gods; whereas if they had received from the Hellenes the name of any divinity, they would naturally have preserved the memory of these most of all, assuming that in those times as now some of the Hellenes were wont to make voyages and were sea-faring folk, as I suppose and as my judgment compels me to think; so that the Egyptians would have learnt the names of these gods even more than that of Heracles. In fact however Heracles is a very ancient Egyptian god; and (as they say themselves) it is seventeen thousand years to the beginning of the reign of Amasis from the time when the twelve gods, of whom they count that Heracles is one, were begotten of the eight gods.

I moreover, desiring to know something certain of these matters so far as might be, made a voyage also to Tyre of Phenicia, hearing that in that place there was a holy temple of Heracles; and I saw that it was richly furnished with many votive offerings besides, and especially there were in it two pillars, the one of pure gold and the other of an emerald stone of such size as to shine by night: and having come to speech with the priests of the god, I asked them how long time it was since their temple had been set up: and these also I found to be at variance with the Hellenes, for they said that at the same time when Tyre was founded, the temple of the god also had been set up, and that it was a period of two thousand three hundred years since their people began to dwell at Tyre. I saw also at Tyre another temple of Heracles, with the surname Thasian; and I came to Thasos also and there I found a temple of Heracles set up by the Phenicians, who had sailed out to seek for Europa and had colonised Thasos; and these things happened full five generations of men before Heracles the son of Amphitryon was born in Hellas. So then my inquiries show clearly that Heracles is an ancient god, and those of the Hellenes seem to me to act most rightly who have two temples of Heracles set up, and who sacrifice to the one as an immortal god and with the title Olympian, and make offerings of the dead to the other as a hero.

Moreover, besides many other stories which the Hellenes tell without due consideration, this tale is especially foolish which they tell about Heracles, namely that when he came to Egypt, the Egyptians put on him wreaths and led him forth in procession to sacrifice him to Zeus; and he for some time kept quiet, but when they were beginning the sacrifice of him at the altar, he betook himself to prowess and slew them all. I for my part am of opinion that the Hellenes when they tell this tale are altogether without knowledge of the nature and customs of the Egyptians; for how should they for whom it is not lawful to sacrifice even beasts, except swine and the males of oxen and calves (such of them as are clean) and geese, how should these sacrifice human beings? Besides this, how is it in nature possible that Heracles, being one person only and moreover a man (as they assert), should slay many myriads? Having said so much of these matters, we pray that we may have grace from both the gods and the heroes for our speech.

Now the reason why those of the Egyptians whom I have mentioned do not sacrifice goats, female or male, is this:—the Mendesians count Pan to be one of the eight gods (now these eight gods they say came into being before the twelve gods), and the painters and image-makers represent in painting and in sculpture the figure of Pan, just as the Hellenes do, with goat's face and legs, not supposing him to be really like this but to resemble the other gods; the cause however why they represent him in this form I prefer not to say. The Mendesians then reverence all goats and the males more than the females (and the goatherds too have greater honour than other herdsmen), but of the goats one especially is reverenced, and when he dies there is great mourning in all the Mendesian district: and both the goat and Pan are called in the Egyptian tongue Mendes. Moreover in my lifetime there happened in that district this marvel, that is to say a he-goat had intercourse with a woman publicly, and this was so done that all men might have evidence of it.

The pig is accounted by the Egyptians an abominable animal; and first, if any of them in passing by touch a pig, he goes into the river and dips himself forthwith in the water together with his garments; and then too swineherds, though they be native Egyptians, unlike all others do not enter any of the temples in Egypt, nor is anyone willing to give his daughter in marriage to one of them or to take a wife from among them; but the swineherds both give in marriage to one another and take from one another. Now to the other gods the Egyptians do not think it right to sacrifice swine; but to the Moon and to Dionysos alone at the same time and on the same full-moon they sacrifice swine, and then eat their flesh: and as to the reason why, when they abominate swine at all their other feasts, they sacrifice them at this, there is a story told by the Egyptians; and this story I know, but it is not a seemly one for me to tell. Now the sacrifice of the swine to the Moon is performed as follows:—when the priest has slain the victim, he puts together the end of the tail and the spleen and the caul, and covers them up with the whole of the fat of the animal which is about the paunch, and then he offers them with fire; and the rest of the flesh they eat on that day of full moon upon which they have held the sacrifice, but on any day after this they will not taste of it: the poor however among them by reason of the scantiness of their means shape pigs of dough and having baked them they offer these as a sacrifice.

Then for Dionysos on the eve of the festival each one kills a pig by cutting its throat before his own doors, and after that he gives the pig to the swineherd who sold it to him, to carry away again; and the rest of the feast of Dionysos is celebrated by the Egyptians in the same way as by the Hellenes in almost all things except choral dances, but instead of the phallos they have invented another contrivance, namely figures of about a cubit in height worked by strings, which women carry about the villages, with the privy member made to move and not much less in size than the rest of the body: and a flute goes before and they follow singing the praises of Dionysos. As to the reason why the figure has this member larger than is natural and moves it, though it moves no other part of the body, about this there is a sacred story told.

Now I think that Melampus the son of Amytheon was not without knowledge of these rites of sacrifice, but was acquainted with them: for Melampus is he who first set forth to the Hellenes the name of Dionysos and the manner of sacrifice and the procession of the phallos. Strictly speaking indeed, he when he made it known did not take in the whole, but those wise men who came after him made it known more at large. Melampus then is he who taught of the phallos which is carried in procession for Dionysos, and from him the Hellenes learnt to do that which they do. I say then that Melampus being a man of ability contrived for himself an art of divination, and having learnt from Egypt he taught the Hellenes many things, and among them those that concern Dionysos, making changes in some few points of them: for I shall not say that that which is done in worship of the god in Egypt came accidentally to be the same with that which is done among the Hellenes, for then these rites would have been in character with the Hellenic worship and not lately brought in; nor certainly shall I say that the Egyptians took from the Hellenes either this or any other customary observance: but I think it most probable that Melampus learnt the matters concerning Dionysos from Cadmos the Tyrian and from those who came with him from Phenicia to the land which we now call Boeotia.

Moreover the naming of almost all the gods has come to Hellas from Egypt: for that it has come from the Barbarians I find by inquiry is true, and I am of opinion that most probably it has come from Egypt, because, except in the case of Poseidon and the Dioscuroi (in accordance with that which I have said before), and also of Hera and Hestia and Themis and the Charites and Nereïds, the Egyptians have had the names of all the other gods in their country for all time. What

I say here is that which the Egyptians think themselves: but as for the gods whose names they profess that they do not know, these I think received their naming from the Pelasgians, except Poseidon; but about this god the Hellenes learnt from the Libyans, for no people except the Libyans have had the name of Poseidon from the first and have paid honour to this god always. Nor, it may be added, have the Egyptians any custom of worshipping heroes.

These observances then, and others besides these which I shall mention, the Hellenes have adopted from the Egyptians; but to make, as they do, the images of Hermes with the phallos they have learnt not from the Egyptians but from the Pelasgians, the custom having been received by the Athenians first of all the Hellenes and from these by the rest; for just at the time when the Athenians were beginning to rank among the Hellenes, the Pelasgians became dwellers with them in their land, and from this very cause it was that they began to be counted as Hellenes. Whosoever has been initiated in the mysteries of the Cabeiroi, which the Samothrakians perform having received them from the Pelasgians, that man knows the meaning of my speech; for these very Pelasgians who became dwellers with the Athenians used to dwell before that time in Samothrake, and from them the Samothrakians received their mysteries. So then the Athenians were the first of the Hellenes who made the images of Hermes with the phallos, having learnt from the Pelasgians; and the Pelasgians told a sacred story about it, which is set forth in the mysteries in Samothrake.

Now the Pelasgians formerly were wont to make all their sacrifices calling upon the gods in prayer, as I know from that which I heard at Dodona, but they gave no title or name to any of them, for they had not yet heard any, but they called them gods ({theous}) from some such notion as this, that they had set ({thentes}) in order all things and so had the distribution of everything. Afterwards, when much time had elapsed, they learnt from Egypt the names of the gods, all except Dionysos, for his name they learnt long afterwards; and after a time the Pelasgians consulted the Oracle at Dodona about the names, for this prophetic seat is accounted to be the most ancient of the Oracles which are among the Hellenes, and at that time it was the only one. So when the Pelasgians asked the Oracle at Dodona whether they should adopt the names which had come from the Barbarians, the Oracle in reply bade them make use of the names. From this time they sacrificed using the names of the gods, and from the Pelasgians the Hellenes afterwards received them: but whence the several gods had their birth, or whether they all were from the beginning, and of what form they are, they did not learn till yesterday, as it were, or the day before: for Hesiod and Homer I suppose were four hundred years before my time and not more, and these are they who made a theogony for the Hellenes and gave the titles to the gods and distributed to them honours and arts, and set forth their forms: but the poets who are said to have been before these men were really in my opinion after them. Of these things the first are said by the priestesses of Dodona, and the latter things, those namely which have regard to Hesiod and Homer, by myself.

As regards the Oracles both that among the Hellenes and that in Libya, the Egyptians tell the following tale. The priests of the Theban Zeus told me that two women in the service of the temple had been carried away from Thebes by Phenicians, and that they had heard that one of them had been sold to go into Libya and the other to the Hellenes; and these women, they said, were they who first founded the prophetic seats among the nations which have been named: and when I inquired whence they knew so perfectly of this tale which they told, they said in reply that a great search had been made by the priests after these women, and that they had not been able to find them, but they had heard afterwards this tale about them which they were telling.

This I heard from the priests at Thebes, and what follows is said by the prophetesses of Dodona. They say that two black doves flew from Thebes to Egypt, and came one of them to Libya and the other to their land. And this latter settled upon an oak-tree and spoke with human voice, saying that it was necessary that a prophetic seat of Zeus should be established in that place; and they supposed that that was of the gods which was announced to them, and made one accordingly: and the dove which went away to the Libyans, they say, bade the Libyans to make an Oracle of Ammon; and this also is of Zeus. The priestesses of Dodona told me these things, of whom the eldest was named Promeneia, the next after her Timarete, and the youngest Nicandra; and the other people of Dodona who were engaged about the temple gave accounts agreeing with theirs.

I however have an opinion about the matter as follows:—If the Phenicians did in truth carry away the consecrated women and sold one of them into Libya and the other into Hellas, I suppose that in the country now called Hellas, which was formerly called Pelasgia, this woman was sold into the land of the Thesprotians; and then being a slave there she set up a sanctuary of Zeus under a real oak-tree; as indeed it was natural that being an attendant of the sanctuary of Zeus at Thebes, she should there, in the place to which she had come, have a memory of him; and after this, when she got understanding of the Hellenic tongue, she established an Oracle, and she reported, I suppose, that her sister had been sold in Libya by the same Phenicians by whom she herself had been sold.

Moreover, I think that the women were called doves by the people of Dodona for the reason that they were Barbarians and because it seemed to them that they uttered voice like birds; but after a time (they say) the dove spoke with human voice, that is when the woman began to speak so that they could understand; but so long as she spoke a Barbarian tongue she seemed to them to be uttering voice like a bird: for had it been really a dove, how could it speak with human voice? And in saying that the dove was black, they indicate that the woman was Egyptian. The ways of delivering oracles too at Thebes in Egypt and at Dodona closely resemble one another, as it happens, and also the method of divination by victims has come from Egypt.

Moreover, it is true also that the Egyptians were the first of men who made solemn assemblies and processions and approaches to the temples, and from them the Hellenes have learnt them, and my evidence for this is that the Egyptian celebrations of these have been held from a very ancient time, whereas the Hellenic were introduced but lately.

The Egyptians hold their solemn assemblies not once in the year but often, especially and with the greatest zeal and devotion at the city of Bubastis for Artemis, and next at Busiris for Isis; for in this last-named city there is a very great temple of Isis, and this city stands in the middle of the Delta of Egypt; now Isis is in the tongue of the Hellenes Demeter: thirdly, they have a solemn assembly at the city of Saïs for Athene, fourthly at Heliopolis for the Sun (Helios), fifthly at the city of Buto in honour of Leto, and sixthly at the city of Papremis for Ares.

Now, when they are coming to the city of Bubastis they do as follows:—they sail men and women together, and a great multitude of each sex in every boat; and some of the women have rattles and rattle with them, while some of the men play the flute during the whole time of the voyage, and the rest, both women and men, sing and clap their hands; and when as they sail they come opposite to any city on the way they bring the boat to land, and some of the women continue to do as I have said, others cry aloud and jeer at the women in that city, some dance, and some stand up and pull up their garments. This they do by every city along the river-bank; and when they come to Bubastis they hold festival celebrating great sacrifices, and more wine of grapes is consumed upon that festival than during the whole of the rest of the year. To this place (so say the natives) they come together year by year even to the number of seventy myriads of men and women, besides children.

. Thus it is done here; and how they celebrate the festival in honour of Isis at the city of Busiris has been told by me before: for, as I said, they beat themselves in mourning after the sacrifice, all of them both men and women, very many myriads of people; but for whom they beat themselves it is not permitted to me by religion to say: and so many as there are of the Carians dwelling in Egypt do this even more than the Egyptians themselves, inasmuch as they cut their foreheads also with knives; and by this it is manifested that they are strangers and not Egyptians.

At the times when they gather together at the city of Saïs for their sacrifices, on a certain night they all kindle lamps many in number in the open air round about the houses; now the lamps are saucers full of salt and oil mixed, and the wick floats by itself on the surface, and this burns during the whole night; and to the festival is given the name Lychnocaia (the lighting of the lamps). Moreover those of the Egyptians who have not come to this solemn assembly observe the night of the festival and themselves also light lamps all of them, and thus not in Saïs alone are they lighted, but over all Egypt: and as to the reason why light and honour are allotted to this night, about this there is a sacred story told.

To Heliopolis and Buto they go year by year and do sacrifice only: but at Papremis they do sacrifice and worship as elsewhere, and besides that, when the sun begins to go down, while some few of the priests are occupied with the image of the god, the greater number of them stand in the entrance of the temple with wooden clubs, and other persons to the number of more than a thousand men with purpose to perform a vow, these also having all of them staves of wood, stand in a body opposite to those: and the image, which is in a small shrine of wood covered over with gold, they take out on the day before to another sacred building. The few then who have been left about the image, draw a wain with four wheels, which bears the shrine and the image that is within the shrine, and the other priests standing in the gateway try to prevent it from entering, and the men who are under a vow come to the assistance of the god and strike them, while the others defend themselves. Then there comes to be a hard fight with staves, and they break one another's heads, and I am of opinion that many even die of the wounds they receive; the Egyptians however told me that no one died. This solemn assembly the people of the place say that they established for the following reason:—the mother of Ares, they say, used to dwell in this temple, and Ares, having been brought up away from her, when he grew up came thither desiring to visit his mother, and the attendants of his mother's temple, not having seen him before, did not permit him to pass in, but kept him away; and he brought men to help him from another city and handled roughly the attendants of the temple, and entered to visit his mother. Hence, they say, this exchange of blows has become the custom in honour of Ares upon his festival.

The Egyptians were the first who made it a point of religion not to lie with women in temples, nor to enter into temples after going away from women without first bathing: for almost all other men except the Egyptians and the Hellenes lie with women in temples and enter into a temple after going away from women without bathing, since they hold that there is no difference in this respect between men and beasts: for they say that they see beasts and the various kinds of birds coupling together both in the temples and in the sacred enclosures of the gods; if then this were not pleasing to the god, the beasts would not do so.

Thus do these defend that which they do, which by me is disallowed: but the Egyptians are excessively careful in their observances, both in other matters which concern the sacred rites and also in those which follow:—Egypt, though it borders upon Libya, does not very much abound in wild animals, but such as they have are one and all accounted by them sacred, some of them living with men and others not. But if I should say for what reasons the sacred animals have been thus dedicated, I should fall into discourse of matters pertaining to the gods, of which I most desire not to speak; and what I have actually said touching slightly upon them, I said because I was constrained by necessity. About these animals there is a custom of this kind:—persons have been appointed of the Egyptians, both men and women, to provide the food for each kind of beast separately, and their office goes down from father to son; and those who dwell in the various cities perform vows to them thus, that is, when they make a vow to the god to whom the animal belongs, they shave the head of their children either the whole or the half or the third part of it, and then set the hair in the balance against silver, and whatever it weighs, this the man gives to the person who provides for the animals, and she cuts up fish of equal value and gives it for food to the animals. Thus food for their support has been appointed: and if any one kill any of these animals, the penalty, if he do it with his own will, is death, and if against his will, such penalty as the priests may appoint: but whosoever shall kill an ibis or a hawk, whether it be with his will or against his will, must die.

Of the animals that live with men there are great numbers, and would be many more but for the accidents which befall the cats. For when the females have produced young they are no longer in the habit of going to the males, and these seeking to be united with them are not able. To this end then they contrive as follows,—they either take away by force or remove secretly the young from the females and kill them (but after killing they do not eat them), and the females being deprived of their young and desiring more, therefore come to the males, for it is a creature that is fond of its young. Moreover when a fire occurs, the cats seem to be divinely possessed; for while the Egyptians stand at intervals and look after the cats, not taking any care to extinguish the fire, the cats slipping through or leaping over the men, jump into the fire; and when this happens, great mourning comes upon the Egyptians. And in whatever houses a cat has died by a natural death, all those who dwell in this house shave their eyebrows only, but those in whose houses a dog has died shave their whole body and also their head.

. The cats when they are dead are carried away to sacred buildings in the city of Bubastis, where after being embalmed they are buried; but the dogs they bury each people in their own city in sacred tombs; and the ichneumons are buried just in the same way as the dogs. The shrew-mice however and the hawks they carry away to the city of Buto, and the ibises to Hermopolis; the bears (which are not commonly seen) and the wolves, not much larger in size than foxes, they bury on the spot where they are found lying.

Of the crocodile the nature is as follows:—during the four most wintry months this creature eats nothing: she has four feet and is an animal belonging to the land and the water both; for she produces and hatches eggs on the land, and the most part of the day she remains upon dry land, but the whole of the night in the river, for the water in truth is warmer than the unclouded open air and the dew. Of all the mortal creatures of which we have knowledge this grows to the greatest bulk from the smallest beginning; for the eggs which she produces are not much larger than those of geese and the newly-hatched young one is in proportion to the egg, but as he grows he becomes as much as seventeen cubits long and sometimes yet larger. He has eyes like those of a pig and teeth large and tusky, in proportion to the size of his body; but unlike all other beasts he grows no tongue, neither does he move his lower jaw, but brings the upper jaw towards the lower, being in this too unlike all other beasts. He has moreover strong claws and a scaly hide upon his back which cannot be pierced; and he is blind in the water, but in the air he is of very keen sight. Since he has his living in the water he keeps his mouth all full within of leeches; and whereas all other birds and beasts fly from him, the trochilus is a creature which is at peace with him, seeing that from her he receives benefit; for the crocodile having come out of the water to the land and then having opened his mouth (this he is wont to do generally towards the West Wind), the trochilus upon that enters into his mouth and swallows down the leeches, and he being benefited is pleased and does no harm to the trochilus.

Now for some of the Egyptians the crocodiles are sacred animals, and for others not so, but they treat them on the contrary as enemies: those however who dwell about Thebes and about the lake of Moiris hold them to be most sacred, and each of these two peoples keeps one crocodile selected from the whole number, which has been trained to tameness, and they put hanging ornaments of molten stone and of gold into the ears of these and anklets round the front feet, and they give them food appointed and victims of sacrifices and treat them as well as possible while they live, and after they are dead they bury them in sacred tombs, embalming them: but those who dwell about the city of Elephantine even eat them, not holding them to be sacred. They are called not crocodiles but champsai, and the Ionians gave them the name of crocodile, comparing their form to that of the crocodiles (lizards) which appear in their country in the stone walls.

There are many ways in use of catching them and of various kinds: I shall describe that which to me seems the most worthy of being told. A man puts the back of a pig upon a hook as bait, and lets it go into the middle of the river, while he himself upon the bank of the river has a young live pig, which he beats; and the crocodile hearing its cries makes for the direction of the sound, and when he finds the pig's back he swallows it down: then they pull, and when he is drawn out to land, first of all the hunter forthwith plasters up his eyes with mud, and having so done he very easily gets the mastery of him, but if he does not do so he has much trouble.

The river-horse is sacred in the district of Papremis, but for the other Egyptians he is not sacred; and this is the appearance which he presents: he is four-footed, cloven-hoofed like an ox, flat-nosed, with a mane like a horse and showing teeth like tusks, with a tail and voice like a horse, and in size as large as the largest ox; and his hide is so exceedingly thick that when it has been dried shafts of javelins are made of it.

There are moreover otters in the river, which they consider to be sacred; and of fish also they esteem that which is called the lepidotos to be sacred, and also the eel; and these they say are sacred to the Nile: and of birds the fox-goose.

There is also another sacred bird called the phoenix which I did not myself see except in painting, for in truth he comes to them very rarely, at intervals, as the people of Heliopolis say, of five hundred years; and these say that he comes regularly when his father dies; and if he be like the painting, he is of this size and nature, that is to say, some of his feathers are of gold colour and others red, and in outline and size he is as nearly as possible like an eagle. This bird they say (but I cannot believe the story) contrives as follows:—setting forth from Arabia he conveys his father, they say, to the temple of the Sun (Helios) plastered up in myrrh, and buries him in the temple of the Sun; and he conveys him thus:—he forms first an egg of myrrh as large as he is able to carry, and then he makes trial of carrying it, and when he has made trial sufficiently, then he hollows out the egg and places his father within it and plasters over with other myrrh that part of the egg where he hollowed it out to put his father in, and when his father is laid in it, it proves (they say) to be of the same weight as it was; and after he has plastered it up, he conveys the whole to Egypt to the temple of the Sun. Thus they say that this bird does.

There are also about Thebes sacred serpents, not at all harmful to men, which are small in size and have two horns growing from the top of the head: these they bury when they die in the temple of Zeus, for to this god they say that they are sacred.

There is a region moreover in Arabia, situated nearly over against the city of Buto, to which place I came to inquire about the winged serpents: and when I came thither I saw bones of serpents and spines in quantity so great that it is impossible to make report of the number, and there were heaps of spines, some heaps large and others less large and others smaller still than these, and these heaps were many in number. This region in which the spines are scattered upon the ground is of the nature of an entrance from a narrow mountain pass to a great plain, which plain adjoins the plain of Egypt; and the story goes that at the beginning of spring winged serpents from Arabia fly towards Egypt, and the birds called ibises meet them at the entrance to this country and do not suffer the serpents to go by but kill them. On account of this deed it is (say the Arabians) that the ibis has come to be greatly honoured by the Egyptians, and the Egyptians also agree that it is for this reason that they honour these birds.

The outward form of the ibis is this:—it is a deep black all over, and has legs like those of a crane and a very curved beak, and in size it is about equal to a rail: this is the appearance of the black kind which fight with the serpents, but of those which most crowd round men's feet (for there are two several kinds of ibises) the head is bare and also the whole of the throat, and it is white in feathering except the head and neck and the extremities of the wings and the rump (in all these parts of which I have spoken it is a deep black), while in legs and in the form of the head it resembles the other. As for the serpent its form is like that of the watersnake; and it has wings not feathered but most nearly resembling the wings of the bat. Let so much suffice as has been said now concerning sacred animals.

Of the Egyptians themselves, those who dwell in the part of Egypt which is sown for crops practise memory more than any other men and are the most learned in history by far of all those of whom I have had experience: and their manner of life is as follows:—For three successive days in each month they purge, hunting after health with emetics and clysters, and they think that all the diseases which exist are produced in men by the food on which they live; for the Egyptians are from other causes also the most healthy of all men next after the Libyans (in my opinion on account of the seasons, because the seasons do not change, for by the changes of things generally, and especially of the seasons, diseases are most apt to be produced in men), and as to their diet, it is as follows:—they eat bread, making loaves of maize, which they call kyllestis, and they use habitually a wine made out of barley, for vines they have not in their land. Of their fish some they dry in the sun and then eat them without cooking, others they eat cured in brine. Of birds they eat quails and ducks and small birds without cooking, after first curing them; and everything else which they have belonging to the class of birds or fishes, except such as have been set apart by them as sacred, they eat roasted or boiled.

In the entertainments of the rich among them, when they have finished eating, a man bears round a wooden figure of a dead body in a coffin, made as like the reality as may be both by painting and carving, and measuring about a cubit or two cubits each way; and this he shows to each of those who are drinking together, saying: "When thou lookest upon this, drink and be merry, for thou shalt be such as this when thou art dead." Thus they do at their carousals.

The customs which they practise are derived from their fathers and they do not acquire others in addition; but besides other customary things among them which are worthy of mention, they have one song, that of Linos, the same who is sung of both in Phenicia and in Cyprus and elsewhere, having however a name different according to the various nations. This song agrees exactly with that which the Hellenes sing calling on the name of Linos, so that besides many other things about which I wonder among those matters which concern Egypt, I wonder especially about this, namely whence they got the song of Linos. It is evident however that they have sung this song from immemorial time, and in the Egyptian tongue Linos is called Maneros. The Egyptians told me that he was the only son of him who first became king of Egypt, and that he died before his time and was honoured with these lamentations by the Egyptians, and that this was their first and only song.

In another respect the Egyptians are in agreement with some of the Hellenes, namely with the Lacedemonians, but not with the rest, that is to say, the younger of them when they meet the elder give way and move out of the path, and when their elders approach they rise out of their seat. In this which follows however they are not in agreement with any of the Hellenes,—instead of addressing one another in the roads they do reverence, lowering their hand down to their knee.

They wear tunics of linen about their legs with fringes, which they call calasiris; above these they have garments of white wool thrown over: woollen garments however are not taken into the temples, nor are they buried with them, for this is not permitted by religion. In these points they are in agreement with the observances called Orphic and Bacchic (which are really Egyptian), and also with those of the Pythagoreans, for one who takes part in these mysteries is also forbidden by religious rule to be buried in woollen garments; and about this there is a sacred story told.

Besides these things the Egyptians have found out also to what god each month and each day belongs, and what fortunes a man will meet with who is born on any particular day, and how he will die, and what kind of a man he will be: and these inventions were taken up by those of the Hellenes who occupied themselves about poesy. Portents too have been found out by them more than by all other men besides; for when a portent has happened, they observe and write down the event which comes of it, and if ever afterwards anything resembling this happens, they believe that the event which comes of it will be similar.

Their divination is ordered thus:—the art is assigned not to any man, but to certain of the gods, for there are in their land Oracles of Heracles, of Apollo, of Athene, of Artemis, of Ares, and of Zeus, and moreover that which they hold most in honour of all, namely the Oracle of Leto which is in the city of Buto. The manner of divination however is not yet established among them according to the same fashion everywhere, but is different in different places.

The art of medicine among them is distributed thus:—each physician is a physician of one disease and of no more; and the whole country is full of physicians, for some profess themselves to be physicians of the eyes, others of the head, others of the teeth, others of the affections of the stomach, and others of the more obscure ailments.

Their fashions of mourning and of burial are these:—Whenever any household has lost a man who is of any regard amongst them, the whole number of women of that house forthwith plaster over their heads or even their faces with mud. Then leaving the corpse within the house they go themselves to and fro about the city and beat themselves, with their garments bound up by a girdle and their breasts exposed, and with them go all the women who are related to the dead man, and on the other side the men beat themselves, they too having their garments bound up by a girdle; and when they have done this, they then convey the body to the embalming.

In this occupation certain persons employ themselves regularly and inherit this as a craft. These, whenever a corpse is conveyed to them, show to those who brought it wooden models of corpses made like reality by painting, and the best of the ways of embalming they say is that of him whose name I think it impiety to mention when speaking of a matter of such a kind; the second which they show is less good than this and also less expensive; and the third is the least expensive of all. Having told them about this, they inquire of them in which way they desire the corpse of their friend to be prepared. Then they after they have agreed for a certain price depart out of the way, and the others being left behind in the buildings embalm according to the best of these ways thus:—First with a crooked iron tool they draw out the brain through the nostrils, extracting it partly thus and partly by pouring in drugs; and after this with a sharp stone of Ethiopia they make a cut along the side and take out the whole contents of the belly, and when they have cleared out the cavity and cleansed it with palm-wine they cleanse it again with spices pounded up: then they fill the belly with pure myrrh pounded up and with cassia and other spices except frankincense, and sew it together again. Having so done they keep it for embalming covered up in natron for seventy days, but for a longer time than this it is not permitted to embalm it; and when the seventy days are past, they wash the corpse and roll its whole body up in fine linen cut into bands, smearing these beneath with gum, which the Egyptians use generally instead of glue. Then the kinsfolk receive it from them and have a wooden figure made in the shape of a man, and when they have had this made they enclose the corpse, and having shut it up within, they store it then in a sepulchral chamber, setting it to stand upright against the wall.

Thus they deal with the corpses which are prepared in the most costly way; but for those who desire the middle way and wish to avoid great cost they prepare the corpse as follows:—having filled their syringes with the oil which is got from cedar-wood, with this they forthwith fill the belly of the corpse, and this they do without having either cut it open or taken out the bowels, but they inject the oil by the breech, and having stopped the drench from returning back they keep it then the appointed number of days for embalming, and on the last of the days they let the cedar oil come out from the belly, which they before put in; and it has such power that it brings out with it the bowels and interior organs of the body dissolved; and the natron dissolves the flesh, so that there is left of the corpse only the skin and the bones. When they have done this they give back the corpse at once in that condition without working upon it any more.

The third kind of embalming, by which are prepared the bodies of those who have less means, is as follows:—they cleanse out the belly with a purge and then keep the body for embalming during the seventy days, and at once after that they give it back to the bringers to carry away.

The wives of men of rank when they die are not given at once to be embalmed, nor such women as are very beautiful or of greater regard than others, but on the third or fourth day after their death (and not before) they are delivered to the embalmers. They do so about this matter in order that the embalmers may not abuse their women, for they say that one of them was taken once doing so to the corpse of a woman lately dead, and his fellow-craftsman gave information.

Whenever any one, either of the Egyptians themselves or of strangers, is found to have been carried off by a crocodile or brought to his death by the river itself, the people of any city by which he may have been cast up on land must embalm him and lay him out in the fairest way they can and bury him in a sacred burial-place, nor may any of his relations or friends besides touch him, but the priests of the Nile themselves handle the corpse and bury it as that of one who was something more than man.

Hellenic usages they will by no means follow, and to speak generally they follow those of no other men whatever. This rule is observed by most of the Egyptians; but there is a large city named Chemmis in the Theban district near Neapolis, and in this city there is a temple of Perseus the son of Danae which is of a square shape, and round it grow date-palms: the gateway of the temple is built of stone and of very great size, and at the entrance of it stand two great statues of stone. Within this enclosure is a temple-house and in it stands an image of Perseus. These people of Chemmis say that Perseus is wont often to appear in their land and often within the temple, and that a sandal which has been worn by him is found sometimes, being in length two cubits, and whenever this appears all Egypt prospers. This they say, and they do in honour of Perseus after Hellenic fashion thus,—they hold an athletic contest, which includes the whole list of games, and they offer in prizes cattle and cloaks and skins: and when I inquired why to them alone Perseus was wont to appear, and wherefore they were separated from all the other Egyptians in that they held an athletic contest, they said that Perseus had been born of their city, for Danaos and Lynkeus were men of Chemmis and had sailed to Hellas, and from them they traced a descent and came down to Perseus: and they told me that he had come to Egypt for the reason which the Hellenes also say, namely to bring from Libya the Gorgon's head, and had then visited them also and recognised all his kinsfolk, and they said that he had well learnt the name of Chemmis before he came to Egypt, since he had heard it from his mother, and that they celebrated an athletic contest for him by his own command.

All these are customs practised by the Egyptians who dwell above the fens: and those who are settled in the fen-land have the same customs for the most part as the other Egyptians, both in other matters and also in that they live each with one wife only, as do the Hellenes; but for economy in respect of food they have invented these things besides:—when the river has become full and the plains have been flooded, there grow in the water great numbers of lilies, which the Egyptians call lotos; these they cut with a sickle and dry in the sun, and then they pound that which grows in the middle of the lotos and which is like the head of a poppy, and they make of it loaves baked with fire. The root also of this lotos is edible and has a rather sweet taste: it is round in shape and about the size of an apple. There are other lilies too, in flower resembling roses, which also grow in the river, and from them the fruit is produced in a separate vessel springing from the root by the side of the plant itself, and very nearly resembles a wasp's comb: in this there grow edible seeds in great numbers of the size of an olive-stone, and they are eaten either fresh or dried. Besides this they pull up from the fens the papyrus which grows every year, and the upper parts of it they cut off and turn to other uses, but that which is left below for about a cubit in length they eat or sell: and those who desire to have the papyrus at its very best bake it in an oven heated red-hot, and then eat it. Some too of these people live on fish alone, which they dry in the sun after having caught them and taken out the entrails, and then when they are dry, they use them for food.

Fish which swim in shoals are not much produced in the rivers, but are bred in the lakes, and they do as follows:—When there comes upon them the desire to breed, they swim out in shoals towards the sea; and the males lead the way shedding forth their milt as they go, while the females, coming after and swallowing it up, from it become impregnated: and when they have become full of young in the sea they swim up back again, each shoal to its own haunts. The same however no longer lead the way as before, but the lead comes now to the females, and they leading the way in shoals do just as the males did, that is to say they shed forth their eggs by a few grains at a time, and the males coming after swallow them up. Now these grains are fish, and from the grains which survive and are not swallowed, the fish grow which afterwards are bred up. Now those of the fish which are caught as they swim out to sea are found to be rubbed on the left side of the head, but those which are caught as they swim up again are rubbed on the right side. This happens to them because as they swim down to the sea they keep close to the land on the left side of the river, and again as they swim up they keep to the same side, approaching and touching the bank as much as they can, for fear doubtless of straying from their course by reason of the stream. When the Nile begins to swell, the hollow places of the land and the depressions by the side of the river first begin to fill, as the water soaks through from the river, and so soon as they become full of water, at once they are all filled with little fishes; and whence these are in all likelihood produced, I think that I perceive. In the preceding year, when the Nile goes down, the fish first lay eggs in the mud and then retire with the last of the retreating waters; and when the time comes round again, and the water once more comes over the land, from these eggs forthwith are produced the fishes of which I speak.

Thus it is as regards the fish. And for anointing those of the Egyptians who dwell in the fens use oil from the castor-berry, which oil the Egyptians call kiki, and thus they do:—they sow along the banks of the rivers and pools these plants, which in a wild form grow of themselves in the land of the Hellenes; these are sown in Egypt and produce berries in great quantity but of an evil smell; and when they have gathered these, some cut them up and press the oil from them, others again roast them first and then boil them down and collect that which runs away from them. The oil is fat and not less suitable for burning than olive-oil, but it gives forth a disagreeable smell.

Against the gnats, which are very abundant, they have contrived as follows:—those who dwell above the fen-land are helped by the towers, to which they ascend when they go to rest; for the gnats by reason of the winds are not able to fly up high: but those who dwell in the fen-land have contrived another way instead of the towers, and this is it:—every man of them has got a casting net, with which by day he catches fish, but in the night he uses it for this purpose, that is to say he puts the casting-net round about the bed in which he sleeps, and then creeps in under it and goes to sleep: and the gnats, if he sleeps rolled up in a garment or a linen sheet, bite through these, but through the net they do not even attempt to bite.

Their boats with which they carry cargoes are made of the thorny acacia, of which the form is very like that of the Kyrenian lotos, and that which exudes from it is gum. From this tree they cut pieces of wood about two cubits in length and arrange them like bricks, fastening the boat together by running a great number of long bolts through the two-cubit pieces; and when they have thus fastened the boat together, they lay cross-pieces over the top, using no ribs for the sides; and within they caulk the seams with papyrus. They make one steering-oar for it, which is passed through the bottom of the boat; and they have a mast of acacia and sails of papyrus. These boats cannot sail up the river unless there be a very fresh wind blowing, but are towed from the shore: down-stream however they travel as follows:—they have a door-shaped crate made of tamarisk wood and reed mats sewn together, and also a stone of about two talents weight bored with a hole; and of these the boatman lets the crate float on in front of the boat, fastened with a rope, and the stone drag behind by another rope. The crate then, as the force of the stream presses upon it, goes on swiftly and draws on the baris (for so these boats are called), while the stone dragging after it behind and sunk deep in the water keeps its course straight. These boats they have in great numbers and some of them carry many thousands of talents' burden.

When the Nile comes over the land, the cities alone are seen rising above the water, resembling more nearly than anything else the islands in the Egean sea; for the rest of Egypt becomes a sea and the cities alone rise above water. Accordingly, whenever this happens, they pass by water not now by the channels of the river but over the midst of the plain: for example, as one sails up from Naucratis to Memphis the passage is then close by the pyramids, whereas the usual passage is not the same even here, but goes by the point of the Delta and the city of Kercasoros; while if you sail over the plain to Naucratis from the sea and from Canobos, you will go by Anthylla and the city called after Archander.

Of these Anthylla is a city of note and is especially assigned to the wife of him who reigns over Egypt, to supply her with sandals, (this is the case since the time when Egypt came to be under the Persians): the other city seems to me to have its name from Archander the son-in-law of Danaos, who was the son of Phthios, the son of Achaios; for it is called the City of Archander. There might indeed be another Archander, but in any case the name is not Egyptian.

Hitherto my own observation and judgment and inquiry are the vouchers for that which I have said; but from this point onwards I am about to tell the history of Egypt according to that which I heard, to which will be added also something of that which I have myself seen.

Of Min, who first became king of Egypt, the priests said that on the one hand he banked off the site of Memphis from the river: for the whole stream of the river used to flow along by the sandy mountain-range on the side of Libya, but Min formed by embankments that bend of the river which lies to the South about a hundred furlongs above Memphis, and thus he dried up the old stream and conducted the river so that it flowed in the middle between the mountains: and even now this bend of the Nile is by the Persians kept under very careful watch, that it may flow in the channel to which it is confined, and the bank is repaired every year; for if the river should break through and overflow in this direction, Memphis would be in danger of being overwhelmed by flood. When this Min, who first became king, had made into dry land the part which was dammed off, on the one hand, I say, he founded in it that city which is now called Memphis; for Memphis too is in the narrow part of Egypt; and outside the city he dug round it on the North and West a lake communicating with the river, for the side towards the East is barred by the Nile itself. Then secondly he established in the city the temple of Hephaistos a great work and most worthy of mention.

After this man the priests enumerated to me from a papyrus roll the names of other kings, three hundred and thirty in number; and in all these generations of men eighteen were Ethiopians, one was a woman, a native Egyptian, and the rest were men and of Egyptian race: and the name of the woman who reigned was the same as that of the Babylonian queen, namely Nitocris. Of her they said that desiring to take vengeance for her brother, whom the Egyptians had slain when he was their king and then, after having slain him, had given his kingdom to her,—desiring, I say, to take vengeance for him, she destroyed by craft many of the Egyptians. For she caused to be constructed a very large chamber under ground, and making as though she would handsel it but in her mind devising other things, she invited those of the Egyptians whom she knew to have had most part in the murder, and gave a great banquet. Then while they were feasting, she let in the river upon them by a secret conduit of large size. Of her they told no more than this, except that, when this had been accomplished, she threw herself into a room full of embers, in order that she might escape vengeance.

As for the other kings, they could tell me of no great works which had been produced by them, and they said that they had no renown except only the last of them, Moris: he (they said) produced as a memorial of himself the gateway of the temple of Hephaistos which is turned towards the North Wind, and dug a lake, about which I shall set forth afterwards how many furlongs of circuit it has, and in it built pyramids of the size which I shall mention at the same time when I speak of the lake itself. He, they said, produced these works, but of the rest none produced any.

Therefore passing these by I shall make mention of the king who came after these, whose name was Sesostris. He (the priests said) first of all set out with ships of war from the Arabian gulf and subdued those who dwelt by the shores of the Erythraian Sea, until as he sailed he came to a sea which could no further be navigated by reason of shoals: then secondly, after he had returned to Egypt, according to the report of the priests he took a great army and marched over the continent, subduing every nation which stood in his way: and those of them whom he found valiant and fighting desperately for their freedom, in their lands he set up pillars which told by inscriptions his own name and the name of his country, and how he had subdued them by his power; but as to those of whose cities he obtained possession without fighting or with ease, on their pillars he inscribed words after the same tenor as he did for the nations which had shown themselves courageous, and in addition he drew upon them the hidden parts of a woman, desiring to signify by this that the people were cowards and effeminate.

Thus doing he traversed the continent, until at last he passed over to Europe from Asia and subdued the Scythians and also the Thracians. These, I am of opinion, were the furthest people to which the Egyptian army came, for in their country the pillars are found to have been set up, but in the land beyond this they are no longer found. From this point he turned and began to go back; and when he came to the river Phasis, what happened then I cannot say for certain, whether the king Sesostris himself divided off a certain portion of his army and left the men there as settlers in the land, or whether some of his soldiers were wearied by his distant marches and remained by the river Phasis.

For the people of Colchis are evidently Egyptian, and this I perceived for myself before I heard it from others. So when I had come to consider the matter I asked them both; and the Colchians had remembrance of the Egyptians more than the Egyptians of the Colchians; but the Egyptians said they believed that the Colchians were a portion of the army of Sesostris. That this was so I conjectured myself not only because they are dark-skinned and have curly hair (this of itself amounts to nothing, for there are other races which are so), but also still more because the Colchians, Egyptians, and Ethiopians alone of all the races of men have practised circumcision from the first. The Phenicians and the Syrians who dwell in Palestine confess themselves that they have learnt it from the Egyptians, and the Syrians about the river Thermodon and the river Parthenios, and the Macronians, who are their neighbours, say that they have learnt it lately from the Colchians. These are the only races of men who practise circumcision, and these evidently practise it in the same manner as the Egyptians. Of the Egyptians themselves however and the Ethiopians, I am not able to say which learnt from the other, for undoubtedly it is a most ancient custom; but that the other nations learnt it by intercourse with the Egyptians, this among others is to me a strong proof, namely that those of the Phenicians who have intercourse with Hellas cease to follow the example of the Egyptians in this matter, and do not circumcise their children.

Now let me tell another thing about the Colchians to show how they resemble the Egyptians:—they alone work flax in the same fashion as the Egyptians, and the two nations are like one another in their whole manner of living and also in their language: now the linen of Colchis is called by the Hellenes Sardonic, whereas that from Egypt is called Egyptian.

The pillars which Sesostris of Egypt set up in the various countries are for the most part no longer to be seen extant; but in Syria Palestine I myself saw them existing with the inscription upon them which I have mentioned and the emblem. Moreover in Ionia there are two figures of this man carved upon rocks, one on the road by which one goes from the land of Ephesos to Phocaia, and the other on the road from Sardis to Smyrna. In each place there is a figure of a man cut in the rock, of four cubits and a span in height, holding in his right hand a spear and in his left a bow and arrows, and the other equipment which he has is similar to this, for it is both Egyptian and Ethiopian: and from the one shoulder to the other across the breast runs an inscription carved in sacred Egyptian characters, saying thus, "This land with my shoulders I won for myself." But who he is and from whence, he does not declare in these places, though in other places he has declared this. Some of those who have seen these carvings conjecture that the figure is that of Memnon, but herein they are very far from the truth.

As this Egyptian Sesostris was returning and bringing back many men of the nations whose lands he had subdued, when he came (said the priests) to Daphnai in the district of Pelusion on his journey home, his brother to whom Sesostris had entrusted the charge of Egypt invited him and with him his sons to a feast; and then he piled the house round with brushwood and set it on fire: and Sesostris when he discovered this forthwith took counsel with his wife, for he was bringing with him (they said) his wife also; and she counselled him to lay out upon the pyre two of his sons, which were six in number, and so to make a bridge over the burning mass, and that they passing over their bodies should thus escape. This, they said, Sesostris did, and two of his sons were burnt to death in this manner, but the rest got away safe with their father.

Then Sesostris, having returned to Egypt and having taken vengeance on his brother, employed the multitude which he had brought in of those whose lands he had subdued, as follows:—these were they who drew the stones which in the reign of this king were brought to the temple of Hephaistos, being of very great size; and also these were compelled to dig all the channels which now are in Egypt; and thus (having no such purpose) they caused Egypt, which before was all fit for riding and driving, to be no longer fit for this from thenceforth: for from that time forward Egypt, though it is plain land, has become all unfit for riding and driving, and the cause has been these channels, which are many and run in all directions. But the reason why the king cut up the land was this, namely because those of the Egyptians who had their cities not on the river but in the middle of the country, being in want of water when the river went down from them, found their drink brackish because they had it from wells.

For this reason Egypt was cut up; and they said that this king distributed the land to all the Egyptians, giving an equal square portion to each man, and from this he made his revenue, having appointed them to pay a certain rent every year: and if the river should take away anything from any man's portion, he would come to the king and declare that which had happened, and the king used to send men to examine and to find out by measurement how much less the piece of land had become, in order that for the future the man might pay less, in proportion to the rent appointed: and I think that thus the art of geometry was found out and afterwards came into Hellas also. For as touching the sun-dial and the gnomon and the twelve divisions of the day, they were learnt by the Hellenes from the Babylonians.

He moreover alone of all the Egyptian kings had rule over Ethiopia; and he left as memorials of himself in front of the temple of Hephaistos two stone statues of thirty cubits each, representing himself and his wife, and others of twenty cubits each representing his four sons: and long afterwards the priest of Hephaistos refused to permit Dareios the Persian to set up a statue of himself in front of them, saying that deeds had not been done by him equal to those which were done by Sesostris the Egyptian; for Sesostris had subdued other nations besides, not fewer than he, and also the Scythians; but Dareios had not been able to conquer the Scythians: wherefore it was not just that he should set up a statue in front of those which Sesostris had dedicated, if he did not surpass him in his deeds. Which speech, they say, Dareios took in good part.

Now after Sesostris had brought his life to an end, his son Pheros, they told me, received in succession the kingdom, and he made no warlike expedition, and moreover it chanced to him to become blind by reason of the following accident:—when the river had come down in flood rising to a height of eighteen cubits, higher than ever before that time, and had gone over the fields, a wind fell upon it and the river became agitated by waves: and this king (they say) moved by presumptuous folly took a spear and cast it into the midst of the eddies of the stream; and immediately upon this he had a disease of the eyes and was by it made blind. For ten years then he was blind, and in the eleventh year there came to him an oracle from the city of Buto saying that the time of his punishment had expired, and that he should see again if he washed his eyes with the water of a woman who had accompanied with her own husband only and had not knowledge of other men: and first he made trial of his own wife, and then, as he continued blind, he went on to try all the women in turn; and when he had at last regained his sight he gathered together all the women of whom he had made trial, excepting her by whose means he had regained his sight, to one city which now is named Erythrabolos, and having gathered them to this he consumed them all by fire, as well as the city itself; but as for her by whose means he had regained his sight, he had her himself to wife. Then after he had escaped the malady of his eyes he dedicated offerings at each one of the temples which were of renown, and especially (to mention only that which is most worthy of mention) he dedicated at the temple of the Sun works which are worth seeing, namely two obelisks of stone, each of a single block, measuring in length a hundred cubits each one and in breadth eight cubits.

After him, they said, there succeeded to the throne a man of Memphis, whose name in the tongue of the Hellenes was Proteus; for whom there is now a sacred enclosure at Memphis, very fair and well ordered, lying on that side of the temple of Hephaistos which faces the North Wind. Round about this enclosure dwell Phenicians of Tyre, and this whole region is called the Camp of the Tyrians. Within the enclosure of Proteus there is a temple called the temple of the "foreign Aphrodite," which temple I conjecture to be one of Helen the daughter of Tyndareus, not only because I have heard the tale how Helen dwelt with Proteus, but also especially because it is called by the name of the "foreign Aphrodite," for the other temples of Aphrodite which there are have none of them the addition of the word "foreign" to the name.

And the priests told me, when I inquired, that the things concerning Helen happened thus:—Alexander having carried off Helen was sailing away from Sparta to his own land, and when he had come to the Egean Sea contrary winds drove him from his course to the Sea of Egypt; and after that, since the blasts did not cease to blow, he came to Egypt itself, and in Egypt to that which is now named the Canobic mouth of the Nile and to Taricheiai. Now there was upon the shore, as still there is now, a temple of Heracles, in which if any man's slave take refuge and have the sacred marks set upon him, giving himself over to the god, it is not lawful to lay hands upon him; and this custom has continued still unchanged from the beginning down to my own time. Accordingly the attendants of Alexander, having heard of the custom which existed about the temple, ran away from him, and sitting down as suppliants of the god, accused Alexander, because they desired to do him hurt, telling the whole tale how things were about Helen and about the wrong done to Menelaos; and this accusation they made not only to the priests but also to the warden of this river-mouth, whose name was Thonis.

Thonis then having heard their tale sent forthwith a message to Proteus at Memphis, which said as follows: "There hath come a stranger, a Teucrian by race, who hath done in Hellas an unholy deed; for he hath deceived the wife of his own host, and is come hither bringing with him this woman herself and very much wealth, having been carried out of his way by winds to thy land. Shall we then allow him to sail out unharmed, or shall we first take away from him that which he brought with him?" In reply to this Proteus sent back a messenger who said thus: "Seize this man, whosoever he may be, who has done impiety to his own host, and bring him away into my presence, that I may know what he will find to say."

Hearing this, Thonis seized Alexander and detained his ships, and after that he brought the man himself up to Memphis and with him Helen and the wealth he had, and also in addition to them the suppliants. So when all had been conveyed up thither, Proteus began to ask Alexander who he was and from whence he was voyaging; and he both recounted to him his descent and told him the name of his native land, and moreover related of his voyage, from whence he was sailing. After this Proteus asked him whence he had taken Helen; and when Alexander went astray in his account and did not speak the truth, those who had become suppliants convicted him of falsehood, relating in full the whole tale of the wrong done. At length Proteus declared to them this sentence, saying, "Were it not that I count it a matter of great moment not to slay any of those strangers who being driven from their course by winds have come to my land hitherto, I should have taken vengeance on thee on behalf of the man of Hellas, seeing that thou, most base of men, having received from him hospitality, didst work against him a most impious deed. For thou didst go in to the wife of thine own host; and even this was not enough for thee, but thou didst stir her up with desire and hast gone away with her like a thief. Moreover not even this by itself was enough for thee, but thou art come hither with plunder taken from the house of thy host. Now therefore depart, seeing that I have counted it of great moment not to be a slayer of strangers. This woman indeed and the wealth which thou hast I will not allow thee to carry away, but I shall keep them safe for the Hellene who was thy host, until he come himself and desire to carry them off to his home; to thyself however and thy fellow-voyagers I proclaim that ye depart from your anchoring within three days and go from my land to some other; and if not, that ye will be dealt with as enemies."

This the priests said was the manner of Helen's coming to Proteus; and I suppose that Homer also had heard this story, but since it was not so suitable to the composition of his poem as the other which he followed, he dismissed it finally, making it clear at the same time that he was acquainted with that story also: and according to the manner in which he described the wanderings of Alexander in the Iliad (nor did he elsewhere retract that which he had said) it is clear that when he brought Helen he was carried out of his course, wandering to various lands, and that he came among other places to Sidon in Phenicia. Of this the poet has made mention in the "prowess of Diomede," and the verses run this:

"There she had robes many-coloured, the works of women of Sidon,

Those whom her son himself the god-like of form Alexander

Carried from Sidon, what time the broad sea-path he sailed over

Bringing back Helene home, of a noble father begotten."

And in the Odyssey also he has made mention of it in these verses:

"Such had the daughter of Zeus, such drugs of exquisite cunning,

Good, which to her the wife of Thon, Polydamna, had given,

Dwelling in Egypt, the land where the bountiful meadow produces

Drugs more than all lands else, many good being mixed, many evil."

And thus too Menelaos says to Telemachos:

"Still the gods stayed me in Egypt, to come back hither desiring,

Stayed me from voyaging home, since sacrifice was due I performed not."

In these lines he makes it clear that he knew of the wandering of Alexander to Egypt, for Syria borders upon Egypt and the Phenicians, of whom is Sidon, dwell in Syria.

By these lines and by this passage it is also most clearly shown that the "Cyprian Epic" was not written by Homer but by some other man: for in this it is said that on the third day after leaving Sparta Alexander came to Ilion bringing with him Helen, having had a "gently-blowing wind and a smooth sea," whereas in the Iliad it says that he wandered from his course when he brought her.

Let us now leave Homer and the "Cyprian" Epic; but this I will say, namely that I asked the priests whether it is but an idle tale which the Hellenes tell of that which they say happened about Ilion; and they answered me thus, saying that they had their knowledge by inquiries from Menelaos himself. After the rape of Helen there came indeed, they said, to the Teucrian land a large army of Hellenes to help Menelaos; and when the army had come out of the ships to land and had pitched its camp there, they sent messengers to Ilion, with whom went also Menelaos himself; and when these entered within the wall they demanded back Helen and the wealth which Alexander had stolen from Menelaos and had taken away; and moreover they demanded satisfaction for the wrongs done: and the Teucrians told the same tale then and afterwards, both with oath and without oath, namely that in deed and in truth they had not Helen nor the wealth for which demand was made, but that both were in Egypt; and that they could not justly be compelled to give satisfaction for that which Proteus the king of Egypt had. The Hellenes however thought that they were being mocked by them and besieged the city, until at last they took it; and when they had taken the wall and did not find Helen, but heard the same tale as before, then they believed the former tale and sent Menelaos himself to Proteus.

And Menelaos having come to Egypt and having sailed up to Memphis, told the truth of these matters, and not only found great entertainment, but also received Helen unhurt, and all his own wealth besides. Then however, after he had been thus dealt with, Menelaos showed himself ungrateful to the Egyptians; for when he set forth to sail away, contrary winds detained him, and as this condition of things lasted long, he devised an impious deed; for he took two children of natives and made sacrifice of them. After this, when it was known that he had done so, he became abhorred, and being pursued he escaped and got away in his ships to Libya; but whither he went besides after this, the Egyptians were not able to tell. Of these things they said that they found out part by inquiries, and the rest, namely that which happened in their own land, they related from sure and certain knowledge.

Thus the priests of the Egyptians told me; and I myself also agree with the story which was told of Helen, adding this consideration, namely that if Helen had been in Ilion she would have been given up to the Hellenes, whether Alexander consented or no; for Priam assuredly was not so mad, nor yet the others of his house, that they were desirous to run risk of ruin for themselves and their children and their city, in order that Alexander might have Helen as his wife: and even supposing that during the first part of the time they had been so inclined, yet when many others of the Trojans besides were losing their lives as often as they fought with the Hellenes, and of the sons of Priam himself always two or three or even more were slain when a battle took place (if one may trust at all to the Epic poets),—when, I say, things were coming thus to pass, I consider that even if Priam himself had had Helen as his wife, he would have given her back to the Achaians, if at least by so doing he might be freed from the evils which oppressed him. Nor even was the kingdom coming to Alexander next, so that when Priam was old the government was in his hands; but Hector, who was both older and more of a man than he, would have received it after the death of Priam; and him it behoved not to allow his brother to go on with his wrong-doing, considering that great evils were coming to pass on his account both to himself privately and in general to the other Trojans. In truth however they lacked the power to give Helen back; and the Hellenes did not believe them, though they spoke the truth; because, as I declare my opinion, the divine power was purposing to cause them utterly to perish, and so make it evident to men that for great wrongs great also are the chastisements which come from the gods. And thus have I delivered my opinion concerning these matters.

After Proteus, they told me, Rhampsinitos received in succession the kingdom, who left as a memorial of himself that gateway to the temple of Hephaistos which is turned towards the West, and in front of the gateway he set up two statues, in height five-and-twenty cubits, of which the one which stands on the North side is called by the Egyptians Summer and the one on the South side Winter; and to that one which they call Summer they do reverence and make offerings, while to the other which is called Winter they do the opposite of these things. (a) This king, they said, got great wealth of silver, which none of the kings born after him could surpass or even come near to; and wishing to store his wealth in safety he caused to be built a chamber of stone, one of the walls whereof was towards the outside of his palace: and the builder of this, having a design against it, contrived as follows, that is, he disposed one of the stones in such a manner that it could be taken out easily from the wall either by two men or even by one. So when the chamber was finished, the king stored his money in it, and after some time the builder, being near the end of his life, called to him his sons (for he had two) and to them he related how he had contrived in building the treasury of the king, and all in forethought for them, that they might have ample means of living. And when he had clearly set forth to them everything concerning the taking out of the stone, he gave them the measurements, saying that if they paid heed to this matter they would be stewards of the king's treasury. So he ended his life, and his sons made no long delay in setting to work, but went to the palace by night, and having found the stone in the wall of the chamber they dealt with it easily and carried forth for themselves great quantity of the wealth within. (b) And the king happening to open the chamber, he marvelled when he saw the vessels falling short of the full amount, and he did not know on whom he should lay the blame, since the seals were unbroken and the chamber had been close shut; but when upon his opening the chamber a second and a third time the money was each time seen to be diminished, for the thieves did not slacken in their assaults upon it, he did as follows:—having ordered traps to be made he set these round about the vessels in which the money was; and when the thieves had come as at former times and one of them had entered, then so soon as he came near to one of the vessels he was straightway caught in the trap: and when he perceived in what evil case he was, straightway calling his brother he showed him what the matter was, and bade him enter as quickly as possible and cut off his head, for fear lest being seen and known he might bring about the destruction of his brother also. And to the other it seemed that he spoke well, and he was persuaded and did so; and fitting the stone into its place he departed home bearing with him the head of his brother. (c) Now when it became day, the king entered into the chamber and was very greatly amazed, seeing the body of the thief held in the trap without his head, and the chamber unbroken, with no way to come in or go out: and being at a loss he hung up the dead body of the thief upon the wall and set guards there, with charge if they saw any one weeping or bewailing himself to seize him and bring him before the king. And when the dead body had been hung up, the mother was greatly grieved, and speaking with the son who survived she enjoined him, in whatever way he could, to contrive means by which he might take down and bring home the body of his dead brother; and if he should neglect to do this, she earnestly threatened that she would go and give information to the king that he had the money. (d) So as the mother dealt hardly with the surviving son, and he though saying many things to her did not persuade her, he contrived for his purpose a device as follows:—Providing himself with asses he filled some skins with wine and laid them upon the asses, and after that he drove them along: and when he came opposite to those who were guarding the corpse hung up, he drew towards him two or three of the necks of the skins and loosened the cords with which they were tied. Then when the wine was running out, he began to beat his head and cry out loudly, as if he did not know to which of the asses he should first turn; and when the guards saw the wine flowing out in streams, they ran together to the road with drinking vessels in their hands and collected the wine that was poured out, counting it so much gain; and he abused them all violently, making as if he were angry, but when the guards tried to appease him, after a time he feigned to be pacified and to abate his anger, and at length he drove his asses out of the road and began to set their loads right. Then more talk arose among them, and one or two of them made jests at him and brought him to laugh with them; and in the end he made them a present of one of the skins in addition to what they had. Upon that they lay down there without more ado, being minded to drink, and they took him into their company and invited him to remain with them and join them in their drinking: so he (as may be supposed) was persuaded and stayed. Then as they in their drinking bade him welcome in a friendly manner, he made a present to them also of another of the skins; and so at length having drunk liberally the guards became completely intoxicated; and being overcome by sleep they went to bed on the spot where they had been drinking. He then, as it was now far on in the night, first took down the body of his brother, and then in mockery shaved the right cheeks of all the guards; and after that he put the dead body upon the asses and drove them away home, having accomplished that which was enjoined him by his mother. (e) Upon this the king, when it was reported to him that the dead body of the thief had been stolen away, displayed great anger; and desiring by all means that it should be found out who it might be who devised these things, did this (so at least they said, but I do not believe the account),—he caused his own daughter to sit in the stews, and enjoined her to receive all equally, and before having commerce with any one to compel him to tell her what was the most cunning and what the most unholy deed which had been done by him in all his life-time; and whosoever should relate that which had happened about the thief, him she must seize and not let him go out. Then as she was doing that which was enjoined by her father, the thief, hearing for what purpose this was done and having a desire to get the better of the king in resource, did thus:—from the body of one lately dead he cut off the arm at the shoulder and went with it under his mantle: and having gone in to the daughter of the king, and being asked that which the others also were asked, he related that he had done the most unholy deed when he cut off the head of his brother, who had been caught in a trap in the king's treasure-chamber, and the most cunning deed in that he made drunk the guards and took down the dead body of his brother hanging up; and she when she heard it tried to take hold of him, but the thief held out to her in the darkness the arm of the corpse, which she grasped and held, thinking that she was holding the arm of the man himself; but the thief left it in her hands and departed, escaping through the door. (f) Now when this also was reported to the king, he was at first amazed at the ready invention and daring of the fellow, and then afterwards he sent round to all the cities and made proclamation granting a free pardon to the thief, and also promising a great reward if he would come into his presence. The thief accordingly trusting to the proclamation came to the king, and Rhampsinitos greatly marvelled at him, and gave him this daughter of his to wife, counting him to be the most knowing of all men; for as the Egyptians were distinguished from all other men, so was he from the other Egyptians.

After these things they said this king went down alive to that place which by the Hellenes is called Hades, and there played at dice with Demeter, and in some throws he overcame her and in others he was overcome by her; and he came back again having as a gift from her a handkerchief of gold: and they told me that because of the going down of Rhampsinitos the Egyptians after he came back celebrated a feast, which I know of my own knowledge also that they still observe even to my time; but whether it is for this cause that they keep the feast or for some other, I am not able to say. However, the priests weave a robe completely on the very day of the feast, and forthwith they bind up the eyes of one of them with a fillet, and having led him with the robe to the way by which one goes to the temple of Demeter, they depart back again themselves. This priest, they say, with his eyes bound up is led by two wolves to the temple of Demeter, which is distant from the city twenty furlongs, and then afterwards the wolves lead him back again from the temple to the same spot.

Now as to the tales told by the Egyptians, any man may accept them to whom such things appear credible; as for me, it is to be understood throughout the whole of the history that I write by hearsay that which is reported by the people in each place. The Egyptians say that Demeter and Dionysos are rulers of the world below; and the Egyptians are also the first who reported the doctrine that the soul of man is immortal, and that when the body dies, the soul enters into another creature which chances then to be coming to the birth, and when it has gone the round of all the creatures of land and sea and of the air, it enters again into a human body as it comes to the birth; and that it makes this round in a period of three thousand years. This doctrine certain Hellenes adopted, some earlier and some later, as if it were of their own invention, and of these men I know the names but I abstain from recording them.

Down to the time when Rhampsinitos was king, they told me there was in Egypt nothing but orderly rule, and Egypt prospered greatly; but after him Cheops became king over them and brought them to every kind of evil: for he shut up all the temples, and having first kept them from sacrificing there, he then bade all the Egyptians work for him. So some were appointed to draw stones from the stone-quarries in the Arabian mountains to the Nile, and others he ordered to receive the stones after they had been carried over the river in boats, and to draw them to those which are called the Libyan mountains; and they worked by a hundred thousand men at a time, for each three months continually. Of this oppression there passed ten years while the causeway was made by which they drew the stones, which causeway they built, and it is a work not much less, as it appears to me, than the pyramid; for the length of it is five furlongs and the breadth ten fathoms and the height, where it is highest, eight fathoms, and it is made of stone smoothed and with figures carved upon it. For this, they said, the ten years were spent, and for the underground chambers on the hill upon which the pyramids stand, which he caused to be made as sepulchral chambers for himself in an island, having conducted thither a channel from the Nile. For the making of the pyramid itself there passed a period of twenty years; and the pyramid is square, each side measuring eight hundred feet, and the height of it is the same. It is built of stone smoothed and fitted together in the most perfect manner, not one of the stones being less than thirty feet in length.

This pyramid was made after the manner of steps, which some call "rows" and others "bases": and when they had first made it thus, they raised the remaining stones with machines made of short pieces of timber, raising them first from the ground to the first stage of the steps, and when the stone got up to this it was placed upon another machine standing on the first stage, and so from this it was drawn to the second upon another machine; for as many as were the courses of the steps, so many machines there were also, or perhaps they transferred one and the same machine, made so as easily to be carried, to each stage successively, in order that they might take up the stones; for let it be told in both ways, according as it is reported. However that may be, the highest parts of it were finished first, and afterwards they proceeded to finish that which came next to them, and lastly they finished the parts of it near the ground and the lowest ranges. On the pyramid it is declared in Egyptian writing how much was spent on radishes and onions and leeks for the workmen, and if I rightly remember that which the interpreter said in reading to me this inscription, a sum of one thousand six hundred talents of silver was spent; and if this is so, how much besides is likely to have been expended upon the iron with which they worked, and upon bread and clothing for the workmen, seeing that they were building the works for the time which has been mentioned and were occupied for no small time besides, as I suppose, in the cutting and bringing of the stones and in working at the excavation under the ground?

Cheops moreover came, they said, to such a pitch of wickedness, that being in want of money he caused his own daughter to sit in the stews, and ordered her to obtain from those who came a certain amount of money (how much it was they did not tell me); but she not only obtained the sum appointed by her father, but also she formed a design for herself privately to leave behind her a memorial, and she requested each man who came in to her to give her one stone upon her building: and of these stones, they told me, the pyramid was built which stands in front of the great pyramid in the middle of the three, each side being one hundred and fifty feet in length.

This Cheops, the Egyptians said, reigned fifty years; and after he was dead his brother Chephren succeeded to the kingdom. This king followed the same manner as the other, both in all the rest and also in that he made a pyramid, not indeed attaining to the measurements of that which was built by the former (this I know, having myself also measured it), and moreover there are no underground chambers beneath nor does a channel come from the Nile flowing to this one as to the other, in which the water coming through a conduit built for it flows round an island within, where they say that Cheops himself is laid: but for a basement he built the first course of Ethiopian stone of divers colours; and this pyramid he made forty feet lower than the other as regards size, building it close to the great pyramid. These stand both upon the same hill, which is about a hundred feet high. And Chephren they said reigned fifty and six years.

Here then they reckon one hundred and six years, during which they say that there was nothing but evil for the Egyptians, and the temples were kept closed and not opened during all that time. These kings the Egyptians by reason of their hatred of them are not very willing to name; nay, they even call the pyramids after the name of Philitis the shepherd, who at that time pastured flocks in those regions.

After him, they said, Mykerinos became king over Egypt, who was the son of Cheops; and to him his father's deeds were displeasing, and he both opened the temples and gave liberty to the people, who were ground down to the last extremity of evil, to return to their own business and to their sacrifices;: also he gave decisions of their causes juster than those of all the other kings besides. In regard to this then they commend this king more than all the other kings who had arisen in Egypt before him; for he not only gave good decisions, but also when a man complained of the decision, he gave him recompense from his own goods and thus satisfied his desire. But while Mykerinos was acting mercifully to his subjects and practising this conduct which has been said, calamities befell him, of which the first was this, namely that his daughter died, the only child whom he had in his house: and being above measure grieved by that which had befallen him, and desiring to bury his daughter in a manner more remarkable than others, he made a cow of wood, which he covered over with gold, and then within it he buried this daughter who, as I said, had died.

This cow was not covered up in the ground, but it might be seen even down to my own time in the city of Saïs, placed within the royal palace in a chamber which was greatly adorned; and they offer incense of all kinds before it every day, and each night a lamp burns beside it all through the night. Near this cow in another chamber stand images of the concubines of Mykerinos, as the priests at Saïs told me; for there are in fact colossal wooden statues, in number about twenty, made with naked bodies; but who they are I am not able to say, except only that which is reported.

Some however tell about this cow and the colossal statues the following tale, namely that Mykerinos was enamoured of his own daughter and afterwards ravished her; and upon this they say that the girl strangled herself for grief, and he buried her in this cow; and her mother cut off the hands of the maids who had betrayed the daughter to her father; wherefore now the images of them have suffered that which the maids suffered in their life. In thus saying they speak idly, as it seems to me, especially in what they say about the hands of the statues; for as to this, even we ourselves saw that their hands had dropped off from lapse of time, and they were to be seen still lying at their feet even down to my time.

. The cow is covered up with a crimson robe, except only the head and the neck, which are seen, overlaid with gold very thickly; and between the horns there is the disc of the sun figured in gold. The cow is not standing up but kneeling, and in size it is equal to a large living cow. Every year it is carried forth from the chamber, at those times, I say, the Egyptians beat themselves for that god whom I will not name upon occasion of such a matter; at these times, I say, they also carry forth the cow to the light of day, for they say that she asked of her father Mykerinos, when she was dying, that she might look upon the sun once in the year.

After the misfortune of his daughter it happened, they said, secondly to this king as follows:—An oracle came to him from the city of Buto, saying that he was destined to live but six years more, in the seventh year to end his life: and he being indignant at it sent to the Oracle a reproach against the god, making complaint in reply that whereas his father and uncle, who had shut up the temples and had not only not remembered the gods, but also had been destroyers of men, had lived for a long time, he himself, who practised piety, was destined to end his life so soon: and from the Oracle there came a second message, which said that it was for this very cause that he was bringing his life to a swift close; for he had not done that which it was appointed for him to do, since it was destined that Egypt should suffer evils for a hundred and fifty years, and the two kings who had risen before him had perceived this, but he had not. Mykerinos having heard this, and considering that this sentence had been passed upon him beyond recall, procured many lamps, and whenever night came on he lighted these and began to drink and take his pleasure, ceasing neither by day nor by night; and he went about to the fen-country and to the woods and wherever he heard there were the most suitable places for enjoyment. This he devised (having a mind to prove that the Oracle spoke falsely) in order that he might have twelve years of life instead of six, the nights being turned into days.

This king also left behind him a pyramid, much smaller than that of his father, of a square shape and measuring on each side three hundred feet lacking twenty, built moreover of Ethiopian stone up to half the height. This pyramid some of the Hellenes say was built by the courtesan Rhodopis, not therein speaking rightly: and besides this it is evident to me that they who speak thus do not even know who Rhodopis was, for otherwise they would not have attributed to her the building of a pyramid like this, on which have been spent (so to speak) innumerable thousands of talents: moreover they do not know that Rhodopis flourished in the reign of Amasis, and not in this king's reign; for Rhodopis lived very many years later than the kings who left behind the pyramids. By descent she was of Thrace, and she was a slave of Iadmon the son of Hephaistopolis a Samian, and a fellow-slave of Esop the maker of fables; for he too was once the slave of Iadmon, as was proved especially in this fact, namely that when the people of Delphi repeatedly made proclamation in accordance with an oracle, to find some one who would take up the blood-money for the death of Esop, no one else appeared, but at length the grandson of Iadmon, called Iadmon also, took it up; and thus it is shown that Esop too was the slave of Iadmon.

As for Rhodopis, she came to Egypt brought by Xanthes the Samian, and having come thither to exercise her calling she was redeemed from slavery for a great sum by a man of Mytilene, Charaxos son of Scamandronymos and brother of Sappho the lyric poet. Thus was Rhodopis set free, and she remained in Egypt and by her beauty won so much liking that she made great gain of money for one like Rhodopis, though not enough to suffice for the cost of such a pyramid as this. In truth there is no need to ascribe to her very great riches, considering that the tithe of her wealth may still be seen even to this time by any one who desires it: for Rhodopis wished to leave behind her a memorial of herself in Hellas, namely to cause a thing to be made such as happens not to have been thought of or dedicated in a temple by any besides, and to dedicate this at Delphi as a memorial of herself. Accordingly with the tithe of her wealth she caused to be made spits of iron of size large enough to pierce a whole ox, and many in number, going as far therein as her tithe allowed her, and she sent them to Delphi: these are even at the present time lying there, heaped all together behind the altar which the Chians dedicated, and just opposite to the cell of the temple. Now at Naucratis, as it happens, the courtesans are rather apt to win credit; for this woman first, about whom the story to which I refer is told, became so famous that all the Hellenes without exception come to know the name of Rhodopis, and then after her one whose name was Archidiche became a subject of song over all Hellas, though she was less talked of than the other. As for Charaxos, when after redeeming Rhodopis he returned back to Mytilene, Sappho in an ode violently abused him. Of Rhodopis then I shall say no more.

After Mykerinos the priests said Asychis became king of Egypt, and he made for Hephaistos the temple gateway which is towards the sunrising, by far the most beautiful and the largest of the gateways; for while they all have figures carved upon them and innumerable ornaments of building besides, this has them very much more than the rest. In this king's reign they told me that, as the circulation of money was very slow, a law was made for the Egyptians that a man might have that money lent to him which he needed, by offering as security the dead body of his father; and there was added moreover to this law another, namely that he who lent the money should have a claim also to the whole sepulchral chamber belonging to him who received it, and that the man who offered that security should be subject to this penalty, if he refused to pay back the debt, namely that neither the man himself should be allowed to have burial when he died, either in that family burial-place or in any other, nor should he be allowed to bury any one of his kinsmen whom he lost by death. This king desiring to surpass the kings of Egypt who had arisen before him left as a memorial of himself a pyramid which he made of bricks, and on it there is an inscription carved in stone and saying thus: "Despise not me in comparison with the pyramids of stone, seeing that I excel them as much as Zeus excels the other gods; for with a pole they struck into the lake, and whatever of the mud attached itself to the pole, this they gathered up and made bricks, and in such manner they finished me."

Such were the deeds which this king performed; and after him reigned a blind man of the city of Anysis, whose name was Anysis. In his reign the Ethiopians and Sabacos the king of the Ethiopians marched upon Egypt with a great host of men; so this blind man departed, flying to the fen-country, and the Ethiopian was king over Egypt for fifty years, during which he performed deeds as follows:—whenever any man of the Egyptians committed any transgression, he would never put him to death, but he gave sentence upon each man according to the greatness of the wrong-doing, appointing them work at throwing up an embankment before that city from whence each man came of those who committed wrong. Thus the cities were made higher still than before; for they were embanked first by those who dug the channels in the reign of Sesostris, and then secondly in the reign of the Ethiopian, and thus they were made very high: and while other cities in Egypt also stood high, I think in the town at Bubastis especially the earth was piled up. In this city there is a temple very well worthy of mention, for though there are other temples which are larger and built with more cost, none more than this is a pleasure to the eyes. Now Bubastis in the Hellenic tongue is Artemis, and her temple is ordered thus:—Except the entrance it is completely surrounded by water; for channels come in from the Nile, not joining one another, but each extending as far as the entrance of the temple, one flowing round on the one side and the other on the other side, each a hundred feet broad and shaded over with trees; and the gateway has a height of ten fathoms, and it is adorned with figures six cubits high, very noteworthy. This temple is in the middle of the city and is looked down upon from all sides as one goes round, for since the city has been banked up to a height, while the temple has not been moved from the place where it was at the first built, it is possible to look down into it: and round it runs a stone wall with figures carved upon it, while within it there is a grove of very large trees planted round a large temple-house, within which is the image of the goddess: and the breadth and length of the temple is a furlong every way. Opposite the entrance there is a road paved with stone for about three furlongs, which leads through the market-place towards the East, with a breadth of about four hundred feet; and on this side and on that grow trees of height reaching to heaven: and the road leads to the temple of Hermes. This temple then is thus ordered.

The final deliverance from the Ethiopian came about (they said) as follows:—he fled away because he had seen in his sleep a vision, in which it seemed to him that a man came and stood by him and counselled him to gather together all the priests of Egypt and cut them asunder in the midst. Having seen this dream, he said that it seemed to him that the gods were foreshowing him this to furnish an occasion against him, in order that he might do an impious deed with respect to religion, and so receive some evil either from the gods or from men: he would not however do so, but in truth (he said) the time had expired, during which it had been prophesied to him that he should rule Egypt before he departed thence. For when he was in Ethiopia the Oracles which the Ethiopians consult had told him that it was fated for him to rule Egypt fifty years: since then this time was now expiring, and the vision of the dream also disturbed him, Sabacos departed out of Egypt of his own free will.

Then when the Ethiopian had gone away out of Egypt, the blind man came back from the fen-country and began to rule again, having lived there during fifty years upon an island which he had made by heaping up ashes and earth: for whenever any of the Egyptians visited him bringing food, according as it had been appointed to them severally to do without the knowledge of the Ethiopian, he bade them bring also some ashes for their gift. This island none was able to find before Amyrtaios; that is, for more than seven hundred years the kings who arose before Amyrtaios were not able to find it. Now the name of this island is Elbo, and its size is ten furlongs each way.

After him there came to the throne the priest of Hephaistos, whose name was Sethos. This man, they said, neglected and held in no regard the warrior class of the Egyptians, considering that he would have no need of them; and besides other slights which he put upon them, he also took from them the yokes of corn-land which had been given to them as a special gift in the reigns of the former kings, twelve yokes to each man. After this, Sanacharib king of the Arabians and of the Assyrians marched a great host against Egypt. Then the warriors of the Egyptians refused to come to the rescue, and the priest, being driven into a strait, entered into the sanctuary of the temple and bewailed to the image of the god the danger which was impending over him; and as he was thus lamenting, sleep came upon him, and it seemed to him in his vision that the god came and stood by him and encouraged him, saying that he should suffer no evil if he went forth to meet the army of the Arabians; for he himself would send him helpers. Trusting in these things seen in sleep, he took with him, they said, those of the Egyptians who were willing to follow him, and encamped in Pelusion, for by this way the invasion came: and not one of the warrior class followed him, but shop-keepers and artisans and men of the market. Then after they came, there swarmed by night upon their enemies mice of the fields, and ate up their quivers and their bows, and moreover the handles of their shields, so that on the next day they fled, and being without defence of arms great numbers fell. And at the present time this king stands in the temple of Hephaistos in stone, holding upon his hand a mouse, and by letters inscribed he says these words: "Let him who looks upon me learn to fear the gods."

So far in the story the Egyptians and the priests were they who made the report, declaring that from the first king down to this priest of Hephaistos who reigned last, there had been three hundred and forty-one generations of men, and that in them there had been the same number of chief-priests and of kings: but three hundred generations of men are equal to ten thousand years, for a hundred years is three generations of men; and in the one-and-forty generations which remain, those I mean which were added to the three hundred, there are one thousand three hundred and forty years. Thus in the period of eleven thousand three hundred and forty years they said that there had arisen no god in human form; nor even before that time or afterwards among the remaining kings who arose in Egypt, did they report that anything of that kind had come to pass. In this time they said that the sun had moved four times from his accustomed place of rising, and where he now sets he had thence twice had his rising, and in the place from whence he now rises he had twice had his setting; and in the meantime nothing in Egypt had been changed from its usual state, neither that which comes from the earth nor that which comes to them from the river nor that which concerns diseases or deaths.

And formerly when Hecataios the historian was in Thebes, and had traced his descent and connected his family with a god in the sixteenth generation before, the priests of Zeus did for him much the same as they did for me (though I had not traced my descent). They led me into the sanctuary of the temple, which is of great size, and they counted up the number, showing colossal wooden statues in number the same as they said; for each chief-priest there sets up in his lifetime an image of himself: accordingly the priests, counting and showing me these, declared to me that each one of them was a son succeeding his own father, and they went up through the series of images from the image of the one who had died last, until they had declared this of the whole number. And when Hecataios had traced his descent and connected his family with a god in the sixteenth generation, they traced a descent in opposition to this, besides their numbering, not accepting it from him that a man had been born from a god; and they traced their counter-descent thus, saying that each one of the statues had been piromis son of piromis, until they had declared this of the whole three hundred and forty-five statues, each one being surnamed piromis; and neither with a god nor a hero did they connect their descent. Now piromis means in the tongue of Hellas "honourable and good man."

From their declaration then it followed, that they of whom the images were had been of form like this, and far removed from being gods: but in the time before these men they said that gods were the rulers in Egypt, not mingling with men, and that of these always one had power at a time; and the last of them who was king over Egypt was Oros the son of Osiris, whom the Hellenes call Apollo: he was king over Egypt last, having deposed Typhon. Now Osiris in the tongue of Hellas is Dionysos.

. Among the Hellenes Heracles and Dionysos and Pan are accounted the latest-born of the gods; but with the Egyptians Pan is a very ancient god, and he is one of those which are called the eight gods, while Heracles is of the second rank, who are called the twelve gods, and Dionysos is of the third rank, namely of those who were born of the twelve gods. Now as to Heracles I have shown already how many years old he is according to the Egyptians themselves, reckoning down to the reign of Amasis, and Pan is said to have existed for yet more years than these, and Dionysos for the smallest number of years as compared with the others; and even for this last they reckon down to the reign of Amasis fifteen thousand years. This the Egyptians say that they know for a certainty, since they always kept a reckoning and wrote down the years as they came. Now the Dionysos who is said to have been born of Semele the daughter of Cadmos, was born about sixteen hundred years before my time, and Heracles who was the son of Alcmene, about nine hundred years, and that Pan who was born of Penelope, for of her and of Hermes Pan is said by the Hellenes to have been born, came into being later than the wars of Troy, about eight hundred years before my time.

Of these two accounts every man may adopt that one which he shall find the more credible when he hears it. I however, for my part, have already declared my opinion about them. For if these also, like Heracles the son of Amphitryon, had appeared before all men's eyes and had lived their lives to old age in Hellas, I mean Dionysos the son of Semele and Pan the son of Penelope, then one would have said that these also had been born mere men, having the names of those gods who had come into being long before: but as it is, with regard to Dionysos the Hellenes say that as soon as he was born Zeus sewed him up in his thigh and carried him to Nysa, which is above Egypt in the land of Ethiopia; and as to Pan, they cannot say whither he went after he was born. Hence it has become clear to me that the Hellenes learnt the names of these gods later than those of the other gods, and trace their descent as if their birth occurred at the time when they first learnt their names.

Thus far then the history is told by the Egyptians themselves; but I will now recount that which other nations also tell, and the Egyptians in agreement with the others, of that which happened in this land: and there will be added to this also something of that which I have myself seen.

Being set free after the reign of the priest of Hephaistos, the Egyptians, since they could not live any time without a king, set up over them twelve kings, having divided all Egypt into twelve parts. These made intermarriages with one another and reigned, making agreement that they would not put down one another by force, nor seek to get an advantage over one another, but would live in perfect friendship: and the reason why they made these agreements, guarding them very strongly from violation, was this, namely that an oracle had been given to them at first when they began to exercise their rule, that he of them who should pour a libation with a bronze cup in the temple of Hephaistos, should be king of all Egypt (for they used to assemble together in all the temples).

Moreover they resolved to join all together and leave a memorial of themselves; and having so resolved they caused to be made a labyrinth, situated a little above the lake of Moiris and nearly opposite to that which is called the City of Crocodiles. This I saw myself, and I found it greater than words can say. For if one should put together and reckon up all the buildings and all the great works produced by the Hellenes, they would prove to be inferior in labour and expense to this labyrinth, though it is true that both the temple at Ephesos and that at Samos are works worthy of note. The pyramids also were greater than words can say, and each one of them is equal to many works of the Hellenes, great as they may be; but the labyrinth surpasses even the pyramids. It has twelve courts covered in, with gates facing one another, six upon the North side and six upon the South, joining on one to another, and the same wall surrounds them all outside; and there are in it two kinds of chambers, the one kind below the ground and the other above upon these, three thousand in number, of each kind fifteen hundred. The upper set of chambers we ourselves saw, going through them, and we tell of them having looked upon them with our own eyes; but the chambers under ground we heard about only; for the Egyptians who had charge of them were not willing on any account to show them, saying that here were the sepulchres of the kings who had first built this labyrinth and of the sacred crocodiles. Accordingly we speak of the chambers below by what we received from hearsay, while those above we saw ourselves and found them to be works of more than human greatness. For the passages through the chambers, and the goings this way and that way through the courts, which were admirably adorned, afforded endless matter for marvel, as we went through from a court to the chambers beyond it, and from the chambers to colonnades, and from the colonnades to other rooms, and then from the chambers again to other courts. Over the whole of these is a roof made of stone like the walls; and the walls are covered with figures carved upon them, each court being surrounded with pillars of white stone fitted together most perfectly; and at the end of the labyrinth, by the corner of it, there is a pyramid of forty fathoms, upon which large figures are carved, and to this there is a way made under ground.

Such is this labyrinth; but a cause for marvel even greater than this is afforded by the lake, which is called the lake of Moiris, along the side of which this labyrinth is built. The measure of its circuit is three thousand six hundred furlongs (being sixty schoines), and this is the same number of furlongs as the extent of Egypt itself along the sea. The lake lies extended lengthwise from North to South, and in depth where it is deepest it is fifty fathoms. That this lake is artificial and formed by digging is self-evident, for about in the middle of the lake stand two pyramids, each rising above the water to a height of fifty fathoms, the part which is built below the water being of just the same height; and upon each is placed a colossal statue of stone sitting upon a chair. Thus the pyramids are a hundred fathoms high; and these hundred fathoms are equal to a furlong of six hundred feet, the fathom being measured as six feet or four cubits, the feet being four palms each, and the cubits six. The water in the lake does not come from the place where it is, for the country there is very deficient in water, but it has been brought thither from the Nile by a canal: and for six months the water flows into the lake, and for six months out into the Nile again; and whenever it flows out, then for the six months it brings into the royal treasury a talent of silver a day from the fish which are caught, and twenty pounds when the water comes in.

The natives of the place moreover said that this lake had an outlet under ground to the Syrtis which is in Libya, turning towards the interior of the continent upon the Western side and running along by the mountain which is above Memphis. Now since I did not see anywhere existing the earth dug out of this excavation (for that was a matter which drew my attention), I asked those who dwelt nearest to the lake where the earth was which had been dug out. These told me to what place it had been carried away; and I readily believed them, for I knew by report that a similar thing had been done at Nineveh, the city of the Assyrians. There certain thieves formed a design once to carry away the wealth of Sardanapallos son of Ninos, the king, which wealth was very great and was kept in treasure-houses under the earth. Accordingly they began from their own dwelling, and making estimate of their direction they dug under ground towards the king's palace; and the earth which was brought out of the excavation they used to carry away, when night came on, to the river Tigris which flows by the city of Nineveh, until at last they accomplished that which they desired. Similarly, as I heard, the digging of the lake in Egypt was effected, except that it was done not by night but during the day; for as they dug the Egyptians carried to the Nile the earth which was dug out; and the river, when it received it, would naturally bear it away and disperse it. Thus is this lake said to have been dug out.

Now the twelve kings continued to rule justly, but in course of time it happened thus:—After sacrifice in the temple of Hephaistos they were about to make libation on the last day of the feast, and the chief-priest, in bringing out for them the golden cups with which they had been wont to pour libations, missed his reckoning and brought eleven only for the twelve kings. Then that one of them who was standing last in order, namely Psammetichos, since he had no cup took off from his head his helmet, which was of bronze, and having held it out to receive the wine he proceeded to make libation: likewise all the other kings were wont to wear helmets and they happened to have them then. Now Psammetichos held out his helmet with no treacherous meaning; but they taking note of that which had been done by Psammetichos and of the oracle, namely how it had been declared to them that whosoever of them should make libation with a bronze cup should be sole king of Egypt, recollecting, I say, the saying of the Oracle, they did not indeed deem it right to slay Psammetichos, since they found by examination that he had not done it with any forethought, but they determined to strip him of almost all his power and to drive him away into the fen-country, and that from the fen-country he should not hold any dealings with the rest of Egypt.

This Psammetichos had formerly been a fugitive from the Ethiopian Sabacos who had killed his father Necos, from him, I say, he had then been a fugitive in Syria; and when the Ethiopian had departed in consequence of the vision of the dream, the Egyptians who were of the district of Saïs brought him back to his own country. Then afterwards, when he was king, it was his fate to be a fugitive a second time on account of the helmet, being driven by the eleven kings into the fen-country. So then holding that he had been grievously wronged by them, he thought how he might take vengeance on those who had driven him out: and when he had sent to the Oracle of Leto in the city of Buto, where the Egyptians have their most truthful Oracle, there was given to him the reply that vengeance would come when men of bronze appeared from the sea. And he was strongly disposed not to believe that bronze men would come to help him; but after no long time had passed, certain Ionians and Carians who had sailed forth for plunder were compelled to come to shore in Egypt, and they having landed and being clad in bronze armour, one of the Egyptians, not having before seen men clad in bronze armour, came to the fen-land and brought a report to Psammetichos that bronze men had come from the sea and were plundering the plain. So he, perceiving that the saying of the Oracle was coming to pass, dealt in a friendly manner with the Ionians and Carians, and with large promises he persuaded them to take his part. Then when he had persuaded them, with the help of those Egyptians who favoured his cause and of these foreign mercenaries he overthrew the kings.

Having thus got power over all Egypt, Psammetichos made for Hephaistos that gateway of the temple at Memphis which is turned towards the South Wind; and he built a court for Apis, in which Apis is kept when he appears, opposite to the gateway of the temple, surrounded all with pillars and covered with figures; and instead of columns there stand to support the roof of the court colossal statues twelve cubits high. Now Apis is in the tongue of the Hellenes Epaphos.

To the Ionians and to the Carians who had helped him Psammetichos granted portions of land to dwell in, opposite to one another with the river Nile between, and these were called "Encampments": these portions of land he gave them, and he paid them besides all that he had promised: moreover he placed with them Egyptian boys to have them taught the Hellenic tongue; and from these, who learnt the language thoroughly, are descended the present class of interpreters in Egypt. Now the Ionians and Carians occupied these portions of land for a long time, and they are towards the sea a little below the city of Bubastis, on that which is called the Pelusian mouth of the Nile. These men king Amasis afterwards removed from thence and established them at Memphis, making them into a guard for himself against the Egyptians: and they being settled in Egypt, we who are Hellenes know by intercourse with them the certainty of all that which happened in Egypt beginning from king Psammetichos and afterwards; for these were the first men of foreign tongue who settled in Egypt: and in the land from which they were removed there still remained down to my time the sheds where their ships were drawn up and the ruins of their houses.

Thus then Psammetichos obtained Egypt: and of the Oracle which is in Egypt I have made mention often before this, and now I will give an account of it, seeing that it is worthy to be described. This Oracle which is in Egypt is sacred to Leto, and it is established in a great city near that mouth of the Nile which is called Sebennytic, as one sails up the river from the sea; and the name of this city where the Oracle is found is Buto, as I have said before in mentioning it. In this Buto there is a temple of Apollo and Artemis; and the temple-house of Leto, in which the Oracle is, is both great in itself and has a gateway of the height of ten fathoms: but that which caused me most to marvel of the things to be seen there, I will now tell. There is in this sacred enclosure a house of Leto made of one single stone as regards both height and length, and of which all the walls are in these two directions equal, each being forty cubits; and for the covering in of the roof there lies another stone upon the top, the cornice measuring four cubits.

This house then of all the things that were to be seen by me in that temple is the most marvellous, and among those which come next is the island called Chemmis. This is situated in a deep and broad lake by the side of the temple at Buto, and it is said by the Egyptians that this island is a floating island. I myself did not see it either floating about or moved from its place, and I feel surprise at hearing of it, wondering if it be indeed a floating island. In this island of which I speak there is a great temple-house of Apollo, and three several altars are set up within, and there are planted in the island many palm-trees and other trees, both bearing fruit and not bearing fruit. And the Egyptians, when they say that it is floating, add this story, namely that in this island, which formerly was not floating, Leto, being one of the eight gods who came into existence first, and dwelling in the city of Buto where she has this Oracle, received Apollo from Isis as a charge and preserved him, concealing him in the island which is said now to be a floating island, at that time when Typhon came after him seeking everywhere and desiring to find the son of Osiris. Now they say that Apollo and Artemis are children of Dionysos and of Isis, and that Leto became their nurse and preserver; and in the Egyptian tongue Apollo is Oros, Demeter is Isis, and Artemis is Bubastis. From this story and from no other Æschylus the son of Euphorion took this which I shall say, wherein he differs from all the preceding poets; he represented namely that Artemis was the daughter of Demeter. For this reason then, they say, it became a floating island.

Such is the story which they tell; but as for Psammetichos, he was king over Egypt for four-and-fifty years, of which for thirty years save one he was sitting before Azotos, a great city of Syria, besieging it, until at last he took it: and this Azotos of all cities about which we have knowledge held out for the longest time under a siege.

The son of Psammetichos was Necos, and he became king of Egypt. This man was the first who attempted the channel leading to the Erythraian Sea, which Dareios the Persian afterwards completed: the length of this is a voyage of four days, and in breadth it was so dug that two triremes could go side by side driven by oars; and the water is brought into it from the Nile. The channel is conducted a little above the city of Bubastis by Patumos the Arabian city, and runs into the Erythraian Sea: and it is dug first along those parts of the plain of Egypt which lie towards Arabia, just above which run the mountains which extend opposite Memphis, where are the stone-quarries,—along the base of these mountains the channel is conducted from West to East for a great way; and after that it is directed towards a break in the hills and tends from these mountains towards the noon-day and the South Wind to the Arabian gulf. Now in the place where the journey is least and shortest from the Northern to the Southern Sea (which is also called Erythraian), that is from Mount Casion, which is the boundary between Egypt and Syria, the distance is exactly a thousand furlongs to the Arabian gulf; but the channel is much longer, since it is more winding; and in the reign of Necos there perished while digging it twelve myriads of the Egyptians. Now Necos ceased in the midst of his digging, because the utterance of an Oracle impeded him, which was to the effect that he was working for the Barbarian: and the Egyptians call all men Barbarians who do not agree with them in speech.

Thus having ceased from the work of the channel, Necos betook himself to waging wars, and triremes were built by him, some for the Northern Sea and others in the Arabian gulf for the Erythraian Sea; and of these the sheds are still to be seen. These ships he used when he needed them; and also on land Necos engaged battle at Magdolos with the Syrians, and conquered them; and after this he took Cadytis, which is a great city of Syria: and the dress which he wore when he made these conquests he dedicated to Apollo, sending it to Branchidai of the Milesians. After this, having reigned in all sixteen years, he brought his life to an end, and handed on the kingdom to Psammis his son.

While this Psammis was king of Egypt, there came to him men sent by the Eleians, who boasted that they ordered the contest at Olympia in the most just and honourable manner possible and thought that not even the Egyptians, the wisest of men, could find out anything besides, to be added to their rules. Now when the Eleians came to Egypt and said that for which they had come, then this king called together those of the Egyptians who were reputed the wisest, and when the Egyptians had come together they heard the Eleians tell of all that which it was their part to do in regard to the contest; and when they had related everything, they said that they had come to learn in addition anything which the Egyptians might be able to find out besides, which was juster than this. They then having consulted together asked the Eleians whether their own citizens took part in the contest; and they said that it was permitted to any one who desired it, both of their own people and of the other Hellenes equally, to take part in the contest: upon which the Egyptians said that in so ordering the games they had wholly missed the mark of justice; for it could not be but that they would take part with the man of their own State, if he was contending, and so act unfairly to the stranger: but if they really desired, as they said, to order the games justly, and if this was the cause for which they had come to Egypt, they advised them to order the contest so as to be for strangers alone to contend in, and that no Eleian should be permitted to contend. Such was the suggestion made by the Egyptians to the Eleians.

When Psammis had been king of Egypt for only six years and had made an expedition to Ethiopia and immediately afterwards had ended his life, Apries the son of Psammis received the kingdom in succession. This man came to be the most prosperous of all the kings up to that time except only his forefather Psammeticos; and he reigned five-and-twenty years, during which he led an army against Sidon and fought a sea-fight with the king of Tyre. Since however it was fated that evil should come upon him, it came by occasion of a matter which I shall relate at greater length in the Libyan history, and at present but shortly. Apries having sent a great expedition against the Kyrenians, met with correspondingly great disaster; and the Egyptians considering him to blame for this revolted from him, supposing that Apries had with forethought sent them out to evident calamity, in order (as they said) that there might be a slaughter of them, and he might the more securely rule over the other Egyptians. Being indignant at this, both these men who had returned from the expedition and also the friends of those who had perished made revolt openly.

Hearing this Apries sent to them Amasis, to cause them to cease by persuasion; and when he had come and was seeking to restrain the Egyptians, as he was speaking and telling them not to do so, one of the Egyptians stood up behind him and put a helmet upon his head, saying as he did so that he put it on to crown him king. And to him this that was done was in some degree not unwelcome, as he proved by his behaviour; for as soon as the revolted Egyptians had set him up as king, he prepared to march against Apries: and Apries hearing this sent to Amasis one of the Egyptians who were about his own person, a man of reputation, whose name was Patarbemis, enjoining him to bring Amasis alive into his presence. When this Patarbemis came and summoned Amasis, the latter, who happened to be sitting on horseback, lifted up his leg and behaved in an unseemly manner, bidding him take that back to Apries. Nevertheless, they say, Patarbemis made demand of him that he should go to the king, seeing that the king had sent to summon him; and he answered him that he had for some time past been preparing to do so, and that Apries would have no occasion to find fault with him. Then Patarbemis both perceiving his intention from that which he said, and also seeing his preparations, departed in haste, desiring to make known as quickly as possible to the king the things which were being done: and when he came back to Apries not bringing Amasis, the king paying no regard to that which he said, but being moved by violent anger, ordered his ears and his nose to be cut off. And the rest of the Egyptians who still remained on his side, when they saw the man of most repute among them thus suffering shameful outrage, waited no longer but joined the others in revolt, and delivered themselves over to Amasis.

Then Apries having heard this also, armed his foreign mercenaries and marched against the Egyptians: now he had about him Carian and Ionian mercenaries to the number of thirty thousand; and his royal palace was in the city of Saïs, of great size and worthy to be seen. So Apries and his army were going against the Egyptians, and Amasis and those with him were going against the mercenaries; and both sides came to the city of Momemphis and were about to make trial of one another in fight.

Now of the Egyptians there are seven classes, and of these one class is called that of the priests, and another that of the warriors, while the others are the cowherds, swineherds, shopkeepers, interpreters, and boatmen. This is the number of the classes of the Egyptians, and their names are given them from the occupations which they follow. Of them the warriors are called Calasirians and Hermotybians, and they are of the following districts, —for all Egypt is divided into districts.

The districts of the Hermotybians are those of Busiris, Saïs, Chemmis, Papremis, the island called Prosopitis, and the half of Natho,—of these districts are the Hermotybians, who reached when most numerous the number of sixteen myriads. Of these not one has learnt anything of handicraft, but they are given up to war entirely.

Again the districts of the Calasirians are those of Thebes, Bubastis, Aphthis, Tanis, Mendes, Sebennytos, Athribis, Pharbaithos, Thmuïs Onuphis, Anytis, Myecphoris,—this last is on an island opposite to the city of Bubastis. These are the districts of the Calasirians; and they reached, when most numerous, to the number of five-and-twenty myriads of men; nor is it lawful for these, any more than for the others, to practise any craft; but they practise that which has to do with war only, handing down the tradition from father to son.

Now whether the Hellenes have learnt this also from the Egyptians, I am not able to say for certain, since I see that the Thracians also and Scythians and Persians and Lydians and almost all the Barbarians esteem those of their citizens who learn the arts, and the descendants of them, as less honourable than the rest; while those who have got free from all practice of manual arts are accounted noble, and especially those who are devoted to war: however that may be, the

Hellenes have all learnt this, and especially the Lacedemonians; but the Corinthians least of all cast slight upon those who practise handicrafts.

The following privilege was specially granted to this class and to none others of the Egyptians except the priests, that is to say, each man had twelve yokes of land specially granted to him free from imposts: now the yoke of land measures a hundred Egyptian cubits every way, and the Egyptian cubit is, as it happens, equal to that of Samos. This, I say, was a special privilege granted to all, and they also had certain advantages in turn and not the same men twice; that is to say, a thousand of the Calasirians and a thousand of the Hermotybians acted as body-guard to the king during each year; and these had besides their yokes of land an allowance given them for each day of five pounds weight of bread to each man, and two pounds of beef, and four half-pints of wine. This was the allowance given to those who were serving as the king's bodyguard for the time being.

So when Apries leading his foreign mercenaries, and Amasis at the head of the whole body of the Egyptians, in their approach to one another had come to the city of Momemphis, they engaged battle: and although the foreign troops fought well, yet being much inferior in number they were worsted by reason of this. But Apries is said to have supposed that not even a god would be able to cause him to cease from his rule, so firmly did he think that it was established. In that battle then, I say, he was worsted, and being taken alive was brought away to the city of Saïs, to that which had formerly been his own dwelling but from thenceforth was the palace of Amasis. There for some time he was kept in the palace, and Amasis dealt well with him; but at last, since the Egyptians blamed him, saying that he acted not rightly in keeping alive him who was the greatest foe both to themselves and to him, therefore he delivered Apries over to the Egyptians; and they strangled him, and after that buried him in the burial-place of his fathers: this is in the temple of Athene, close to the sanctuary, on the left hand as you enter. Now the men of Saïs buried all those of this district who had been kings, within the temple; for the tomb of Amasis also, though it is further from the sanctuary than that of Apries and his forefathers, yet this too is within the court of the temple, and it consists of a colonnade of stone of great size, with pillars carved to imitate date-palms, and otherwise sumptuously adorned; and within the colonnade are double-doors, and inside the doors a sepulchral chamber.

Also at Saïs there is the burial-place of him whom I account it not pious to name in connexion with such a matter, which is in the temple of Athene behind the house of the goddess, stretching along the whole wall of it; and in the sacred enclosure stand great obelisks of stone, and near them is a lake adorned with an edging of stone and fairly made in a circle, being in size, as it seemed to me, equal to that which is called the "Round Pool" in Delos.

On this lake they perform by night the show of his sufferings, and this the Egyptians call Mysteries. Of these things I know more fully in detail how they take place, but I shall leave this unspoken; and of the mystic rites of Demeter, which the Hellenes call thesmophoria, of these also, although I know, I shall leave unspoken all except so much as piety permits me to tell. The daughters of Danaos were they who brought this rite out of Egypt and taught it to the women of the Pelasgians; then afterwards when all the inhabitants of Peloponnese were driven out by the Dorians, the rite was lost, and only those who were left behind of the Peloponnesians and not driven out, that is to say the Arcadians, preserved it.

Apries having thus been overthrown, Amasis became king, being of the district of Saïs, and the name of the city whence he was is Siuph. Now at the first the Egyptians despised Amasis and held him in no great regard, because he had been a man of the people and was of no distinguished family; but afterwards Amasis won them over to himself by wisdom and not wilfulness. Among innumerable other things of price which he had, there was a foot-basin of gold in which both Amasis himself and all his guests were wont always to wash their feet. This he broke up, and of it he caused to be made the image of a god, and set it up in the city, where it was most convenient; and the Egyptians went continually to visit the image and did great reverence to it. Then Amasis, having learnt that which was done by the men of the city, called together the Egyptians and made known to them the matter, saying that the image had been produced from the foot-basin, into which formerly the Egyptians used to vomit and make water, and in which they washed their feet, whereas now they did to it great reverence; and just so, he continued, had he himself now fared, as the foot-basin; for though formerly he was a man of the people, yet now he was their king, and he bade them accordingly honour him and have regard for him.

In such manner he won the Egyptians to himself, so that they consented to be his subjects; and his ordering of affairs was thus:—In the early morning, and until the time of the filling of the market he did with a good will the business which was brought before him; but after this he passed the time in drinking and in jesting at his boon-companions, and was frivolous and playful. And his friends being troubled at it admonished him in some such words as these: "O king, thou dost not rightly govern thyself in thus letting thyself descend to behaviour so trifling; for thou oughtest rather to have been sitting throughout the day stately upon a stately throne and administering thy business; and so the Egyptians would have been assured that they were ruled by a great man, and thou wouldest have had a better report: but as it is, thou art acting by no means in a kingly fashion." And he answered them thus: "They who have bows stretch them at such time as they wish to use them, and when they have finished using them they loose them again; for if they were stretched tight always they would break, so that the men would not be able to use them when they needed them. So also is the state of man: if he should always be in earnest and not relax himself for sport at the due time, he would either go mad or be struck with stupor before he was aware; and knowing this well, I distribute a portion of the time to each of the two ways of living." Thus he replied to his friends.

It is said however that Amasis, even when he was in a private station, was a lover of drinking and of jesting, and not at all seriously disposed; and whenever his means of livelihood failed him through his drinking and luxurious living, he would go about and steal; and they from whom he stole would charge him with having their property, and when he denied it would bring him before the judgment of an Oracle, whenever there was one in their place; and many times he was convicted by the Oracles and many times he was absolved: and then when finally he became king he did as follows:—as many of the gods as had absolved him and pronounced him not to be a thief, to their temples he paid no regard, nor gave anything for the further adornment of them, nor even visited them to offer sacrifice, considering them to be worth nothing and to possess lying Oracles; but as many as had convicted him of being a thief, to these he paid very great regard, considering them to be truly gods, and to present Oracles which did not lie.

First in Saïs he built and completed for Athene a temple-gateway which is a great marvel, and he far surpassed herein all who had done the like before, both in regard to height and greatness, so large are the stones and of such quality. Then secondly he dedicated great colossal statues and man-headed sphinxes very large, and for restoration he brought other stones of monstrous size. Some of these he caused to be brought from the stone-quarries which are opposite Memphis, others of very great size from the city of Elephantine, distant a voyage of not less than twenty days from Saïs: and of them all I marvel most at this, namely a monolith chamber which he brought from the city of Elephantine; and they were three years engaged in bringing this, and two thousand men were appointed to convey it, who all were of the class of boatmen. Of this house the length outside is one-and-twenty cubits, the breadth is fourteen cubits, and the height eight. These are the measures of the monolith house outside; but the length inside is eighteen cubits and five-sixths of a cubit, the breadth twelve cubits, and the height five cubits. This lies by the side of the entrance to the temple; for within the temple they did not draw it, because, as it said, while the house was being drawn along, the chief artificer of it groaned aloud, seeing that much time had been spent and he was wearied by the work; and Amasis took it to heart as a warning and did not allow them to draw it further onwards. Some say on the other hand that a man was killed by it, of those who were heaving it with levers, and that it was not drawn in for that reason.

Amasis also dedicated in all the other temples which were of repute, works which are worth seeing for their size, and among them also at Memphis the colossal statue which lies on its back in front of the temple of Hephaistos, whose length is five-and-seventy feet; and on the same base made of the same stone are set two colossal statues, each of twenty feet in length, one on this side and the other on that side of the large statue. There is also another of stone of the same size in Saïs, lying in the same manner as that at Memphis. Moreover Amasis was he who built and finished for Isis her temple at Memphis, which is of great size and very worthy to be seen.

In the reign of Amasis it is said that Egypt became more prosperous than at any other time before, both in regard to that which comes to the land from the river and in regard to that which comes from the land to its inhabitants, and that at this time the inhabited towns in it numbered in all twenty thousand. It was Amasis too who established the law that every year each one of the Egyptians should declare to the ruler of his district, from what source he got his livelihood, and if any man did not do this or did not make declaration of an honest way of living, he should be punished with death. Now Solon the Athenian received from Egypt this law and had it enacted for the Athenians, and they have continued to observe it, since it is a law with which none can find fault.

Moreover Amasis became a lover of the Hellenes; and besides other proofs of friendship which he gave to several among them, he also granted the city of Naucratis for those of them who came to Egypt to dwell in; and to those who did not desire to stay, but who made voyages thither, he granted portions of land to set up altars and make sacred enclosures for their gods. Their greatest enclosure and that one which has most name and is most frequented is called the Hellenion, and this was established by the following cities in common:—of the Ionians Chios, Teos, Phocaia, Clazomenai, of the Dorians Rhodes, Cnidos, Halicarnassos, Phaselis, and of the Aiolians Mytilene alone. To these belongs this enclosure and these are the cities which appoint superintendents of the port; and all other cities which claim a share in it, are making a claim without any right. Besides this the Eginetans established on their own account a sacred enclosure dedicated to Zeus, the Samians one to Hera, and the Milesians one to Apollo.

Now in old times Naucratis alone was an open trading-place, and no other place in Egypt: and if any one came to any other of the Nile mouths, he was compelled to swear that he came not thither of his own will, and when he had thus sworn his innocence he had to sail with his ship to the Canobic mouth, or if it were not possible to sail by reason of contrary winds, then he had to carry his cargo round the head of the Delta in boats to Naucratis: thus highly was Naucratis privileged.

Moreover when the Amphictyons had let out the contract for building the temple which now exists at Delphi, agreeing to pay a sum of three hundred talents, (for the temple which formerly stood there had been burnt down of itself), it fell to the share of the people of Delphi to provide the fourth part of the payment; and accordingly the Delphians went about to various cities and collected contributions. And when they did this they got from Egypt as much as from any place, for Amasis gave them a thousand talents' weight of alum, while the Hellenes who dwelt in Egypt gave them twenty pounds of silver.

Also with the people of Kyrene Amasis made an agreement for friendship and alliance; and he resolved too to marry a wife from thence, whether because he desired to have a wife of Hellenic race, or apart from that, on account of friendship for the people of Kyrene: however that may be, he married, some say the daughter of Battos, others of Arkesilaos, and others of Critobulos, a man of repute among the citizens; and her name was Ladike. Now whenever Amasis lay with her he found himself unable to have intercourse, but with his other wives he associated as he was wont; and as this happened repeatedly, Amasis said to his wife, whose name was Ladike: "Woman, thou hast given me drugs, and thou shalt surely perish more miserably than any other woman." Then Ladike, when by her denials Amasis was not at all appeased in his anger against her, made a vow in her soul to Aphrodite, that if Amasis on that night had intercourse with her (seeing that this was the remedy for her danger), she would send an image to be dedicated to her at Kyrene; and after the vow immediately Amasis had intercourse, and from thenceforth whenever Amasis came in to her he had intercourse with her; and after this he became very greatly attached to her. And Ladike paid the vow that she had made to the goddess; for she had an image made and sent it to Kyrene, and it was still preserved even to my own time, standing with its face turned away from the city of the Kyrenians. This Ladike Cambyses, having conquered Egypt and heard from her who she was, sent back unharmed to Kyrene.

Amasis also dedicated offerings in Hellas, first at Kyrene an image of Athene covered over with gold and a figure of himself made like by painting; then in the temple of Athene at Lindson two images of stone and a corslet of linen worthy to be seen; and also at Samos two wooden figures of himself dedicated to Hera, which were standing even to my own time in the great temple, behind the doors. Now at Samos he dedicated offerings because of the guest-friendship between himself and Polycrates the son of Aiakes; at Lindos for no guest-friendship but because the temple of Athene at Lindos is said to have been founded by the daughters of Danaos, who had touched land there at the time when they were fleeing from the sons of Aigyptos. These offerings were dedicated by Amasis; and he was the first of men who conquered Cyprus and subdued it so that it paid him tribute.

Book III

The Third Book of the Histories, Called Thaleia

Against this Amasis then Cambyses the son of Cyrus was making his march, taking with him not only other nations of which he was ruler, but also Hellenes, both Ionians and Aiolians: and the cause of the expedition was as follows:—Cambyses sent an envoy to Egypt and asked Amasis to give him his daughter; and he made the request by counsel of an Egyptian, who brought this upon Amasis having a quarrel with him for the following reason:—at the time when Cyrus sent to Amasis and asked him for a physician of the eyes, whosoever was the best of those in Egypt, Amasis had selected him from all the physicians in Egypt and had torn him away from his wife and children and delivered him up to Persia. Having, I say, this cause of quarrel, the Egyptian urged Cambyses on by his counsel bidding him ask Amasis for his daughter, in order that he might either be grieved if he gave her, or if he refused to give her, might offend Cambyses. So Amasis, who was vexed by the power of the Persians and afraid of it, knew neither how to give nor how to refuse: for he was well assured that Cambyses did not intend to have her as his wife but as a concubine. So making account of the matter thus, he did as follows:—there was a daughter of Apries the former king, very tall and comely of form and the only person left of his house, and her name was Nitetis. This girl Amasis adorned with raiment and with gold, and sent her away to Persia as his own daughter: but after a time, when Cambyses saluted her calling her by the name of her father, the girl said to him: "O king, thou dost not perceive how thou hast been deceived by Amasis; for he adorned me with ornaments and sent me away giving me to thee as his own daughter, whereas in truth I am the daughter of Apries against whom Amasis rose up with the Egyptians and murdered him, who was his lord and master." These words uttered and this occasion having arisen, led Cambyses the son of Cyrus against Egypt, moved to very great anger.

Such is the report made by the Persians; but as for the Egyptians they claim Cambyses as one of themselves, saying that he was born of this very daughter of Apries; for they say that Cyrus was he who sent to Amasis for his daughter, and not Cambyses. In saying this however they say not rightly; nor can they have failed to observe (for the Egyptians fully as well as any other people are acquainted with the laws and customs of the Persians), first that it is not customary among them for a bastard to become king, when there is a son born of a true marriage, and secondly that Cambyses was the son of Cassandane the daughter of Pharnaspes, a man of the Achaimenid family, and not the son of the Egyptian woman: but they pervert the truth of history, claiming to be kindred with the house of Cyrus. Thus it is with these matters; and the following story is also told, which for my part I do not believe, namely that one of the Persian women came in to the wives of Cyrus, and when she saw standing by the side of Cassandane children comely of form and tall, she was loud in her praises of them, expressing great admiration; and Cassandane, who was the wife of Cyrus, spoke as follows: "Nevertheless, though I am the mother of such children of these, Cyrus treats me with dishonour and holds in honour her whom he has brought in from Egypt." Thus she spoke, they say, being vexed by Nitetis, and upon that Cambyses the elder of her sons said: "For this cause, mother, when I am grown to be a man, I will make that which is above in Egypt to be below, and that which is below above." This he is reported to have said when he was perhaps about ten years old, and the women were astonished by it: and he, they say, kept it ever in mind, and so at last when he had become a man and had obtained the royal power, he made the expedition against Egypt.

Another thing also contributed to this expedition, which was as follows:—There was among the foreign mercenaries of Amasis a man who was by race of Halicarnassos, and his name was Phanes, one who was both capable in judgment and valiant in that which pertained to war. This Phanes, having (as we may suppose) some quarrel with Amasis, fled away from Egypt in a ship, desiring to come to speech with Cambyses: and as he was of no small repute among the mercenaries and was very closely acquainted with all the affairs of Egypt, Amasis pursued him and considered it a matter of some moment to capture him: and he pursued by sending after him the most trusted of his eunuchs with a trireme, who captured him in Lykia; but having captured him he did not bring him back to Egypt, since Phanes got the better of him by cunning; for he made his guards drunk and escaped to Persia. So when Cambyses had made his resolve to march upon Egypt, and was in difficulty about the march, as to how he should get safely through the waterless region, this man came to him and besides informing of the other matters of Amasis, he instructed him also as to the march, advising him to send to the king of the Arabians and ask that he would give him safety of passage through this region.

Now by this way only is there a known entrance to Egypt: for from Phenicia to the borders of the city of Cadytis belongs to the Syrians who are called of Palestine, and from Cadytis, which is a city I suppose not much less than Sardis, from this city the trading stations on the sea-coast as far as the city of Ienysos belong to the king of Arabia, and then from Ienysos again the country belongs to the Syrians as far as the Serbonian lake, along the side of which Mount Casion extends towards the Sea. After that, from the Serbonian lake, in which the story goes that Typhon is concealed, from this point onwards the land is Egypt. Now the region which lies between the city of Ienysos on the one hand and Mount Casion and the Serbonian lake on the other, which is of no small extent but as much as a three days' journey, is grievously destitute of water.

. And one thing I shall tell of, which few of those who go in ships to Egypt have observed, and it is this:—into Egypt from all parts of Hellas and also from Phenicia are brought twice every year earthenware jars full of wine, and yet it may almost be said that you cannot see there one single empty wine-jar.

In what manner, then, it will be asked, are they used up? This also I will tell. The head-man of each place must collect all the earthenware jars from his own town and convey them to Memphis, and those at Memphis must fill them with water and convey them to these same waterless regions of Syria: this the jars which come regularly to Egypt and are emptied there, are carried to Syria to be added to that which has come before. It was the Persians who thus prepared this approach to Egypt, furnishing it with water in the manner which has been said, from the time when they first took possession of Egypt: but at the time of which I speak, seeing that water was not yet provided, Cambyses, in accordance with what he was told by his Halicarnassian guest, sent envoys to the Arabian king and from him asked and obtained the safe passage, having given him pledges of friendship and received them from him in return.

Now the Arabians have respect for pledges of friendship as much as those men in all the world who regard them most; and they give them in the following manner:—A man different from those who desire to give the pledges to one another, standing in the midst between the two, cuts with a sharp stone the inner parts of the hands, along by the thumbs, of those who are giving the pledges to one another, and then he takes a thread from the cloak of each one and smears with the blood seven stones laid in the midst between them; and as he does this he calls upon Dionysos and Urania. When the man has completed these ceremonies, he who has given the pledges commends to the care of his friends the stranger (or the fellow-tribesman, if he is giving the pledges to one who is a member of his tribe), and the friends think it right that they also should have regard for the pledges given. Of gods they believe in Dionysos and Urania alone: moreover they say that the cutting of their hair is done after the same fashion as that of Dionysos himself; and they cut their hair in a circle round, shaving away the hair of the temples. Now they call Dionysos Orotalt and Urania they call Alilat.

So then when the Arabian king had given the pledge of friendship to the men who had come to him from Cambyses, he contrived as follows:—he took skins of camels and filled them with water and loaded them upon the backs of all the living camels that he had; and having so done he drove them to the waterless region and there awaited the army of Cambyses. This which has been related is the more credible of the accounts given, but the less credible must also be related, since it is a current account. There is a great river in Arabia called Corys, and this runs out into the Sea which is called Erythraian. From this river then it is said that the king of the Arabians, having got a conduit pipe made by sewing together raw ox-hides and other skins, of such a length as to reach to the waterless region, conducted the water through these forsooth, and had great cisterns dug in the waterless region, that they might receive the water and preserve it. Now it is a journey of twelve days from the river to this waterless region; and moreover the story says that he conducted the water by three conduit-pipes to three different parts of it.

Meanwhile Psammenitos the son of Amasis was encamped at the Pelusian mouth of the Nile waiting for the coming of Cambyses: for Cambyses did not find Amasis yet living when he marched upon Egypt, but Amasis had died after having reigned forty and four years during which no great misfortune had befallen him: and when he had died and had been embalmed he was buried in the burial-place in the temple, which he had built for himself. Now when Psammenitos son of Amasis was reigning as king, there happened to the Egyptians a prodigy, the greatest that had ever happened: for rain fell at Thebes in Egypt, where never before had rain fallen nor afterwards down to my time, as the Thebans themselves say; for in the upper parts of Egypt no rain falls at all: but at the time of which I speak rain fell at Thebes in a drizzling shower.

Now when the Persians had marched quite through the waterless region and were encamped near the Egyptians with design to engage battle, then the foreign mercenaries of the Egyptian king, who were Hellenes and Carians, having a quarrel with Phanes because he had brought against Egypt an army of foreign speech, contrived against him as follows:—Phanes had children whom he had left behind in Egypt: these they brought to their camp and into the sight of their father, and they set up a mixing-bowl between the two camps, and after that they brought up the children one by one and cut their throats so that the blood ran into the bowl. Then when they had gone through the whole number of the children, they brought and poured into the bowl both wine and water, and not until the mercenaries had all drunk of the blood, did they engage battle. Then after a battle had been fought with great stubbornness, and very many had fallen of both the armies, the Egyptians at length turned to flight.

I was witness moreover of a great marvel, being informed of it by the natives of the place; for of the bones scattered about of those who fell in this fight, each side separately, since the bones of the Persians were lying apart on one side according as they were divided at first, and those of the Egyptians on the other, the skulls of the Persians are so weak that if you shall hit them only with a pebble you will make a hole in them, while those of the Egyptians are so exceedingly strong that you would hardly break them if you struck them with a large stone. The cause of it, they say, was this, and I for my part readily believe them, namely that the Egyptians beginning from their early childhood shave their heads, and the bone is thickened by exposure to the sun: and this is also the cause of their not becoming bald-headed; for among the Egyptians you see fewer bald-headed men than among any other race. This then is the reason why these have their skulls strong; and the reason why the Persians have theirs weak is that they keep them delicately in the shade from the first by wearing tiaras, that is felt caps. So far of this: and I saw also a similar thing to this at Papremis, in the case of those who were slain together with Achaimenes the son of Dareios, by Inaros the Libyan.

The Egyptians when they turned to flight from the battle fled in disorder: and they being shut up in Memphis, Cambyses sent a ship of Mytilene up the river bearing a Persian herald, to summon the Egyptians to make terms of surrender; but they, when they saw the ship had entered into Memphis, pouring forth in a body from the fortress both destroyed the ship and also tore the men in it limb from limb, and so bore them into the fortress. After this the Egyptians being besieged, in course of time surrendered themselves; and the Libyans who dwell on the borders of Egypt, being struck with terror by that which had happened to Egypt, delivered themselves up without resistance, and they both laid on themselves a tribute and sent presents: likewise also those of Kyrene and Barca, being struck with terror equally with the Libyans, acted in a similar manner: and Cambyses accepted graciously the gifts which came from the Libyans, but as for those which came from the men of Kyrene, finding fault with them, as I suppose, because they were too small in amount (for the Kyrenians sent in fact five hundred pounds' weight of silver), he took the silver by handfuls and scattered it with his own hand among his soldiers.

On the tenth day after that on which he received the surrender of the fortress of Memphis, Cambyses set the king of the Egyptians Psammenitos, who had been king for six months, to sit in the suburb of the city, to do him dishonour,—him I say with other Egyptians he set there, and he proceeded to make trial of his spirit as follows:—having arrayed his daughter in the clothing of a slave, he sent her forth with a pitcher to fetch water, and with her he sent also other maidens chosen from the daughters of the chief men, arrayed as was the daughter of the king: and as the maidens were passing by their fathers with cries and lamentation, the other men all began to cry out and lament aloud, seeing that their children had been evilly entreated, but Psammenitos when he saw it before his eyes and perceived it bent himself down to the earth. Then when the water-bearers had passed by, next Cambyses sent his son with two thousand Egyptians besides who were of the same age, with ropes bound round their necks and bits placed in their mouths; and these were being led away to execution to avenge the death of the Mytilenians who had been destroyed at Memphis with their ship: for the Royal Judges had decided that for each man ten of the noblest Egyptians should lose their lives in retaliation. He then, when he saw them passing out by him and perceived that his son was leading the way to die, did the same as he had done with respect to his daughter, while the other Egyptians who sat round him were lamenting and showing signs of grief. When these also had passed by, it chanced that a man of his table companions, advanced in years, who had been deprived of all his possessions and had nothing except such things as a beggar possesses, and was asking alms from the soldiers, passed by Psammenitos the son of Amasis and the Egyptians who were sitting in the suburb of the city: and when Psammenitos saw him he uttered a great cry of lamentation, and he called his companion by name and beat himself upon the head. Now there was, it seems, men set to watch him, who made known to Cambyses all that he did on the occasion of each going forth: and Cambyses marvelled at that which he did, and he sent a messenger and asked him thus: "Psammenitos, thy master Cambyses asks thee for what reason, when thou sawest thy daughter evilly entreated and thy son going to death, thou didst not cry aloud nor lament for them, whereas thou didst honour with these signs of grief the beggar who, as he hears from others, is not in any way related to thee?" Thus he asked, and the other answered as follows: "O son of Cyrus, my own troubles were too great for me to lament them aloud, but the trouble of my companion was such as called for tears, seeing that he has been deprived of great wealth, and has come to beggary upon the threshold of old age." When this saying was reported by the messenger, it seemed to them that it was well spoken; and, as is reported by the Egyptians, Croesus shed tears (for he also, as fortune would have it, had accompanied Cambyses to Egypt) and the Persians who were present shed tears also; and there entered some pity into Cambyses himself, and forthwith he bade them save the life of the son of Psammenitos from among those who were being put to death, and also he bade them raise Psammenitos himself from his place in the suburb of the city and bring him into his own presence.

As for the son, those who went for him found that he was no longer alive, but had been cut down first of all, but Psammenitos himself they raised from his place and brought him into the presence of Cambyses, with whom he continued to live for the rest of his time without suffering any violence; and if he had known how to keep himself from meddling with mischief, he would have received Egypt so as to be ruler of it, since the Persians are wont to honour the sons of kings, and even if the kings have revolted from them, they give back the power into the hands of their sons. Of this, namely that it is their established rule to act so, one may judge by many instances besides and especially by the case of Thannyras the son of Inaros, who received back the power which his father had, and by that of Pausiris the son of Amyrtaios, for he too received back the power of his father: yet it is certain that no men ever up to this time did more evil to the Persians than Inaros and Amyrtaios. As it was, however, Psammenitos devised evil and received the due reward: for he was found to be inciting the Egyptians to revolt; and when this became known to Cambyses, Psammenitos drank bull's blood and died forthwith. Thus he came to his end.

From Memphis Cambyses came to the city of Saïs with the purpose of doing that which in fact he did: for when he had entered into the palace of Amasis, he forthwith gave command to bring the corpse of Amasis forth out of his burial-place; and when this had been accomplished, he gave command to scourge it and pluck out the hair and stab it, and to do to it dishonour in every possible way besides: and when they had done this too until they were wearied out, for the corpse being embalmed held out against the violence and did not fall to pieces in any part, Cambyses gave command to consume it with fire, enjoining thereby a thing which was not permitted by religion: for the Persians hold fire to be a god. To consume corpses with fire then is by no means according to the custom of either people, of the Persians for the reason which has been mentioned, since they say that it is not right to give the dead body of a man to a god; while the Egyptians have the belief established that fire is a living wild beast, and that it devours everything which it catches, and when it is satiated with the food it dies itself together with that which it devours: but it is by no means their custom to give the corpse of a man to wild beasts, for which reason they embalm it, that it may not be eaten by worms as it lies in the tomb. Thus then Cambyses was enjoining them to do that which is not permitted by the customs of either people. However, the Egyptians say that it was not Amasis who suffered this outrage, but another of the Egyptians who was of the same stature of body as Amasis; and that to him the Persians did outrage, thinking that they were doing it to Amasis: for they say that Amasis learnt from an Oracle that which was about to happen with regard to himself after his death; and accordingly, to avert the evil which threatened to come upon him, he buried the dead body of this man who was scourged within his own sepulchral chamber near the doors, and enjoined his son to lay his own body as much as possible in the inner recess of the chamber. These injunctions, said to have been given by Amasis with regard to his burial and with regard to the man mentioned, were not in my opinion really given at all, but I think that the Egyptians make pretence of it from pride and with no good ground.

After this Cambyses planned three several expeditions, one against the Carthaginians, another against the Ammonians, and a third against the "Long-lived" Ethiopians, who dwell in that part of Libya which is by the Southern Sea: and in forming these designs he resolved to send his naval force against the Carthaginians, and a body chosen from his land-army against the Ammonians; and to the Ethiopians to send spies first, both to see whether the table of the Sun existed really, which is said to exist among these Ethiopians, and in addition to this to spy out all else, but pretending to be bearers of gifts for their king.

. Now the table of the Sun is said to be as follows:—there is a meadow in the suburb of their city full of flesh-meat boiled of all four-footed creatures; and in this, it is said, those of the citizens who are in authority at the time place the flesh by night, managing the matter carefully, and by day any man who wishes comes there and feasts himself; and the natives (it is reported) say that the earth of herself produces these things continually.

Of such nature is the so-called table of the Sun said to be. So when Cambyses had resolved to send the spies, forthwith he sent for those men of the Ichthyophagoi who understood the Ethiopian tongue, to come from the city of Elephantine: and while they were going to fetch these men, he gave command to the fleet to sail against Carthage: but the Phenicians said that they would not do so, for they were bound not to do so by solemn vows, and they would not be acting piously if they made expedition against their own sons: and as the Phenicians were not willing, the rest were rendered unequal to the attempt. Thus then the Carthaginians escaped being enslaved by the Persians; for Cambyses did not think it right to apply force to compel the Phenicians, both because they had delivered themselves over to the

Persians of their own accord and because the whole naval force was dependent upon the Phenicians. Now the men of Cyprus also had delivered themselves over to the Persians, and were joining in the expedition against Egypt.

Then as soon as the Ichthyophagoi came to Cambyses from Elephantine, he sent them to the Ethiopians, enjoining them what they should say and giving them gifts to bear with them, that is to say a purple garment, and a collar of twisted gold with bracelets, and an alabaster box of perfumed ointment, and a jar of palm-wine. Now these Ethiopians to whom Cambyses was sending are said to be the tallest and the most beautiful of all men; and besides other customs which they are reported to have different from other men, there is especially this, it is said, with regard to their regal power,—whomsoever of the men of their nation they judge to be the tallest and to have strength in proportion to his stature, this man they appoint to reign over them.

So when the Ichthyophagoi had come to this people they presented their gifts to the king who ruled over them, and at the same time they said as follows: "The king of the Persians Cambyses, desiring to become a friend and guest to thee, sent us with command to come to speech with thee, and he gives thee for gifts these things which he himself most delights to use." The Ethiopian however, perceiving that they had come as spies, spoke to them as follows: "Neither did the king of the Persians send you bearing gifts because he thought it a matter of great moment to become my guest-friend, nor do ye speak true things (for ye have come as spies of my kingdom), nor again is he a righteous man; for if he had been righteous he would not have coveted a land other than his own, nor would he be leading away into slavery men at whose hands he has received no wrong. Now however give him this bow and speak to him these words: The king of the Ethiopians gives this counsel to the king of the Persians, that when the Persians draw their bows (of equal size to mine) as easily as I do this, then he should march against the Long-lived Ethiopians, provided that he be superior in numbers; but until that time he should feel gratitude to the gods that they do not put it into the mind of the sons of the Ethiopians to acquire another land in addition to their own."

Having thus said and having unbent the bow, he delivered it to those who had come. Then he took the garment of purple and asked what it was and how it had been made: and when the Ichthyophagoi had told him the truth about the purple-fish and the dyeing of the tissue, he said that the men were deceitful and deceitful also were their garments. Then secondly he asked concerning the twisted gold of the collar and the bracelets; and when the Ichthyophagoi were setting forth to him the manner in which it was fashioned, the king broke into a laugh and said, supposing them to be fetters, that they had stronger fetters than those in their country. Thirdly he asked about the perfumed ointment, and when they had told him of the manner of its making and of the anointing with it, he said the same as he had said before about the garment. Then when he came to the wine, and had learned about the manner of its making, being exceedingly delighted with the taste of the drink he asked besides what food the king ate, and what was the longest time that a Persian man lived. They told him that he ate bread, explaining to him first the manner of growing the wheat, and they said that eighty years was the longest term of life appointed for a Persian man. In answer to this the Ethiopian said that he did not wonder that they lived but a few years, when they fed upon dung; for indeed they would not be able to live even so many years as this, if they did not renew their vigour with the drink, indicating to the Ichthyophagoi the wine; for in regard to this, he said, his people were much behind the Persians.

Then when the Ichthyophagoi asked the king in return about the length of days and the manner of life of his people, he answered that the greater number of them reached the age of a hundred and twenty years, and some surpassed even this; and their food was boiled flesh and their drink was milk. And when the spies marvelled at the number of years, he conducted them to a certain spring, in the water of which they washed and became more sleek of skin, as if it were a spring of oil; and from it there came a scent as it were of violets: and the water of this spring, said the spies, was so exceedingly weak that it was not possible for anything to float upon it, either wood or any of those things which are lighter than wood, but they all went to the bottom. If this water which they have be really such as it is said to be, it would doubtless be the cause why the people are long-lived, as making use of it for all the purposes of life. Then when they departed from this spring, he led them to a prison-house for men, and there all were bound in fetters of gold. Now among these Ethiopians bronze is the rarest and most precious of all things. Then when they had seen the prison-house they saw also the so-called table of the Sun:

, and after this they saw last of all their receptacles of dead bodies, which are said to be made of crystal in the following manner:—when they have dried the corpse, whether it be after the Egyptian fashion or in some other way, they cover it over completely with plaster and then adorn it with painting, making the figure as far as possible like the living man. After this they put about it a block of crystal hollowed out; for this they dig up in great quantity and it is very easy to work: and the dead body being in the middle of the block is visible through it, but produces no unpleasant smell nor any other effect which is unseemly, and it has all its parts visible like the dead body itself. For a year then they who are most nearly related to the man keep the block in their house, giving to the dead man the first share of everything and offering to him sacrifices: and after this period they carry it out and set it up round about the city.

After they had seen all, the spies departed to go back; and when they reported these things, forthwith Cambyses was enraged and proceeded to march his army against the Ethiopians, not having ordered any provision of food nor considered with himself that he was intending to march an army to the furthest extremities of the earth; but as one who is mad and not in his right senses, when he heard the report of the Ichthyophagoi he began the march, ordering those of the Hellenes who were present to remain behind in Egypt, and taking with him his whole land force: and when in the course of his march he had arrived at Thebes, he divided off about fifty thousand of his army, and these he enjoined to make slaves of the Ammonians and to set fire to the seat of the Oracle of Zeus, but he himself with the remainder of his army went on against the Ethiopians. But before the army had passed over the fifth part of the way, all that they had of provisions came to an end completely; and then after the provisions the beasts of burden also were eaten up and came to an end. Now if Cambyses when he perceived this had changed his plan and led his army back, he would have been a wise man in spite of his first mistake; as it was, however, he paid no regard, but went on forward without stopping. The soldiers accordingly, so long as they were able to get anything from the ground, prolonged their lives by eating grass; but when they came to the sand, some did a fearful deed, that is to say, out of each company of ten they selected by lot one of themselves and devoured him: and Cambyses, when he heard it, being alarmed by this eating of one another gave up the expedition against the Ethiopians and set forth to go back again; and he arrived at Thebes having suffered loss of a great number of his army. Then from Thebes he came down to Memphis and allowed the Hellenes to sail away home.

Thus fared the expedition against the Ethiopians: and those of the Persians who had been sent to march against the Ammonians set forth from Thebes and went on their way with guides; and it is known that they arrived at the city of Oasis, which is inhabited by Samians said to be of the Aischrionian tribe, and is distant seven days' journey from Thebes over sandy desert: now this place is called in the speech of the Hellenes the "Isle of the Blessed." It is said that the army reached this place, but from that point onwards, except the Ammonians themselves and those who have heard the account from them, no man is able to say anything about them; for they neither reached the Ammonians nor returned back. This however is added to the story by the Ammonians themselves:—they say that as the army was going from this Oasis through the sandy desert to attack them, and had got to a point about mid-way between them and the Oasis, while they were taking their morning meal a violent South Wind blew upon them, and bearing with it heaps of the desert sand it buried them under it, and so they disappeared and were seen no more. Thus the Ammonians say that it came to pass with regard to this army.

When Cambyses arrived at Memphis, Apis appeared to the Egyptians, whom the Hellenes call Epaphos: and when he had appeared, forthwith the Egyptians began to wear their fairest garments and to have festivities. Cambyses accordingly seeing the Egyptians doing thus, and supposing that they were certainly acting so by way of rejoicing because he had fared ill, called for the officers who had charge of Memphis; and when they had come into his presence, he asked them why when he was at Memphis on the former occasion, the Egyptians were doing nothing of this kind, but only now, when he came there after losing a large part of his army. They said that a god had appeared to them, who was wont to appear at intervals of long time, and that whenever he appeared, then all the Egyptians rejoiced and kept festival. Hearing this Cambyses said that they were lying, and as liars he condemned them to death.

Having put these to death, next he called the priests into his presence; and when the priests answered him after the same manner, he said that it should not be without his knowledge if a tame god had come to the Egyptians; and having so said he bade the priests bring Apis away into his presence: so they went to bring him. Now this Apis-Epaphos is a calf born of a cow who after this is not permitted to conceive any other offspring; and the Egyptians say that a flash of light comes down from heaven upon this cow, and of this she produces Apis. This calf which is called Apis is black and has the following signs, namely a white square upon the forehead, and on the back the likeness of an eagle, and in the tail the hairs are double, and on the tongue there is a mark like a beetle.

When the priests had brought Apis, Cambyses being somewhat affected with madness drew his dagger, and aiming at the belly of Apis, struck his thigh: then he laughed and said to the priests: "O ye wretched creatures, are gods born such as this, with blood and flesh, and sensible of the stroke of iron weapons? Worthy indeed of Egyptians is such a god as this. Ye however at least shall not escape without punishment for making a mock of me." Having thus spoken he ordered those whose duty it was to do such things, to scourge the priests without mercy, and to put to death any one of the other Egyptians whom they should find keeping the festival. Thus the festival of the Egyptians had been brought to an end, and the priests were being chastised, and Apis wounded by the stroke in his thigh lay dying in the temple.

Him, when he had brought his life to an end by reason of the wound, the priests buried without the knowledge of Cambyses: but Cambyses, as the Egyptians say, immediately after this evil deed became absolutely mad, not having been really in his right senses even before that time: and the first of his evil deeds was that he put to death his brother Smerdis, who was of the same father and the same mother as himself. This brother he had sent away from Egypt to Persia in envy, because alone of all the Persians he had been able to draw the bow which the Ichthyophagoi brought from the Ethiopian king, to an extent of about two finger-breadths; while of the other Persians not one had proved able to do this. Then when Smerdis had gone away to Persia, Cambyses saw a vision in his sleep of this kind:—it seemed to him that a messenger came from Persia and reported that Smerdis sitting upon the royal throne had touched the heaven with his head. Fearing therefore with regard to this lest his brother might slay him and reign in his stead, he sent Prexaspes to Persia, the man whom of all the Persians he trusted most, with command to slay him. He accordingly went up to Susa and slew Smerdis; and some say that he took him out of the chase and so slew him, others that he brought him to the Erythraian Sea and drowned him.

This they say was the first beginning of the evil deeds of Cambyses; and next after this he put to death his sister, who had accompanied him to Egypt, to whom also he was married, she being his sister by both parents. Now he took her to wife in the following manner (for before this the Persians had not been wont at all to marry their sisters):—Cambyses fell in love with one of his sisters, and desired to take her to wife; so since he had it in mind to do that which was not customary, he called the Royal Judges and asked them whether there existed any law which permitted him who desired it to marry his sister. Now the Royal Judges are men chosen out from among the Persians, and hold their office until they die or until some injustice is found in them, so long and no longer. These pronounce decisions for the Persians and are the expounders of the ordinances of their fathers, and all matters are referred to them. So when Cambyses asked them, they gave him an answer which was both upright and safe, saying that they found no law which permitted a brother to marry his sister, but apart from that they had found a law to the effect that the king of the Persians might do whatsoever he desired. Thus on the one hand they did not tamper with the law for fear of Cambyses, and at the same time, that they might not perish themselves in maintaining the law, they found another law beside that which was asked for, which was in favour of him who wished to marry his sisters. So Cambyses at that time took to wife her with whom he was in love, but after no long time he took another sister. Of these it was the younger whom he put to death, she having accompanied him to Egypt.

About her death, as about the death of Smerdis, two different stories are told. The Hellenes say that Cambyses had matched a lion's cub in fight with a dog's whelp, and this wife of his was also a spectator of it; and when the whelp was being overcome, another whelp, its brother, broke its chain and came to help it; and having become two instead of one, the whelps then got the better of the cub: and Cambyses was pleased at the sight, but she sitting by him began to weep; and Cambyses perceived it and asked wherefore she wept; and she said that she had wept when she saw that the whelp had come to the assistance of its brother, because she remembered Smerdis and perceived that there was no one who would come to his assistance. The Hellenes say that it was for this saying that she was killed by Cambyses: but the Egyptians say that as they were sitting round at table, the wife took a lettuce and pulled off the leaves all round, and then asked her husband whether the lettuce was fairer when thus plucked round or when covered with leaves, and he said "when covered with leaves": she then spoke thus: "Nevertheless thou didst once produce the likeness of this lettuce, when thou didst strip bare the house of Cyrus." And he moved to anger leapt upon her, being with child, and she miscarried and died.

These were the acts of madness done by Cambyses towards those of his own family, whether the madness was produced really on account of Apis or from some other cause, as many ills are wont to seize upon men; for it is said moreover that Cambyses had from his birth a certain grievous malady, that which is called by some the "sacred" disease: and it was certainly nothing strange that when the body was suffering from a grievous malady, the mind should not be sound either.

The following also are acts of madness which he did to the other Persians:—To Prexaspes, the man whom he honoured most and who used to bear his messages (his son also was cup-bearer to Cambyses, and this too was no small honour),—to him it is said that he spoke as follows: "Prexaspes, what kind of a man do the Persians esteem me to be, and what speech do they hold concerning me?" and he said: "Master, in all other respects thou art greatly commended, but they say that thou art overmuch given to love of wine." Thus he spoke concerning the Persians; and upon that Cambyses was roused to anger, and answered thus: "It appears then that the Persians say I am given to wine, and that therefore I am beside myself and not in my right mind; and their former speech then was not sincere." For before this time, it seems, when the Persians and Croesus were sitting with him in council, Cambyses asked what kind of a man they thought he was as compared with his father Cyrus; and they answered that he was better than his father, for he not only possessed all that his father had possessed, but also in addition to this had acquired Egypt and the Sea. Thus the Persians spoke; but Croesus, who was present and was not satisfied with their judgment, spoke thus to Cambyses: "To me, O son of Cyrus, thou dost not appear to be equal to thy father, for not yet hast thou a son such as he left behind him in you." Hearing this Cambyses was pleased, and commended the judgment of Croesus.

So calling to mind this, he said in anger to Prexaspes: "Learn then now for thyself whether the Persians speak truly, or whether when they say this they are themselves out of their senses: for if I, shooting at thy son there standing before the entrance of the chamber, hit him in the very middle of the heart, the Persians will be proved to be speaking falsely, but if I miss, then thou mayest say that the Persians are speaking the truth and that I am not in my right mind." Having thus said he drew his bow and hit the boy; and when the boy had fallen down, it is said that he ordered them to cut open his body and examine the place where he was hit; and as the arrow was found to be sticking in the heart, he laughed and was delighted, and said to the father of the boy: "Prexaspes, it has now been made evident, as thou seest, that I am not mad, but that it is the Persians who are out of their senses; and now tell me, whom of all men didst thou ever see before this time hit the mark so well in shooting?" Then Prexaspes, seeing that the man was not in his right senses and fearing for himself, said: "Master, I think that not even God himself could have hit the mark so fairly." Thus he did at that time: and at another time he condemned twelve of the Persians, men equal to the best, on a charge of no moment, and buried them alive with the head downwards.

When he was doing these things, Croesus the Lydian judged it right to admonish him in the following words: "O king, do not thou indulge the heat of thy youth and passion in all things, but retain and hold thyself back: it is a good thing to be prudent, and forethought is wise. Thou however are putting to death men who are of thine own people, condemning them on charges of no moment, and thou art putting to death men's sons also. If thou do many such things, beware lest the Persians make revolt from thee. As for me, thy father Cyrus gave me charge, earnestly bidding me to admonish thee, and suggest to thee that which I should find to be good." Thus he counselled him, manifesting goodwill towards him; but Cambyses answered: "Dost thou venture to counsel me, who excellently well didst rule thine own country, and well didst counsel my father, bidding him pass over the river Araxes and go against the Massagetai, when they were willing to pass over into our land, and so didst utterly ruin thyself by ill government of thine own land, and didst utterly ruin Cyrus, who followed thy counsel. However thou shalt not escape punishment now, for know that before this I had very long been desiring to find some occasion against thee." Thus having said he took his bow meaning to shoot him, but Croesus started up and ran out: and so since he could not shoot him, he gave orders to his attendants to take and slay him. The attendants however, knowing his moods, concealed Croesus, with the intention that if Cambyses should change his mind and seek to have Croesus again, they might produce him and receive gifts as the price of saving his life; but if he did not change his mind nor feel desire to have him back, then they might kill him. Not long afterwards Cambyses did in fact desire to have Croesus again, and the attendants perceiving this reported to him that he was still alive: and Cambyses said that he rejoiced with Croesus that he was still alive, but that they who had preserved him should not get off free, but he would put them to death: and thus he did.

Many such acts of madness did he both to Persians and allies, remaining at Memphis and opening ancient tombs and examining the dead bodies. Likewise also he entered into the temple of Hephaistos and very much derided the image of the god: for the image of Hephaistos very nearly resembles the Phenician Pataicoi, which the Phenicians carry about on the prows of their triremes; and for him who has not seen these, I will indicate its nature,—it is the likeness of a dwarfish man. He entered also into the temple of the Cabeiroi, into which it is not lawful for any one to enter except the priest only, and the images there he even set on fire, after much mockery of them. Now these also are like the images of Hephaistos, and it is said that they are the children of that god.

It is clear to me therefore by every kind of proof that Cambyses was mad exceedingly; for otherwise he would not have attempted to deride religious rites and customary observances. For if one should propose to all men a choice, bidding them select the best customs from all the customs that there are, each race of men, after examining them all, would select those of his own people; thus all think that their own customs are by far the best: and so it is not likely that any but a madman would make a jest of such things. Now of the fact that all men are thus wont to think about their customs, we may judge by many other proofs and more specially by this which follows:—Dareios in the course of his reign summoned those of the Hellenes who were present in his land, and asked them for what price they would consent to eat up their fathers when they died; and they answered that for no price would they do so. After this Dareios summoned those Indians who are called Callatians, who eat their parents, and asked them in presence of the Hellenes, who understood what they said by help of an interpreter, for what payment they would consent to consume with fire the bodies of their fathers when they died; and they cried out aloud and bade him keep silence from such words. Thus then these things are established by usage, and I think that Pindar spoke rightly in his verse, when he said that "of all things law is king."

Now while Cambyses was marching upon Egypt, the Lacedemonians also had made an expedition against Samos and against Polycrates the son of Aiakes, who had risen against the government and obtained rule over Samos. At first he had divided the State into three parts and had given a share to his brothers Pantagnotos and Syloson; but afterwards he put to death one of these, and the younger, namely Syloson, he drove out, and so obtained possession of the whole of Samos. Then, being in possession, he made a guest-friendship with Amasis the king of Egypt, sending him gifts and receiving gifts in return from him. After this straightway within a short period of time the power of Polycrates increased rapidly, and there was much fame of it not only in Ionia, but also over the rest of Hellas: for to whatever part he directed his forces, everything went fortunately for him: and he had got for himself a hundred fifty-oared galleys and a thousand archers, and he plundered from all, making no distinction of any; for it was his wont to say that he would win more gratitude from his friend by giving back to him that which he had taken, than by not taking at all. So he had conquered many of the islands and also many cities of the continent, and besides other things he gained the victory in a sea-fight over the Lesbians, as they were coming to help the Milesians with their forces, and conquered them: these men dug the whole trench round the wall of the city of Samos working in chains.

Now Amasis, as may be supposed, did not fail to perceive that Polycrates was very greatly fortunate, and it was to him an object of concern; and as much more good fortune yet continued to come to Polycrates, he wrote upon a paper these words and sent them to Samos: "Amasis to Polycrates thus saith:—It is a pleasant thing indeed to hear that one who is a friend and guest is faring well; yet to me thy great good fortune is not pleasing, since I know that the Divinity is jealous; and I think that I desire, both for myself and for those about whom I have care, that in some of our affairs we should be prosperous and in others should fail, and thus go through life alternately faring well and ill, rather than that we should be prosperous in all things: for never yet did I hear tell of any one who was prosperous in all things and did not come to an utterly evil end at the last. Now therefore do thou follow my counsel and act as I shall say with respect to thy prosperous fortunes. Take thought and consider, and that which thou findest to be the most valued by thee, and for the loss of which thou wilt most be vexed in thy soul, that take and cast away in such a manner that it shall never again come to the sight of men; and if in future from that time forward good fortune does not befall thee in alternation with calamities, apply remedies in the manner by me suggested."

Polycrates, having read this and having perceived by reflection that Amasis suggested to him good counsel, sought to find which one of his treasures he would be most afflicted in his soul to lose; and seeking he found this which I shall say:—he had a signet which he used to wear, enchased in gold and made of an emerald stone; and it was the work of Theodoros the son of Telecles of Samos. Seeing then that he thought it good to cast this away, he did thus:—he manned a fifty-oared galley with sailors and went on board of it himself; and then he bade them put out into the deep sea. And when he had got to a distance from the island, he took off the signet-ring, and in the sight of all who were with him in the ship he threw it into the sea. Thus having done he sailed home; and when he came to his house he mourned for his loss.

But on the fifth or sixth day after these things it happened to him as follows:—a fisherman having caught a large and beautiful fish, thought it right that this should be given as a gift to Polycrates. He bore it therefore to the door of the palace and said that he desired to come into the presence of Polycrates, and when he had obtained this he gave him the fish, saying: "O king, having taken this fish I did not think fit to bear it to the market, although I am one who lives by the labour of his hands; but it seemed to me that it was worthy of thee and of thy monarchy: therefore I bring it and present it to thee." He then, being pleased at the words spoken, answered thus: "Thou didst exceedingly well, and double thanks are due to thee, for thy words and also for thy gift; and we invite thee to come to dinner." The fisherman then, thinking this a great thing, went away to this house; and the servants as they were cutting up the fish found in its belly the signet-ring of Polycrates. Then as soon as they had seen it and taken it up, they bore it rejoicing to Polycrates, and giving him the signet-ring they told him in what manner it had been found: and he perceiving that the matter was of God, wrote upon paper all that he had done and all that had happened to him, and having written he despatched it to Egypt.

Then Amasis, when he had read the paper which had come from Polycrates, perceived that it was impossible for man to rescue man from the event which was to come to pass, and that Polycrates was destined not to have a good end, being prosperous in all things, seeing that he found again even that which he cast away. Therefore he sent an envoy to him in Samos and said that he broke off the guest-friendship; and this he did lest when a fearful and great mishap befell Polycrates, he might himself be grieved in his soul as for a man who was his guest.

It was this Polycrates then, prosperous in all things, against whom the Lacedemonians were making an expedition, being invited by those Samians who afterwards settled at Kydonia in Crete, to come to their assistance. Now Polycrates had sent an envoy to Cambyses the son of Cyrus without the knowledge of the Samians, as he was gathering an army to go against Egypt, and had asked him to send to him in Samos and to ask for an armed force. So Cambyses hearing this very readily sent to Samos to ask Polycrates to send a naval force with him against Egypt: and Polycrates selected of the citizens those whom he most suspected of desiring to rise against him and sent them away in forty triremes, charging Cambyses not to send them back.

Now some say that those of the Samians who were sent away by Polycrates never reached Egypt, but when they arrived on their voyage at Carpathos, they considered with themselves, and resolved not to sail on any further: others say that they reached Egypt and being kept under guard there, they made their escape from thence. Then, as they were sailing in to Samos, Polycrates encountered them with ships and engaged battle with them; and those who were returning home had the better and landed in the island; but having fought a land-battle in the island, they were worsted, and so sailed to Lacedemon. Some however say that those from Egypt defeated Polycrates in the battle; but this in my opinion is not correct, for there would have been no need for them to invite the assistance of the Lacedemonians if they had been able by themselves to bring Polycrates to terms. Moreover, it is not reasonable either, seeing that he had foreign mercenaries and native archers very many in number, to suppose that he was worsted by the returning Samians, who were but few. Then Polycrates gathered together the children and wives of his subjects and confined them in the ship-sheds, keeping them ready so that, if it should prove that his subjects deserted to the side of the returning exiles, he might burn them with the sheds.

When those of the Samians who had been driven out by Polycrates reached Sparta, they were introduced before the magistrates and spoke at length, being urgent in their request. The magistrates however at the first introduction replied that they had forgotten the things which had been spoken at the beginning, and did not understand those which were spoken at the end. After this they were introduced a second time, and bringing with them a bag they said nothing else but this, namely that the bag was in want of meal; to which the others replied that they had overdone it with the bag. However, they resolved to help them.

Then the Lacedemonians prepared a force and made expedition to Samos, in repayment of former services, as the Samians say, because the Samians had first helped them with ships against the Messenians; but the Lacedemonians say that they made the expedition not so much from desire to help the Samians at their request, as to take vengeance on their own behalf for the robbery of the mixing-bowl which they had been bearing as a gift to Croesus, and of the corslet which Amasis the king of Egypt had sent as a gift to them; for the Samians had carried off the corslet also in the year before they took the bowl; and it was of linen with many figures woven into it and embroidered with gold and with cotton; and each thread of this corslet is worthy of admiration, for that being itself fine it has in it three hundred and sixty fibres, all plain to view. Such another as this moreover is that which Amasis dedicated as an offering to Athene at Lindos.

The Corinthians also took part with zeal in this expedition against Samos, that it might be carried out; for there had been an offence perpetrated against them also by the Samians a generation before the time of this expedition and about the same time as the robbery of the bowl. Periander the son of Kypselos had despatched three hundred sons of the chief men of Corcyra to Alyattes at Sardis to be made eunuchs; and when the Corinthians who were conducting the boys had put in to Samos, the Samians, being informed of the story and for what purpose they were being conducted to Sardis, first instructed the boys to lay hold of the temple of Artemis, and then they refused to permit the Corinthians to drag the suppliants away from the temple: and as the Corinthians cut the boys off from supplies of food, the Samians made a festival, which they celebrate even to the present time in the same manner: for when night came on, as long as the boys were suppliants they arranged dances of maidens and youths, and in arranging the dances they made it a rule of the festival that sweet cakes of sesame and honey should be carried, in order that the Corcyrean boys might snatch them and so have support; and this went on so long that at last the Corinthians who had charge of the boys departed and went away; and as for the boys, the Samians carried them back to Corcyra.

Now, if after the death of Periander the Corinthians had been on friendly terms with the Corcyreans, they would not have joined in the expedition against Samos for the cause which has been mentioned; but as it is, they have been ever at variance with one another since they first colonised the island. This then was the cause why the Corinthians had a grudge against the Samians.

Now Periander had chosen out the sons of the chief men of Corcyra and was sending them to Sardis to be made eunuchs, in order that he might have revenge; since the Corcyreans had first begun the offence and had done to him a deed of reckless wrong. For after Periander had killed his wife Melissa, it chanced to him to experience another misfortune in addition to that which had happened to him already, and this was as follows:—He had by Melissa two sons, the one of seventeen and the other of eighteen years. These sons their mother's father Procles, who was despot of Epidauros, sent for to himself and kindly entertained, as was to be expected seeing that they were the sons of his own daughter; and when he was sending them back, he said in taking leave of them: "Do ye know, boys, who it was that killed your mother?" Of this saying the elder of them took no account, but the younger, whose name was Lycophron, was grieved so greatly at hearing it, that when he reached Corinth again he would neither address his father, nor speak to him when his father would have conversed with him, nor give any reply when he asked questions, regarding him as the murderer of his mother. At length Periander being enraged with his son drove him forth out of his house.

And having driven him forth, he asked of the elder son what his mother's father had said to them in his conversation. He then related how Procles had received them in a kindly manner, but of the saying which he had uttered when he parted from them he had no remembrance, since he had taken no note of it. So Periander said that it could not be but that he had suggested to them something, and urged him further with questions; and he after that remembered, and told of this also. Then Periander taking note of it and not desiring to show any indulgence, sent a messenger to those with whom the son who had been driven forth was living at that time, and forbade them to receive him into their houses; and whenever having been driven away from one house he came to another, he was driven away also from this, since Periander threatened those who received him, and commanded them to exclude him; and so being driven away again he would go to another house, where persons lived who were his friends, and they perhaps received him because he was the son of Periander, notwithstanding that they feared.

At last Periander made a proclamation that whosoever should either receive him into their houses or converse with him should be bound to pay a fine to Apollo, stating the amount that it should be. Accordingly, by reason of this proclamation no one was willing either to converse with him or to receive him into their house; and moreover even he himself did not think it fit to attempt it, since it had been forbidden, but he lay about in the porticoes enduring exposure: and on the fourth day after this, Periander seeing him fallen into squalid misery and starvation felt pity for him; and abating his anger he approached him and began to say: "Son, which of these two is to be preferred, the fortune which thou dost now experience and possess, or to inherit the power and wealth which I possess now, by being submissive to thy father's will? Thou however, being my son and the prince of wealthy Corinth, didst choose nevertheless the life of a vagabond by making opposition and displaying anger against him with whom it behoved thee least to deal so; for if any misfortune happened in those matters, for which cause thou hast suspicion against me, this has happened to me first, and I am sharer in the misfortune more than others, inasmuch as I did the deed myself. Do thou however, having learnt by how much to be envied is better than to be pitied, and at the same time what a grievous thing it is to be angry against thy parents and against those who are stronger than thou, come back now to the house." Periander with these words endeavoured to restrain him; but he answered nothing else to his father, but said only that he ought to pay a fine to the god for having come to speech with him. Then Periander, perceiving that the malady of his son was hopeless and could not be overcome, despatched a ship to Corcyra, and so sent him away out of his sight, for he was ruler also of that island; and having sent him away, Periander proceeded to make war against his father-in-law Procles, esteeming him most to blame for the condition in which he was; and he took Epidauros and took also Procles himself and made him a prisoner.

When however, as time went on, Periander had passed his prime and perceived within himself that he was no longer able to overlook and manage the government of the State, he sent to Corcyra and summoned Lycophron to come back and take the supreme power; for in the elder of his sons he did not see the required capacity, but perceived clearly that he was of wits too dull. Lycophron however did not deign even to give an answer to the bearer of his message. Then Periander, clinging still in affection to the youth, sent to him next his own daughter, the sister of Lycophron, supposing that he would yield to her persuasion more than to that of others; and she arrived there and spoke to him thus: "Boy, dost thou desire that both the despotism should fall to others, and also the substance of thy father, carried off as plunder, rather than that thou shouldest return back and possess them? Come back to thy home: cease to torment thyself. Pride is a mischievous possession. Heal not evil with evil. Many prefer that which is reasonable to that which is strictly just; and many ere now in seeking the things of their mother have lost the things of their father. Despotism is an insecure thing, and many desire it: moreover he is now an old man and past his prime. Give not thy good things unto others." She thus said to him the most persuasive things, having been before instructed by her father: but he in answer said, that he would never come to Corinth so long as he heard that his father was yet alive. When she had reported this,

Periander the third time sent an envoy, and said that he desired himself to come to Corcyra, exhorting Lycophron at the same time to come back to Corinth and to be his successor on the throne. The son having agreed to return on these terms, Periander was preparing to sail to Corcyra and his son to Corinth; but the Corcyreans, having learnt all that had taken place, put the young man to death, in order that Periander might not come to their land. For this cause it was that Periander took vengeance on those of Corcyra.

The Lacedemonians then had come with a great armament and were besieging Samos; and having made an attack upon the wall, they occupied the tower which stands by the sea in the suburb of the city, but afterwards when Polycrates came up to the rescue with a large body they were driven away from it. Meanwhile by the upper tower which is upon the ridge of the mountain there had come out to the fight the foreign mercenaries and many of the Samians themselves, and these stood their ground against the Lacedemonians for a short while and then began to fly backwards; and the Lacedemonians followed and were slaying them.

Now if the Lacedemonians there present had all been equal on that day to Archias and Lycopas, Samos would have been captured; for Archias and Lycopas alone rushed within the wall together with the flying Samians, and being shut off from retreat were slain within the city of the Samians. I myself moreover had converse in Pitane (for to that deme he belonged) with the third in descent from this Archias, another Archias the son of Samios the son of Archias, who honoured the Samians of all strangers most; and not only so, but he said that his own father had been called Samios because his father Archias had died by a glorious death in Samos; and he said that he honoured Samians because his grandfather had been granted a public funeral by the Samians.

The Lacedemonians then, when they had been besieging Samos for forty days and their affairs made no progress, set forth to return to Peloponnesus. But according to the less credible account which has been put abroad of these matters Polycrates struck in lead a quantity of a certain native coin, and having gilded the coins over, gave them to the Lacedemonians, and they received them and upon that set forth to depart. This was the first expedition which the Lacedemonians (being Dorians) made into Asia.

Those of the Samians who had made the expedition against Polycrates themselves also sailed away, when the Lacedemonians were about to desert them, and came to Siphnos: for they were in want of money, and the people of Siphnos were then at their greatest height of prosperity and possessed wealth more than all the other islanders, since they had in their island mines of gold and silver, so that there is a treasury dedicated at Delphi with the tithe of the money which came in from these mines, and furnished in a manner equal to the wealthiest of these treasuries: and the people used to divide among themselves the money which came in from the mines every year. So when they were establishing the treasury, they consulted the Oracle as to whether their present prosperity was capable of remaining with them for a long time, and the Pythian prophetess gave them this reply:

"But when with white shall be shining the hall of the city

in Siphnos,

And when the market is white of brow, one wary is needed

Then, to beware of an army of wood and a red-coloured herald."

Now just at that time the market-place and city hall of the Siphnians had been decorated with Parian marble.

This oracle they were not able to understand either then at first or when the Samians had arrived: for as soon as the Samians were putting in to Siphnos they sent one of their ships to bear envoys to the city: now in old times all ships were painted with red, and this was that which the Pythian prophetess was declaring beforehand to the Siphnians, bidding them guard against the "army of wood" and the "red-coloured herald." The messengers accordingly came and asked the Siphnians to lend them ten talents; and as they refused to lend to them, the Samians began to lay waste their lands: so when they were informed of it, forthwith the Siphnians came to the rescue, and having engaged battle with them were defeated, and many of them were cut off by the Samians and shut out of the city; and the Samians after this imposed upon them a payment of a hundred talents.

Then from the men of Hermion they received by payment of money the island of Hydrea, which is near the coast of Peloponnese, and they gave it in charge to the Troizenians, but they themselves settled at Kydonia which is in Crete, not sailing thither for that purpose but in order to drive the Zakynthians out of the island. Here they remained and were prosperous for five years, so much so that they were the builders of the temples which are now existing in Kydonia, and also of the house of Dictyna. In the sixth year however the Eginetans together with the Cretans conquered them in a sea-fight and brought them to slavery; and they cut off the prows of their ships, which were shaped like boars, and dedicated them in the temple of Athene in Egina. This the Eginetans did because they had a grudge against the Samians; for the Samians had first made expedition against Egina, when Amphicrates was king in Samos, and had done much hurt to the Eginetans and suffered much hurt also from them. Such was the cause of this event: and about the Samians I have spoken at greater length, because they have three works which are greater than any others that have been made by Hellenes: first a passage beginning from below and open at both ends, dug through a mountain not less than a hundred and fifty fathoms in height; the length of the passage is seven furlongs and the height and breadth each eight feet, and throughout the whole of it another passage has been dug twenty cubits in depth and three feet in breadth, through which the water is conducted and comes by the pipes to the city, brought from an abundant spring: and the designer of this work was a Megarian, Eupalinos the son of Naustrophos. This is one of the three; and the second is a mole in the sea about the harbour, going down to a depth of as much as twenty fathoms; and the length of the mole is more than two furlongs. The third work which they have executed is a temple larger than all the other temples of which we know. Of this the first designer was Rhoicos the son of Philes, a native of Samos. For this reason I have spoken at greater length of the Samians.

Now while Cambyses the son of Cyrus was spending a long time in Egypt and had gone out of his right mind, there rose up against him two brothers, Magians, of whom the one had been left behind by Cambyses as caretaker of his household. This man, I say, rose up against him perceiving that the occurrence of the death of Smerdis was being kept secret, and that there were but few of the Persians who were aware of it, while the greater number believed without doubt that he was still alive. Therefore he endeavoured to obtain the kingdom, and he formed his plan as follows:—he had a brother (that one who, as I said, rose up with him against Cambyses), and this man in form very closely resembled Smerdis the son of Cyrus, whom Cambyses had slain, being his own brother. He was like Smerdis, I say, in form, and not only so but he had the same name, Smerdis. Having persuaded this man that he would manage everything for him, the Magian Patizeithes brought him and seated him upon the royal throne: and having so done he sent heralds about to the various provinces, and among others one to the army in Egypt, to proclaim to them that they must obey Smerdis the son of Cyrus for the future instead of Cambyses.

So then the other heralds made this proclamation, and also the one who was appointed to go to Egypt, finding Cambyses and his army at Agbatana in Syria, stood in the midst and began to proclaim that which had been commanded to him by the Magian. Hearing this from the herald, and supposing that the herald was speaking the truth and that he had himself been betrayed by Prexaspes, that is to say, that when Prexaspes was sent to kill Smerdis he had not done so, Cambyses looked upon Prexaspes and said: "Prexaspes, was it thus that thou didst perform for me the thing which I gave over to thee to do?" and he said: "Master, the saying is not true that Smerdis thy brother has risen up against thee, nor that thou wilt have any contention arising from him, either great or small: for I myself, having done that which thou didst command me to do, buried him with my own hands. If therefore the dead have risen again to life, then thou mayest expect that Astyages also the Mede will rise up against thee; but if it is as it was beforetime, there is no fear now that any trouble shall spring up for you, at least from him. Now therefore I think it well that some should pursue after the herald and examine him, asking from whom he has come to proclaim to us that we are to obey Smerdis as king."

When Prexaspes had thus spoken, Cambyses was pleased with the advice, and accordingly the herald was pursued forthwith and returned. Then when he had come back, Prexaspes asked him as follows: "Man, thou sayest that thou art come as a messenger from Smerdis the son of Cyrus: now therefore speak the truth and go away in peace. I ask thee whether Smerdis himself appeared before thine eyes and charged thee to say this, or some one of those who serve him." He said: "Smerdis the son of Cyrus I have never yet seen, since the day that king Cambyses marched to Egypt: but the Magian whom Cambyses appointed to be guardian of his household, he, I say, gave me this charge, saying that Smerdis the son of Cyrus was he who laid the command upon me to speak these things to you." Thus he spoke to them, adding no falsehoods to the first, and Cambyses said: "Prexaspes, thou hast done that which was commanded thee like an honest man, and hast escaped censure; but who of the Persians may this be who has risen up against me and usurped the name of Smerdis?" He said: "I seem to myself, O king, to have understanding of this which has come to pass: the Magians have risen against thee, Patizeithes namely, whom thou didst leave as caretaker of thy household, and his brother Smerdis."

Then Cambyses, when he heard the name of Smerdis, perceived at once the true meaning of this report and of the dream, for he thought in his sleep that some one had reported to him that Smerdis was sitting upon the royal throne and had touched the heaven with his head: and perceiving that he had slain his brother without need, he began to lament for Smerdis; and having lamented for him and sorrowed greatly for the whole mishap, he was leaping upon his horse, meaning as quickly as possible to march his army to Susa against the Magian; and as he leapt upon his horse, the cap of his sword-sheath fell off, and the sword being left bare struck his thigh. Having been wounded then in the same part where he had formerly struck Apis the god of the Egyptians, and believing that he had been struck with a mortal blow, Cambyses asked what was the name of that town, and they said "Agbatana." Now even before this he had been informed by the Oracle at the city of Buto that in Agbatana he should bring his life to an end: and he supposed that he should die of old age in Agbatana in Media, where was his chief seat of power; but the oracle, it appeared, meant in Agbatana of Syria. So when by questioning now he learnt the name of the town, being struck with fear both by the calamity caused by the Magian and at the same time by the wound, he came to his right mind, and understanding the meaning of the oracle he said: "Here it is fated that Cambyses the son of Cyrus shall end his life."

So much only he said at that time; but about twenty days afterwards he sent for the most honourable of the Persians who were with him, and said to them as follows: "Persians, it has become necessary for me to make known to you the thing which I was wont to keep concealed beyond all other things. Being in Egypt I saw a vision in my sleep, which I would I had never seen, and it seemed to me that a messenger came from home and reported to me that Smerdis was sitting upon the royal throne and had touched the heaven with his head. Fearing then lest I should be deprived of my power by my brother, I acted quickly rather than wisely; for it seems that it is not possible for man to avert that which is destined to come to pass. I therefore, fool that I was, sent away Prexaspes to Susa to kill Smerdis; and when this great evil had been done, I lived in security, never considering the danger that some other man might at some time rise up against me, now that Smerdis had been removed: and altogether missing the mark of that which was about to happen, I have both made myself the murderer of my brother, when there was no need, and I have been deprived none the less of the kingdom; for it was in fact Smerdis the Magian of whom the divine power declared to me beforehand in the vision that he should rise up against me. So then, as I say, this deed has been done by me, and ye must imagine that ye no longer have Smerdis the son of Cyrus alive: but it is in truth the Magians who are masters of your kingdom, he whom I left as guardian of my household and his brother Smerdis. The man then who ought above all others to have taken vengeance on my behalf for the dishonour which I have suffered from the Magians, has ended his life by an unholy death received from the hands of those who were his nearest of kin; and since he is no more, it becomes most needful for me, as the thing next best of those which remain, to charge you, O Persians, with that which dying I desire should be done for me. This then I lay upon you, calling upon the gods of the royal house to witness it,—upon you and most of all upon those of the Achaemenidai who are present here,—that ye do not permit the return of the chief power to the Medes, but that if they have acquired it by craft, by craft they be deprived of it by you, or if they have conquered it by any kind of force, by force and by a strong hand ye recover it. And if ye do this, may the earth bring forth her produce and may your wives and your cattle be fruitful, while ye remain free for ever; but if ye do not recover the power nor attempt to recover it, I pray that curses the contrary of these blessings may come upon you, and moreover that each man of the Persians may have an end to his life like that which has come upon me." Then as soon as he had finished speaking these things, Cambyses began to bewail and make lamentation for all his fortunes.

And the Persians, when they saw that the king had begun to bewail himself, both rent the garments which they wore and made lamentation without stint. After this, when the bone had become diseased and the thigh had mortified, Cambyses the son of Cyrus was carried off by the wound, having reigned in all seven years and five months, and being absolutely childless both of male and female offspring. The Persians meanwhile who were present there were very little disposed to believe that the power was in the hands of the Magians: on the contrary, they were surely convinced that Cambyses had said that which he said about the death of Smerdis to deceive them, in order that all the Persians might be moved to war against him. These then were surely convinced that Smerdis the son of Cyrus was established to be king; for Prexaspes also very strongly denied that he had slain Smerdis, since it was not safe, now that Cambyses was dead, for him to say that he had destroyed with his own hand the son of Cyrus.

. Thus when Cambyses had brought his life to an end, the Magian became king without disturbance, usurping the place of his namesake Smerdis the son of Cyrus; and he reigned during the seven months which were wanting yet to Cambyses for the completion of the eight years: and during them he performed acts of great benefit to all his subjects, so that after his death all those in Asia except the Persians themselves mourned for his loss: for the Magian sent messengers abroad to every nation over which he ruled, and proclaimed freedom from military service and from tribute for three years.

This proclamation, I say, he made at once when he established himself upon the throne: but in the eighth month it was discovered who he was in the following manner:—There was one Otanes the son of Pharnaspes, in birth and in wealth not inferior to any of the Persians. This Otanes was the first who had had suspicion of the Magian, that he was not Smerdis the son of Cyrus but the person that he really was, drawing his inference from these facts, namely that he never went abroad out of the fortress, and that he did not summon into his presence any of the honourable men among the Persians: and having formed a suspicion of him, he proceeded to do as follows:—Cambyses had taken to wife his daughter, whose name was Phaidyme; and this same daughter the Magian at that time was keeping as his wife and living with her as with all the rest also of the wives of Cambyses. Otanes therefore sent a message to this daughter and asked her who the man was by whose side she slept, whether Smerdis the son of Cyrus or some other. She sent back word to him saying that she did not know, for she had never seen Smerdis the son of Cyrus, nor did she know otherwise who he was who lived with her. Otanes then sent a second time and said: "If thou dost not thyself know Smerdis the son of Cyrus, then do thou ask of Atossa who this man is, with whom both she and thou live as wives; for assuredly it must be that she knows her own brother."

To this the daughter sent back word: "I am not able either to come to speech with Atossa or to see any other of the women who live here with me; for as soon as this man, whosoever he may be, succeeded to the kingdom, he separated us and placed us in different apartments by ourselves." When Otanes heard this, the matter became more and more clear to him, and he sent another message in to her, which said: "Daughter, it is right for thee, nobly born as thou art, to undertake any risk which thy father bids thee take upon thee: for if in truth this is not Smerdis the son of Cyrus but the man whom I suppose, he ought not to escape with impunity either for taking thee to his bed or for holding the dominion of Persians, but he must pay the penalty. Now therefore do as I say. When he sleeps by thee and thou perceivest that he is sound asleep, feel his ears; and if it prove that he has ears, then believe that thou art living with Smerdis the son of Cyrus, but if not, believe that it is with the Magian Smerdis." To this Phaidyme sent an answer saying that, if she should do so, she would run a great risk; for supposing that he should chance not to have his ears, and she were detected feeling for them, she was well assured that he would put her to death; but nevertheless she would do this. So she undertook to do this for her father: but as for this Magian Smerdis, he had had his ears cut off by Cyrus the son of Cambyses when he was king, for some grave offence. This Phaidyme then, the daughter of Otanes, proceeding to perform all that she had undertaken for her father, when her turn came to go to the Magian (for the wives of the Persians go in to them regularly each in her turn), came and lay down beside him: and when the Magian was in deep sleep, she felt his ears; and perceiving not with difficulty but easily that her husband had no ears, so soon as it became day she sent and informed her father of that which had taken place.

Then Otanes took to him Aspathines and Gobryas, who were leading men among the Persians and also his own most trusted friends, and related to them the whole matter: and they, as it then appeared, had suspicions also themselves that it was so; and when Otanes reported this to them, they readily accepted his proposals. Then it was resolved by them that each one should associate with himself that man of the Persians whom he trusted most; so Otanes brought in Intaphrenes, Gobryas brought in Megabyzos, and Aspathines brought in Hydarnes. When they had thus become six, Dareios the son of Hystaspes arrived at Susa, having come from the land of Persia, for of this his father was governor. Accordingly when he came, the six men of the Persians resolved to associate Dareios also with themselves.

These then having come together, being seven in number, gave pledges of faith to one another and deliberated together; and when it came to Dareios to declare his opinion, he spoke to them as follows: "I thought that I alone knew this, namely that it was the Magian who was reigning as king and that Smerdis the son of Cyrus had brought his life to an end; and for this very reason I am come with earnest purpose to contrive death for the Magian. Since however it has come to pass that ye also know and not I alone, I think it well to act at once and not to put the matter off, for that is not the better way." To this replied Otanes: "Son of Hystaspes, thou art the scion of a noble stock, and thou art showing thyself, as it seems, in no way inferior to thy father: do not however hasten this enterprise so much without consideration, but take it up more prudently; for we must first become more in numbers, and then undertake the matter." In answer to this Dareios said: "Men who are here present, if ye shall follow the way suggested by Otanes, know that ye will perish miserably; for some one will carry word to the Magian, getting gain thereby privately for himself. Your best way would have been to do this action upon your own risk alone; but since it seemed good to you to refer the matter to a greater number, and ye communicated it to me, either let us do the deed to-day, or be ye assured that if this present day shall pass by, none other shall prevent me as your accuser, but I will myself tell these things to the Magian."

To this Otanes, when he saw Dareios in violent haste, replied: "Since thou dost compel us to hasten the matter and dost not permit us to delay, come expound to us thyself in what manner we shall pass into the palace and lay hands upon them: for that there are guards set in various parts, thou knowest probably thyself as well as we, if not from sight at least from hearsay; and in what manner shall we pass through these?" Dareios made reply with these words: "Otanes, there are many things in sooth which it is not possible to set forth in speech, but only in deed; and other things there are which in speech can be set forth, but from them comes no famous deed. Know ye however that the guards which are set are not difficult to pass: for in the first place, we being what we are, there is no one who will not let us go by, partly, as may be supposed, from having respect for us, and partly also perhaps from fear; and secondly I have myself a most specious pretext by means of which we may pass by; for I shall say that I am just now come from the Persian land and desire to declare to the king a certain message from my father: for where it is necessary that a lie be spoken, let it be spoken; seeing that we all aim at the same object, both they who lie and they who always speak the truth; those lie whenever they are likely to gain anything by persuading with their lies, and these tell the truth in order that they may draw to themselves gain by the truth, and that things may be entrusted to them more readily. Thus, while practising different ways, we aim all at the same thing. If however they were not likely to make any gain by it, the truth-teller would lie and the liar would speak the truth, with indifference. Whosoever then of the door-keepers shall let us pass by of his own free will, for him it shall be the better afterwards; but whosoever shall endeavour to oppose our passage, let him then and there be marked as our enemy, and after that let us push in and set about our work."

Then said Gobryas: "Friends, at what time will there be a fairer opportunity for us either to recover our rule, or, if we are not able to get it again, to die? seeing that we being Persians on the one hand lie under the rule of a Mede, a Magian, and that too a man whose ears have been cut off. Moreover all those of you who stood by the side of Cambyses when he was sick remember assuredly what he laid upon the Persians as he was bringing his life to an end, if they should not attempt to win back the power; and this we did not accept then, but supposed that Cambyses had spoken in order to deceive us. Now therefore I give my vote that we follow the opinion of Dareios, and that we do not depart from this assembly to go anywhither else but straight to attack the Magian." Thus spoke Gobryas, and they all approved of this proposal.

Now while these were thus taking counsel together, it was coming to pass by coincidence as follows:—The Magians taking counsel together had resolved to join Prexaspes with themselves as a friend, both because he had suffered grievous wrong from Cambyses, who had killed his son by shooting him, and because he alone knew for a certainty of the death of Smerdis the son of Cyrus, having killed him with his own hands, and finally because Prexaspes was in very great repute among the Persians. For these reasons they summoned him and endeavoured to win him to be their friend, engaging him by pledge and with oaths, that he would assuredly keep to himself and not reveal to any man the deception which had been practised by them upon the Persians, and promising to give him things innumerable in return. After Prexaspes had promised to do this, the Magians, having persuaded him so far, proposed to him a second thing, and said that they would call together all the Persians to come up to the wall of the palace, and bade him go up upon a tower and address them, saying that they were living under the rule of Smerdis the son of Cyrus and no other. This they so enjoined because they supposed that he had the greatest credit among the Persians, and because he had frequently declared the opinion that Smerdis the son of Cyrus was still alive, and had denied that he had slain him.

When Prexaspes said that he was ready to do this also, the Magians having called together the Persians caused him to go up upon a tower and bade him address them. Then he chose to forget those things which they asked of him, and beginning with Achaimenes he traced the descent of Cyrus on the father's side, and then, when he came down to Cyrus, he related at last what great benefits he had conferred upon the Persians; and having gone through this recital he proceeded to declare the truth, saying that formerly he kept it secret, since it was not safe for him to tell of that which had been done, but at the present time he was compelled to make it known. He proceeded to say how he had himself slain Smerdis the son of Cyrus, being compelled by Cambyses, and that it was the Magians who were now ruling. Then he made imprecation of many evils on the Persians, if they did not win back again the power and take vengeance upon the Magians, and upon that he let himself fall down from the tower head foremost. Thus Prexaspes ended his life, having been throughout his time a man of repute.

. Now the seven of the Persians, when they had resolved forthwith to lay hands upon the Magians and not to delay, made prayer to the gods and went, knowing nothing of that which had been done with regard to Prexaspes: and as they were going and were in the middle of their course, they heard that which had happened about Prexaspes. Upon that they retired out of the way and again considered with themselves, Otanes and his supporters strongly urging that they should delay and not set to the work when things were thus disturbed, while Dareios and those of his party urged that they should go forthwith and do that which had been resolved, and not delay. Then while they were contending, there appeared seven pairs of hawks pursuing two pairs of vultures, plucking out their feathers and tearing them. Seeing this the seven all approved the opinion of Dareios and thereupon they went to the king's palace, encouraged by the sight of the birds.

When they appeared at the gates, it happened nearly as Dareios supposed, for the guards, having respect for men who were chief among the Persians, and not suspecting that anything would be done by them of the kind proposed, allowed them to pass in under the guiding of heaven, and none asked them any question. Then when they had passed into the court, they met the eunuchs who bore in the messages to the king; and these inquired of them for what purpose they had come, and at the same time they threatened with punishment the keepers of the gates for having let them pass in, and tried to stop the seven when they attempted to go forward. Then they gave the word to one another and drawing their daggers stabbed these men there upon the spot, who tried to stop them, and themselves went running on towards the chamber of the men.

Now the Magians happened both of them to be there within, consulting about that which had been done by Prexaspes. So when they saw that the eunuchs had been attacked and were crying aloud, they ran back both of them, and perceiving that which was being done they turned to self-defence: and one of them got down his bow and arrows before he was attacked, while the other had recourse to his spear. Then they engaged in combat with one another; and that one of them who had taken up his bow and arrows found them of no use, since his enemies were close at hand and pressed hard upon him, but the other defended himself with his spear, and first he struck Aspathines in the thigh, and then Intaphrenes in the eye; and Intaphrenes lost his eye by reason of the wound, but his life he did not lose. These then were wounded by one of the Magians, but the other, when his bow and arrows proved useless to him, fled into a bedchamber which opened into the chamber of the men, intending to close the door; and with him there rushed in two of the seven, Dareios and Gobryas. And when Gobryas was locked together in combat with the Magian, Dareios stood by and was at a loss what to do, because it was dark, and he was afraid lest he should strike Gobryas. Then seeing him standing by idle, Gobryas asked why he did not use his hands, and he said: "Because I am afraid lest I may strike thee": and Gobryas answered: "Thrust with thy sword even though it stab through us both." So Dareios was persuaded, and he thrust with his danger and happened to hit the Magian.

So when they had slain the Magians and cut off their heads, they left behind those of their number who were wounded, both because they were unable to go, and also in order that they might take charge of the fortress, and the five others taking with them the heads of the Magians ran with shouting and clashing of arms and called upon the other Persians to join them, telling them of that which had been done and showing the heads, and at the same time they proceeded to slay every one of the Magians who crossed their path. So the Persians when they heard of that which had been brought to pass by the seven and of the deceit of the Magians, thought good themselves also to do the same, and drawing their daggers they killed the Magians wherever they found one; so that if night had not come on and stopped them, they would not have left a single Magian alive. This day the Persians celebrate in common more than all other days, and upon it they keep a great festival which is called by the Persians the festival of the slaughter of the Magians, on which no Magian is permitted to appear abroad, but the Magians keep themselves within their houses throughout that day.

When the tumult had subsided and more than five days had elapsed, those who had risen against the Magians began to take counsel about the general state, and there were spoken speeches which some of the Hellenes do not believe were really uttered, but spoken they were nevertheless. On the one hand Otanes urged that they should resign the government into the hands of the whole body of the Persians, and his words were as follows: "To me it seems best that no single one of us should henceforth be ruler, for that is neither pleasant nor profitable. Ye saw the insolent temper of Cambyses, to what lengths it went, and ye have had experience also of the insolence of the Magian: and how should the rule of one alone be a well-ordered thing, seeing that the monarch may do what he desires without rendering any account of his acts? Even the best of all men, if he were placed in this disposition, would be caused by it to change from his wonted disposition: for insolence is engendered in him by the good things which he possesses, and envy is implanted in man from the beginning; and having these two things, he has all vice: for he does many deeds of reckless wrong, partly moved by insolence proceeding from satiety, and partly by envy. And yet a despot at least ought to have been free from envy, seeing that he has all manner of good things. He is however naturally in just the opposite temper towards his subjects; for he grudges to the nobles that they should survive and live, but delights in the basest of citizens, and he is more ready than any other man to receive calumnies. Then of all things he is the most inconsistent; for if you express admiration of him moderately, he is offended that no very great court is paid to him, whereas if you pay court to him extravagantly, he is offended with you for being a flatterer. And the most important matter of all is that which I am about to say:—he disturbs the customs handed down from our fathers, he is a ravisher of women, and he puts men to death without trial. On the other hand the rule of many has first a name attaching to it which is the fairest of all names, that is to say 'Equality'; next, the multitude does none of those things which the monarch does: offices of state are exercised by lot, and the magistrates are compelled to render account of their action: and finally all matters of deliberation are referred to the public assembly. I therefore give as my opinion that we let monarchy go and increase the power of the multitude; for in the many is contained everything."

This was the opinion expressed by Otanes; but Megabyzos urged that they should entrust matters to the rule of a few, saying these words: "That which Otanes said in opposition to a tyranny, let it be counted as said for me also, but in that which he said urging that we should make over the power to the multitude, he has missed the best counsel: for nothing is more senseless or insolent than a worthless crowd; and for men flying from the insolence of a despot to fall into that of unrestrained popular power, is by no means to be endured: for he, if he does anything, does it knowing what he does, but the people cannot even know; for how can that know which has neither been taught anything noble by others nor perceived anything of itself, but pushes on matters with violent impulse and without understanding, like a torrent stream? Rule of the people then let them adopt who are foes to the Persians; but let us choose a company of the best men, and to them attach the chief power; for in the number of these we shall ourselves also be, and it is likely that the resolutions taken by the best men will be the best."

This was the opinion expressed by Megabyzos; and thirdly Dareios proceeded to declare his opinion, saying: "To me it seems that in those things which Megabyzos said with regard to the multitude he spoke rightly, but in those which he said with regard to the rule of a few, not rightly: for whereas there are three things set before us, and each is supposed to be the best in its own kind, that is to say a good popular government, and the rule of a few, and thirdly the rule of one, I say that this last is by far superior to the others; for nothing better can be found than the rule of an individual man of the best kind; seeing that using the best judgment he would be guardian of the multitude without reproach; and resolutions directed against enemies would so best be kept secret. In an oligarchy however it happens often that many, while practising virtue with regard to the commonwealth, have strong private enmities arising among themselves; for as each man desires to be himself the leader and to prevail in counsels, they come to great enmities with one another, whence arise factions among them, and out of the factions comes murder, and from murder results the rule of one man; and thus it is shown in this instance by how much that is the best. Again, when the people rules, it is impossible that corruption should not arise, and when corruption arises in the commonwealth, there arise among the corrupt men not enmities but strong ties of friendship: for they who are acting corruptly to the injury of the commonwealth put their heads together secretly to do so. And this continues so until at last some one takes the leadership of the people and stops the course of such men. By reason of this the man of whom I speak is admired by the people, and being so admired he suddenly appears as monarch. Thus he too furnishes herein an example to prove that the rule of one is the best thing. Finally, to sum up all in a single word, whence arose the liberty which we possess, and who gave it to us? Was it a gift of the people or of an oligarchy or of a monarch? I therefore am of opinion that we, having been set free by one man, should preserve that form of rule, and in other respects also that we should not annul the customs of our fathers which are ordered well; for that is not the better way."

These three opinions then had been proposed, and the other four men of the seven gave their assent to the last. So when Otanes, who was desirous to give equality to the Persians, found his opinion defeated, he spoke to those assembled thus: "Partisans, it is clear that some one of us must become king, selected either by casting lots, or by entrusting the decision to the multitude of the Persians and taking him whom it shall choose, or by some other means. I therefore shall not be a competitor with you, for I do not desire either to rule or to be ruled; and on this condition I withdraw from my claim to rule, namely that I shall not be ruled by any of you, either I myself or my descendants in future time." When he had said this, the six made agreement with him on those terms, and he was no longer a competitor with them, but withdrew from the assembly; and at the present time this house remains free alone of all the Persian houses, and submits to rule only so far as it wills to do so itself, not transgressing the laws of the Persians.

The rest however of the seven continued to deliberate how they should establish a king in the most just manner; and it was resolved by them that to Otanes and his descendants in succession, if the kingdom should come to any other of the seven, there should be given as special gifts a Median dress every year and all those presents which are esteemed among the Persians to be the most valuable: and the reason why they determined that these things should be given to him, was because he first suggested to them the matter and combined them together. These were special gifts for Otanes; and this they also determined for all in common, namely that any one of the seven who wished might pass in to the royal palaces without any to bear in a message, unless the king happened to be sleeping with his wife; and that it should not be lawful for the king to marry from any other family, but only from those of the men who had made insurrection with him: and about the kingdom they determined this, namely that the man whose horse should first neigh at sunrise in the suburb of the city when they were mounted upon their horses, he should have the kingdom.

Now Dareios had a clever horse-keeper, whose name was Oibares. To this man, when they had left their assembly, Dareios spoke these words: "Oibares, we have resolved to do about the kingdom thus, namely that the man whose horse first neighs at sunrise, when we are mounted upon our horses he shall be king. Now therefore, if thou hast any cleverness, contrive that we may obtain this prize, and not any other man." Oibares replied thus: "If, my master, it depends in truth upon this whether thou be king or no, have confidence so far as concerns this and keep a good heart, for none other shall be king before thee; such charms have I at my command." Then Dareios said: "If then thou hast any such trick, it is time to devise it and not to put things off, for our trial is to-morrow." Oibares therefore hearing this did as follows:—when night was coming on he took one of the mares, namely that one which the horse of Dareios preferred, and this he led into the suburb of the city and tied her up: then he brought to her the horse of Dareios, and having for some time led him round her, making him go so close by so as to touch the mare, at last he let the horse mount.

Now at dawn of day the six came to the place as they had agreed, riding upon their horses; and as they rode through by the suburb of the city, when they came near the place where the mare had been tied up on the former night, the horse of Dareios ran up to the place and neighed; and just when the horse had done this, there came lightning and thunder from a clear sky: and the happening of these things to Dareios consummated his claim, for they seemed to have come to pass by some design, and the others leapt down from their horses and did obeisance to Dareios.

Some say that the contrivance of Oibares was this, but others say as follows (for the story is told by the Persians in both ways), namely that he touched with his hands the parts of this mare and kept his hand hidden in his trousers; and when at sunrise they were about to let the horses go, this Oibares pulled out his hand and applied it to the nostrils of the horse of Dareios; and the horse, perceiving the smell, snorted and neighed.

So Dareios the son of Hystaspes had been declared king; and in Asia all except the Arabians were his subjects, having been subdued by Cyrus and again afterwards by Cambyses. The Arabians however were never obedient to the Persians under conditions of subjection, but had become guest-friends when they let Cambyses pass by to Egypt: for against the will of the Arabians the Persians would not be able to invade Egypt. Moreover Dareios made the most noble marriages possible in the estimation of the Persians; for he married two daughters of Cyrus, Atossa and Artystone, of whom the one, Arossa, had before been the wife of Cambyses her brother and then afterwards of the Magian, while Artystone was a virgin; and besides them he married the daughter of Smerdis the son of Cyrus, whose name was Parmys; and he also took to wife the daughter of Otanes, he who had discovered the Magian; and all things became filled with his power. And first he caused to be a carving in stone, and set it up; and in it there was the figure of a man on horseback, and he wrote upon it writing to this effect: "Dareios son of Hystaspes by the excellence of his horse," mentioning the name of it, "and of his horse-keeper Oibares obtained the kingdom of the Persians."

Having so done in Persia, he established twenty provinces, which the Persians themselves call satrapies; and having established the provinces and set over them rulers, he appointed tribute to come to him from them according to races, joining also to the chief races those who dwelt on their borders, or passing beyond the immediate neighbours and assigning to various races those which lay more distant. He divided the provinces and the yearly payment of tribute as follows: and those of them who brought in silver were commanded to pay by the standard of the Babylonian talent, but those who brought in gold by the Euboïc talent; now the Babylonian talent is equal to eight-and-seventy Euboïc pounds. For in the reign of Cyrus, and again of Cambyses, nothing was fixed about tribute, but they used to bring gifts: and on account of this appointing of tribute and other things like this, the Persians say that Dareios was a shopkeeper, Cambyses a master, and Cyrus a father; the one because he dealt with all his affairs like a shopkeeper, the second because he was harsh and had little regard for any one, and the other because he was gentle and contrived for them all things good.

From the Ionians and the Magnesians who dwell in Asia and the Aiolians, Carians, Lykians, Milyans and Pamphylians (for one single sum was appointed by him as tribute for all these) there came in four hundred talents of silver. This was appointed by him to be the first division. From the Mysians and Lydians and Lasonians and Cabalians and Hytennians there came in five hundred talents: this is the second division. From the Hellespontians who dwell on the right as one sails in and the Phrygians and the Thracians who dwell in Asia and the Paphlagonians and Mariandynoi and Syrians the tribute was three hundred and sixty talents: this is the third division. From the Kilikians, besides three hundred and sixty white horses, one for every day in the year, there came also five hundred talents of silver; of these one hundred and forty talents were spent upon the horsemen which served as a guard to the Kilikian land, and the remaining three hundred and sixty came in year by year to Dareios: this is the fourth division.

From that division which begins with the city of Posideion, founded by Amphilochos the son of Amphiaraos on the borders of the Kilikians and the Syrians, and extends as far as Egypt, not including the territory of the Arabians (for this was free from payment), the amount was three hundred and fifty talents; and in this division are the whole of Phenicia and Syria which is called Palestine and Cyprus: this is the fifth division. From Egypt and the Libyans bordering upon Egypt, and from Kyrene and Barca, for these were so ordered as to belong to the Egyptian division, there came in seven hundred talents, without reckoning the money produced by the lake of Moiris, that is to say from the fish; without reckoning this, I say, or the corn which was contributed in addition by measure, there came in seven hundred talents; for as regards the corn, they contribute by measure one hundred and twenty thousand bushels for the use of those Persians who are established in the "White Fortress" at Memphis, and for their foreign mercenaries: this is the sixth division. The Sattagydai and Gandarians and Dadicans and Aparytai, being joined together, brought in one hundred and seventy talents: this is the seventh division. From Susa and the rest of the land of the Kissians there came in three hundred: this is the eighth division.

From Babylon and from the rest of Assyria there came in to him a thousand talents of silver and five hundred boys for eunuchs: this is the ninth division. From Agbatana and from the rest of Media and the Paricanians and Orthocorybantians, four hundred and fifty talents: this is the tenth division. The Caspians and Pausicans and Pantimathoi and Dareitai, contributing together, brought in two hundred talents: this is the eleventh division. From the Bactrians as far as the Aigloi the tribute was three hundred and sixty talents: this is the twelfth division.

From Pactyïke and the Armenians and the people bordering upon them as far as the Euxine, four hundred talents: this is the thirteenth division. From the Sagartians and Sarangians and Thamanaians and Utians and Mycans and those who dwell in the islands of the Erythraian Sea, where the king settles those who are called the "Removed," from all these together a tribute was produced of six hundred talents: this is the fourteenth division. The Sacans and the Caspians brought in two hundred and fifty talents: this is the fifteenth division. The Parthians and Chorasmians and Sogdians and Areians three hundred talents: this is the sixteenth division.

The Paricanians and Ethiopians in Asia brought in four hundred talents: this is the seventeenth division. To the Matienians and Saspeirians and Alarodians was appointed a tribute of two hundred talents: this is the eighteenth division. To the Moschoi and Tibarenians and Macronians and Mossynoicoi and Mares three hundred talents were ordered: this is the nineteenth division. Of the Indians the number is far greater than that of any other race of men of whom we know; and they brought in a tribute larger than all the rest, that is to say three hundred and sixty talents of gold-dust: this is the twentieth division.

Now if we compare Babylonian with Euboïc talents, the silver is found to amount to nine thousand eight hundred and eighty talents; and if we reckon the gold at thirteen times the value of silver, weight for weight, the gold-dust is found to amount to four thousand six hundred and eighty Euboïc talents. These being all added together, the total which was collected as yearly tribute for Dareios amounts to fourteen thousand five hundred and sixty Euboïc talents: the sums which are less than these I pass over and do not mention.

This was the tribute which came in to Dareios from Asia and from a small part of Libya: but as time went on, other tribute came in also from the islands and from those who dwell in Europe as far as Thessaly. This tribute the king stores up in his treasury in the following manner:—he melts it down and pours it into jars of earthenware, and when he has filled the jars he takes off the earthenware jar from the metal; and when he wants money he cuts off so much as he needs on each occasion.

These were the provinces and the assessments of tribute: and the Persian land alone has not been mentioned by me as paying a contribution, for the Persians have their land to dwell in free from payment. The following moreover had no tribute fixed for them to pay, but brought gifts, namely the Ethiopians who border upon Egypt, whom Cambyses subdued as he marched against the Long-lived Ethiopians, those who dwell about Nysa, which is called "sacred," and who celebrate the festivals in honour of Dionysos: these Ethiopians and those who dwell near them have the same kind of seed as the Callantian Indians, and they have underground dwellings. These both together brought every other year, and continue to bring even to my own time, two quart measures of unmelted gold and two hundred blocks of ebony and five Ethiopian boys and twenty large elephant tusks. The Colchians also had set themselves among those who brought gifts, and with them those who border upon them extending as far as the range of the Caucasus (for the Persian rule extends as far as these mountains, but those who dwell in the parts beyond Caucasus toward the North

Wind regard the Persians no longer),—these, I say, continued to bring the gifts which they had fixed for themselves every four years even down to my own time, that is to say, a hundred boys and a hundred maidens. Finally, the Arabians brought a thousand talents of frankincense every year. Such were the gifts which these brought to the king apart from the tribute.

Now this great quantity of gold, out of which the Indians bring in to the king the gold-dust which has been mentioned, is obtained by them in a manner which I shall tell:—That part of the Indian land which is towards the rising sun is sand; for of all the peoples in Asia of which we know or about which any certain report is given, the Indians dwell furthest away towards the East and the sunrising; seeing that the country to the East of the Indians is desert on account of the sand. Now there are many tribes of Indians, and they do not agree with one another in language; and some of them are pastoral and others not so, and some dwell in the swamps of the river and feed upon raw fish, which they catch by fishing from boats made of cane; and each boat is made of one joint of cane. These Indians of which I speak wear clothing made of rushes: they gather and cut the rushes from the river and then weave them together into a kind of mat and put it on like a corslet.

Others of the Indians, dwelling to the East of these, are pastoral and eat raw flesh: these are called Padaians, and they practise the following customs:—whenever any of their tribe falls ill, whether it be a woman or a man, if a man then the men who are his nearest associates put him to death, saying that he is wasting away with the disease and his flesh is being spoilt for them: and meanwhile he denies stoutly and says that he is not ill, but they do not agree with him; and after they have killed him they feast upon his flesh: but if it be a woman who falls ill, the women who are her greatest intimates do to her in the same manner as the men do in the other case. For in fact even if a man has come to old age they slay him and feast upon him; but very few of them come to be reckoned as old, for they kill every one who falls into sickness, before he reaches old age.

Other Indians have on the contrary a manner of life as follows:—they neither kill any living thing nor do they sow any crops nor is it their custom to possess houses; but they feed on herbs, and they have a grain of the size of millet, in a sheath, which grows of itself from the ground; this they gather and boil with the sheath, and make it their food: and whenever any of them falls into sickness, he goes to the desert country and lies there, and none of them pay any attention either to one who is dead or to one who is sick.

The sexual intercourse of all these Indians of whom I have spoken is open like that of cattle, and they have all one colour of skin, resembling that of the Ethiopians: moreover the seed which they emit is not white like that of other races, but black like their skin; and the Ethiopians also are similar in this respect. These tribes of Indians dwell further off than the Persian power extends, and towards the South Wind, and they never became subjects of Dareios.

Others however of the Indians are on the borders of the city of Caspatyros and the country of Pactyïke, dwelling towards the North of the other Indians; and they have a manner of living nearly the same as that of the Bactrians: these are the most warlike of the Indians, and these are they who make expeditions for the gold. For in the parts where they live it is desert on account of the sand; and in this desert and sandy tract are produced ants, which are in size smaller than dogs but larger than foxes, for there are some of them kept at the residence of the king of Persia, which are caught here. These ants then make their dwelling under ground and carry up the sand just in the same manner as the ants found in the land of the Hellenes, which they themselves also very much resemble in form; and the sand which is brought up contains gold. To obtain this sand the Indians make expeditions into the desert, each one having yoked together three camels, placing a female in the middle and a male like a trace-horse to draw by each side. On this female he mounts himself, having arranged carefully that she shall be taken to be yoked from young ones, the more lately born the better. For their female camels are not inferior to horses in speed, and moreover they are much more capable of bearing weights.

As to the form of the camel, I do not here describe it, since the Hellenes for whom I write are already acquainted with it, but I shall tell that which is not commonly known about it, which is this:—the camel has in the hind legs four thighs and four knees, and its organs of generation are between the hind legs, turned towards the tail.

The Indians, I say, ride out to get the gold in the manner and with the kind of yoking which I have described, making calculations so that they may be engaged in carrying it off at the time when the greatest heat prevails; for the heat causes the ants to disappear underground. Now among these nations the sun is hottest in the morning hours, not at midday as with others, but from sunrise to the time of closing the market: and during this time it produces much greater heat than at midday in Hellas, so that it is said that then they drench themselves with water. Midday however has about equal degree of heat with the Indians as with other men, while after midday their sun becomes like the morning sun with other men, and after this, as it goes further away, it produces still greater coolness, until at last at sunset it makes the air very cool indeed.

When the Indians have come to the place with bags, they fill them with the sand and ride away back as quickly as they can, for forthwith the ants, perceiving, as the Persians allege, by the smell, begin to pursue them: and this animal, they say, is superior to every other creature in swiftness, so that unless the Indians got a start in their course, while the ants were gathering together, not one of them would escape. So then the male camels, for they are inferior in speed of running to the females, if they drag behind are even let loose from the side of the female, one after the other; the females however, remembering the young which they left behind, do not show any slackness in their course. Thus it is that the Indians get most part of the gold, as the Persians say; there is however other gold also in their land obtained by digging, but in smaller quantities.

It seems indeed that the extremities of the inhabited world had allotted to them by nature the fairest things, just as it was the lot of Hellas to have its seasons far more fairly tempered than other lands: for first, India is the most distant of inhabited lands towards the East, as I have said a little above, and in this land not only the animals, birds as well as four-footed beasts, are much larger than in other places (except the horses, which are surpassed by those of Media called Nessaian), but also there is gold in abundance there, some got by digging, some brought down by rivers, and some carried off as I explained just now: and there also the trees which grow wild produce wool which surpasses in beauty and excellence that from sheep, and the Indians wear clothing obtained from these trees.

Then again Arabia is the furthest of inhabited lands in the direction of the midday, and in it alone of all lands grow frankincense and myrrh and cassia and cinnamon and gum-mastich. All these except myrrh are got with difficulty by the Arabians. Frankincense they collect by burning the storax, which is brought thence to the Hellenes by the Phenicians, by burning this, I say, so as to produce smoke they take it; for these trees which produce frankincense are guarded by winged serpents, small in size and of various colours, which watch in great numbers about each tree, of the same kind as those which attempt to invade Egypt: and they cannot be driven away from the trees by any other thing but only the smoke of storax.

The Arabians say also that all the world would have been by this time filled with these serpents, if that did not happen with regard to them which I knew happened with regard to vipers: and it seems that the Divine Providence, as indeed was to be expected, seeing that it is wise, has made all those animals prolific which are of cowardly spirit and good for food, in order that they may not be all eaten up and their race fail, whereas it has made those which are bold and noxious to have small progeny. For example, because the hare is hunted by every beast and bird as well as by man, therefore it is so very prolific as it is: and this is the only one of all beasts which becomes pregnant again before the former young are born, and has in its womb some of its young covered with fur and others bare; and while one is just being shaped in the matrix, another is being conceived. Thus it is in this case; whereas the lioness, which is the strongest and most courageous of creatures, produces one cub once only in her life; for when she produces young she casts out her womb together with her young; and the cause of it is this:—when the cub being within the mother begins to move about, then having claws by far sharper than those of any other beast he tears the womb, and as he grows larger he proceeds much further in his scratching: at last the time of birth approaches and there is now nothing at all left of it in a sound condition.

Just so also, if vipers and the winged serpents of the Arabians were produced in the ordinary course of their nature, man would not be able to live upon the earth; but as it is, when they couple with one another and the male is in the act of generation, as he lets go from him the seed, the female seizes hold of his neck, and fastening on to it does not relax her hold till she has eaten it through. The male then dies in the manner which I have said, but the female pays the penalty of retribution for the male in this manner:—the young while they are still in the womb take vengeance for their father by eating through their mother, and having eaten through her belly they thus make their way out for themselves. Other serpents however, which are not hurtful to man, produce eggs and hatch from them a very large number of offspring. Now vipers are distributed over all the earth; but the others, which are winged, are found in great numbers together in Arabia and in no other land: therefore it is that they appear to be numerous.

This frankincense then is obtained thus by the Arabians; and cassia is obtained as follows:—they bind up in cows'-hide and other kinds of skins all their body and their face except only the eyes, and then go to get the cassia. This grows in a pool not very deep, and round the pool and in it lodge, it seems, winged beasts nearly resembling bats, and they squeak horribly and are courageous in fight. These they must keep off from their eyes, and so cut the cassia.

Cinnamon they collect in a yet more marvellous manner than this: for where it grows and what land produces it they are not able to tell, except only that some say (and it is a probable account) that it grows in those regions where Dionysos was brought up; and they say that large birds carry those dried sticks which we have learnt from the Phenicians to call cinnamon, carry them, I say, to nests which are made of clay and stuck on to precipitous sides of mountains, which man can find no means of scaling. With regard to this then the Arabians practise the following contrivance:—they divide up the limbs of the oxen and asses that die and of their other beasts of burden, into pieces as large as convenient, and convey them to these places, and when they have laid them down not far from the nests, they withdraw to a distance from them: and the birds fly down and carry the limbs of the beasts of burden off to their nests; and these are not able to bear them, but break down and fall to the earth; and the men come up to them and collect the cinnamon. Thus cinnamon is collected and comes from this nation to the other countries of the world.

Gum-mastich however, which the Arabians call ladanon, comes in a still more extraordinary manner; for though it is the most sweet-scented of all things, it comes in the most evil-scented thing, since it is found in the beards of he-goats, produced there like resin from wood: this is of use for the making of many perfumes, and the Arabians use it more than anything else as incense.

Let what we have said suffice with regard to spices; and from the land of Arabia there blows a scent of them most marvellously sweet. They have also two kinds of sheep which are worthy of admiration and are not found in any other land: the one kind has the tail long, not less than three cubits in length; and if one should allow these to drag these after them, they would have sores from their tails being worn away against the ground; but as it is, every one of the shepherds knows enough of carpentering to make little cars, which they tie under the tails, fastening the tail of each animal to a separate little car. The other kind of sheep has the tail broad, even as much as a cubit in breadth.

As one passes beyond the place of the midday, the Ethiopian land is that which extends furthest of all inhabited lands towards the sunset. This produces both gold in abundance and huge elephants and trees of all kinds growing wild and ebony, and men who are of all men the tallest, the most beautiful and the most long-lived.

These are the extremities in Asia and in Libya; but as to the extremities of Europe towards the West, I am not able to speak with certainty: for neither do I accept the tale that there is a river called in Barbarian tongue Eridanos, flowing into the sea which lies towards the North Wind, whence it is said that amber comes; nor do I know of the real existence of "Tin Islands" from which tin comes to us: for first the name Eridanos itself declares that it is Hellenic and that it does not belong to a Barbarian speech, but was invented by some poet; and secondly I am not able to hear from any one who has been an eye-witness, though I took pains to discover this, that there is a sea on the other side of Europe. However that may be, tin and amber certainly come to us from the extremity of Europe.

Then again towards the North of Europe, there is evidently a quantity of gold by far larger than in any other land: as to how it is got, here again I am not able to say for certain, but it is said to be carried off from the griffins by Arimaspians, a one-eyed race of men. But I do not believe this tale either, that nature produces one-eyed men which in all other respects are like other men. However, it would seem that the extremities which bound the rest of the world on every side and enclose it in the midst, possess the things which by us are thought to be the most beautiful and the most rare.

Now there is a plain in Asia bounded by mountains on all sides, and through the mountains there are five clefts. This plain belonged once to the Chorasmians, and it lies on the borders of the Chorasmians themselves, the Hyrcanians, Parthians, Sarangians, and Thamanaians; but from the time that the Persians began to bear rule it belongs to the king. From this enclosing mountain of which I speak there flows a great river, and its name is Akes. This formerly watered the lands of these nations which have been mentioned, being divided into five streams and conducted through a separate cleft in the mountains to each separate nation; but from the time that they have come to be under the Persians they have suffered as follows:—the king built up the clefts in the mountains and set gates at each cleft; and so, since the water has been shut off from its outlet, the plain within the mountains is made into a sea, because the river runs into it and has no way out in any direction. Those therefore who in former times had been wont to make use of the water, not being able now to make use of it are in great trouble: for during the winter they have rain from heaven, as also other men have, but in the summer they desire to use the water when they sow millet and sesame seed. So then, the water not being granted to them, they come to the Persians both themselves and their wives, and standing at the gates of the king's court they cry and howl; and the king orders that for those who need it most, the gates which lead to their land shall be opened; and when their land has become satiated with drinking in the water, these gates are closed, and he orders the gates to be opened for others, that is to say those most needing it of the rest who remain: and, as I have heard, he exacts large sums of money for opening them, besides the regular tribute.

Thus it is with these matters: but of the seven men who had risen against the Magian, it happened to one, namely Intaphrenes, to be put to death immediately after their insurrection for an outrage which I shall relate. He desired to enter into the king's palace and confer with the king; for the law was in fact so, that those who had risen up against the Magian were permitted to go in to the king's presence without any one to announce them, unless the king happened to be lying with his wife. Accordingly Intaphrenes did not think it fit that any one should announce his coming; but as he was one of the seven, he desired to enter. The gatekeeper however and the bearer of messages endeavoured to prevent him, saying that the king was lying with his wife: but Intaphrenes believing that they were not speaking the truth, drew his sword and cut off their ears and their noses, and stringing these upon his horse's bridle he tied them round their necks and so let them go.

Upon this they showed themselves to the king and told the cause for which they had suffered this; and Dareios, fearing that the six might have done this by common design, sent for each one separately and made trial of his inclinations, as to whether he approved of that which had been done: and when he was fully assured that Intaphrenes had not done this in combination with them, he took both Intaphrenes himself and his sons and all his kinsmen, being much disposed to believe that he was plotting insurrection against him with the help of his relations; and having seized them he put them in bonds as for execution. Then the wife of Intaphrenes, coming constantly to the doors of the king's court, wept and bewailed herself; and by doing this continually after the same manner she moved Dareios to pity her. Accordingly he sent a messenger and said to her: "Woman, king Dareios grants to thee to save from death one of thy kinsmen who are lying in bonds, whomsoever thou desirest of them all." She then, having considered with herself, answered thus: "If in truth the king grants me the life of one, I choose of them all my brother." Dareios being informed of this, and marvelling at her speech, sent and addressed her thus: "Woman, the king asks thee what was in thy mind, that thou didst leave thy husband and thy children to die, and didst choose thy brother to survive, seeing that he is surely less near to thee in blood than thy children, and less dear to thee than thy husband." She made answer: "O king, I might, if heaven willed, have another husband and other children, if I should lose these; but another brother I could by no means have, seeing that my father and my mother are no longer alive. This was in my mind when I said those words." To Dareios then it seemed that the woman had spoken well, and he let go not only him for whose life she asked, but also the eldest of her sons because he was pleased with her: but all the others he slew. One therefore of the seven had perished immediately in the manner which has been related.

Now about the time of the sickness of Cambyses it had come to pass as follows:—There was one Oroites, a Persian, who had been appointed by Cyrus to be governor of the province of Sardis. This man had set his desire upon an unholy thing; for though from Polycrates the Samian he had never suffered anything nor heard any offensive word nor even seen him before that time, he desired to take him and put him to death for a reason of this kind, as most who report the matter say:—while Oroites and another Persian whose name was Mitrobates, ruler of the province of Daskyleion, were sitting at the door of the king's court, they came from words to strife with one another; and as they debated their several claims to excellence, Mitrobates taunting Oroites said: "Dost thou count thyself a man, who didst never yet win for the king the island of Samos, which lies close to thy province, when it is so exceedingly easy of conquest that one of the natives of it rose up against the government with fifteen men-at-arms and got possession of the island, and is now despot of it?" Some say that because he heard this and was stung by the reproach, he formed the desire, not so much to take vengeance on him who said this, as to bring Polycrates to destruction at all costs, since by reason of him he was ill spoken of: the lesser number however of those who tell the tale say that Oroites sent a herald to Samos to ask for something or other, but what it was is not mentioned; and Polycrates happened to be lying down in the men's chamber of his palace, and Anacreon also of Teos was present with him: and somehow, whether it was by intention and because he made no account of the business of Oroites, or whether some chance occurred to bring it about, it happened that the envoy of Oroites came into his presence and spoke with him, and Polycrates, who chanced to be turned away towards the wall, neither turned round at all nor made any answer.

The cause then of the death of Polycrates is reported in these two different ways, and we may believe whichever of them we please. Oroites however, having his residence at that Magnesia which is situated upon the river Maiander, sent Myrsos the son of Gyges, a Lydian, to Samos bearing a message, since he had perceived the designs of Polycrates. For Polycrates was the first of the Hellenes of whom we have any knowledge, who set his mind upon having command of the sea, excepting Minos the Cnossian and any other who may have had command of the sea before his time. Of that which we call mortal race Polycrates was the first; and he had great expectation of becoming ruler of Ionia and of the islands. Oroites accordingly, having perceived that he had this design, sent a message to him and said thus: "Oroites to Polycrates saith as follows: I hear that thou art making plans to get great power, and that thou hast not wealth according to thy high thoughts. Now therefore if thou shalt do as I shall say, thou wilt do well for thyself on the one hand, and also save me from destruction: for king Cambyses is planning death for me, and this is reported to me so that I cannot doubt it. Do thou then carry away out of danger both myself and with me my wealth; and of this keep a part for thyself and a part let me keep, and then so far as wealth may bring it about, thou shalt be ruler of all Hellas. And if thou dost not believe that which I say about the money, send some one, whosoever happens to be most trusted by thee, and to him I will show it."

Polycrates having heard this rejoiced, and was disposed to agree; and as he had a great desire, it seems, for wealth, he first sent Maiandrios the son of Maiandrios, a native of Samos who was his secretary, to see it: this man was the same who not long after these events dedicated all the ornaments of the men's chamber in the palace of Polycrates, ornaments well worth seeing, as an offering to the temple of Hera. Oroites accordingly, having heard that the person sent to examine might be expected soon to come, did as follows, that is to say, he filled eight chests with stones except a small depth at the very top of each, and laid gold above upon the stones; then he tied up the chests and kept them in readiness. So Maiandrios came and looked at them and brought back word to Polycrates: and he upon that prepared to set out thither, although the diviners and also his friends strongly dissuaded him from it, and in spite moreover of a vision which his daughter had seen in sleep of this kind,—it seemed to her that her father was raised up on high and was bathed by Zeus and anointed by the Sun. Having seen this vision, she used every kind of endeavour to dissuade Polycrates from leaving his land to go to Oroites, and besides that, as he was going to his fifty-oared galley she accompanied his departure with prophetic words: and he threatened her that if he should return safe, she should remain unmarried for long; but she prayed that this might come to pass, for she desired rather, she said, to be unmarried for long than to be an orphan, having lost her father.

Polycrates however neglected every counsel and set sail to go to Oroites, taking with him, besides many others of his friends, Demokedes also the son of Calliphon, a man of Croton, who was a physician and practised his art better than any other man of his time. Then when he arrived at Magnesia, Polycrates was miserably put to death in a manner unworthy both of himself and of his high ambition: for excepting those who become despots of the Syracusans, not one besides of the Hellenic despots is worthy to be compared with Polycrates in magnificence. And when he had killed him in a manner not fit to be told, Oroites impaled his body: and of those who accompanied him, as many as were Samians he released, bidding them be grateful to him that they were free men; but all those of his company who were either allies or servants, he held in the estimation of slaves and kept them. Polycrates then being hung up accomplished wholly the vision of his daughter, for he was bathed by Zeus whenever it rained, and anointed by the Sun, giving forth moisture himself from his body.

To this end came the great prosperity of Polycrates, as Amasis the king of Egypt had foretold to him: but not long afterwards retribution overtook Oroites in his turn for the murder of Polycrates. For after the death of Cambyses and the reign of the Magians Oroites remained at Sardis and did no service to the Persians, when they had been deprived of their empire by the Medes; moreover during this time of disturbance he slew Mitrobates the governor in Daskyleion, who had brought up against him the matter of Polycrates as a reproach; and he slew also Cranaspes the son of Mitrobates, both men of repute among the Persians: and besides other various deeds of insolence, once when a bearer of messages had come to him from Dareios, not being pleased with the message which he brought he slew him as he was returning, having set men to lie in wait for him by the way; and having slain him he made away with the bodies both of the man and of his horse.

Dareios accordingly, when he had come to the throne, was desirous of taking vengeance upon Oroites for all his wrongdoings and especially for the murder of Mitrobates and his son. However he did not think it good to act openly and to send an army against him, since his own affairs were still in a disturbed state and he had only lately come to the throne, while he heard that the strength of Oroites was great, seeing that he had a bodyguard of a thousand Persian spearmen and was in possession of the divisions of Phrygia and Lydia and Ionia. Therefore Dareios contrived as follows:—having called together those of the Persians who were of most repute, he said to them: "Persians, which of you all will undertake to perform this matter for me with wisdom, and not by force or with tumult? for where wisdom is wanted, there is no need of force. Which of you, I say, will either bring Oroites alive to me or slay him? for he never yet did any service to the Persians, and on the other hand he has done to them great evil. First he destroyed two of us, Mitrobates and his son; then he slays the men who go to summon him, sent by me, displaying insolence not to be endured. Before therefore he shall accomplish any other evil against the Persians, we must check his course by death."

Thus Dareios asked, and thirty men undertook the matter, each one separately desiring to do it himself; and Dareios stopped their contention and bade them cast lots: so when they cast lots, Bagaios the son of Artontes obtained the lot from among them all. Bagaios accordingly, having obtained the lot, did thus:—he wrote many papers dealing with various matters and on them set the seal of Dareios, and with them he went to Sardis. When he arrived there and came into the presence of Oroites, he took the covers off the papers one after another and gave them to the Royal Secretary to read; for all the governors of provinces have Royal Secretaries. Now Bagaios thus gave the papers in order to make trial of the spearmen of the guard, whether they would accept the motion to revolt from Oroites; and seeing that they paid great reverence to the papers and still more to the words which were recited from them, he gave another paper in which were contained these words: "Persians, king Dareios forbids you to serve as guards to Oroites": and they hearing this lowered to him the points of their spears. Then Bagaios, seeing that in this they were obedient to the paper, took courage upon that and gave the last of the papers to the secretary; and in it was written: "King Dareios commands the Persians who are in Sardis to slay Oroites." So the spearmen of the guard, when they heard this, drew their swords and slew him forthwith. Thus did retribution for the murder of Polycrates the Samian overtake Oroites.

When the wealth of Oroites had come or had been carried up to Susa, it happened not long after, that king Dareios while engaged in hunting wild beasts twisted his foot in leaping off his horse, and it was twisted, as it seems, rather violently, for the ball of his ankle-joint was put out of the socket. Now he had been accustomed to keep about him those of the Egyptians who were accounted the first in the art of medicine, and he made use of their assistance then: but these by wrenching and forcing the foot made the evil continually greater. For seven days then and seven nights Dareios was sleepless owing to the pain which he suffered; and at last on the eighth day, when he was in a wretched state, some one who had heard talk before while yet at Sardis of the skill of Demokedes of Croton, reported this to Dareios; and he bade them bring him forthwith into his presence. So having found him somewhere unnoticed among the slaves of Oroites, they brought him forth into the midst dragging fetters after him and clothed in rags.

When he had been placed in the midst of them, Dareios asked him whether he understood the art; but he would not admit it, fearing lest, if he declared himself to be what he was, he might lose for ever the hope of returning to Hellas: and it was clear to Dareios that he understood that art but was practising another, and he commanded those who had brought him thither to produce scourges and pricks. Accordingly upon that he spoke out, saying that he did not understand it precisely, but that he had kept company with a physician and had some poor knowledge of the art. Then after this, when Dareios had committed the case to him, by using Hellenic drugs and applying mild remedies after the former violent means, he caused him to get sleep, and in a short time made him perfectly well, though he had never hoped to be sound of foot again. Upon this Dareios presented him with two pairs of golden fetters; and he asked him whether it was by design that he had given to him a double share of his suffering, because he had made him well. Being pleased by this saying, Dareios sent him to visit his wives, and the eunuchs in bringing him in said to the women that this was he who had restored to the king his life. Then each one of them plunged a cup into the gold-chest and presented Demokedes with so abundant a gift that his servant, whose name was Skiton, following and gathering up the coins which fell from the cups, collected for himself a very large sum of gold.

This Demokedes came from Croton, and became the associate of Polycrates in the following manner:—at Croton he lived in strife with his father, who was of a harsh temper, and when he could no longer endure him, he departed and came to Egina. Being established there he surpassed in the first year all the other physicians, although he was without appliances and had none of the instruments which are used in the art. In the next year the Eginetan State engaged him for a payment of one talent, in the third year he was engaged by the Athenians for a hundred pounds weight of silver, and in the fourth by Polycrates for two talents. Thus he arrived in Samos; and it was by reason of this man more than anything else that the physicians of Croton got their reputation: for this event happened at the time when the physicians of Croton began to be spoken of as the first in Hellas, while the Kyrenians were reputed to have the second place. About this same time also the Argives had the reputation of being the first musicians in Hellas.

Then Demokedes having healed king Dareios had a very great house in Susa, and had been made a table-companion of the king; and except the one thing of returning to the land of the Hellenes, he had everything. And first as regards the Egyptian physicians who tried to heal the king before him, when they were about to be impaled because they had proved inferior to a physician who was a Hellene, he asked their lives of the king and rescued them from death: then secondly, he rescued an Eleian prophet, who had accompanied Polycrates and had remained unnoticed among the slaves. In short Demokedes was very great in the favour of the king.

Not long time after this another thing came to pass which was this:—Atossa the daughter of Cyrus and wife of Dareios had a tumour upon her breast, which afterwards burst and then was spreading further: and so long as it was not large, she concealed it and said nothing to anybody, because she was ashamed; but afterwards when she was in evil case, she sent for Demokedes and showed it to him: and he said that he would make her well, and caused her to swear that she would surely do for him in return that which he should ask of her; and he would ask, he said, none of such things as are shameful.

So when after this by his treatment he had made her well, then Atossa instructed by Demokedes uttered to Dareios in his bedchamber some such words as these: "O king, though thou hast such great power, thou dost sit still, and dost not win in addition any nation or power for the Persians: and yet it is reasonable that a man who is both young and master of much wealth should be seen to perform some great deed, in order that the Persians may know surely that he is a man by whom they are ruled. It is expedient indeed in two ways that thou shouldest do so, both in order that the Persians may know that their ruler is a man, and in order that they may be worn down by war and not have leisure to plot against thee. For now thou mightest display some great deed, while thou art still young; seeing that as the body grows the spirit grows old also with it, and is blunted for every kind of action." Thus she spoke according to instructions received, and he answered thus: "Woman, thou hast said all the things which I myself have in mind to do; for I have made the plan to yoke together a bridge from this continent to the other and to make expedition against the Scythians, and these designs will be by way of being fulfilled within a little time." Then Atossa said: "Look now,— forbear to go first against the Scythians, for these will be in thy power whenever thou desirest: but do thou, I pray thee, make an expedition against Hellas; for I am desirous to have Lacedemonian women and Argive and Athenian and Corinthian, for attendants, because I hear of them by report: and thou hast the man who of all men is most fitted to show thee all things which relate to Hellas and to be thy guide, that man, I mean, who healed thy foot." Dareios made answer: "Woman, since it seems good to thee that we should first make trial of Hellas, I think it better to send first to them men of the Persians together with him of whom thou speakest, to make investigation, that when these have learnt and seen, they may report each several thing to us; and then I shall go to attack them with full knowledge of all."

Thus he said, and he proceeded to do the deed as he spoke the word: for as soon as day dawned, he summoned fifteen Persians, men of repute, and bade them pass through the coasts of Hellas in company with Demokedes, and take care not to let Demokedes escape from them, but bring him back at all costs. Having thus commanded them, next he summoned Demokedes himself and asked him to act as a guide for the whole of Hellas and show it to the Persians, and then return back: and he bade him take all his movable goods and carry them as gifts to his father and his brothers, saying that he would give him in their place many times as much; and besides this, he said, he would contribute to the gifts a merchant ship filled with all manner of goods, which should sail with him. Dareios, as it seems to me, promised him these things with no crafty design; but Demokedes was afraid that Dareios was making trial of him, and did not make haste to accept all that was offered, but said that he would leave his own things where they were, so that he might have them when he came back; he said however that he accepted the merchant ship which Dareios promised him for the presents to his brothers. Dareios then, having thus given command to him also, sent them away to the sea.

So these, when they had gone down to Phenicia and in Phenicia to the city of Sidon, forthwith manned two triremes, and besides them they also filled a large ship of burden with all manner of goods. Then when they had made all things ready they set sail for Hellas, and touching at various places they saw the coast regions of it and wrote down a description, until at last, when they had seen the greater number of the famous places, they came to Taras in Italy. There from complaisance to Demokedes Aristophilides the king of the Tarentines unfastened and removed the steering-oars of the Median ships, and also confined the Persians in prison, because, as he alleged, they came as spies. While they were being thus dealt with, Demokedes went away and reached Croton; and when he had now reached his own native place, Aristophilides set the Persians free and gave back to them those parts of their ships which he had taken away.

The Persians then sailing thence and pursuing Demokedes reached Croton, and finding him in the market-place they laid hands upon him; and some of the men of Croton fearing the Persian power were willing to let him go, but others took hold of him and struck with their staves at the Persians, who pleaded for themselves in these words: "Men of Croton, take care what ye are about: ye are rescuing a man who was a slave of king Dareios and who ran away from him. How, think you, will king Dareios be content to receive such an insult; and how shall this which ye do be well for you, if ye take him away from us? Against what city, think you, shall we make expedition sooner than against this, and what city before this shall we endeavour to reduce to slavery?" Thus saying they did not however persuade the men of Croton, but having had Demokedes rescued from them and the ship of burden which they were bringing with them taken away, they set sail to go back to Asia, and did not endeavour to visit any more parts of Hellas or to find out about them, being now deprived of their guide. This much however Demokedes gave them as a charge when they were putting forth to sea, bidding them say to Dareios that Demokedes was betrothed to the daughter of Milon: for the wrestler Milon had a great name at the king's court; and I suppose that Demokedes was urgent for this marriage, spending much money to further it, in order that Dareios might see that he was held in honour also in his own country.

The Persians however, after they had put out from Croton, were cast away with their ships in Iapygia; and as they were remaining there as slaves, Gillos a Tarentine exile rescued them and brought them back to king Dareios. In return for this Dareios offered to give him whatsoever thing he should desire; and Gillos chose that he might have the power of returning to Taras, narrating first the story of his misfortune: and in order that he might not disturb all Hellas, as would be the case if on his account a great armament should sail to invade Italy, he said it was enough for him that the men of Cnidos should be those who brought him back, without any others; because he supposed that by these, who were friends with the Tarentines, his return from exile would most easily be effected. Dareios accordingly having promised proceeded to perform; for he sent a message to Cnidos and bade them being back Gillos to Taras: and the men of Cnidos obeyed Dareios, but nevertheless they did not persuade the Tarentines, and they were not strong enough to apply force. Thus then it happened with regard to these things; and these were the first Persians who came from Asia to Hellas, and for the reason which has been mentioned these were sent as spies.

After this king Dareios took Samos before all other cities, whether of Hellenes or Barbarians, and for a cause which was as follows:—When Cambyses the son of Cyrus was marching upon Egypt, many Hellenes arrived in Egypt, some, as might be expected, joining in the campaign to make profit, and some also coming to see the land itself; and among these was Syoloson the son of Aiakes and brother of Polycrates, an exile from Samos. To this Syloson a fortunate chance occurred, which was this:—he had taken and put upon him a flame-coloured mantle, and was about the market-place in Memphis; and Dareios, who was then one of the spearmen of Cambyses and not yet held in any great estimation, seeing him had a desire for the mantle, and going up to him offered to buy it. Then Syloson, seeing that Dareios very greatly desired the mantle, by some divine inspiration said: "I will not sell this for any sum, but I will give it thee for nothing, if, as it appears, it must be thine at all costs." To this Dareios agreed and received from him the garment.

Now Syloson supposed without any doubt that he had altogether lost this by easy simplicity; but when in course of time Cambyses was dead, and the seven Persians had risen up against the Magian, and of the seven Dareios had obtained the kingdom, Syloson heard that the kingdom had come about to that man to whom once in Egypt he had given the garment at his request: accordingly he went up to Susa and sat down at the entrance of the king's palace, and said that he was a benefactor of Dareios. The keeper of the door hearing this reported it to the king; and he marvelled at it and said to him: "Who then of the Hellenes is my benefactor, to whom I am bound by gratitude? seeing that it is now but a short time that I possess the kingdom, and as yet scarcely one of them has come up to our court; and I may almost say that I have no debt owing to a Hellene. Nevertheless bring him in before me, that I may know what he means when he says these things." Then the keeper of the door brought Syloson before him, and when he had been set in the midst, the interpreters asked him who he was and what he had done, that he called himself the benefactor of the king. Syloson accordingly told all that had happened about the mantle, and how he was the man who had given it; to which Dareios made answer: "O most noble of men, thou art he who when as yet I had no power gavest me a gift, small it may be, but nevertheless the kindness is counted with me to be as great as if I should now receive some great thing from some one. Therefore I will give thee in return gold and silver in abundance, that thou mayest not ever repent that thou didst render a service to Dareios the son of Hystaspes." To this Syloson replied: "To me, O king, give neither gold nor silver, but recover and give to me my fatherland Samos, which now that my brother Polycrates has been slain by Oroites is possessed by our slave. This give to me without bloodshed or selling into slavery."

Dareios having heard this prepared to send an expedition with Otanes as commander of it, who had been one of the seven, charging him to accomplish for Syloson all that which he had requested. Otanes then went down to the sea-coast and was preparing the expedition.

Now Maiandrios the son of Maiandrios was holding the rule over Samos, having received the government as a trust from Polycrates; and he, though desiring to show himself the most righteous of men, did not succeed in so doing: for when the death of Polycrates was reported to him, he did as follows:—first he founded an altar to Zeus the Liberator and marked out a sacred enclosure round it, namely that which exists still in the suburb of the city: then after he had done this he gathered together an assembly of all the citizens and spoke these words: "To me, as ye know as well as I, has been entrusted the sceptre of Polycrates and all his power; and now it is open to me to be your ruler; but that for the doing of which I find fault with my neighbour, I will myself refrain from doing, so far as I may: for as I did not approve of Polycrates acting as master of men who were not inferior to himself, so neither do I approve of any other who does such things. Now Polycrates for his part fulfilled his own appointed destiny, and I now give the power into the hands of the people, and proclaim to you equality. These privileges however I think it right to have assigned to me, namely that from the wealth of Polycrates six talents should be taken out and given to me as a special gift; and in addition to this I choose for myself and for my descendants in succession the priesthood of Zeus the Liberator, to whom I myself founded a temple, while I bestow liberty upon you." He, as I say, made these offers to the Samians; but one of them rose up and said: "Nay, but unworthy too art thou to be our ruler, seeing that thou art of mean birth and a pestilent fellow besides. Rather take care that thou give an account of the money which thou hadst to deal with."

Thus said one who was a man of repute among the citizens, whose name was Telesarchos; and Maiandrios perceiving that if he resigned the power, some other would be set up as despot instead of himself, did not keep the purpose at all of resigning it; but having retired to the fortress he sent for each man separately, pretending that he was going to give an account of the money, and so seized them and put them in bonds. These then had been put in bonds; but Maiandrios after this was overtaken by sickness, and his brother, whose name was Lycaretos, expecting that he would die, put all the prisoners to death, in order that he might himself more easily get possession of the power over Samos: and all this happened because, as it appears, they did not choose to be free.

So when the Persians arrived at Samos bringing Syloson home from exile, no one raised a hand against them, and moreover the party of Maiandrios and Maiandrios himself said that they were ready to retire out of the island under a truce. Otanes therefore having agreed on these terms and having made a treaty, the most honourable of the Persians had seats placed for them in front of the fortress and were sitting there.

Now the despot Maiandrios had a brother who was somewhat mad, and his name was Charilaos. This man for some offence which he had been committed had been confined in an underground dungeon, and at this time of which I speak, having heard what was being done and having put his head through out of the dungeon, when he saw the Persians peacefully sitting there he began to cry out and said that he desired to come to speech with Maiandrios. So Maiandrios hearing his voice bade them loose him and bring him into his presence; and as soon as he was brought he began to abuse and revile him, trying to persuade him to attack the Persians, and saying thus: "Thou basest of men, didst thou put me in bonds and judge me worthy of the dungeon under ground, who am thine own brother and did no wrong worthy of bonds, and when thou seest the Persians casting thee forth from the land and making thee homeless, dost thou not dare to take any revenge, though they are so exceedingly easy to be overcome? Nay, but if in truth thou art afraid of them, give me thy mercenaries and I will take vengeance on them for their coming here; and thyself I am willing to let go out of the island."

Thus spoke Charilaos, and Maiandrios accepted that which he said, not, as I think, because he had reached such a height of folly as to suppose that his own power would overcome that of the king, but rather because he grudged Syloson that he should receive from him the State without trouble, and with no injury inflicted upon it. Therefore he desired to provoke the Persians to anger and make the Samian power as feeble as possible before he gave it up to him, being well assured that the Persians, when they had suffered evil, would be likely to be as bitter against the Samians as well as against those who did the wrong, and knowing also that he had a safe way of escape from the island whenever he desired: for he had had a secret passage made under ground, leading from the fortress to the sea. Maiandrios then himself sailed out from Samos; but Charilaos armed all the mercenaries, and opening wide the gates sent them out upon the Persians, who were not expecting any such thing, but supposed that all had been arranged: and the mercenaries falling upon them began to slay those of the Persians who had seats carried for them and were of most account. While these were thus engaged, the rest of the Persian force came to the rescue, and the mercenaries were hard pressed and forced to retire to the fortress.

Then Otanes the Persian commander, seeing that the Persians had suffered greatly, purposely forgot the commands which Dareios gave him when he sent him forth, not to kill any one of the Samians nor to sell any into slavery, but to restore the island to Syloson free from all suffering of calamity,—these commands, I say, he purposely forgot, and gave the word to his army to slay every one whom they should take, man or boy, without distinction. So while some of the army were besieging the fortress, others were slaying every one who came in their way, in sanctuary or out of sanctuary equally.

Meanwhile Maiandrios had escaped from Samos and was sailing to Lacedemon; and having come thither and caused to be brought up to the city the things which he had taken with him when he departed, he did as follows:—first, he would set out his cups of silver and of gold, and then while the servants were cleaning them, he would be engaged in conversation with Cleomenes the son of Anaxandrides, then king of Sparta, and would bring him on to his house; and when Cleomenes saw the cups he marvelled and was astonished at them, and Maiandrios would bid him take away with him as many of them as he pleased. Maiandrios said this twice or three times, but Cleomenes herein showed himself the most upright of men; for he not only did not think fit to take that which was offered, but perceiving that Maiandrios would make presents to others of the citizens, and so obtain assistance for himself, he went to the Ephors and said that it was better for Sparta that the stranger of Samos should depart from Peloponnesus, lest he might persuade either himself or some other man of the Spartans to act basely. They accordingly accepted his counsel, and expelled Maiandrios by proclamation.

As to Samos, the Persians, after sweeping the population off it, delivered it to Syloson stripped of men. Afterwards however the commander Otanes even joined in settling people there, moved by a vision of a dream and by a disease which seized him, so that he was diseased in the genital organs.

After a naval force had thus gone against Samos, the Babylonians made revolt, being for this exceedingly well prepared; for during all the time of the reign of the Magian and of the insurrection of the seven, during all this time and the attendant confusion they were preparing themselves for the siege of their city: and it chanced by some means that they were not observed to be doing this. Then when they made open revolt, they did as follows:—after setting apart their mothers first, each man set apart also for himself one woman, whosoever he wished of his own household, and all the remainder they gathered together and killed by suffocation. Each man set apart the one who has been mentioned to serve as a maker of bread, and they suffocated the rest in order that they might not consume their provisions.

Dareios being informed of this and having gathered together all his power, made expedition against them, and when he had marched his army up to Babylon he began to besiege them; but they cared nothing about the siege, for the Babylonians used to go up to the battlements of the wall and show contempt of Dareios and of his army by gestures and by words; and one of them uttered this saying: "Why, O Persians, do ye remain sitting here, and not depart? For then only shall ye capture us, when mules shall bring forth young." This was said by one of the Babylonians, not supposing that a mule would ever bring forth young.

So when a year and seven months had now passed by, Dareios began to be vexed and his whole army with him, not being able to conquer the Babylonians. And yet Dareios had used against them every kind of device and every possible means, but not even so could he conquer them, though besides other devices he had attempted it by that also with which Cyrus conquered them; but the Babylonians were terribly on their guard and he was not able to conquer them.

Then in the twentieth month there happened to Zopyros the son of that Megabyzos who had been of the seven men who slew the Magian, to this Zopyros, I say, son of Megabyzos there happened a prodigy,—one of the mules which served as bearers of provisions for him produced young: and when this was reported to him, and Zopyros had himself seen the foal, because he did not believe the report, he charged those who had seen it not to tell that which had happened to any one, and he considered with himself what to do. And having regard to the words spoken by the Babylonian, who had said at first that when mules should produce young, then the wall would be taken, having regard (I say) to this ominous saying, it seemed to Zopyros that Babylon could be taken: for he thought that both the man had spoken and his mule had produced young by divine dispensation.

Since then it seemed to him that it was now fated that Babylon should be captured, he went to Dareios and inquired of him whether he thought it a matter of very great moment to conquer Babylon; and hearing in answer that he thought it of great consequence, he considered again how he might be the man to take it and how the work might be his own: for among the Persians benefits are accounted worthy of a very high degree of honour. He considered accordingly that he was not able to make conquest of it by any other means, but only if he should maltreat himself and desert to their side. So, making light esteem of himself, he maltreated his own body in a manner which could not be cured; for he cut off his nose and his ears, and shaved his hair round in an unseemly way, and scourged himself, and so went into the presence of Dareios.

And Dareios was exceedingly troubled when he saw the man of most repute with him thus maltreated; and leaping up from his seat he cried aloud and asked him who was the person who had maltreated him, and for what deed. He replied: "That man does not exist, excepting thee, who has so great power as to bring me into this condition; and not any stranger, O king, has done this, but I myself to myself, accounting it a very grievous thing that the Assyrians should make a mock of the Persians." He made answer: "Thou most reckless of men, thou didst set the fairest name to the foulest deed when thou saidest that on account of those who are besieged thou didst bring thyself into a condition which cannot be cured. How, O thou senseless one, will the enemy surrender to us more quickly, because thou hast maltreated thyself? Surely thou didst wander out of thy senses in thus destroying thyself." And he said, "If I had communicated to thee that which I was about to do, thou wouldst not have permitted me to do it; but as it was, I did it on my own account. Now therefore, unless something is wanting on thy part, we shall conquer Babylon: for I shall go straightway as a deserter to the wall; and I shall say to them that I suffered this treatment at thy hands: and I think that when I have convinced them that this is so, I shall obtain the command of a part of their forces. Do thou then on the tenth day from that on which I shall enter within the wall take of those troops about which thou wilt have no concern if they be destroyed,—of these, I say, get a thousand by the gate of the city which is called the gate of Semiramis; and after this again on the seventh day after the tenth set, I pray thee, two thousand by the gate which is called the gate of the Ninevites; and after this seventh day let twenty days elapse, and then lead other four thousand and place them by the gate called the gate of the Chaldeans: and let neither the former men nor these have any weapons to defend them except daggers, but this weapon let them have. Then after the twentieth day at once bid the rest of the army make an attack on the wall all round, and set the Persians, I pray thee, by those gates which are called the gate of Belos and the gate of Kissia: for, as I think, when I have displayed great deeds of prowess, the Babylonians will entrust to me, besides their other things, also the keys which draw the bolts of the gates. Then after that it shall be the care of myself and the Persians to do that which ought to be done."

Having thus enjoined he proceeded to go to the gate of the city, turning to look behind him as he went, as if he were in truth a deserter; and those who were set in that part of the wall, seeing him from the towers ran down, and slightly opening one wing of the gate asked who he was, and for what purpose he had come. And he addressed them and said that he was Zopyros, and that he came as a deserter to them. The gate-keepers accordingly when they heard this led him to the public assembly of the Babylonians; and being introduced before it he began to lament his fortunes, saying that he had in fact suffered at his own hands, and that he had suffered this because he had counselled the king to withdraw his army, since in truth there seemed to be no means of taking the town: "And now," he went on to say, "I am come for very great good to you, O Babylonians, but for very great evil to Dareios and his army, and to the Persians, for he shall surely not escape with impunity for having thus maltreated me; and I know all the courses of his counsels."

Thus he spoke, and the Babylonians, when they saw the man of most reputation among the Persians deprived of nose and ears and smeared over with blood from scourging, supposing assuredly that he was speaking the truth and had come to be their helper, were ready to put in his power that for which he asked them, and he asked them that he might command a certain force. Then when he had obtained this from them, he did that which he had agreed with Dareios that he would do; for he led out on the tenth day the army of the Babylonians, and having surrounded the thousand men whom he had enjoined Dareios first to set there, he slew them. The Babylonians accordingly, perceiving that the deeds which he displayed were in accordance with his words, were very greatly rejoiced and were ready to serve him in all things: and after the lapse of the days which had been agreed upon, he again chose men of the Babylonians and led them out and slew the two thousand men of the troops of Dareios. Seeing this deed also, the Babylonians all had the name of Zopyros upon their tongues, and were loud in his praise. He then again, after the lapse of the days which had been agreed upon, led them out to the place appointed, and surrounded the four thousand and slew them. When this also had been done, Zopyros was everything among the Babylonians, and he was appointed both commander of their army and guardian of their walls.

But when Dareios made an attack according to the agreement on every side of the wall, then Zopyros discovered all his craft: for while the Babylonians, having gone up on the wall, were defending themselves against the attacks of the army of Dareios, Zopyros opened the gates called the gates of Kissia and of Belos, and let in the Persians within the wall. And of the Babylonians those who saw that which was done fled to the temple of Zeus Belos, but those who did not see remained each in his own appointed place, until at last they also learnt that they had been betrayed.

Thus was Babylon conquered for the second time: and Dareios when he had overcome the Babylonians, first took away the wall from round their city and pulled down all the gates; for when Cyrus took Babylon before him, he did neither of these things: and secondly Dareios impaled the leading men to the number of about three thousand, but to the rest of the Babylonians he gave back their city to dwell in: and to provide that the Babylonians should have wives, in order that their race might be propagated, Dareios did as follows (for their own wives, as has been declared at the beginning, the Babylonians had suffocated, in provident care for their store of food):—he ordered the nations who dwelt round to bring women to Babylon, fixing a certain number for each nation, so that the sum total of fifty thousand women was brought together, and from these women the present Babylonians are descended.

As for Zopyros, in the judgment of Dareios no one of the Persians surpassed him in good service, either of those who came after or of those who had gone before, excepting Cyrus alone; for to Cyrus no man of the Persians ever yet ventured to compare himself: and Dareios is said to have declared often that he would rather that Zopyros were free from the injury than that he should have twenty Babylons added to his possession in addition to that one which he had. Moreover he gave him great honours; for not only did he give him every year those things which by the Persians are accounted the most honourable, but also he granted him Babylon to rule free from tribute, so long as he should live; and he added many other gifts. The son of this Zopyros was Megabyzos, who was made commander in Egypt against the Athenians and their allies; and the son of this Megabyzos was Zopyros, who went over to Athens as a deserter from the Persians.

Book IV

The Fourth Book of the Histories, Called Melpomene

After Babylon had been taken, the march of Dareios himself against the Scythians took place: for now that Asia was flourishing in respect of population, and large sums were being gathered in as revenue, Dareios formed the desire to take vengeance upon the Scythians, because they had first invaded the Median land and had overcome in fight those who opposed them; and thus they had been the beginners of wrong. The Scythians in truth, as I have before said, had ruled over Upper Asia for eight-and-twenty years; for they had invaded Asia in their pursuit of the Kimmerians, and they had deposed the Medes from their rule, who had rule over Asia before the Scythians came. Now when the Scythians had been absent from their own land for eight-and-twenty years, as they were returning to it after that interval of time, they were met by a contest not less severe than that which they had had with the Medes, since they found an army of no mean size opposing them. For the wives of the Scythians, because their husbands were absent from them for a long time, had associated with the slaves.

Now the Scythians put out the eyes of all their slaves because of the milk which they drink; and they do as follows:—they take blow-pipes of bone just like flutes, and these they insert into the vagina of the mare and blow with their mouths, and others milk while they blow: and they say that they do this because the veins of the mare are thus filled, being blown out, and so the udder is let down. When they had drawn the milk they pour it into wooden vessels hollowed out, and they set the blind slaves in order about the vessels and agitate the milk. Then that which comes to the top they skim off, considering it the more valuable part, whereas they esteem that which settles down to be less good than the other. For this reason the Scythians put out the eyes of all whom they catch; for they are not tillers of the soil but nomads.

From these their slaves then, I say, and from their wives had been born and bred up a generation of young men, who having learnt the manner of their birth set themselves to oppose the Scythians as they were returning from the Medes. And first they cut off their land by digging a broad trench extending from the Tauric mountains to the Maiotian lake, at the point where this is broadest; then afterwards when the Scythians attempted to invade the land, they took up a position against them and fought; and as they fought many times, and the Scythians were not able to get any advantage in the fighting, one of them said: "What a thing is this that we are doing, Scythians! We are fighting against our own slaves, and we are not only becoming fewer in number ourselves by being slain in battle, but also we are killing them, and so we shall have fewer to rule over in future. Now therefore to me it seems good that we leave spears and bows and that each one take his horse-whip and so go up close to them: for so long as they saw us with arms in our hands, they thought themselves equal to us and of equal birth; but when they shall see that we have whips instead of arms, they will perceive that they are our slaves, and having acknowledged this they will not await our onset."

When they heard this, the Scythians proceeded to do that which he said, and the others being panic-stricken by that which was done forgot their fighting and fled. Thus the Scythians had ruled over Asia; and in such manner, when they were driven out again by the Medes, they had returned to their own land. For this Dareios wished to take vengeance upon them, and was gathering together an army to go against them.

. Now the Scythians say that their nation is the youngest of all nations, and that this came to pass as follows:—The first man who ever existed in this region, which then was desert, was one named Targitaos: and of this Targitaos they say, though I do not believe it for my part, however they say the parents were Zeus and the daughter of the river Borysthenes. Targitaos, they report, was produced from some such origin as this, and of him were begotten three sons, Lipoxaïs and Arpoxaïs and the youngest Colaxaïs. In the reign of these there came down from heaven certain things wrought of gold, a plough, a yoke, a battle-axe, and a cup, and fell in the Scythian land: and first the eldest saw and came near them, desiring to take them, but the gold blazed with fire when he approached it: then when he had gone away from it, the second approached, and again it did the same thing. These then the gold repelled by blazing with fire; but when the third and youngest came up to it, the flame was quenched, and he carried them to his own house. The elder brothers then, acknowledging the significance of this thing, delivered the whole of the kingly power to the youngest.

From Lixopaïs, they say, are descended those Scythians who are called the race of the Auchatai; from the middle brother Arpoxaïs those who are called Catiaroi and Traspians, and from the youngest of them the "Royal" tribe, who are called Paralatai: and the whole together are called, they say, Scolotoi, after the name of their king; but the Hellenes gave them the name of Scythians.

Thus the Scythians say they were produced; and from the time of their origin, that is to say from the first king Targitaos, to the passing over of Dareios against them, they say that there is a period of a thousand years and no more. Now this sacred gold is guarded by the kings with the utmost care, and they visit it every year with solemn sacrifices of propitiation: moreover if any one goes to sleep while watching in the open air over this gold during the festival, the Scythians say that he does not live out the year; and there is given him for this so much land as he shall ride round himself on his horse in one day. Now as the land was large, Colaxaïs, they say, established three kingdoms for his sons; and of these he made one larger than the rest, and in this the gold is kept. But as to the upper parts which lie on the North side of those who dwell above this land, they say one can neither see nor pass through any further by reason of feathers which are poured down; for both the earth and the air are full of feathers, and this is that which shuts off the view.

Thus say the Scythians about themselves and about the region above them; but the Hellenes who dwell about the Pontus say as follows:—Heracles driving the cattle of Geryones came to this land, then desert, which the Scythians now inhabit; and Geryones, says the tale, dwelt away from the region of the Pontus, living in the island called by the Hellenes Erytheia, near Gadeira which is outside the Pillars of Heracles by the Ocean.—As to the Ocean, they say indeed that it flows round the whole earth beginning from the place of the sunrising, but they do not prove this by facts.—From thence Heracles came to the land now called Scythia; and as a storm came upon him together with icy cold, he drew over him his lion's skin and went to sleep. Meanwhile the mares harnessed in his chariot disappeared by a miraculous chance, as they were feeding.

Then when Heracles woke he sought for them; and having gone over the whole land, at last he came to the region which is called Hylaia; and there he found in a cave a kind of twofold creature formed by the union of a maiden and a serpent, whose upper parts from the buttocks upwards were those of a woman, but her lower parts were those of a snake. Having seen her and marvelled at her, he asked her then whether she had seen any mares straying anywhere; and she said that she had them herself and would not give them up until he lay with her; and Heracles lay with her on condition of receiving them. She then tried to put off the giving back of the mares, desiring to have Heracles with her as long as possible, while he on the other hand desired to get the mares and depart; and at last she gave them back and said: "These mares when they came hither I saved for thee, and thou didst give me reward for saving them; for I have by thee three sons. Tell me then, what must I do with these when they shall be grown to manhood, whether I shall settle them here, for over this land I have power alone, or send them away to thee?" She thus asked of him, and he, they say, replied: "When thou seest that the boys are grown to men, do this and thou shalt not fail of doing right:—whichsoever of them thou seest able to stretch this bow as I do now, and to be girded with this girdle, him cause to be the settler of this land; but whosoever of them fails in the deeds which I enjoin, send him forth out of the land: and if thou shalt do thus, thou wilt both have delight thyself and perform that which has been enjoined to thee."

Upon this he drew one of his bows (for up to that time Heracles, they say, was wont to carry two) and showed her the girdle, and then he delivered to her both the bow and the girdle, which had at the end of its clasp a golden cup; and having given them he departed. She then, when her sons had been born and had grown to be men, gave them names first, calling one of them Agathyrsos and the next Gelonos and the youngest Skythes; then bearing in mind the charge given to her, she did that which was enjoined. And two of her sons, Agathyrsos and Gelonos, not having proved themselves able to attain to the task set before them, departed from the land, being cast out by her who bore them; but Skythes the youngest of them performed the task and remained in the land: and from Skythes the son of Heracles were descended, they say, the succeeding kings of the Scythians (Skythians): and they say moreover that it is by reason of the cup that the Scythians still even to this day wear cups attached to their girdles: and this alone his mother contrived for Skythes. Such is the story told by the Hellenes who dwell about the Pontus.

There is however also another story, which is as follows, and to this I am most inclined myself. It is to the effect that the nomad Scythians dwelling in Asia, being hard pressed in war by the Massagetai, left their abode and crossing the river Araxes came towards the Kimmerian land (for the land which now is occupied by the Scythians is said to have been in former times the land of the Kimmerians); and the Kimmerians, when the Scythians were coming against them, took counsel together, seeing that a great host was coming to fight against them; and it proved that their opinions were divided, both opinions being vehemently maintained, but the better being that of their kings: for the opinion of the people was that it was necessary to depart and that they ought not to run the risk of fighting against so many, but that of the kings was to fight for their land with those who came against them: and as neither the people were willing by means to agree to the counsel of the kings nor the kings to that of the people, the people planned to depart without fighting and to deliver up the land to the invaders, while the kings resolved to die and to be laid in their own land, and not to flee with the mass of the people, considering the many goods of fortune which they had enjoyed, and the many evils which it might be supposed would come upon them, if they fled from their native land. Having resolved upon this, they parted into two bodies, and making their numbers equal they fought with one another: and when these had all been killed by one another's hands, then the people of the Kimmerians buried them by the bank of the river Tyras (where their burial-place is still to be seen), and having buried them, then they made their way out from the land, and the Scythians when they came upon it found the land deserted of its inhabitants.

And there are at the present time in the land of Scythia Kimmerian walls, and a Kimmerian ferry; and there is also a region which is called Kimmeria, and the so-called Kimmerian Bosphorus. It is known moreover that the Kimmerians, in their flight to Asia from the Scythians, also made a settlement on that peninsula on which now stands the Hellenic city of Sinope; and it is known too that the Scythians pursued them and invaded the land of Media, having missed their way; for while the Kimmerians kept ever along by the sea in their flight, the Scythians pursued them keeping Caucasus on their right hand, until at last they invaded Media, directing their course inland. This then which has been told is another story, and it is common both to Hellenes and Barbarians.

Aristeas however the son of Caÿstrobios, a man of Proconnesos, said in the verses which he composed, that he came to the land of the Issedonians being possessed by Phoebus, and that beyond the Issedonians dwelt Arimaspians, a one-eyed race, and beyond these the gold-guarding griffins, and beyond them the Hyperboreans extending as far as the sea: and all these except the Hyperboreans, beginning with the Arimaspians, were continually making war on their neighbours, and the Issedonians were gradually driven out of their country by the Arimaspians and the Scythians by the Issedonians, and so the Kimmerians, who dwelt on the Southern Sea, being pressed by the Scythians left their land. Thus neither does he agree in regard to this land with the report of the Scythians.

As to Aristeas who composed this, I have said already whence he was; and I will tell also the tale which I heard about him in Proconnesos and Kyzicos. They say that Aristeas, who was in birth inferior to none of the citizens, entered into a fuller's shop in Proconnesos and there died; and the fuller closed his workshop and went away to report the matter to those who were related to the dead man. And when the news had been spread abroad about the city that Aristeas was dead, a man of Kyzicos who had come from the town of Artake entered into controversy with those who said so, and declared that he had met him going towards Kyzicos and had spoken with him: and while he was vehement in dispute, those who were related to the dead man came to the fuller's shop with the things proper in order to take up the corpse for burial; and when the house was opened, Aristeas was not found there either dead or alive. In the seventh year after this he appeared at Proconnesos and composed those verses which are now called by the Hellenes the Arimaspeia, and having composed them he disappeared the second time.

So much is told by these cities; and what follows I know happened to the people of Metapontion in Italy two hundred and forty years after the second disappearance of Aristeas, as I found by putting together the evidence at Proconnesos and Metapontion. The people of Metapontion say that Aristeas himself appeared in their land and bade them set up an altar of Apollo and place by its side a statue bearing the name of Aristeas of Proconnesos; for he told them that to their land alone of all the Italiotes Apollo had come, and he, who now was Aristeas, was accompanying him, being then a raven when he accompanied the god. Having said this he disappeared; and the Metapontines say that they sent to Delphi and asked the god what the apparition of the man meant: and the Pythian prophetess bade them obey the command of the apparition, and told them that if they obeyed, it would be the better for them. They therefore accepted this answer and performed the commands; and there stands a statue now bearing the name of Aristeas close by the side of the altar dedicated to Apollo, and round it stand laurel trees; and the altar is set up in the market-place. Let this suffice which has been said about Aristeas.

Now of the land about which this account has been begun, no one knows precisely what lies beyond it: for I am not able to hear of any one who alleges that he knows as an eye-witness; and even Aristeas, the man of whom I was making mention just now, even he, I say, did not allege, although he was composing verse, that he went further than the Issedonians; but that which is beyond them he spoke of by hearsay, and reported that it was the Issedonians who said these things. So far however as we were able to arrive at certainty by hearsay, carrying inquiries as far as possible, all this shall be told.

Beginning with the trading station of the Borysthenites,—for of the parts along the sea this is the central point of all Scythia,—beginning with this, the first regions are occupied by the Callipidai, who are Hellenic Scythians; and above these is another race, who are called Alazonians. These last and the Callipidai in all other respects have the same customs as the Scythians, but they both sow corn and use it as food, and also onions, leeks, lentils and millet. Above the Alazonians dwell Scythians who till the ground, and these sow their corn not for food but to sell.

Beyond them dwell the Neuroi; and beyond the Neuroi towards the North Wind is a region without inhabitants, as far as we know. These races are along the river Hypanis to the West of the Borysthenes; but after crossing the Borysthenes, first from the sea-coast is Hylaia, and beyond this as one goes up the river dwell agricultural Scythians, whom the Hellenes who live upon the river Hypanis call Borysthenites, calling themselves at the same time citizens of Olbia. These agricultural Scythians occupy the region which extends Eastwards for a distance of three days' journey, reaching to a river which is called Panticapes, and Northwards for a distance of eleven days' sail up the Borysthenes. Then immediately beyond these begins the desert and extends for a great distance; and on the other side of the desert dwell the Androphagoi, a race apart by themselves and having no connection with the Scythians. Beyond them begins a region which is really desert and has no race of men in it, as far as we know.

The region which lies to the East of these agricultural Scythians, after one has crossed the river Panticapes, is occupied by nomad Scythians, who neither sow anything nor plough the earth; and this whole region is bare of trees except Hylaia. These nomads occupy a country which extends to the river Gerros, a distance of fourteen days' journey Eastwards.

Then on the other side of the Gerros we have those parts which are called the "Royal" lands and those Scythians who are the bravest and most numerous and who esteem the other Scythians their slaves. These reach Southwards to the Tauric land, and Eastwards to the trench which those who were begotten of the blind slaves dug, and to the trading station which is called Cremnoi upon the Maiotian lake; and some parts of their country reach to the river Tanaïs. Beyond the Royal Scythians towards the North Wind dwell the Melanchlainoi, of a different race and not Scythian. The region beyond the Melanchlainoi is marshy and not inhabited by any, so far as we know.

After one has crossed the river Tanaïs the country is no longer Scythia, but the first of the divisions belongs to the Sauromatai, who beginning at the corner of the Maiotian lake occupy land extending towards the North Wind fifteen days' journey, and wholly bare of trees both cultivated and wild. Above these, holding the next division of land, dwell the Budinoi, who occupy a land wholly overgrown with forest consisting of all kinds of trees.

Then beyond the Budinoi towards the North, first there is desert for seven days' journey; and after the desert turning aside somewhat more towards the East Wind we come to land occupied by the Thyssagetai, a numerous people and of separate race from the others. These live by hunting; and bordering upon them there are settled also in these same regions men who are called Irycai, who also live by hunting, which they practise in the following manner:—the hunter climbs up a tree and lies in wait there for his game (now trees are abundant in all this country), and each has a horse at hand, which has been taught to lie down upon its belly in order that it may make itself low, and also a dog: and when he sees the wild animal from the tree, he first shoots his arrow and then mounts upon his horse and pursues it, and the dog seizes hold of it. Above these in a direction towards the East dwell other Scythians, who have revolted from the Royal Scythians and so have come to this region.

As far as the country of these Scythians the whole land which has been described is level plain and has a deep soil; but after this point it is stony and rugged. Then when one has passed through a great extent of this rugged country, there dwell in the skirts of lofty mountains men who are said to be all bald-headed from their birth, male and female equally, and who have flat noses and large chins and speak a language of their own, using the Scythian manner of dress, and living on the produce of trees. The tree on the fruit of which they live is called the Pontic tree, and it is about the size of a fig-tree: this bears a fruit the size of a bean, containing a stone. When the fruit has ripened, they strain it through cloths and there flows from it a thick black juice, and this juice which flows from it is called as-chy. This they either lick up or drink mixed with milk, and from its lees, that is the solid part, they make cakes and use them for food; for they have not many cattle, since the pastures there are by no means good. Each man has his dwelling under a tree, in winter covering the tree all round with close white felt-cloth, and in summer without it. These are injured by no men, for they are said to be sacred, and they possess no weapon of war. These are they also who decide the disputes rising among their neighbours; and besides this, whatever fugitive takes refuge with them is injured by no one: and they are called Argippaians.

Now as far as these bald-headed men there is abundantly clear information about the land and about the nations on this side of them; for not only do certain of the Scythians go to them, from whom it is not difficult to get information, but also some of the Hellenes who are at the trading-station of the Borysthenes and the other trading-places of the Pontic coast: and those of the Scythians who go to them transact their business through seven interpreters and in seven different languages.

So far as these, I say, the land is known; but concerning the region to the North of the bald-headed men no one can speak with certainty, for lofty and impassable mountains divide it off, and no one passes over them. However these bald-headed men say (though I do not believe it) that the mountains are inhabited by men with goats' feet; and that after one has passed beyond these, others are found who sleep through six months of the year. This I do not admit at all as true. However, the country to the East of the bald-headed men is known with certainty, being inhabited by the Issedonians, but that which lies beyond both the bald-headed men and the Issedonians towards the North Wind is unknown, except so far as we know it from the accounts given by these nations which have just been mentioned.

The Issedonians are said to have these customs:—when a man's father is dead, all the relations bring cattle to the house, and then having slain them and cut up the flesh, they cut up also the dead body of the father of their entertainer, and mixing all the flesh together they set forth a banquet. His skull however they strip of the flesh and clean it out and then gild it over, and after that they deal with it as a sacred thing and perform for the dead man great sacrifices every year. This each son does for his father, just as the Hellenes keep the day of memorial for the dead. In other respects however this race also is said to live righteously, and their women have equal rights with the men.

These then also are known; but as to the region beyond them, it is the Issedonians who report that there are there one-eyed men and gold-guarding griffins; and the Scythians report this having received it from them, and from the Scythians we, that is the rest of mankind, have got our belief; and we call them in Scythian language Arimaspians, for the Scythians call the number one arima and the eye spu.

This whole land which has been described is so exceedingly severe in climate, that for eight months of the year there is frost so hard as to be intolerable; and during these if you pour out water you will not be able to make mud, but only if you kindle a fire can you make it; and the sea is frozen and the whole of the Kimmerian Bosphorus, so that the Scythians who are settled within the trench make expeditions and drive their waggons over into the country of the Sindians. Thus it continues to be winter for eight months, and even for the remaining four it is cold in those parts. This winter is distinguished in its character from all the winters which come in other parts of the world; for in it there is no rain to speak of at the usual season for rain, whereas in summer it rains continually; and thunder does not come at the time when it comes in other countries, but is very frequent, in the summer; and if thunder comes in winter, it is marvelled at as a prodigy: just so, if an earthquake happens, whether in summer or in winter, it is accounted a prodigy in Scythia. Horses are able to endure this winter, but neither mules nor asses can endure it at all, whereas in other countries horses if they stand in frost lose their limbs by mortification, while asses and mules endure it.

I think also that it is for this reason that the hornless breed of oxen in that country have no horns growing; and there is a verse of Homer in the Odyssey supporting my opinion, which runs this:—

"Also the Libyan land, where the sheep very quickly grow hornèd,"

for it is rightly said that in hot regions the horns come quickly, whereas in extreme cold the animals either have no horns growing at all, or hardly any.

In that land then this takes place on account of the cold; but (since my history proceeded from the first seeking occasions for digression) I feel wonder that in the whole land of Elis mules cannot be bred, though that region is not cold, nor is there any other evident cause. The Eleians themselves say that in consequence of some curse mules are not begotten in their land; but when the time approaches for the mares to conceive, they drive them out into the neighbouring lands and there in the land of their neighbours they admit to them the he-asses until the mares are pregnant, and then they drive them back.

As to the feathers of which the Scythians say that the air is full, and that by reason of them they are not able either to see or to pass through the further parts of the continent, the opinion which I have is this:—in the parts beyond this land it snows continually, though less in summer than in winter, as might be supposed. Now whomsoever has seen close at hand snow falling thickly, knows what I mean without further explanation, for the snow is like feathers: and on account of this wintry weather, being such as I have said, the Northern parts of this continent are uninhabitable. I think therefore that by the feathers the Scythians and those who dwell near them mean symbolically the snow. This then which has been said goes to the furthest extent of the accounts given.

About a Hyperborean people the Scythians report nothing, nor do any of those who dwell in this region, unless it be the Issedonians: but in my opinion neither do these report anything; for if they did the Scythians also would report it, as they do about the one-eyed people. Hesiod however has spoken of Hyperboreans, and so also has Homer in the poem of the "Epigonoi," at least if Homer was really the composer of that Epic.

But much more about them is reported by the people of Delos than by any others. For these say that sacred offerings bound up in wheat straw are carried from the land of the Hyperboreans and come to the Scythians, and then from the Scythians the neighbouring nations in succession receive them and convey them Westwards, finally as far as the Adriatic: thence they are sent forward towards the South, and the people of Dodona receive them first of all the Hellenes, and from these they come down to the Malian gulf and are passed over to Euboea, where city sends them on to city till they come to Carystos. After this Andros is left out, for the Carystians are those who bring them to Tenos, and the Tenians to Delos. Thus they say that these sacred offerings come to Delos; but at first, they say, the Hyperboreans sent two maidens bearing the sacred offerings, whose names, say the Delians, were Hyperoche and Laodike, and with them for their protection the Hyperboreans sent five men of their nation to attend them, those namely who are now called Perphereës and have great honours paid to them in Delos. Since however the Hyperboreans found that those who were sent away did not return back, they were troubled to think that it would always befall them to send out and not to receive back; and so they bore the offerings to the borders of their land bound up in wheat straw, and laid a charge upon their neighbours, bidding them send these forward from themselves to another nation. These things then, they say, come to Delos being thus sent forward; and I know of my own knowledge that a thing is done which has resemblance to these offerings, namely that the women of Thrace and Paionia, when they sacrifice to Artemis "the Queen," do not make their offerings without wheat straw.

These I know do as I have said; and for those maidens from the Hyperboreans, who died in Delos, both the girls and the boys of the Delians cut off their hair: the former before marriage cut off a lock and having wound it round a spindle lay it upon the tomb (now the tomb is on the left hand as one goes into the temple of Artemis, and over it grows an olive-tree), and all the boys of the Delians wind some of their hair about a green shoot of some tree, and they also place it upon the tomb.

The maidens, I say, have this honour paid them by the dwellers in Delos: and the same people say that Arge and Opis also, being maidens, came to Delos, passing from the Hyperboreans by the same nations which have been mentioned, even before Hyperoche and Laodike. These last, they say, came bearing for Eileithuia the tribute which they had laid upon themselves for the speedy birth, but Arge and Opis came with the divinities themselves, and other honours have been assigned to them by the people of Delos: for the women, they say, collect for them, naming them by their names in the hymn which Olen a man of Lykia composed in their honour; and both the natives of the other islands and the Ionians have learnt from them to sing hymns naming Opis and Arge and collecting:—now this Olen came from Lukia and composed also the other ancient hymns which are sung in Delos:—and moreover they say that when the thighs of the victim are consumed upon the altar, the ashes of them are used to cast upon the grave of Opis and Arge. Now their grave is behind the temple of Artemis, turned towards the East, close to the banqueting hall of the Keïeans.

Let this suffice which has been said of the Hyperboreans; for the tale of Abaris, who is reported to have been a Hyperborean, I do not tell, namely how he carried the arrow about all over the earth, eating no food. If however there are any Hyperboreans, it follows that there are also Hypernotians; and I laugh when I see that, though many before this have drawn maps of the Earth, yet no one has set the matter forth in an intelligent way; seeing that they draw Ocean flowing round the Earth, which is circular exactly as if drawn with compasses, and they make Asia equal in size to Europe. In a few words I shall declare the size of each division and of what nature it is as regards outline.

The Persians inhabit Asia extending to the Southern Sea, which is called the Erythraian; and above these towards the North Wind dwell the Medes, and above the Medes the Saspeirians, and above the Saspeirians the Colchians, extending to the Northern Sea, into which the river Phasis runs. These four nations inhabit from sea to sea.

From them Westwards two peninsulas stretch out from Asia into the sea, and these I will describe. The first peninsula on the one of its sides, that is the Northern, stretches along beginning from the Phasis and extending to the sea, going along the Pontus and the Hellespont as far as Sigeion in the land of Troy; and on the Southern side the same peninsula stretches from the Myriandrian gulf, which lies near Phenicia, in the direction of the sea as far as the headland Triopion; and in this peninsula dwell thirty races of men.

This then is one of the peninsulas, and the other beginning from the land of the Persians stretches along to the Erythraian Sea, including Persia and next after it Assyria, and Arabia after Assyria: and this ends, or rather is commonly supposed to end, at the Arabian gulf, into which Dareios conducted a channel from the Nile. Now in the line stretching to Phenicia from the land of the Persians the land is broad and the space abundant, but after Phenicia this peninsula goes by the shore of our Sea along Palestine, Syria, and Egypt, where it ends; and in it there are three nations only.

These are the parts of Asia which tend towards the West from the Persian land; but as to those which lie beyond the Persians and Medes and Saspeirians and Colchians towards the East and the sunrising, on one side the Erythraian Sea runs along by them, and on the North both the Caspian Sea and the river Araxes, which flows towards the rising sun: and Asia is inhabited as far as the Indian land; but from this onwards towards the East it becomes desert, nor can any one say what manner of land it is.

Such and so large is Asia: and Libya is included in the second peninsula; for after Egypt Libya succeeds at once. Now about Egypt this peninsula is narrow, for from our Sea to the Erythraian Sea is a distance there of ten myriads of fathoms, which would amount to a thousand furlongs; but after this narrow part, the portion of the peninsula which is called Libya is, as it chances, extremely broad.

I wonder then at those who have parted off and divided the world into Libya, Asia, and Europe, since the difference between these is not small; for in length Europe extends along by both, while in breadth it is clear to me that it is beyond comparison larger; for Libya furnishes proofs about itself that it is surrounded by sea, except so much of it as borders upon Asia; and this fact was shown by Necos king of the Egyptians first of all those about whom we have knowledge. He when he had ceased digging the channel which goes through from the Nile to the Arabian gulf, sent Phenicians with ships, bidding them sail and come back through the Pillars of Heracles to the Northern Sea and so to Egypt. The Phenicians therefore set forth from the Erythraian Sea and sailed through the Southern Sea; and when autumn came, they would put to shore and sow the land, wherever in Libya they might happen to be as they sailed, and then they waited for the harvest: and having reaped the corn they would sail on, so that after two years had elapsed, in the third year they turned through the Pillars of Heracles and arrived again in Egypt. And they reported a thing which I cannot believe, but another man may, namely that in sailing round Libya they had the sun on their right hand.

Thus was this country first known to be what it is, and after this it is the Carthaginians who make report of it; for as to Sataspes the son of Teaspis the Achaimenid, he did not sail round Libya, though he was sent for this very purpose, but was struck with fear by the length of the voyage and the desolate nature of the land, and so returned back and did not accomplish the task which his mother laid upon him. For this man had outraged a daughter of Zopyros the son of Megabyzos, a virgin; and then when he was about to be impaled by order of king Xerxes for this offence, the mother of Sataspes, who was a sister of Dareios, entreated for his life, saying that she would herself lay upon him a greater penalty than Xerxes; for he should be compelled (she said) to sail round Libya, until in sailing round it he came to the Arabian gulf. So then Xerxes having agreed upon these terms, Sataspes went to Egypt, and obtaining a ship and sailors from the Egyptians, he sailed to the Pillars of Heracles; and having sailed through them and turned the point of Libya which is called the promontory of Soloeis, he sailed on towards the South. Then after he had passed over much sea in many months, as there was needed ever more and more voyaging, he turned about and sailed back again to Egypt: and having come from thence into the presence of king Xerxes, he reported saying that at the furthest point which he reached he was sailing by dwarfish people, who used clothing made from the palm-tree, and who, whenever they came to land with their ship, left their towns and fled away to the mountains: and they, he said, did no injury when they entered into the towns, but took food from them only. And the cause, he said, why he had not completely sailed round Libya was that the ship could not advance any further but stuck fast. Xerxes however did not believe that he was speaking the truth, and since he had not performed the appointed task, he impaled him, inflicting upon him the penalty pronounced before. A eunuch belonging to this Sataspes ran away to Samos as soon as he heard that his master was dead, carrying with him large sums of money; and of this a man of Samos took possession, whose name I know, but I purposely pass it over without mention.

Of Asia the greater part was explored by Dareios, who desiring to know of the river Indus, which is a second river producing crocodiles of all the rivers in the world,—to know, I say, of this river where it runs out into the sea, sent with ships, besides others whom he trusted to speak the truth, Skylax also, a man of Caryanda. These starting from the city of Caspatyros and the land of Pactyïke, sailed down the river towards the East and the sunrising to the sea; and then sailing over the sea Westwards they came in the thirtieth month to that place from whence the king of the Egyptians had sent out the Phenicians of whom I spoke before, to sail round Libya. After these had made their voyage round the coast, Dareios both subdued the Indians and made use of this sea. Thus Asia also, excepting the parts of it which are towards the rising sun, has been found to be similar to Libya.

As to Europe, however, it is clearly not known by any, either as regards the parts which are towards the rising sun or those towards the North, whether it be surrounded by sea: but in length it is known to stretch along by both the other divisions. And I am not able to understand for what reason it is that to the Earth, which is one, three different names are given derived from women, and why there were set as boundaries to divide it the river Nile of Egypt and the Phasis in Colchis (or as some say the Maiotian river Tanaïs and the Kimmerian ferry); nor can I learn who those persons were who made the boundaries, or for what reason they gave the names. Libya indeed is said by most of the Hellenes to have its name from Libya a woman of that country, and Asia from the wife of Prometheus: but this last name is claimed by the Lydians, who say that Asia has been called after Asias the son of Cotys the son of Manes, and not from Asia the wife of Prometheus; and from him too they say the Asian tribe in Sardis has its name. As to Europe however, it is neither known by any man whether it is surrounded by sea, nor does it appear whence it got this name or who he was who gave it, unless we shall say that the land received its name from Europa the Tyrian; and if so, it would appear that before this it was nameless like the rest. She however evidently belongs to Asia and did not come to this land which is now called by the Hellenes Europe, but only from Phenicia to Crete, and from Crete to Lykia. Let this suffice now which has been said about these matters; for we will adopt those which are commonly accepted of the accounts.

Now the region of the Euxine upon which Dareios was preparing to march has, apart from the Scythian race, the most ignorant nations within it of all lands: for we can neither put forward any nation of those who dwell within the region of Pontus as eminent in ability, nor do we know of any man of learning having arisen there, apart from the Scythian nation and Anacharsis. By the Scythian race one thing which is the most important of all human things has been found out more cleverly than by any other men of whom we know; but in other respects I have no great admiration for them: and that most important thing which they have discovered is such that none can escape again who has come to attack them, and if they do not desire to be found, it is not possible to catch them: for they who have neither cities founded nor walls built, but all carry their houses with them and are mounted archers, living not by the plough but by cattle, and whose dwellings are upon cars, these assuredly are invincible and impossible to approach.

This they have found out, seeing that their land is suitable to it and at the same time the rivers are their allies: for first this land is plain land and is grassy and well watered, and then there are rivers flowing through it not much less in number than the channels in Egypt. Of these as many as are noteworthy and also can be navigated from the sea, I will name: there is Ister with five mouths, and after this Tyras, Hypanis, Borysthenes, Panticapes, Kypakyris, Gerros and Tanaïs. These flow as I shall now describe.

The Ister, which is the greatest of all the rivers which we know, flows always with equal volume in summer and winter alike. It is the first towards the West of all the Scythian rivers, and it has become the greatest of all rivers because other rivers flow into it. And these are they which make it great: —five in number are those which flow through the Scythian land, namely that which the Scythians call Porata and the Hellenes Pyretos, and besides this, Tiarantos and Araros and Naparis and Ordessos. The first-mentioned of these is a great river lying towards the East, and there it joins waters with the Ister, the second Tiarantos is more to the West and smaller, and the Araros and Naparis and Ordessos flow into the Ister going between these two.

These are the native Scythian rivers which join to swell its stream, while from the Agathyrsians flows the Maris and joins the Ister, and from the summits of Haimos flow three other great rivers towards the North Wind and fall into it, namely Atlas and Auras and Tibisis. Through Thrace and the Thracian Crobyzians flow the rivers Athrys and Noes and Artanes, running into the Ister; and from the Paionians and Mount Rhodope the river Kios, cutting through Haimos in the midst, runs into it also. From the Illyrians the river Angros flows Northwards and runs out into the Triballian plain and into the river Brongos, and the Brongos flows into the Ister; thus the Ister receives both these, being great rivers. From the region which is above the Ombricans, the river Carpis and another river, the Alpis, flow also towards the North Wind and run into it; for the Ister flows in fact through the whole of Europe, beginning in the land of the Keltoi, who after the Kynesians dwell furthest towards the sun-setting of all the peoples of Europe; and thus flowing through all Europe it falls into the sea by the side of Scythia.

So then it is because these which have been named and many others join their waters together, that Ister becomes the greatest of rivers; since if we compare the single streams, the Nile is superior in volume of water; for into this no river or spring flows, to contribute to its volume. And the Ister flows at an equal level always both in summer and in winter for some such cause as this, as I suppose:—in winter it is of the natural size, or becomes only a little larger than its nature, seeing that this land receives very little rain in winter, but constantly has snow; whereas in summer the snow which fell in the winter, in quantity abundant, melts and runs from all parts into the Ister. This snow of which I speak, running into the river helps to swell its volume, and with it also many and violent showers of rain, for it rains during the summer: and thus the waters which mingle with the Ister are more copious in summer than they are in winter by about as much as the water which the Sun draws to himself in summer exceeds that which he draws in winter; and by the setting of these things against one another there is produced a balance; so that the river is seen to be of equal volume always.

One, I say, of the rivers which the Scythians have is the Ister; and after it the Tyras, which starts from the North and begins its course from a large lake which is the boundary between the land of the Scythians and that of the Neuroi. At its mouth are settled those Hellenes who are called Tyritai.

The third river is the Hypanis, which starts from Scythia and flows from a great lake round which feed white wild horses; and this lake is rightly called "Mother of Hypanis." From this then the river Hypanis takes its rise and for a distance of five days' sail it flows shallow and with sweet water still; but from this point on towards the sea for four days' sail it is very bitter, for there flows into it the water of a bitter spring, which is so exceedingly bitter that, small as it is, it changes the water of the Hypanis by mingling with it, though that is a river to which few are equal in greatness. This spring is on the border between the lands of the agricultural Scythians and of the Alazonians, and the name of the spring and of the place from which it flows is in Scythian Exampaios, and in the Hellenic tongue Hierai Hodoi. Now the Tyras and the Hypanis approach one another in their windings in the land of the Alazonians, but after this each turns off and widens the space between them as they flow.

. Fourth is the river Borysthenes, which is both the largest of these after the Ister, and also in our opinion the most serviceable not only of the Scythian rivers but also of all the rivers of the world besides, excepting only the Nile of Egypt, for to this it is not possible to compare any other river: of the rest however the Borysthenes is the most serviceable, seeing that it provides both pastures which are the fairest and the richest for cattle, and fish which are better by far and more numerous than those of any other river, and also it is the sweetest water to drink, and flows with clear stream, though others beside it are turbid, and along its banks crops are produced better than elsewhere, while in parts where it is not sown, grass grows deeper. Moreover at its mouth salt forms of itself in abundance, and it produces also huge fish without spines, which they call antacaioi, to be used for salting, and many other things also worthy of wonder. Now as far as the region of the Gerrians, to which it is a voyage of forty days, the Borysthenes is known as flowing from the North Wind; but above this none can tell through what nations it flows: it is certain however that it runs through desert to the land of the agricultural Scythians; for these Scythians dwell along its banks for a distance of ten days' sail. Of this river alone and of the Nile I cannot tell where the sources are, nor, I think, can any of the Hellenes. When the Borysthenes comes near the sea in its course, the Hypanis mingles with it, running out into the same marsh; and the space between these two rivers, which is as it were a beak of land, is called the point of Hippoles, and in it is placed a temple of the Mother, and opposite the temple upon the river Hypanis are settled the Borysthenites.

This is that which has to do with these rivers; and after these there is a fifth river besides, called Panticapes. This also flows both from the North and from a lake, and in the space between this river and the Borysthenes dwell the agricultural Scythians: it runs out into the region of Hylaia, and having passed by this it mingles with the Borysthenes.

Sixth comes the river Hypakyris, which starts from a lake, and flowing through the midst of the nomad Scythians runs out into the sea by the city of Carkinitis, skirting on its right bank the region of Hylaia and the so-called racecourse of Achilles.

Seventh is the Gerros, which parts off from the Borysthenes near about that part of the country where the Borysthenes ceases to be known,—it parts off, I say, in this region and has the same name which this region itself has, namely Gerros; and as it flows to the sea it borders the country of the nomad and that of the Royal Scythians, and runs out into the Hypakyris.

The eighth is the river Tanaïs, which starts in its flow at first from a large lake, and runs out into a still larger lake called Maiotis, which is the boundary between the Royal Scythians and the Sauromatai. Into this Tanaïs falls another river, whose name is Hyrgis.

. So many are the rivers of note with which the Scythians are provided: and for cattle the grass which comes up in the land of Scythia is the most productive of bile of any grass which we know; and that this is so you may judge when you open the bodies of the cattle.

Thus abundant supply have they of that which is most important; and as for the rest their customs are as follows. The gods whom they propitiate by worship are these only:—Hestia most of all, then Zeus and the Earth, supposing that Earth is the wife of Zeus, and after these Apollo, and Aphrodite Urania, and Heracles, and Ares. Of these all the Scythians have the worship established, and the so-called Royal Scythians sacrifice also to Poseidon. Now Hestia is called in Scythian Tabiti, and Zeus, being most rightly named in my opinion, is called Papaios, and Earth Api, and Apollo Oitosyros, and Aphrodite Urania is called Argimpasa, and Poseidon Thagimasidas. It is not their custom however to make images, altars or temples to any except Ares, but to him it is their custom to make them.

They have all the same manner of sacrifice established for all their religious rites equally, and it is thus performed:—the victim stands with its fore-feet tied, and the sacrificing priest stands behind the victim, and by pulling the end of the cord he throws the beast down; and as the victim falls, he calls upon the god to whom he is sacrificing, and then at once throws a noose round its neck, and putting a small stick into it he turns it round and so strangles the animal, without either lighting a fire or making any first offering from the victim or pouring any libation over it: and when he has strangled it and flayed off the skin, he proceeds to boil it.

Now as the land of Scythia is exceedingly ill wooded, this contrivance has been invented for the boiling of the flesh:—having flayed the victims, they strip the flesh off the bones and then put it into caldrons, if they happen to have any, of native make, which very much resemble Lesbian mixing-bowls except that they are much larger,—into these they put the flesh and boil it by lighting under it the bones of the victim: if however thy have not at hand the caldron, they put all the flesh into the stomachs of the victims and adding water they light the bones under them; and these blaze up beautifully, and the stomachs easily hold the flesh when it has been stripped off the bones: thus an ox is made to boil itself, and the other kinds of victims each boil themselves also. Then when the flesh is boiled, the sacrificer takes a first offering of the flesh and of the vital organs and casts it in front of him. And they sacrifice various kinds of cattle, but especially horses.

To the others of the gods they sacrifice thus and these kinds of beasts, but to Ares as follows:—In each district of the several governments they have a temple of Ares set up in this way:—bundles of brushwood are heaped up for about three furlongs in length and in breadth, but less in height; and on the top of this there is a level square made, and three of the sides rise sheer but by the remaining one side the pile may be ascended. Every year they pile on a hundred and fifty waggon-loads of brushwood, for it is constantly settling down by reason of the weather. Upon this pile of which I speak each people has an ancient iron sword set up, and this is the sacred symbol of Ares. To this sword they bring yearly offerings of cattle and of horses; and they have the following sacrifice in addition, beyond what they make to the other gods, that is to say, of all the enemies whom they take captive in war they sacrifice one man in every hundred, not in the same manner as they sacrifice cattle, but in a different manner: for they first pour wine over their heads, and after that they cut the throats of the men, so that the blood runs into a bowl; and then they carry this up to the top of the pile of brushwood and pour the blood over the sword. This, I say, they carry up; and meanwhile below by the side of the temple they are doing thus:—they cut off all the right arms of the slaughtered men with the hands and throw them up into the air, and then when they have finished offering the other victims, they go away; and the arm lies wheresoever it has chanced to fall, and the corpse apart from it.

Such are the sacrifices which are established among them; but of swine these make no use, nor indeed are they wont to keep them at all in their land.

That which relates to war is thus ordered with them:—When a Scythian has slain his first man, he drinks some of his blood: and of all those whom he slays in the battle he bears the heads to the king; for if he has brought a head he shares in the spoil which they have taken, but otherwise not. And he takes off the skin of the head by cutting it round about the ears and then taking hold of the scalp and shaking it off; afterwards he scrapes off the flesh with the rib of an ox, and works the skin about with his hands; and when he has thus tempered it, he keeps it as a napkin to wipe the hands upon, and hangs it from the bridle of the horse on which he himself rides, and takes pride in it; for whosoever has the greatest number of skins to wipe the hands upon, he is judged to be the bravest man. Many also make cloaks to wear of the skins stripped off, sewing them together like shepherds' cloaks of skins; and many take the skin together with the finger-nails off the right hands of their enemies when they are dead, and make them into covers for their quivers: now human skin it seems is both thick and glossy in appearance, more brilliantly white than any other skin. Many also take the skins off the whole bodies of men and stretch them on pieces of wood and carry them about on their horses.

Such are their established customs about these things; and to the skulls themselves, not of all but of their greatest enemies, they do thus:—the man saws off all below the eyebrows and clears out the inside; and if he is a poor man he only stretches ox-hide round it and then makes use of it; but if he be rich, besides stretching the ox-hide he gilds it over within, and makes use of it as a drinking-cup. They do this also if any of their own family have been at variance with them and the man gets the better of his adversary in trial before the king; and when strangers come to him whom he highly esteems, he sets these skulls before them, and adds the comment that they being of his own family had made war against him, and that he had got the better of them; and this they hold to be a proof of manly virtue.

Once every year each ruler of a district mixes in his own district a bowl of wine, from which those of the Scythians drink by whom enemies have been slain; but those by whom this has not been done do not taste of the wine, but sit apart dishonoured; and this is the greatest of all disgraces among them: but those of them who have slain a very great number of men, drink with two cups together at the same time.

Diviners there are many among the Scythians, and they divine with a number of willow rods in the following manner:—they bring large bundles of rods, and having laid them on the ground they unroll them, and setting each rod by itself apart they prophesy; and while speaking thus, they roll the rods together again, and after that they place them in order a second time one by one. This manner of divination they have from their fathers: but the Enareës or "man-women" say that Aphrodite gave them the gift of divination, and they divine accordingly with the bark of the linden-tree. Having divided the linden-bark into three strips, the man twists them together in his fingers and untwists them again, and as he does this he utters the oracle.

When the king of the Scythians is sick, he sends for three of the diviners, namely those who are most in repute, who divine in the manner which has been said: and these say for the most part something like this, namely that so and so has sworn falsely by the hearth of the king, and they name one of the citizens, whosoever it may happen to be: now it is the prevailing custom of the Scythians to swear by the hearth of the king at the times when they desire to swear the most solemn oath. He then who they say has sworn falsely, is brought forthwith held fast on both sides; and when he has come the diviners charge him with this, that he is shown by their divination to have sworn falsely by the hearth of the king, and that for this reason the king is suffering pain: and he denies and says that he did not swear falsely, and complains indignantly: and when he denies it, the king sends for other diviners twice as many in number, and if these also by looking into their divination pronounce him guilty of having sworn falsely, at once they cut off the man's head, and the diviners who came first part his goods among them by lot; but if the diviners who came in afterwards acquit him, other diviners come in, and again others after them. If then the greater number acquit the man, the sentence is that the first diviners shall themselves be put to death.

They put them to death accordingly in the following manner:—first they fill a waggon with brushwood and yoke oxen to it; then having bound the feet of the diviners and tied their hands behind them and stopped their mouths with gags, they fasten them down in the middle of the brushwood, and having set fire to it they scare the oxen and let them go: and often the oxen are burnt to death together with the diviners, and often they escape after being scorched, when the pole to which they are fastened has been burnt: and they burn the diviners in the manner described for other causes also, calling them false prophets. Now when the king puts any to death, he does not leave alive their sons either, but he puts to death all the males, not doing any hurt to the females.

In the following manner the Scythians make oaths to whomsoever they make them:—they pour wine into a great earthenware cup and mingle with it blood of those who are taking the oath to one another, either making a prick with an awl or cutting with a dagger a little way into their body, and then they dip into the cup a sword and arrows and a battle-axe and a javelin; and having done this, they invoke many curses on the breaker of the oath, and afterwards they drink it off, both they who are making the oath and the most honourable of their company.

The burial-place of the kings is in the land of the Gerrians, the place up to which the Borysthenes is navigable. In this place, when their king has died, they make a large square excavation in the earth; and when they have made this ready, they take up the corpse (the body being covered over with wax and the belly ripped up and cleansed, and then sewn together again, after it has been filled with kyperos cut up and spices and parsley-seed and anise), and they convey it in a waggon to another nation. Then those who receive the corpse thus conveyed to them do the same as the Royal Scythians, that is they cut off a part of their ear and shave their hair round about and cut themselves all over the arms and tear their forehead and nose and pass arrows through their left hand. Thence they convey in the waggon the corpse of the king to another of the nations over whom they rule; and they to whom they came before accompany them: and when they have gone round to all conveying the corpse, then they are in the land of the Gerrians, who have their settlements furthest away of all the nations over whom they rule, and they have reached the spot where the burial place is. After that, having placed the corpse in the tomb upon a bed of leaves, they stick spears along on this side and that of the corpse and stretch pieces of wood over them, and then they cover the place in with matting. Then they strangle and bury in the remaining space of the tomb one of the king's mistresses, his cup-bearer, his cook, his horse-keeper, his attendant, and his bearer of messages, and also horses, and a first portion of all things else, and cups of gold; for silver they do not use at all, nor yet bronze. Having thus done they all join together to pile up a great mound, vying with one another and zealously endeavouring to make it as large as possible.

Afterwards, when the year comes round again, they do as follows:—they take the most capable of the remaining servants,—and these are native Scythians, for those serve him whom the king himself commands to do so, and his servants are not bought for money,—of these attendants then they strangle fifty and also fifty of the finest horses; and when they have taken out their bowels and cleansed the belly, they fill it with chaff and sew it together again. Then they set the half of a wheel upon two stakes with the hollow side upwards, and the other half of the wheel upon other two stakes, and in this manner they fix a number of these; and after this they run thick stakes through the length of the horses as far as the necks, and they mount them upon the wheels; and the front pieces of wheel support the shoulders of the horses, while those behind bear up their bellies, going by the side of the thighs; and both front and hind legs hang in the air. On the horses they put bridles and bits, and stretch the bridles tight in front of them and then tie them up to pegs: and of the fifty young men who have been strangled they mount each one upon his horse, having first run a straight stake through each body along by the spine up to the neck; and a part of this stake projects below, which they fasten into a socket made in the other stake that runs through the horse. Having set horsemen such as I have described in a circle round the tomb, they then ride away.

Thus they bury their kings; but as for the other Scythians, when they die their nearest relations carry them round laid in waggons to their friends in succession; and of them each one when he receives the body entertains those who accompany it, and before the corpse they serve up of all things about the same quantity as before the others. Thus private persons are carried about for forty days, and then they are buried: and after burying them the Scythians cleanse themselves in the following way:—they soap their heads and wash them well, and then, for their body, they set up three stakes leaning towards one another and about them they stretch woollen felt coverings, and when they have closed them as much as possible they throw stones heated red-hot into a basin placed in the middle of the stakes and the felt coverings.

Now they have hemp growing in their land, which is very like flax except in thickness and in height, for in these respects the hemp is much superior. This grows both of itself and with cultivation; and of it the Thracians even make garments, which are very like those made of flaxen thread, so that he who was not specially conversant with it would not be able to decide whether the garments were of flax or of hemp; and he who had not before seen stuff woven of hemp would suppose that the garment was made of flax.

The Scythians then take the seed of this hemp and creep under the felt coverings, and then they throw the seed upon the stones which have been heated red-hot: and it burns like incense and produces a vapour so thick that no vapour-bath in Hellas would surpass it: and the Scythians being delighted with the vapour-bath howl like wolves. This is to them instead of washing, for in fact they do not wash their bodies at all in water. Their women however pound with a rough stone the wood of the cypress and cedar and frankincense tree, pouring in water with it, and then with this pounded stuff, which is thick, they plaster over all their body and also their face; and not only does a sweet smell attach to them by reason of this, but also when they take off the plaster on the next day, their skin is clean and shining.

This nation also is very averse to adopting strange customs, rejecting even those of other tribes among themselves, but especially those of the Hellenes, as the history of Anacharsis and also afterwards of Skyles proved. For as to Anacharsis first, when he was returning to the abodes of the Scythians, after having visited many lands and displayed in them much wisdom, as he sailed through the Hellespont he put in to Kyzicos: and since he found the people of Kyzicos celebrating a festival very magnificently in honour of the Mother of the gods, Anacharsis vowed to the Mother that if he should return safe and sound to his own land, he would both sacrifice to her with the same rites as he saw the men of Kyzicos do, and also hold a night festival. So when he came to Scythia he went down into the region called Hylaia (this is along by the side of the racecourse of Achilles and is quite full, as it happens, of trees of all kinds),—into this, I say, Anacharsis went down, and proceeded to perform all the ceremonies of the festival in honour of the goddess, with a kettle-drum and with images hung about himself. And one of the Scythians perceived him doing this and declared it to Saulios the king; and the king came himself also, and when he saw Anacharsis doing this, he shot him with an arrow and killed him. Accordingly at the present time if one asks about Anacharsis, the Scythians say that they do not know him, and for this reason, because he went out of his own country to Hellas and adopted foreign customs. And as I heard from Tymnes the steward of Ariapeithes, he was the uncle on the father's side of Idanthyrsos king of the Scythians, and the son of Gnuros, the son of Lycos, the son of Spargapeithes. If then Anacharsis was of this house, let him know that he died by the hand of his brother, for Idanthyrsos was the son of Saulios, and Saulios was he who killed Anacharsis.

However I have heard also another story, told by the Peloponnesians, that Anacharsis was sent out by the king of the Scythians, and so made himself a disciple of Hellas; and that when he returned back he said to him that had sent him forth, that the Hellenes were all busied about every kind of cleverness except the Lacedemonians; but these alone knew how to exchange speech sensibly. This story however has been invented without any ground by the Hellenes themselves; and however that may be, the man was slain in the way that was related above.

This man then fared thus badly by reason of foreign customs and communication with Hellenes; and very many years afterwards Skyles the son of Ariapeithes suffered nearly the same fate as he. For Ariapeithes the king of the Scythians with other sons had Skyles born to him: and he was born of a woman who was of Istria, and certainly not a native of Scythia; and this mother taught him the language and letters of Hellas. Afterwards in course of time Ariapeithes was brought to his end by treachery at the hands of Spargapeithes the king of the Agathyrsians, and Skyles succeeded to the kingdom; and he took not only that but also the wife of his father, whose name was Opoia: this Opoia was a native Scythian and from her was born Oricos to Ariapeithes. Now when Skyles was king of the Scythians, he was by no means satisfied with the Scythian manner of life, but was much more inclined towards Hellenic ways because of the training with which he had been brought up, and he used to do somewhat as follows:—When he came with the Scythians in arms to the city of the Borysthenites (now these Borysthenites say that they are of Miletos),—when Skyles came to these, he would leave his band in the suburbs of the city and go himself within the walls and close the gates. After that he would lay aside his Scythian equipments and take Hellenic garments, and wearing them he would go about in the market-place with no guards or any other man accompanying him (and they watched the gates meanwhile, that none of the Scythians might see him wearing this dress): and while in other respects too he adopted Hellenic manners of life, he used also to perform worship to the gods according to the customs of the Hellenes. Then having stayed a month or more than that, he would put on the Scythian dress and depart. This he did many times, and he both built for himself a house in Borysthenes and also took to it a woman of the place as his wife.

Since however it was fated that evil should happen to him, it happened by an occasion of this kind:—he formed a desire to be initiated in the rites of Bacchus-Dionysos, and as he was just about to receive the initiation, there happened a very great portent. He had in the city of the Borysthenites a house of great size and built with large expense, of which also I made mention a little before this, and round it were placed sphinxes and griffins of white stone: on this house Zeus caused a bolt to fall; and the house was altogether burnt down, but Skyles none the less for this completed his initiation. Now the Scythians make the rites of Bacchus a reproach against the Hellenes, for they say that it is not fitting to invent a god like this, who impels men to frenzy. So when Skyles had been initiated into the rites of Bacchus, one of the Borysthenites went off to the Scythians and said: "Whereas ye laugh at us, O Scythians, because we perform the rite of Bacchus and because the god seizes us, now this divinity has seized also your king; and he is both joining in the rite of Bacchus and maddened by the influence of the god. And if ye disbelieve me, follow and I will show you." The chief men of the Scythians followed him, and the Borysthenite led them secretly into the town and set them upon a tower. So when Skyles passed by with the company of revellers, and the Scythians saw him joining in the rite of Bacchus, they were exceedingly grieved at it, and they went out and declared to the whole band that which they had seen.

After this when Skyles was riding out again to his own abode, the Scythians took his brother Octamasades for their leader, who was a son of the daughter of Teres, and made insurrection against Skyles. He then when he perceived that which was being done to his hurt and for what reason it was being done, fled for refuge to Thrace; and Octamasades being informed of this, proceeded to march upon Thrace. So when he had arrived at the river Ister, the Thracians met him; and as they were about to engage battle, Sitalkes sent a messenger to Octamasades and said: "Why must we make trial of one another in fight? Thou art my sister's son and thou hast in thy power my brother. Do thou give him back to me, and I will deliver to thee thy brother Skyles: and let us not either of us set our armies in peril, either thou or I." Thus Sitalkes proposed to him by a herald; for there was with Octamasades a brother of Sitalkes, who had gone into exile for fear of him. And Octamasades agreed to this, and by giving up his own mother's brother to Sitalkes he received his brother Skyles in exchange: and Sitalkes when he received his brother led him away as a prisoner, but Octamasades cut off the head of Skyles there upon the spot. Thus do the Scythians carefully guard their own customary observances, and such are the penalties which they inflict upon those who acquire foreign customs besides their own.

How many the Scythians are I was not able to ascertain precisely, but I heard various reports of the number: for reports say both that they are very many in number and also that they are few, at least as regards the true Scythians.

Thus far however they gave me evidence of my own eyesight:—there is between the river Borysthenes and the Hypanis a place called Exampaios, of which also I made mention somewhat before this, saying that there was in it a spring of bitter water, from which the water flows and makes the river Hypanis unfit to drink. In this place there is set a bronze bowl, in size at least six times as large as the mixing-bowl at the entrance of the Pontus, which Pausanias the son of Cleombrotos dedicated: and for him who has never seen that, I will make the matter clear by saying that the bowl in Scythia holds easily six hundred amphors, and the thickness of this Scythian bowl is six fingers. This then the natives of the place told me had been made of arrow-heads: for their king, they said, whose name was Ariantas, wishing to know how many the Scythians were, ordered all the Scythians to bring one arrow-head, each from his own arrow, and whosoever should not bring one, he threatened with death. So a great multitude of arrow-heads was brought, and he resolved to make of them a memorial and to leave it behind him: from these then, they said, he made this bronze bowl and dedicated it in this place Exampaios.

This is what I heard about the number of the Scythians. Now this land has no marvellous things except that it has rivers which are by far larger and more numerous than those of any other land. One thing however shall be mentioned which it has to show, and which is worthy of wonder even besides the rivers and the greatness of the plain, that is to say, they point out a footprint of Heracles in the rock by the bank of the river Tyras, which in shape is like the mark of a man's foot but in size is two cubits long. This then is such as I have said; and I will go back now to the history which I was about to tell at first.

While Dareios was preparing to go against the Scythians and was sending messengers to appoint to some the furnishing of a land-army, to others that of ships, and to others the bridging over of the Thracian Bosphorus, Artabanos, the son of Hystaspes and brother of Dareios, urged him by no means to make the march against the Scythians, telling him how difficult the Scythians were to deal with. Since however he did not persuade him, though he gave him good counsel, he ceased to urge; and Dareios, when all his preparations had been made, began to march his army forth from Susa.

Then one of the Persians, Oiobazos, made request to Dareios that as he had three sons and all were serving in the expedition, one might be left behind for him: and Dareios said that as he was a friend and made a reasonable request, he would leave behind all the sons. So Oiobazos was greatly rejoiced, supposing that his sons had been freed from service, but Dareios commanded those who had the charge of such things to put to death all the sons of Oiobazos.

. These then were left, having been slain upon the spot where they were: and Dareios meanwhile set forth from Susa and arrived at the place on the Bosphorus where the bridge of ships had been made, in the territory of Chalcedon; and there he embarked in a ship and sailed to the so-called Kyanean rocks, which the Hellenes say formerly moved backwards and forwards; and taking his seat at the temple he gazed upon the Pontus, which is a sight well worth seeing. Of all seas indeed it is the most marvellous in its nature. The length of it is eleven thousand one hundred furlongs, and the breadth, where it is broadest, three thousand three hundred: and of this great Sea the mouth is but four furlongs broad, and the length of the mouth, that is of the neck of water which is called Bosphorus, where, as I said, the bridge of ships had been made, is not less than a hundred and twenty furlongs. This Bosphorus extends to the Propontis; and the Propontis, being in breadth five hundred furlongs and in length one thousand four hundred, has its outlet into the Hellespont, which is but seven furlongs broad at the narrowest place, though it is four hundred furlongs in length: and the Hellespont runs out into that expanse of sea which is called the Egean.

These measurements I have made as follows:—a ship completes on an average in a long day a distance of seventy thousand fathoms, and in a night sixty thousand. Now we know that to the river Phasis from the mouth of the Sea (for it is here that the Pontus is longest) is a voyage of nine days and eight nights, which amounts to one hundred and eleven myriads of fathoms; and these fathoms are eleven thousand one hundred furlongs. Then from the land of the Sindians to Themiskyra on the river Thermodon (for here is the broadest part of the Pontus) it is a voyage of three days and two nights, which amounts to thirty-three myriads of fathoms or three thousand three hundred furlongs. This Pontus then and also the Bosphorus and the Hellespont have been measured by me thus, and their nature is such as has been said: and this Pontus also has a lake which has its outlet into it, which lake is not much less in size than the Pontus itself, and it is called Maiotis and "Mother of the Pontus."

Dareios then having gazed upon the Pontus sailed back to the bridge, of which Mandrocles a Samian had been chief constructor; and having gazed upon the Bosphorus also, he set up two pillars by it of white stone with characters cut upon them, on the one Assyrian and on the other Hellenic, being the names of all the nations which he was leading with him: and he was leading with him all over whom he was ruler. The whole number of them without the naval force was reckoned to be seventy myriads including cavalry, and ships had been gathered together to the number of six hundred.

These pillars the Byzantians conveyed to their city after the events of which I speak, and used them for the altar of Artemis Orthosia, excepting one stone, which was left standing by the side of the temple of Dionysos in Byzantion, covered over with Assyrian characters. Now the place on the Bosphorus where Dareios made his bridge is, as I conclude, midway between Byzantion and the temple at the mouth of the Pontus.

After this Dareios being pleased with the floating bridge rewarded the chief constructor of it, Mandrocles the Samian, with gifts tenfold; and as an offering from these Mandrocles had a painting made of figures to present the whole scene of the bridge over the Bosphorus and king Dareios sitting in a prominent seat and his army crossing over; this he caused to be painted and dedicated it as an offering in the temple of Hera, with the following inscription:

"Bosphorus having bridged over, the straits fish-abounding, to Hera

   Mandrocleës dedicates this, of his work to record;

 A crown on himself he set, and he brought to the Samians glory,

And for Dareios performed everything after his mind."

This memorial was made of him who constructed the bridge: and Dareios, after he had rewarded Mandrocles with gifts, passed over into Europe, having first commanded the Ionians to sail into the Pontus as far as the river Ister, and when they arrived at the Ister, there to wait for him, making a bridge meanwhile over the river; for the chief of his naval force were the Ionians, the Aiolians and the Hellespontians. So the fleet sailed through between the Kyanean rocks and made straight for the Ister; and then they sailed up the river a two days' voyage from the sea and proceeded to make a bridge across the neck, as it were, of the river, where the mouths of the Ister part off. Dareios meanwhile, having crossed the Bosphorus on the floating bridge, was advancing through Thrace, and when he came to the sources of the river Tearos he encamped for three days.

. Now the Tearos is said by those who dwell near it to be the best of all rivers, both in other respects which tend to healing and especially for curing diseases of the skin both in men and in horses: and its springs are thirty-eight in number, flowing all from the same rock, of which some are cold and others warm. The way to them is of equal length from the city of Heraion near Perinthos and from Apollonia upon the Euxine Sea, that is to say two days' journey by each road. This Tearos runs into the river Contadesdos and the Contadesdos into the Agrianes and the Agrianes into the Hebros, which flows into the sea by the city of Ainos.

Dareios then, having come to this river and having encamped there, was pleased with the river and set up a pillar there also, with an inscription as follows: "The head-springs of the river Tearos give the best and fairest water of all rivers; and to them came leading an army against the Scythians the best and fairest of all men, Dareios the son of Hystaspes, of the Persians and of all the Continent king." These were the words which were there written.

Dareios then set out from thence and came to another river whose name is Artescos, which flows through the land of the Odrysians. Having come to this river he did as follows:—he appointed a place for his army and bade every man as he passed out by it place one stone in this appointed place: and when the army had performed this, then he marched away his army leaving behind great mounds of these stones.

But before he came to the Ister he conquered first the Getai, who believe in immortality: for the Thracians who occupy Salmydessos and are settled above the cities of Apollonian and Mesambria, called the Kyrmianai and the Nipsaioi, delivered themselves over to Dareios without fighting; but the Getai, who are the bravest and the most upright in their dealings of all the Thracians, having betaken themselves to obstinacy were forthwith subdued.

And their belief in immortality is of this kind, that is to say, they hold that they do not die, but that he who is killed goes to Salmoxis, a divinity, whom some of them call Gebeleizis; and at intervals of four years they send one of themselves, whomsoever the lot may select, as a messenger to Salmoxis, charging him with such requests as they have to make on each occasion; and they send him thus:—certain of them who are appointed for this have three javelins, and others meanwhile take hold on both sides of him who is being sent to Salmoxis, both by his hands and his feet, and first they swing him up, then throw him into the air so as to fall upon the spear-points: and if when he is pierced through he is killed, they think that the god is favourable to them; but if he is not killed, they find fault with the messenger himself, calling him a worthless man, and then having found fault with him they send another: and they give him the charge beforehand, while he is yet alive. These same Thracians also shoot arrows up towards the sky when thunder and lightning come, and use threats to the god, not believing that there exists any other god except their own.

This Salmoxis I hear from the Hellenes who dwell about the Hellespont and the Pontus, was a man, and he became a slave in Samos, and was in fact a slave of Pythagoras the son of Mnesarchos. Then having become free he gained great wealth, and afterwards returned to his own land: and as the Thracians both live hardly and are rather simple-minded, this Salmoxis, being acquainted with the Ionian way of living and with manners more cultivated than the Thracians were used to see, since he had associated with Hellenes (and not only that but with Pythagoras, not the least able philosopher of the Hellenes), prepared a banqueting-hall, where he received and feasted the chief men of the tribe and instructed them meanwhile that neither he himself nor his guests nor their descendants in succession after them would die; but that they would come to a place where they would live for ever and have all things good. While he was doing that which has been mentioned and was saying these things, he was making for himself meanwhile a chamber under the ground; and when his chamber was finished, he disappeared from among the Thracians and went down into the underground chamber, where he continued to live for three years: and they grieved for his loss and mourned for him as dead. Then in the fourth year he appeared to the Thracians, and in this way the things which Salmoxis said became credible to them.

Thus they say that he did; but as to this matter and the chamber under ground, I neither disbelieve it nor do I very strongly believe, but I think that this Salmoxis lived many years before Pythagoras. However, whether there ever lived a man Salmoxis, or whether he is simply a native deity of the Getai, let us bid farewell to him now.

These, I say, having such manners as I have said, were subdued by the Persians and accompanied the rest of the army: and when Dareios and with him the land-army arrived at the Ister, then after all had passed over, Dareios commanded the Ionians to break up the floating bridge and to accompany him by land, as well as the rest of the troops which were in the ships: and when the Ionians were just about to break it up and to do that which he commanded, Coës the son of Erxander, who was commander of the Mytilenians, said thus to Dareios, having first inquired whether he was disposed to listen to an opinion from one who desired to declare it: "O king, seeing that thou art about to march upon a land where no cultivated ground will be seen nor any inhabited town, do thou therefore let this bridge remain where it is, leaving to guard it those same men who constructed it. Then, if we find the Scythians and fare as we desire, we have a way of return; and also even if we shall not be able to find them, at least our way of return is secured: for that we should be worsted by the Scythians in fight I never feared yet, but rather that we might not be able to find them, and might suffer some disaster in wandering about. Perhaps some one will say that in speaking thus I am speaking for my own advantage, in order that I may remain behind; but in truth I am bringing forward, O king, the opinion which I found best for thee, and I myself will accompany thee and not be left behind." With this opinion Dareios was very greatly pleased and made answer to him in these words: "Friend from Lesbos, when I have returned safe to my house, be sure that thou appear before me, in order that I may requite thee with good deeds for good counsel."

Having thus said and having tied sixty knots in a thong, he called the despots of the Ionians to speak with him and said as follows: "Men of Ionia, know that I have given up the opinion which I formerly declared with regard to the bridge; and do ye keep this thong and do as I shall say:—so soon as ye shall have seen me go forward against the Scythians, from that time begin, and untie a knot on each day: and if within this time I am not here, and ye find that the days marked by the knots have passed by, then sail away to your own lands. Till then, since our resolve has thus been changed, guard the floating bridge, showing all diligence to keep it safe and to guard it. And thus acting, ye will do for me a very acceptable service." Thus said Dareios and hastened on his march forwards.

Now in front of Scythia in the direction towards the sea lies Thrace; and where a bay is formed in this land, there begins Scythia, into which the Ister flows out, the mouth of the river being turned towards the South-East Wind. Beginning at the Ister then I am about to describe the coast land of the true Scythia, with regard to measurement. At once from the Ister begins this original land of Scythia, and it lies towards the midday and the South Wind, extending as far as the city called Carkinitis. After this the part which lies on the coast of the same sea still, a country which is mountainous and runs out in the direction of the Pontus, is occupied by the Tauric race, as far as the peninsula which is called the "Rugged Chersonese"; and this extends to the sea which lies towards the East Wind: for two sides of the Scythian boundaries lie along by the sea, one by the sea on the South, and the other by that on the East, just as it is with Attica: and in truth the Tauroi occupy a part of Scythia which has much resemblance to Attica; it is as if in Attica another race and not the Athenians occupied the hill region of Sunion, supposing it to project more at the point into the sea, that region namely which is cut off by a line from Thoricos to Anaphlystos. Such I say, if we may be allowed to compare small things such as this with great, is the form of the Tauric land. For him however who has not sailed along this part of the coast of Attica I will make it clear by another comparison:—it is as if in Iapygia another race and not the Iapygians had cut off for themselves and were holding that extremity of the land which is bounded by a line beginning at the harbour of Brentesion and running to Taras. And in mentioning these two similar cases I am suggesting many other things also to which the Tauric land has resemblance.

After the Tauric land immediately come Scythians again, occupying the parts above the Tauroi and the coasts of the Eastern sea, that is to say the parts to the West of the Kimmerian Bosphorus and of the Maiotian lake, as far as the river Tanaïs, which runs into the corner of this lake. In the upper parts which tend inland Scythia is bounded (as we know) by the Agathyrsians first, beginning from the Ister, and then by the Neuroi, afterwards by the Androphagoi, and lastly by the Melanchlainoi.

Scythia then being looked upon as a four-sided figure with two of its sides bordered by the sea, has its border lines equal to one another in each direction, that which tends inland and that which runs along by the sea: for from Ister to the Borysthenes is ten days' journey, and from the Borysthenes to the Maiotian lake ten days' more; and the distance inland to the Melanchlainoi, who are settled above the Scythians, is a journey of twenty days. Now I have reckoned the day's journey at two hundred furlongs: and by this reckoning the cross lines of Scythia would be four thousand furlongs in length, and the perpendiculars which tend inland would be the same number of furlongs. Such is the size of this land.

The Scythians meanwhile having considered with themselves that they were not able to repel the army of Dareios alone by a pitched battle, proceeded to send messengers to those who dwelt near them: and already the kings of these nations had come together and were taking counsel with one another, since so great an army was marching towards them. Now those who had come together were the kings of the Tauroi, Agathyrsians, Neuroi, Androphagoi, Melanchlainoi, Gelonians, Budinoi and Sauromatai.

Of these the Tauroi have the following customs:—they sacrifice to the "Maiden" both ship-wrecked persons and also those Hellenes whom they can capture by putting out to sea against them; and their manner of sacrifice is this:—when they have made the first offering from the victim they strike his head with a club: and some say that they push the body down from the top of the cliff (for it is upon a cliff that the temple is placed) and set the head up on a stake; but others, while agreeing as to the heads, say nevertheless that the body is not pushed down from the top of the cliff, but buried in the earth. This divinity to whom they sacrifice, the Tauroi themselves say is Iphigeneia the daughter of Agamemnon. Whatsoever enemies they have conquered they treat in this fashion:—each man cuts off a head and bears it away to his house; then he impales it on a long stake and sets it up above his house raised to a great height, generally above the chimney; and they say that these are suspended above as guards to preserve the whole house. This people has its living by plunder and war.

The Agathyrsians are the most luxurious of men and wear gold ornaments for the most part: also they have promiscuous intercourse with their women, in order that they may be brethren to one another and being all nearly related may not feel envy or malice one against another. In their other customs they have come to resemble the Thracians.

The Neuroi practise the Scythian customs: and one generation before the expedition of Dareios it so befell them that they were forced to quit their land altogether by reason of serpents: for their land produced serpents in vast numbers, and they fell upon them in still larger numbers from the desert country above their borders; until at last being hard pressed they left their own land and settled among the Budinoi. These men it would seem are wizards; for it is said of them by the Scythians and by the Hellenes who are settled in the Scythian land that once in every year each of the Neuroi becomes a wolf for a few days and then returns again to his original form. For my part I do not believe them when they say this, but they say it nevertheless, and swear it moreover.

The Androphagoi have the most savage manners of all human beings, and they neither acknowledge any rule of right nor observe any customary law. They are nomads and wear clothing like that of the Scythians, but have a language of their own; and alone of all these nations they are man-eaters.

The Melanchlainoi wear all of them black clothing, whence also they have their name; and they practise the customs of the Scythians.

The Budinoi are a very great and numerous race, and are all very blue-eyed and fair of skin: and in their land is built a city of wood, the name of which is Gelonos, and each side of the wall is thirty furlongs in length and lofty at the same time, all being of wood; and the houses are of wood also and the temples; for there are in it temples of Hellenic gods furnished after Hellenic fashion with sacred images and altars and cells, all of wood; and they keep festivals every other year to Dionysos and celebrate the rites of Bacchus: for the Gelonians are originally Hellenes, and they removed from the trading stations on the coast and settled among the Budinoi; and they use partly the Scythian language and partly the Hellenic. The Budinoi however do not use the same language as the Gelonians, nor is their manner of living the same: for the Budinoi are natives of the soil and a nomad people, and alone of the nations in these parts feed on fir-cones; but the Gelonians are tillers of the ground and feed on corn and have gardens, and resemble them not at all either in appearance or in complexion of skin. However by the Hellenes the Budinoi also are called Gelonians, not being rightly so called. Their land is all thickly overgrown with forests of all kinds of trees, and in the thickest forest there is a large and deep lake, and round it marshy ground and reeds. In this are caught otters and beavers and certainly other wild animals with square-shaped faces. The fur of these is sewn as a fringe round their coats of skin, and the testicles are made use of by them for curing diseases of the womb.

About the Sauromatai the following tale is told:—When the Hellenes had fought with the Amazons,—now the Amazons are called by the Scythians Oiorpata, which name means in the Hellenic tongue "slayers of men," for "man" they call oior, and pata means "to slay,"—then, as the story goes, the Hellenes, having conquered them in the battle at the Thermodon, were sailing away and conveying with them in three ships as many Amazons as they were able to take prisoners. These in the open sea set upon the men and cast them out of the ships; but they knew nothing about ships, nor how to use rudders or sails or oars, and after they had cast out the men they were driven about by wave and wind and came to that part of the Maiotian lake where Cremnoi stands; now Cremnoi is in the land of the free Scythians. There the Amazons disembarked from their ships and made their way into the country, and having met first with a troop of horses feeding they seized them, and mounted upon these they plundered the property of the Scythians.

The Scythians meanwhile were not able to understand the matter, for they did not know either their speech or their dress or the race to which they belonged, but were in wonder as to whence they had come and thought that they were men, of an age corresponding to their appearance: and finally they fought a battle against them, and after the battle the Scythians got possession of the bodies of the dead, and thus they discovered that they were women. They took counsel therefore and resolved by no means to go on trying to kill them, but to send against them the youngest men from among themselves, making conjecture of the number so as to send just as many men as there were women. These were told to encamp near them, and do whatsoever they should do; if however the women should come after them, they were not to fight but to retire before them, and when the women stopped, they were to approach near and encamp. This plan was adopted by the Scythians because they desired to have children born from them.

The young men accordingly were sent out and did that which had been commanded them: and when the Amazons perceived that they had not come to do them any harm, they let them alone; and the two camps approached nearer to one another every day: and the young men, like the Amazons, had nothing except their arms and their horses, and got their living, as the Amazons did, by hunting and by taking booty.

Now the Amazons at midday used to scatter abroad either one by one or by two together, dispersing to a distance from one another to ease themselves; and the Scythians also having perceived this did the same thing: and one of the Scythians came near to one of those Amazons who were apart by themselves, and she did not repulse him but allowed him to lie with her: and she could not speak to him, for they did not understand one another's speech, but she made signs to him with her hand to come on the following day to the same place and to bring another with him, signifying to him that there should be two of them, and that she would bring another with her. The young man therefore, when he returned, reported this to the others; and on the next day he came himself to the place and also brought another, and he found the Amazon awaiting him with another in her company. Then hearing this the rest of the young men also in their turn tamed for themselves the remainder of the Amazons; and after this they joined their camps and lived together, each man having for his wife her with whom he had had dealings at first; and the men were not able to learn the speech of the women, but the women came to comprehend that of the men. So when they understood one another, the men spoke to the Amazons as follows: "We have parents and we have possessions; now therefore let us no longer lead a life of this kind, but let us go away to the main body of our people and dwell with them; and we will have you for wives and no others." They however spoke thus in reply: "We should not be able to live with your women, for we and they have not the same customs. We shoot with bows and hurl javelins and ride horses, but the works of women we never learnt; whereas your women do none of these things which we said, but stay in the waggons and work at the works of women, neither going out to the chase nor anywhither else. We therefore should not be able to live in agreement with them: but if ye desire to keep us for your wives and to be thought honest men, go to your parents and obtain from them your share of the goods, and then let us go and dwell by ourselves."

The young men agreed and did this; and when they had obtained the share of the goods which belonged to them and had returned back to the Amazons, the women spoke to them as follows: "We are possessed by fear and trembling to think that we must dwell in this place, having not only separated you from your fathers, but also done great damage to your land. Since then ye think it right to have us as your wives, do this together with us,—come and let us remove from this land and pass over the river Tanaïs and there dwell."

The young men agreed to this also, and they crossed over the Tanaïs and made their way towards the rising sun for three days' journey from Tanaïs, and also towards the North Wind for three days' journey from the Maiotian lake: and having arrived at the place where they are now settled, they took up their abode there: and from thenceforward the women of the Sauromatai practise their ancient way of living, going out regularly on horseback to the chase both in company with the men and apart from them, and going regularly to war, and wearing the same dress as the men.

And the Sauromatai make use of the Scythian tongue, speaking it barbarously however from the first, since the Amazons did not learn it thoroughly well. As regards marriages their rule is this, that no maiden is married until she has slain a man of their enemies; and some of them even grow old and die before they are married, because they are not able to fulfil the requirement of the law.

To the kings of these nations then, which have been mentioned in order, the messengers of the Scythians came, finding them gathered together, and spoke declaring to them how the Persian king, after having subdued all things to himself in the other continent, had laid a bridge over the neck of the Bosphorus and had crossed over to that continent, and having crossed over and subdued the Thracians, was making a bridge over the river Ister, desiring to bring under his power all these regions also. "Do ye therefore," they said, "by no means stand aloof and allow us to be destroyed, but let us become all of one mind and oppose him who is coming against us. If ye shall not do so, we on our part shall either be forced by necessity to leave our land, or we shall stay in it and make a treaty with the invader; for what else can we do if ye are not willing to help us? and for you after this it will be in no respect easier; for the Persian has come not at all less against you than against us, nor will it content him to subdue us and abstain from you. And of the truth of that which we say we will mention a strong evidence: if the Persian had been making his expedition against us alone, because he desired to take vengeance for the former servitude, he ought to have abstained from all the rest and to have come at once to invade our land, and he would thus have made it clear to all that he was marching to fight against the Scythians and not against the rest. In fact however, ever since he crossed over to this continent, he has compelled all who came in his way to submit to him, and he holds under him now not only the other Thracians but also the Getai, who are our nearest neighbours."

When the Scythians proposed this, the kings who had come from the various nations took counsel together, and their opinions were divided. The kings of the Gelonians, of the Budinoi and of the Sauromatai agreed together and accepted the proposal that they should help the Scythians, but those of the Agathyrsians, Neuroi, Androphagoi, Melanchlainoi and Tauroi returned answer to the Scythians as follows: "If ye had not been the first to do wrong to the Persians and to begin war, then we should have surely thought that ye were speaking justly in asking for those things for which ye now ask, and we should have yielded to your request and shared your fortunes. As it is however, ye on the one hand made invasion without us into their land, and bare rule over the Persians for so long a time as God permitted you; and they in their turn, since the same God stirs them up, are repaying you with the like. As for us however, neither at that time did we do any wrong to these men nor now shall we attempt to do any wrong to them unprovoked: if however the Persians shall come against our land also, and do wrong first to us, we also shall refuse to submit : but until we shall see this, we shall remain by ourselves, for we are of opinion that the Persians have come not against us, but against those who were the authors of the wrong."

When the Scythians heard this answer reported, they planned not to fight a pitched battle openly, since these did not join them as allies, but to retire before the Persians and to drive away their cattle from before them, choking up with earth the wells and the springs of water by which they passed and destroying the grass from off the ground, having parted themselves for this into two bodies; and they resolved that the Sauromatai should be added to one of their divisions, namely that over which Scopasis was king, and that these should move on, if the Persians turned in that direction, straight towards the river Tanaïs, retreating before him by the shore of the Maiotian lake; and when the Persian marched back again, they should come after and pursue him. This was one division of their kingdom, appointed to go by the way which has been said; and the other two of the kingdoms, the large one over which Idanthyrsos was king, and the third of which Taxakis was king, were to join together in one, with the Gelonians and the Budinoi added to them, and they also were to retire before the Persians one day's march in front of them, going on out of their way and doing that which had been planned. First they were to move on straight for the countries which had refused to give their alliance, in order that they might involve these also in the war, and though these had not voluntarily undertaken the war with the Persians, they were to involve them in it nevertheless against their will; and after that they were to return to their own land and attack the enemy, if it should seem good to them in council so to do.

Having formed this plan the Scythians went to meet the army of Dareios, sending off the best of their horsemen before them as scouts; but all the waggons in which their children and their women lived they sent on, and with them all their cattle (leaving only so much as was sufficient to supply them with food), and charged them that they should proceed continually towards the North Wind. These, I say, were being carried on before: but when the scouts who went in front of the Scythians discovered the Persians distant about three days' march from Ister, then the Scythians having discovered them continued to pitch their camp one day's march in front, destroying utterly that which grew from the ground: and when the Persians saw that the horsemen of the Scythians had made their appearance, they came after them following in their track, while the Scythians continually moved on. After this, since they had directed their march towards the first of the divisions, the Persians continued to pursue towards the East and the river Tanaïs; and when the Scythians crossed over the river Tanaïs, the Persians crossed over after them and continued still to pursue, until they had passed quite through the land of the Sauromatai and had come to that of the Budinoi.

Now so long as the Persians were passing through Scythia and the land of the Sauromatai, they had nothing to destroy, seeing that the land was bare, but when they invaded the land of the Budinoi, then they fell in with the wooden wall, which had been deserted by the Budinoi and left wholly unoccupied, and this they destroyed by fire. Having done so they continued to follow on further in the tracks of the enemy, until they had passed through the whole of this land and had arrived at the desert. This desert region is occupied by no men, and it lies above the land of the Budinoi, extending for a seven days' journey; and above this desert dwell the Thyssagetai, and four large rivers flow from them through the land of the Maiotians and run into that which is called the Maiotian lake, their names being as follows,—Lycos, Oaros, Tanaïs, Syrgis.

When therefore Dareios came to the desert region, he ceased from his course and halted his army upon the river Oaros. Having so done he began to build eight large fortifications at equal distances from one another, that is to say about sixty furlongs, of which the ruins still existed down to my time; and while he was occupied in this, the Scythians whom he was pursuing came round by the upper parts and returned back to Scythia. Accordingly, since these had altogether disappeared and were no longer seen by the Persians at all, Dareios left those fortifications half finished, and turning back himself began to go towards the West, supposing that these were the whole body of the Scythians and that they were flying towards the West.

And marching his army as quickly as possible, when he came to Scythia he met with the two divisions of the Scythians together, and having fallen in with these he continued to pursue them, while they retired out of his way one day's journey in advance: and as Dareios did not cease to come after them, the Scythians according to the plan which they had made continued to retire before him towards the land of those who had refused to give their alliance, and first towards that of the Melanchlainoi; and when Scythians and Persians both together had invaded and disturbed these, the Scythians led the way to the country of the Androphagoi; and when these had also been disturbed, they proceeded to the land of the Neuroi; and while these too were being disturbed, the Scythians went on retiring before the enemy to the Agathyrsians. The Agathyrsians however, seeing that their next neighbours also were flying from the Scythians and had been disturbed, sent a herald before the Scythians invaded their land and proclaimed to the Scythians not to set foot upon their confines, warning them that if they should attempt to invade the country, they would first have to fight with them. The Agathyrsians then having given this warning came out in arms to their borders, meaning to drive off those who were coming upon them; but the Melanchlainoi and Androphagoi and Neuroi, when the Persians and Scythians together invaded them, did not betake themselves to brave defence but forgot their former threat and fled in confusion ever further towards the North to the desert region. The Scythians however, when the Agathyrsians had warned them off, did not attempt any more to come to these, but led the Persians from the country of the Neuroi back to their own land.

Now as this went on for a long time and did not cease, Dareios sent a horseman to Idanthyrsos king of the Scythians and said as follows: "Thou most wondrous man, why dost thou fly for ever, when thou mightest do of these two things one?—if thou thinkest thyself able to make opposition to my power, stand thou still and cease from wandering abroad, and fight; but if thou dost acknowledge thyself too weak, cease then in that case also from thy course, and come to speech with thy master, bringing to him gifts of earth and water."

To this the king of the Scythians Idanthyrsos made answer thus: "My case, O Persian, stands thus:—Never yet did I fly because I was afraid, either before this time from any other man, or now from thee; nor have I done anything different now from that which I was wont to do also in time of peace: and as to the cause why I do not fight with thee at once, this also I will declare to thee. We have neither cities nor land sown with crops, about which we should fear lest they should be captured or laid waste, and so join battle more speedily with you; but if it be necessary by all means to come to this speedily, know that we have sepulchres in which our fathers are buried; therefore come now, find out these and attempt to destroy them, and ye shall know then whether we shall fight with you for the sepulchres or whether we shall not fight. Before that however, unless the motion comes upon us, we shall not join battle with thee. About fighting let so much as has been said suffice; but as to masters, I acknowledge none over me but Zeus my ancestor and Hestia the queen of the Scythians. To thee then in place of gifts of earth and water I shall send such things as it is fitting that thou shouldest receive; and in return for thy saying that thou art my master, for that I say, woe betide thee." This is the proverbial "saying of the Scythians."

The herald then had departed to report this to Dareios; and the kings of the Scythians, having heard mention of subjection to a master, were filled with wrath. They sent accordingly the division which was appointed to be joined with the Sauromatai, that division of which Scopasis was in command, bidding them come to speech with the Ionians, namely those who were guarding the bridge of the Ister, and meanwhile they who were left behind resolved not to lead the Persians wandering about any more, but to attack them constantly as they were getting provisions. Therefore they observed the soldiers of Dareios as they got provisions, and did that which they had determined: and the cavalry of the Scythians always routed that of the enemy, but the Persian horsemen as they fled fell back upon the men on foot, and these would come up to their assistance; and meanwhile the Scythians when they had driven in the cavalry turned back, fearing the men on foot. Also by night the Scythians used to make similar attacks: and the thing which, strange to say, most helped the Persians and hindered the Scythians in their attacks upon the camp of Dareios, I will mention, namely the voice of the asses and the appearance of the mules; for Scythia produces neither ass nor mule, as I have declared before, nor is there at all in the Scythian country either ass or mule on account of the cold. The asses accordingly by riotously braying used to throw into confusion the cavalry of the Scythians; and often, as they were in the middle of riding against the Persians, when the horses heard the voice of the asses they turned back in confusion and were possessed with wonder, pricking up their ears, because they had never heard such a voice nor seen the form of the creature before.

. So far then the Persians had the advantage for a small part of the war. But the Scythians, whenever they saw that the Persians were disquieted, then in order that they might remain a longer time in Scythia and in remaining might suffer by being in want of everything, would leave some of their own cattle behind with the herdsmen, while they themselves rode out of the way to another place, and the Persians would come upon the cattle and take them, and having taken them they were elated at what they had done.

As this happened often, at length Dareios began to be in straits; and the kings of the Scythians perceiving this sent a herald bearing as gifts to Dareios a bird and a mouse and a frog and five arrows. The Persians accordingly asked the bearer of the gifts as to the meaning of the gifts which were offered; but he said that nothing more had been commanded to him but to give them and get away as speedily as possible; and he bade the Persians find out for themselves, if they had wisdom, that which the gifts were meant to express.

Having heard this the Persians took counsel with one another; and the opinion of Dareios was that the Scythians were giving to him both themselves and also earth and water, making his conjecture by this, namely that a mouse is produced in the earth and feeds on the same produce of the earth as man, and a frog in the water, while a bird has great resemblance to a horse; and moreover that in giving the arrows they were delivering up their own might in battle. This was the opinion expressed by Dareios; but the opinion of Gobryas, one of the seven men who killed the Magian, was at variance with it, for he conjectured that the gifts expressed this: "Unless ye become birds and fly up into the heaven, O Persians, or become mice and sink down under the earth, or become frogs and leap into the lakes, ye shall not return back home, but shall be smitten by these arrows."

The Persians then, I say, were making conjecture of the gifts: and meanwhile the single division of the Scythians, that which had been appointed at first to keep guard along the Maiotian lake and then to go to the Ister and come to speech with the Ionians, when they arrived at the bridge spoke as follows: "Ionians, we have come bringing you freedom, if at least ye are willing to listen to us; for we are informed that Dareios gave you command to guard the bridge for sixty days only, and then, if he had not arrived within that time, to get you away to your own land. Now therefore, if ye do as we say, ye will be without blame from his part and without blame also from ours: stay the appointed days and then after that get you away." They then, when the Ionians had engaged themselves to do this, hastened back again by the quickest way: and meanwhile, after the coming of the gifts to Dareios, the Scythians who were left had arrayed themselves against the Persians with both foot and horse, meaning to engage battle. Now when the Scythians had been placed in battle-array, a hare darted through them into the space between the two armies, and each company of them, as they saw the hare, began to run after it. When the Scythians were thus thrown into disorder and were raising loud cries, Dareios asked what was this clamour arising from the enemy; and hearing that they were running after the hare, he said to those men to whom he was wont to say things at other times: "These men have very slight regard for us, and I perceive now that Gobryas spoke rightly about the Scythian gifts. Seeing then that now I myself too think that things are so, we have need of good counsel, in order that our retreat homewards may be safely made." To this replied Gobryas and said: "O king, even by report I was almost assured of the difficulty of dealing with these men; and when I came I learnt it still more thoroughly, since I saw that they were mocking us. Now therefore my opinion is, that as soon as night comes on, we kindle the camp-fires as we are wont to do at other times also, and deceive with a false tale those of our men who are weakest to endure hardships, and tie up all the asses and get us away, before either the Scythians make for the Ister to destroy the bridge or something be resolved by the Ionians which may be our ruin."

Thus Gobryas advised; and after this, when night came on, Dareios acted on this opinion. Those of his men who were weakened by fatigue and whose loss was of least account, these he left behind in the camp, and the asses also tied up: and for the following reasons he left behind the asses and the weaker men of his army,—the asses in order that they might make a noise which should be heard, and the men really because of their weakness, but on a pretence stated openly that he was about to attack the Scythians with the effective part of the army, and that they meanwhile were to be defenders of the camp. Having thus instructed those who were left behind, and having kindled camp-fires, Dareios hastened by the quickest way towards the Ister: and the asses, having no longer about them the usual throng, very much more for that reason caused their voice to be heard; so the Scythians, hearing the asses, supposed surely that the Persians were remaining in their former place.

But when it was day, those who were left behind perceived that they had been betrayed by Dareios, and they held out their hands in submission to the Scythians, telling them what their case was; and the Scythians, when they heard this, joined together as quickly as possible, that is to say the two combined divisions of the Scythians and the single division, and also the Sauromatai, Budinoi, and Gelonians, and began to pursue the Persians, making straight for the Ister: but as the Persian army for the most part consisted of men on foot, and was not acquainted with the roads (the roads not being marked with tracks), while the Scythian army consisted of horsemen and was acquainted with the shortest cuts along the way, they missed one another and the Scythians arrived at the bridge much before the Persians. Then having learnt that the Persians had not yet arrived, they said to the Ionians who were in the ships: "Ionians, the days of your number are past, and ye are not acting uprightly in that ye yet remain waiting: but as ye stayed before from fear, so now break up the passage as quickly as ye may, and depart free and unhurt, feeling thankfulness both to the gods and to the Scythians: and him who was formerly your master we will so convince, that he shall never again march with an army upon any nation."

. Upon this the Ionians took counsel together; and Miltiades the Athenian on the one hand, who was commander and despot of the men of the Chersonese in Hellespont, was of opinion that they should follow the advice of the Scythians and set Ionia free: but Histiaios the Milesian was of the opposite opinion to this; for he said that at the present time it was by means of Dareios that each one of them was ruling as despot over a city; and if the power of Dareios should be destroyed, neither he himself would be able to bear rule over the Milesians, nor would any other of them be able to bear rule over any other city; for each of the cities would choose to have popular rather than despotic rule. When Histiaios declared his opinion thus, forthwith all turned to this opinion, whereas at the first they were adopting that of Miltiades.

Now these were they who gave the vote between the two opinions, and were men of consequence in the eyes of the king, —first the despots of the Hellespontians, Daphnis of Abydos, Hippoclos of Lampsacos, Herophantos of Parion, Metrodoros of Proconnesos, Aristagoras of Kyzicos, and Ariston of Byzantion, these were those from the Hellespont; and from Ionia, Strattis of Chios, Aiakes of Samos, Laodamas of Phocaia, and Histiaios of Miletos, whose opinion had been proposed in opposition to that of Miltiades; and of the Aiolians the only man of consequence there present was Aristagoras of Kyme.

When these adopted the opinion of Histiaios, they resolved to add to it deeds and words as follows, namely to break up that part of the bridge which was on the side towards the Scythians, to break it up, I say, for a distance equal to the range of an arrow, both in order that they might be thought to be doing something, though in fact they were doing nothing, and for fear that the Scythians might make an attempt using force and desiring to cross the Ister by the bridge: and in breaking up that part of the bridge which was towards Scythia they resolved to say that they would do all that which the Scythians desired. This they added to the opinion proposed, and then Histiaios coming forth from among them made answer to the Scythians as follows: "Scythians, ye are come bringing good news, and it is a timely haste that ye make to bring it; and ye on your part give us good guidance, while we on ours render to you suitable service. For, as ye see, we are breaking up the passage, and we shall show all zeal in our desire to be free: and while we are breaking up the bridge, it is fitting that ye should be seeking for those of whom ye speak, and when ye have found them, that ye should take vengeance on them on behalf of us as well as of yourselves in such manner as they deserve."

The Scythians then, believing for the second time that the Ionians were speaking the truth, turned back to make search for the Persians, but they missed altogether their line of march through the land. Of this the Scythians themselves were the cause, since they had destroyed the pastures for horses in that region and had choked up with earth the springs of water; for if they had not done this, it would have been possible for them easily, if they desired it, to discover the Persians: but as it was, by those things wherein they thought they had taken their measures best, they failed of success. The Scythians then on their part were passing through those regions of their own land where there was grass for the horses and springs of water, and were seeking for the enemy there, thinking that they too were taking a course in their retreat through such country as this; while the Persians in fact marched keeping carefully to the track which they had made before, and so they found the passage of the river, though with difficulty: and as they arrived by night and found the bridge broken up, they were brought to the extreme of fear, lest the Ionians should have deserted them.

Now there was with Dareios an Egyptian who had a voice louder than that of any other man on earth, and this man Dareios ordered to take his stand upon the bank of the Ister and to call Histiaios of Miletos. He accordingly proceeded to do so; and Histiaios, hearing the first hail, produced all the ships to carry the army over and also put together the bridge.

Thus the Persians escaped, and the Scythians in their search missed the Persians the second time also: and their judgment of the Ionians is that on the one hand, if they be regarded as free men, they are the most worthless and cowardly of all men, but on the other hand, if regarded as slaves, they are the most attached to their master and the least disposed to run away of all slaves. This is the reproach which is cast against the Ionians by the Scythians.

Dareios then marching through Thrace arrived at Sestos in the Chersonese; and from that place, he passed over himself in his ships to Asia, but to command his army in Europe he left Megabazos a Persian, to whom Dareios once gave honour by uttering in the land of Persia this saying:—Dareios was beginning to eat pomegranates, and at once when he opened the first of them, Artabanos his brother asked him of what he would desire to have as many as there were seeds in the pomegranate: and Dareios said that he would desire to have men like Megabazos as many as that in number, rather than to have Hellas subject to him. In Persia, I say, he honoured him by saying these words, and at this time he left him in command with eight myriads of his army.

This Megabazos uttered one saying whereby he left of himself an imperishable memory with the peoples of Hellespont: for being once at Byzantion he heard that the men of Calchedon had settled in that region seventeen years before the Byzantians, and having heard it he said that those of Calchedon at that time chanced to be blind; for assuredly they would not have chosen the worse place, when they might have settled in that which was better, if they had not been blind. This Megabazos it was who was left in command at that time in the land of the Hellespontians, and he proceeded to subdue all who did not take the side of the Medes.

He then was doing thus; and at this very same time a great expedition was being made also against Libya, on an occasion which I shall relate when I have first related this which follows.—The children's children of those who voyaged in the Argo, having been driven forth by those Pelasgians who carried away at Brauron the women of the Athenians,—having been driven forth I say by these from Lemnos, had departed and sailed to Lacedemon, and sitting down on Mount Taÿgetos they kindled a fire. The Lacedemonians seeing this sent a messenger to inquire who they were and from whence; and they answered the question of the messenger saying that they were Minyai and children of heroes who sailed in the Argo, for these, they said, had put in to Lemnos and propagated the race of which they sprang. The Lacedemonians having heard the story of the descent of the Minyai, sent a second time and asked for what purpose they had come into the country and were causing a fire to blaze. They said that they had been cast out by the Pelasgians, and were come now to the land of their fathers, for most just it was that this should so be done; and they said that their request was to be permitted to dwell with these, having a share of civil rights and a portion allotted to them of the land. And the Lacedemonians were content to receive the Minyai upon the terms which they themselves desired, being most of all impelled to do this by the fact that the sons of Tyndareus were voyagers in the Argo. So having received the Minyai they gave them a share of land and distributed them in the tribes; and they forthwith made marriages, and gave in marriage to others the women whom they brought with them from Lemnos.

However, when no very long time had passed, the Minyai forthwith broke out into insolence, asking for a share of the royal power and also doing other impious things: therefore the Lacedemonians resolved to put them to death; and having seized them they cast them into a prison. Now the Lacedemonians put to death by night all those whom they put to death, but no man by day. When therefore they were just about to kill them, the wives of the Minyai, being native Spartans and daughters of the first citizens of Sparta, entreated to be allowed to enter the prison and come to speech every one with her own husband: and they let them pass in, not supposing that any craft would be practised by them. They however, when they had entered, delivered to their husbands all the garments which they were wearing, and themselves received those of their husbands: thus the Minyai having put on the women's clothes went forth out of prison as women, and having escaped in this manner they went again to Taÿgetos and sat down there.

Now at this very same time Theras the son of Autesion, the son of Tisamenos, the son of Thersander, the son of Polyneikes, was preparing to set forth from Lacedemon to found a settlement. This Theras, who was of the race of Cadmos, was mother's brother to the sons of Aristodemos, Eurysthenes and Procles; and while these sons were yet children, Theras as their guardian held the royal power in Sparta. When however his nephews were grown and had taken the power into their hands, then Theras, being grieved that he should be ruled by others after he had tasted of rule himself, said that he would not remain in Lacedemon, but would sail away to his kinsmen. Now there were in the island which is now called Thera, but formerly was called Callista, descendants of Membliaros the son of Poikiles, a Phenician: for Cadmos the son of Agenor in his search for Europa put in to land at the island which is now called Thera; and, whether it was that the country pleased him when he had put to land, or whether he chose to do so for any other reason, he left in this island, besides other Phenicians, Membliaros also, of his own kinsmen. These occupied the island called Callista for eight generations of men, before Theras came from Lacedemon.

To these then, I say, Theras was preparing to set forth, taking with him people from the tribes, and intending to settle together with those who have been mentioned, not with any design to drive them out, but on the contrary claiming them very strongly as kinfolk. And when the Minyai after having escaped from the prison went and sat down on Taÿgetos, Theras entreated of the Lacedemonians, as they were proposing to put them to death, that no slaughter might take place, and at the same time he engaged himself to take them forth out of the land. The Lacedemonians having agreed to this proposal, he sailed away with three thirty-oared galleys to the descendants of Membliaros, not taking with him by any means all the Minyai, but a few only; for the greater number of them turned towards the land of the Paroreatai and Caucones, and having driven these out of their country, they parted themselves into six divisions and founded in their territory the following towns,—Lepreon, Makistos, Phrixai, Pyrgos, Epion, Nudion; of these the Eleians sacked the greater number within my own lifetime. The island meanwhile got its name of Thera after Theras who led the settlement.

And since his son said that he would not sail with him, therefore he said that he would leave him behind as a sheep among wolves; and in accordance with that saying this young man got the name of Oiolycos, and it chanced that this name prevailed over his former name: then from Oiolycos was begotten Aigeus, after whom are called the Aigeidai, a powerful clan in Sparta: and the men of this tribe, since their children did not live to grow up, established by the suggestion of an oracle a temple to the Avenging Deities of Laïos and OEdipus, and after this the same thing was continued in Thera by the descendants of these men.

Up to this point of the story the Lacedemonians agree in their report with the men of Thera; but in what is to come it is those of Thera alone who report that it happened as follows. Grinnos the son of Aisanios, a descendant of the Theras who has been mentioned, and king of the island of Thera, came to Delphi bringing the offering of a hecatomb from his State; and there were accompanying him, besides others of the citizens, also Battos the son of Polymnestos, who was by descent of the family of Euphemos of the race of the Minyai. Now when Grinnos the king of the Theraians was consulting the Oracle about other matters, the Pythian prophetess gave answer bidding him found a city in Libya; and he made reply saying: "Lord, I am by this time somewhat old and heavy to stir, but do thou bid some one of these younger ones do this." As he thus said he pointed towards Battos. So far at that time: but afterwards when he had come away they were in difficulty about the saying of the Oracle, neither having any knowledge of Libya, in what part of the earth it was, nor venturing to send a colony to the unknown.

Then after this for seven years there was no rain in Thera, and in these years all the trees in their island were withered up excepting one: and when the Theraians consulted the Oracle, the Pythian prophetess alleged this matter of colonising Libya to be the cause. As then they had no remedy for their evil, they sent messengers to Crete, to find out whether any of the Cretans or of the sojourners in Crete had ever come to Libya. These as they wandered round about the country came also the city of Itanos, and there they met with a fisher for purple named Corobios, who said that he had been carried away by winds and had come to Libya, and in Libya to the island of Platea. This man they persuaded by payment of money and took him to Thera, and from Thera there set sail men to explore, at first not many in number; and Corobios having guided them to this same island of Platea, they left Corobios there, leaving behind with him provisions for a certain number of months, and sailed themselves as quickly as possible to make report about the island to the men of Thera.

Since however these stayed away longer than the time appointed, Corobios found himself destitute; and after this a ship of Samos, of which the master was Colaios, while sailing to Egypt was carried out of its course and came to this island of Platea; and the Samians hearing from Corobios the whole story left him provisions for a year. They themselves then put out to sea from the island and sailed on, endeavouring to reach Egypt but carried away continually by the East Wind; and as the wind did not cease to blow, they passed through the Pillars of Heracles and came to Tartessos, guided by divine providence. Now this trading-place was at that time untouched by any, so that when these returned back home they made profit from their cargo greater than any other Hellenes of whom we have certain knowledge, with the exception at least of Sostratos the son of Laodamas the Eginetan, for with him it is not possible for any other man to contend. And the Samians set apart six talents, the tenth part of their gains, and had a bronze vessel made like an Argolic mixing-bowl with round it heads of griffins projecting in a row; and this they dedicated as an offering in the temple of Hera, setting as supports under it three colossal statues of bronze seven cubits in height, resting upon their knees. By reason first of this deed great friendship was formed by those of Kyrene and Thera with the Samians.

The Theraians meanwhile, when they arrived at Thera after having left Corobios in the island, reported that they had colonised an island on the coast of Libya: and the men of Thera resolved to send one of every two brothers selected by lot and men besides taken from all the regions of the island, which are seven in number; and further that Battos should be both their leader and their king. Thus then they sent forth two fifty-oared galleys to Platea.

This is the report of the Theraians; and for the remainder of the account from this point onwards the Theraians are in agreement with the men of Kyrene: from this point onwards, I say, since in what concerns Battos the Kyrenians tell by no means the same tale as those of Thera; for their account is this:—There is in Crete a city called Oäxos in which one Etearchos became king, who when he had a daughter, whose mother was dead, named Phronime, took to wife another woman notwithstanding. She having come in afterwards, thought fit to be a stepmother to Phronime in deed as well as in name, giving her evil treatment and devising everything possible to her hurt; and at last she brings against her a charge of lewdness and persuades her husband that the truth is so. He then being convinced by his wife, devised an unholy deed against the daughter: for there was in Oäxos one Themison, a merchant of Thera, whom Etearchos took to himself as a guest-friend and caused him to swear that he would surely serve him in whatsoever he should require: and when he had caused him to swear this, he brought and delivered to him his daughter and bade him take her away and cast her into the sea. Themison then was very greatly vexed at the deceit practised in the matter of the oath, and he dissolved his guest-friendship and did as follows, that is to say, he received the girl and sailed away, and when he got out into the open sea, to free himself from blame as regards the oath which Etearchos had made him swear, he tied her on each side with ropes and let her down into the sea, and then drew her up and came to Thera.

After that, Polymnestos, a man of repute among the Theraians, received Phronime from him and kept her as his concubine; and in course of time there was born to him from her a son with an impediment in his voice and lisping, to whom, as both Theraians and Kyrenians say, was given the name Battos, but I think that some other name was then given, and he was named Battos instead of this after he came to Libya, taking for himself this surname from the oracle which was given to him at Delphi and from the rank which he had obtained; for the Libyans call a king battos: and for this reason, I think, the Pythian prophetess in her prophesying called him so, using the Libyan tongue, because she knew that he would be a king in Libya. For when he had grown to be a man, he came to Delphi to inquire about his voice; and when he asked, the prophetess thus answered him:

"For a voice thou camest, O Battos, but thee lord Phoebus Apollo

  Sendeth as settler forth to the Libyan land sheep-abounding,"

just as if she should say using the Hellenic tongue, "For a voice thou camest, O king." He thus made answer: "Lord, I came to thee to inquire concerning my voice, but thou answerest me other things which are not possible, bidding me go as a settler to Libya; but with what power, or with what force of men should I go?" Thus saying he did not at all persuade her to give him any other reply; and as she was prophesying to him again the same things as before, Battos departed while she was yet speaking, and went away to Thera.

After this there came evil fortune both to himself and to the other men of Thera; and the Theraians, not understanding that which befell them, sent to Delphi to inquire about the evils which they were suffering: and the Pythian prophetess gave them reply that if they joined with Battos in founding Kyrene in Libya, they would fare the better. After this the Theraians sent Battos with two fifty-oared galleys; and these sailed to Libya, and then came away back to Thera, for they did not know what else to do: and the Theraians pelted them with missiles when they endeavoured to land, and would not allow them to put to shore, but bade them sail back again. They accordingly being compelled sailed away back, and they made a settlement in an island lying near the coast of Libya, called, as was said before, Platea. This island is said to be of the same size as the now existing city of Kyrene.

In this they continued to dwell two years; but as they had no prosperity, they left one of their number behind and all the rest sailed away to Delphi, and having come to the Oracle they consulted it, saying that they were dwelling in Libya and that, though they were dwelling there, they fared none the better: and the Pythian prophetess made answer to them thus:

"Better than I if thou knowest the Libyan land sheep-abounding,

 Not having been there than I who have been, at thy wisdom I wonder."

Having heard this Battos and his companions sailed away back again; for in fact the god would not let them off from the task of settlement till they had come to Libya itself: and having arrived at the island and taken up him whom they had left, they made a settlement in Libya itself at a spot opposite the island, called Aziris, which is enclosed by most fair woods on both sides and a river flows by it on one side.

In this spot they dwelt for six years; and in the seventh year the Libyans persuaded them to leave it, making request and saying that they would conduct them to a better region. So the Libyans led them from that place making them start towards evening; and in order that the Hellenes might not see the fairest of all the regions as they passed through it, they led them past it by night, having calculated the time of daylight: and this region is called Irasa. Then having conducted them to the so-called spring of Apollo, they said, "Hellenes, here is a fit place for you to dwell, for here the heaven is pierced with holes."

Now during the lifetime of the first settler Battos, who reigned forty years, and of his son Arkesilaos, who reigned sixteen years, the Kyrenians continued to dwell there with the same number as when they first set forth to the colony; but in the time of the third king, called Battos the Prosperous, the Pythian prophetess gave an oracle wherein she urged the Hellenes in general to sail and join with the Kyrenians in colonising Libya. For the Kyrenians invited them, giving promise of a division of land; and the oracle which she uttered was as follows:

"Who to the land much desirèd, to Libya, afterwards cometh,

 After the land be divided, I say he shall some day repent it."

Then great numbers were gathered at Kyrene, and the Libyans who dwelt round had much land cut off from their possessions; therefore they with their king whose name was Adicran, as they were not only deprived of their country but also were dealt with very insolently by the Kyrenians, sent to Egypt and delivered themselves over to Apries king of Egypt. He then having gathered a great army of Egyptians, sent it against Kyrene; and the men of Kyrene marched out to the region of Irasa and to the spring Theste, and there both joined battle with the Egyptians and defeated them in the battle: for since the Egyptians had not before made trial of the Hellenes in fight and therefore despised them, they were so slaughtered that but few of them returned back to Egypt. In consequence of this and because they laid the blame of it upon Apries, the Egyptians revolted from him.

This Battos had a son called Arkesilaos, who first when he became king made a quarrel with his own brothers, until they finally departed to another region of Libya, and making the venture for themselves founded that city which was then and is now called Barca; and at the same time as they founded this, they induced the Libyans to revolt from the Kyrenians. After this, Arkesilaos made an expedition against those Libyans who had received them and who had also revolted from Kyrene, and the Libyans fearing him departed and fled towards the Eastern tribes of Libyans: and Arkesilaos followed after them as they fled, until he arrived in his pursuit at Leucon in Libya, and there the Libyans resolved to attack him. Accordingly they engaged battle and defeated the Kyrenians so utterly that seven thousand hoplites of the Kyrenians fell there. After this disaster Arkesilaos, being sick and having swallowed a potion, was strangled by his brother Haliarchos, and Haliarchos was killed treacherously by the wife of Arkesilaos, whose name was Eryxo.

Then Battos the son of Arkesilaos succeeded to the kingdom, who was lame and not sound in his feet: and the Kyrenians with a view to the misfortune which had befallen them sent men to Delphi to ask what form of rule they should adopt, in order to live in the best way possible; and the Pythian prophetess bade them take to themselves a reformer of their State from Mantineia of the Arcadians. The men of Kyrene accordingly made request, and those of Mantineia gave them the man of most repute among their citizens, whose name was Demonax. This man therefore having come to Kyrene and having ascertained all things exactly, in the first place caused them to have three tribes, distributing them thus:—one division he made of the Theraians and their dependants, another of the Peloponnesians and Cretans, and a third of all the islanders. Then secondly for the king Battos he set apart domains of land and priesthoods, but all the other powers which the kings used to possess before, he assigned as of public right to the people.

During the reign of this Battos things continued to be thus, but in the reign of his son Arkesilaos there arose much disturbance about the offices of the State: for Arkesilaos son of Battos the Lame and of Pheretime said that he would not suffer it to be according as the Mantineian Demonax had arranged, but asked to have back the royal rights of his forefathers. After this, stirring up strife he was worsted and went as an exile to Samos, and his mother to Salamis in Cyprus. Now at that time the ruler of Salamis was Euelthon, the same who dedicated as an offering the censer at Delphi, a work well worth seeing, which is placed in the treasury of the Corinthians. To him having come, Pheretime asked him for an army to restore herself and her son to Kyrene. Euelthon however was ready to give her anything else rather than that; and she when she received that which he gave her said that this too was a fair gift, but fairer still would be that other gift of an army for which she was asking. As she kept saying this to every thing which was given, at last Euelthon sent out to her a present of a golden spindle and distaff, with wool also upon it: and when Pheretime uttered again the same saying about this present, Euelthon said that such things as this were given as gifts to women and not an army.

Arkesilaos meanwhile, being in Samos, was gathering every one together by a promise of dividing land; and while a great host was being collected, Arkesilaos set out to Delphi to inquire of the Oracle about returning from exile: and the Pythian prophetess gave him this answer: "For four named Battos and four named Arkesilaos, eight generations of men, Loxias grants to you to be kings of Kyrene, but beyond this he counsels you not even to attempt it. Thou however must keep quiet when thou hast come back to thy land; and if thou findest the furnace full of jars, heat not the jars fiercely, but let them go with a fair wind: if however thou heat the furnace fiercely, enter not thou into the place flowed round by water; for if thou dost thou shalt die, both thou and the bull which is fairer than all the rest."

Thus the Pythian prophetess gave answer to Arkesilaos; and he, having taken to him those in Samos, made his return to Kyrene; and when he had got possession of the power, he did not remember the saying of the Oracle but endeavoured to exact penalties from those of the opposite faction for having driven him out. Of these some escaped out of the country altogether, but some Arkesilaos got into his power and sent them away to Cyprus to be put to death. These were driven out of their course to Cnidos, and the men of Cnidos rescued them and sent them away to Thera. Some others however of the Kyrenians fled to a great tower belonging to Aglomachos a private citizen, and Arkesilaos burnt them by piling up brushwood round. Then after he had done the deed he perceived that the Oracle meant this, in that the Pythian prophetess forbade him, if he found the jars in the furnace, to heat them fiercely; and he voluntarily kept away from the city of the Kyrenians, fearing the death which had been prophesied by the Oracle and supposing that Kyrene was flowed round by water. Now he had to wife a kinswoman of his own, the daughter of the king of Barca whose name was Alazeir: to him he came, and men of Barca together with certain of the exiles from Kyrene, perceiving him going about in the market-place, killed him, and also besides him his father-in-law Alazeir. Arkesilaos accordingly, having missed the meaning of the oracle, whether with his will or against his will, fulfilled his own destiny.

His mother Pheretime meanwhile, so long as Arkesilaos having worked evil for himself dwelt at Barca, herself held the royal power of her son at Kyrene, both exercising his other rights and also sitting in council: but when she heard that her son had been slain in Barca, she departed and fled to Egypt: for she had on her side services done for Cambyses the son of Cyrus by Arkesilaos, since this was the Arkesilaos who had given over Kyrene to Cambyses and had laid a tribute upon himself. Pheretime then having come to Egypt sat down as a suppliant of Aryandes, bidding him help her, and alleging as a reason that it was on account of his inclination to the side of the Medes that her son had been slain. . Now this Aryandes had been appointed ruler of the province of Egypt by Cambyses; and after the time of these events he lost his life because he would measure himself with Dareios. For having heard and seen that Dareios desired to leave behind him as a memorial of himself a thing which had not been made by any other king, he imitated him, until at last he received his reward: for whereas Dareios refined gold and made it as pure as possible, and of this caused coins to be struck, Aryandes, being ruler of Egypt, did the same thing with silver; and even now the purest silver is that which is called Aryandic. Dareios then having learnt that he was doing this put him to death, bringing against him another charge of attempting rebellion.

Now at the time of which I speak this Aryandes had compassion on Pheretime and gave her all the troops that were in Egypt, both the land and the sea forces, appointing Amasis a Maraphian to command the land-army and Badres, of the race of the Pasargadai, to command the fleet: but before he sent away the army, Aryandes despatched a herald to Barca and asked who it was who had killed Arkesilaos; and the men of Barca all took it upon themselves, for they said they suffered formerly many great evils at his hands. Having heard this, Aryandes at last sent away the army together with Pheretime. This charge then was the pretext alleged; but in fact the army was being sent out (as I believe) for the purpose of subduing Libya: for of the Libyans there are many nations of nations of various kinds, and but few of them are subject to the king, while the greater number paid no regard to Dareios.

Now the Libyans have their dwelling as follows:—Beginning from Egypt, first of the Libyans are settled the Adyrmachidai, who practise for the most part the same customs as the Egyptians, but wear clothing similar to that of the other Libyans. Their women wear a bronze ring upon each leg, and they have long hair on their heads, and when they catch their lice, each one bites her own in retaliation and then throws them away. These are the only people of the Lybians who do this; and they alone display to the king their maidens when they are about to be married, and whosoever of them proves to be pleasing to the king is deflowered by him. These Adyrmachidai extend along the coast from Egypt as far as the port which is called Plynos.

Next after these come the Giligamai, occupying the country towards the West as far as the island of Aphrodisias. In the space within this limit lies off the coast the island of Platea, where the Kyrenians made their settlement; and on the coast of the mainland there is Port Menelaos, and Aziris, where the Kyrenians used to dwell. From this point begins the silphion and it extends along the coast from the island of Platea as far as the entrance of the Syrtis. This nation practises customs nearly resembling those of the rest.

Next to the Giligamai on the West are the Asbystai: these dwell above Kyrene, and the Asbystai do not reach down the sea, for the region along the sea is occupied by Kyrenians. These most of all the Libyans are drivers of four-horse chariots, and in the greater number of their customs they endeavour to imitate the Kyrenians.

Next after the Asbystai on the West come the Auchisai: these dwell above Barca and reach down to the sea by Euesperides: and in the middle of the country of the Auchisai dwell the Bacales, a small tribe, who reach down to the sea by the city of Taucheira in the territory of Barca: these practise the same customs as those above Kyrene.

Next after these Auschisai towards the West come the Nasamonians, a numerous race, who in the summer leave their flocks behind by the sea and go up to the region of Augila to gather the fruit of the date-palms, which grow in great numbers and very large and are all fruit-bearing: these hunt the wingless locusts, and they dry them in the sun and then pound them up, and after that they sprinkle them upon milk and drink them. Their custom is for each man to have many wives, and they make their intercourse with them common in nearly the same manner as the Massagetai, that is they set up a staff in front of the door and so have intercourse. When a Nasamonian man marries his first wife, the custom is for the bride on the first night to go through the whole number of the guests having intercourse with them, and each man when he has lain with her gives a gift, whatsoever he has brought with him from his house. The forms of oath and of divination which they use are as follows:—they swear by the men among themselves who are reported to have been the most righteous and brave, by these, I say, laying hands upon their tombs; and they divine by visiting the sepulchral mounds of their ancestors and lying down to sleep upon them after having prayed; and whatsoever thing the man sees in his dream, this he accepts. They practise also the exchange of pledges in the following manner, that is to say, one gives the other to drink from his hand, and drinks himself from the hand of the other; and if they have no liquid, they take of the dust from the ground and lick it.

Adjoining the Nasamonians is the country of the Psylloi. These have perished utterly in the following manner:—The South Wind blowing upon them dried up all their cisterns of water, and their land was waterless, lying all within the Syrtis. They then having taken a resolve by common consent, marched in arms against the South Wind (I report that which is reported by the Libyans), and when they had arrived at the sandy tract, the South Wind blew and buried them in the sand. These then having utterly perished, the Nasamonians from that time forward possess their land.

Above these towards the South Wind in the region of wild beasts dwell the Garamantians, who fly from every man and avoid the company of all; and they neither possess any weapon of war, nor know how to defend themselves against enemies.

These dwell above the Nasamonians; and next to the Nasamonians along the sea coast towards the West come the Macai, who shave their hair so as to leave tufts, letting the middle of their hair grow long, but round this on all sides shaving it close to the skin; and for fighting they carry shields made of ostrich skins. Through their land the river Kinyps runs out into the sea, flowing from a hill called the "Hill of the Charites." This Hill of the Charites is overgrown thickly with wood, while the rest of Libya which has been spoken of before is bare of trees; and the distance from the sea to this hill is two hundred furlongs.

Next to these Macai are the Gindanes, whose women wear each of them a number of anklets made of the skins of animals, for the following reason, as it is said:—for every man who has commerce with her she binds on an anklet, and the woman who has most is esteemed the best, since she has been loved by the greatest number of men.

In a peninsula which stands out into the sea from the land of these Gindanes dwell the Lotophagoi, who live by eating the fruit of the lotos only. Now the fruit of the lotos is in size like that of the mastich-tree, and in flavour it resembles that of the date-palm. Of this fruit the Lotophagoi even make for themselves wine.

Next after the Lotophagoi along the sea-coast are the Machlyans, who also make use of the lotos, but less than those above mentioned. These extend to a great river named the river Triton, and this runs out into a great lake called Tritonis, in which there is an island named Phla. About this island they say there was an oracle given to the Lacedemonians that they should make a settlement in it.

The following moreover is also told, namely that Jason, when the Argo had been completed by him under Mount Pelion, put into it a hecatomb and with it also a tripod of bronze, and sailed round Pelopponese, desiring to come to Delphi; and when in sailing he got near Malea, a North Wind seized his ship and carried it off to Libya, and before he caught sight of land he had come to be in the shoals of the lake Tritonis. Then as he was at a loss how he should bring his ship forth, the story goes that Triton appeared to him and bade Jason give him the tripod, saying that he would show them the right course and let them go away without hurt: and when Jason consented to it, then Triton showed them the passage out between the shoals and set the tripod in his own temple, after having first uttered a prophecy over the tripod and having declared to Jason and his company the whole matter, namely that whensoever one of the descendants of those who sailed with him in the Argo should carry away this tripod, then it was determined by fate that a hundred cities of Hellenes should be established about the lake Tritonis. Having heard this the native Libyans concealed the tripod.

Next to these Machlyans are the Auseans. These and the Machlyans dwell round the lake Tritonis, and the river Triton is the boundary between them: and while the Machlyans grow their hair long at the back of the head, the Auseans do so in front. At a yearly festival of Athene their maidens take their stand in two parties and fight against one another with stones and staves, and they say that in doing so they are fulfilling the rites handed down by their fathers for the divinity who was sprung from that land, whom we call Athene: and those of the maidens who die of the wounds received they call "false-maidens." But before they let them begin the fight they do this:—all join together and equip the maiden who is judged to be the fairest on each occasion, with a Corinthian helmet and with full Hellenic armour, and then causing her to go up into a chariot they conduct her round the lake. Now I cannot tell with what they equipped the maidens in old time, before the Hellenes were settled near them; but I suppose that they used to be equipped with Egyptian armour, for it is from Egypt that both the shield and the helmet have come to the Hellenes, as I affirm. They say moreover that Athene is the daughter of Poseidon and of the lake Tritonis, and that she had some cause of complaint against her father and therefore gave herself to Zeus, and Zeus made her his own daughter. Such is the story which these tell; and they have their intercourse with women in common, not marrying but having intercourse like cattle: and when the child of any woman has grown big, he is brought before a meeting of the men held within three months of that time, and whomsoever of the men the child resembles, his son he is accounted to be.

Thus then have been mentioned those nomad Libyans who live along the sea-coast: and above these inland is the region of Libya which has wild beasts; and above the wild-beast region there stretches a raised belt of sand, extending from Thebes of the Egyptians to the Pillars of Heracles. In this belt at intervals of about ten days' journey there are fragments of salt in great lumps forming hills, and at the top of each hill there shoots up from the middle of the salt a spring of water cold and sweet; and about the spring dwell men, at the furthest limit towards the desert, and above the wild-beast region. First, at a distance of ten days' journey from Thebes, are the Ammonians, whose temple is derived from that of the Theban Zeus, for the image of Zeus in Thebes also, as I have said before, has the head of a ram. These, as it chances, have also other water of a spring, which in the early morning is warm; at the time when the market fills, cooler; when midday comes, it is quite cold, and then they water their gardens; but as the day declines, it abates from its coldness, until at last, when the sun sets, the water is warm; and it continues to increase in heat still more until it reaches midnight, when it boils and throws up bubbles; and when midnight passes, it becomes cooler gradually till dawn of day. This spring is called the fountain of the Sun.

After the Ammonians, as you go on along the belt of sand, at an interval again of ten days' journey there is a hill of salt like that of the Ammonians, and a spring of water, with men dwelling about it; and the name of this place is Augila. To this the Nasamonians come year by year to gather the fruit of the date-palms.

From Augila at a distance again of ten days' journey there is another hill of salt and spring of water and a great number of fruit-bearing date-palms, as there are also in the other places: and men dwell here who are called the Garmantians, a very great nation, who carry earth to lay over the salt and then sow crops. From this point is the shortest way to the Lotophagoi, for from these it is a journey of thirty days to the country of the Garmantians. Among them also are produced the cattle which feed backwards; and they feed backwards for this reason, because they have their horns bent down forwards, and therefore they walk backwards as they feed; for forwards they cannot go, because the horns run into the ground in front of them; but in nothing else do they differ from other cattle except in this and in the thickness and firmness to the touch of their hide. These Garamantians of whom I speak hunt the "Cave-dwelling" Ethiopians with their four-horse chariots, for the Cave-dwelling Ethiopians are the swiftest of foot of all men about whom we hear report made: and the Cave-dwellers feed upon serpents and lizards and such creeping things, and they use a language which resembles no other, for in it they squeak just like bats.

From the Garmantians at a distance again of ten days' journey there is another hill of salt and spring of water, and men dwell round it called Atarantians, who alone of all men about whom we know are nameless; for while all taken together have the name Atarantians, each separate man of them has no name given to him. These utter curses against the Sun when he is at his height, and moreover revile him with all manner of foul terms, because he oppresses them by his burning heat, both themselves and their land. After this at a distance of ten days' journey there is another hill of salt and spring of water, and men dwell round it. Near this salt hill is a mountain named Atlas, which is small in circuit and rounded on every side; and so exceedingly lofty is it said to be, that it is not possible to see its summits, for clouds never leave them either in the summer or in the winter. This the natives say is the pillar of the heaven. After this mountain these men got their name, for they are called Atlantians; and it is said that they neither eat anything that has life nor have any dreams.

As far as these Atlantians I am able to mention in order the names of those who are settled in the belt of sand; but for the parts beyond these I can do so no more. However, the belt extends as far as the Pillars of Heracles and also in the parts outside them: and there is a mine of salt in it at a distance of ten days' journey from the Atlantians, and men dwelling there; and these all have their houses built of the lumps of salt, since these parts of Libya which we have now reached are without rain; for if it rained, the walls being made of salt would not be able to last: and the salt is dug up there both white and purple in colour. Above the sand-belt, in the parts which are in the direction of the South Wind and towards the interior of Libya, the country is uninhabited, without water and without wild beasts, rainless and treeless, and there is no trace of moisture in it.

I have said that from Egypt as far as the lake Tritonis Libyans dwell who are nomads, eating flesh and drinking milk; and these do not taste at all of the flesh of cows, for the same reason as the Egyptians also abstain from it, nor do they keep swine. Moreover the women of the Kyrenians too think it not right to eat cows' flesh, because of the Egyptian Isis, and they even keep fasts and celebrate festivals for her; and the women of Barca, in addition from cows' flesh, do not taste of swine either.

Thus it is with these matters: but in the region to the West of lake Tritonis the Libyans cease to be nomads, and they do not practise the same customs, nor do to their children anything like that which the nomads are wont to do; for the nomad Libyans, whether all of them I cannot say for certain, but many of them, do as follows:—when their children are four years old, they burn with a greasy piece of sheep's wool the veins in the crowns of their heads, and some of them burn the veins of the temples, so that for all their lives to come the cold humour may not run down from their heads and do them hurt: and for this reason it is (they say) that they are so healthy; for the Libyans are in truth the most healthy of all races concerning which we have knowledge, whether for this reason or not I cannot say for certain, but the most healthy they certainly are: and if, when they burn the children, a convulsion comes on, they have found out a remedy for this; for they pour upon them the water of a he-goat and so save them. I report that which is reported by the Libyans themselves.

The following is the manner of sacrifice which the nomads have:—they cut off a part of the animal's ear as a first offering and throw it over the house, and having done this they twist its neck. They sacrifice only to the Sun and the

Moon; that is to say, to these all the Libyans sacrifice, but those who dwell round the lake Tritonis sacrifice most of all to Athene, and next to Triton and Poseidon.

It would appear also that the Hellenes made the dress and the aigis of the images of Athene after the model of the Libyan women; for except that the dress of the Libyan women is of leather, and the tassels which hang from their aigis are not formed of serpents but of leather thongs, in all other respects Athene is dressed like them. Moreover the name too declares that the dress of the figures of Pallas has come from Libya, for the Libyan women wear over their other garments bare goat-skins (aigeas) with tasselled fringes and coloured over with red madder, and from the name of these goat-skins the Hellenes formed the name aigis. I think also that in these regions first arose the practice of crying aloud during the performance of sacred rites, for the Libyan women do this very well. The Hellenes learnt from the Libyans also the yoking together of four horses.

The nomads bury those who die just in the same manner as the Hellenes, except only the Nasamonians: these bury bodies in a sitting posture, taking care at the moment when the man expires to place him sitting and not to let him die lying down on his back. They have dwellings composed of the stems of asphodel entwined with rushes, and so made that they can be carried about. Such are the customs followed by these tribes.

On the West of the river Triton next after the Auseans come Libyans who are tillers of the soil, and whose custom it is to possess fixed habitations; and they are called Maxyans. They grow their hair long on the right side of their heads and cut it short upon the left, and smear their bodies over with red ochre. These say that they are of the men who came from Troy.

This country and the rest of Libya which is towards the West is both much more frequented by wild beasts and much more thickly wooded than the country of the nomads: for whereas the part of Libya which is situated towards the East, where the nomads dwell, is low-lying and sandy up to the river Triton, that which succeeds it towards the West, the country of those who till the soil, is exceedingly mountainous and thickly-wooded and full of wild beasts: for in the land of these are found both the monstrous serpent and the lion and the elephant, and bears and venomous snakes and horned asses, besides the dog-headed men, and the headless men with their eyes set in their breasts (at least so say the Libyans about them), and the wild men and wild women, and a great multitude of other beasts which are not fabulous like these.

In the land of the nomads however there exist none of these, but other animals as follows:—white-rump antelopes, gazelles, buffaloes, asses, not the horned kind but others which go without water (for in fact these never drink), oryes, whose horns are made into the sides of the Phenician lyre (this animal is in size about equal to an ox), small foxes, hyenas, porcupines, wild rams, wolves, jackals, panthers, boryes, land-crocodiles about three cubits in length and very much resembling lizards, ostriches, and small snakes, each with one horn: these wild animals there are in this country, as well as those which exist elsewhere, except the stag and the wild-boar; but Libya has no stags nor wild boars at all. Also there are in this country three kinds of mice, one is called the "two-legged" mouse, another the zegeris (a name which is Libyan and signifies in the Hellenic tongue a "hill"), and a third the "prickly" mouse. There are also weasels produced in the silphion, which are very like those of Tartessos. Such are the wild animals which the land of the Libyans possesses, so far as we were able to discover by inquiries extended as much as possible.

Next to the Maxyan Libyans are the Zauekes, whose women drive their chariots for them to war.

Next to these are the Gyzantes, among whom honey is made in great quantity by bees, but in much greater quantity still it is said to be made by men, who work at it as a trade. However that may be, these all smear themselves over with red ochre and eat monkeys, which are produced in very great numbers upon their mountains.

Opposite these, as the Carthaginians say, there lies an island called Kyrauis, two hundred furlongs in length but narrow, to which one may walk over from the mainland; and it is full of olives and vines. In it they say there is a pool, from which the native girls with birds' feathers smeared over with pitch bring up gold-dust out of the mud. Whether this is really so I do not know, but I write that which is reported; and nothing is impossible, for even in Zakynthos I saw myself pitch brought up out of a pool of water. There are there several pools, and the largest of them measures seventy feet each way and is two fathoms in depth. Into this they plunge a pole with a myrtle-branch bound to it, and then with the branch of the myrtle they bring up pitch, which has the smell of asphalt, but in other respects it is superior to the pitch of Pieria. This they pour into a pit dug near the pool; and when they have collected a large quantity, then they pour it into the jars from the pit: and whatever thing falls into the pool goes under ground and reappears in the sea, which is distant about four furlongs from the pool. Thus then the report about the island lying near the coast of Libya is also probably enough true.

The Carthaginians say also this, namely that there is a place in Libya and men dwelling there, outside the Pillars of Heracles, to whom when they have come and have taken the merchandise forth from their ships, they set it in order along the beach and embark again in their ships, and after that they raise a smoke; and the natives of the country seeing the smoke come to the sea, and then they lay down gold as an equivalent for the merchandise and retire to a distance away from the merchandise. The Carthaginians upon that disembark and examine it, and if the gold is in their opinion sufficient for the value of the merchandise, they take it up and go their way; but if not, they embark again in their ships and sit there; and the others approach and straightway add more gold to the former, until they satisfy them: and they say that neither party wrongs the other; for neither do the Carthaginians lay hands on the gold until it is made equal to the value of their merchandise, nor do the others lay hands on the merchandise until the Carthaginians have taken the gold.

These are the Libyan tribes whom we are able to name; and of these the greater number neither now pay any regard to the king of the Medes nor did they then. Thus much also I have to say about this land, namely that it is occupied by four races and no more, so far as we know; and of these races two are natives of the soil and the other two not so; for the Libyans and the Ethiopians are natives, the one race dwelling in the Northern parts of Libya and the other in the Southern, while the Phenicians and the Hellenes are strangers.

I think moreover that (besides other things) in goodness of soil Libya does not very greatly excel as compared with Asia or Europe, except only the region of Kinyps, for the same name is given to the land as to the river. This region is equal to the best of lands in bringing forth the fruit of Demeter, nor does it at all resemble the rest of Libya; for it has black soil and is watered by springs, and neither has it fear of drought nor is it hurt by drinking too abundantly of rain; for rain there is in this part of Libya. Of the produce of the crops the same measures hold good here as for the Babylonian land. And that is good land also which the Euesperites occupy, for when it bears best it produces a hundred-fold, but the land in the region of Kinyps produces sometimes as much as three-hundred-fold.

Moreover the land of Kyrene, which is the highest land of the part of Libya which is occupied by nomads, has within its confines three seasons of harvest, at which we may marvel: for the parts by the sea-coasts first have their fruits ripe for reaping and for gathering the vintage; and when these have been gathered in, the parts which lie above the sea-side places, those situated in the middle, which they call the hills, are ripe for the gathering in; and as soon as this middle crop has been gathered in, that in the highest part of the land comes to perfection and is ripe; so that by the time the first crop has been eaten and drunk up, the last is just coming in. Thus the harvest for the Kyrenians lasts eight months. Let so much as has been said suffice for these things.

Now when the Persian helpers of Pheretime, having been sent from Egypt by Aryandes, had arrived at Barca, they laid siege to the city, proposing to the inhabitants that they should give up those who were guilty of the murder of Arkesilaos: but as all their people had taken a share in the guilt, they did not accept the proposals. Then they besieged Barca for nine months, both digging underground passages which led to the wall and making vigorous attacks upon it. Now the passages dug were discovered by a worker of bronze with a shield covered over with bronze, who had thought of a plan as follows:—carrying it round within the wall he applied it to the ground in the city, and whereas the other places to which he applied it were noiseless, at those places where digging was going on the bronze of the shield gave a sound; and the men of Barca would make a countermine there and slay the Persians who were digging mines. This then was discovered as I have said, and the attacks were repulsed by the men of Barca.

Then as they were suffering hardship for a long time and many were falling on both sides, and especially on that of the Persians, Amasis the commander of the land-army contrived as follows:—perceiving that the Barcaians were not to be conquered by force but might be conquered by guile, he dug by night a broad trench and over it he laid timber of no great strength, and brought earth and laid it above on the top of the timber, making it level with the rest of the ground: then at daybreak he invited the men of Barca to a parley; and they gladly consented, and at last they agreed to make a treaty: and the treaty they made with one another was taken over the hidden trench, namely that so long as this earth should continue to be as it was, so long the oath should remain firm, and that the men of Barca should promise to pay tribute of due amount to the king, and the Persians should do no further violence to the men of Barca. After the oath the men of Barca trusting to these engagements both went forth themselves from their city and let any who desired it of the enemy pass within their walls, having opened all the gates; but the Persians first broke down the concealed bridge and then began to run inside the city wall. And the reason why they broke down the bridge which they had made was that they might keep their oaths, since they had sworn to the men of Barca that the oath should remain firm continually for so long time as the earth should remain as it then was, but after that they had broken it down, the oath no longer remained firm.

Now the most guilty of the Barcaians, when they were delivered to her by the Persians, Pheretime impaled in a ring round about the wall; and she cut off the breasts of their wives and set the wall round with these also in order: but the rest of the men of Barca she bade the Persians carry off as spoil, except so many of them as were of the house of Battos and not sharers in the guilt of the murder; and to these Pheretime gave the city in charge.

So the Persians having made slaves of the rest of the Barcaians departed to go back: and when they appeared at the gates of the city of Kyrene, the Kyrenians let them go through their town in order to avoid neglect of some oracle. Then as the army was going through, Badres the commander of the fleet urged that they should capture the city, but Amasis the commander of the land-army would not consent to it; for he said that they had been sent against no other city of the Hellenes except Barca. When however they had passed through and were encamping on the hill of Zeus Lycaios, they repented of not having taken possession of Kyrene; and they endeavoured again to pass into it, but the men of Kyrene would not allow them. Then upon the Persians, although no one fought against them, there fell a sudden panic, and they ran away for about sixty furlongs and then encamped. And when the camp had been placed here, there came to it a messenger from Aryandes summoning them back; so the Persians asked the Kyrenians to give them provisions for their march and obtained their request; and having received these, they departed to go to Egypt. After this the Libyans took them up, and killed for the sake of their clothes and equipment those of them who at any time were left or straggled behind, until at last they came to Egypt.

This army of the Persians reached Euesperides, and this was their furthest point in Libya: and those of the Barcaians whom they had reduced to slavery they removed again from Egypt and brought them to the king, and king Dareios gave them a village in the land of Bactria in which to make a settlement. To this village they gave the name of Barca, and it still continued to be inhabited by them even down to my own time, in the land of Bactria.

Pheretime however did not bring her life happily to an end any more than they: for as soon as she had returned from Libya to Egypt after having avenged herself on the Barcaians, she died an evil death, having become suddenly full of worms while yet alive: for, as it seems, too severe punishments inflicted by men prove displeasing to the gods. Such and so great was the punishment inflicted by Pheretime the wife of Battos on the men of Barca.

CPSIA information can be obtained
at www.ICGtesting.com
Printed in the USA
LVOW09s1949110517
534161LV00007B/363/P

9 781536 824001